TERROR FROM THE EXTREME RIGHT

CASS SERIES ON POLITICAL VIOLENCE

Series Editors -   DAVID C. RAPOPORT, University of California, Los Angeles
                         PAUL WILKINSON, University of St Andrews, Scotland

1. *Terror from the Extreme Right*, edited by Tore Bjørgo
2. *Millennialism and Violence*, edited by Michael Barkun
3. *Violence in Southern Africa*, edited by J.E. Spence
4. *April 19 and Right-Wing Violence in America*, edited by David. C. Rapoport

TERROR
FROM THE
EXTREME RIGHT

Edited by
TORE BJØRGO

FRANK CASS • LONDON

First published in 1995 in Great Britain by
FRANK CASS & CO. LTD.
900 Eastern Avenue, London
IG2 7HH, England

and in the United States of America by
FRANK CASS
c/o International Specialized Book Services, Inc.
5804 N.E. Hassalo Street, Portland, Oregon 97213–3644

Transferred to Digital Printing 2004

British Library Cataloguing in Publication Data
A catalogue record for this book is available from
the British Library.
ISBN 0-7146-4663-6 (cloth)
ISBN 0-7146-4196-0 (paper)

Library of Congress Cataloging in Publication Data
A catalog record for this book is available from the Library
of Congress.

Typeset by Frank Cass & Co. Ltd.

CONTENTS

Series Foreword

Terror from the Extreme Right is the first volume in the new series
POLITICAL VIOLENCE published by Frank Cass. The decision to begin with
this volume, originally planned as a special issue of the *Journal of
Terrorism and Political Violence* (Spring 1995), was made before the
Oklahoma City Bombing (19 April 1995). The Journal's interest in violent
right-wing groups had been strong, publishing eight articles on the subject
in the last three years. So when Tore Bjørgo suggested a conference to
bring people interested in the Extreme Right together, the Editors were
delighted to help promote the project, one largely subsidized by the
Norwegian Ministry of Foreign Affairs. The result is a fascinating volume
which is at the same time the first comparative international analysis of
right-wing violence.

DAVID C. RAPOPORT
PAUL WILKINSON
Editors, CASS SERIES ON POLITICAL VIOLENCE
May 1995

Editor's Preface

As this volume was about to go to press, a large car bomb devastated a US federal office building in Oklahoma City on 19 April 1995, killing 169 people and wounding more than 400 at the heart of continental America. It was the single most lethal terrorist attack in the country's domestic history, and possible also the most lethal act of right-wing terrorism world-wide (with the exception of wartime atrocities). Immediately after the blast, some politicians and commentators blamed Islamic terrorists as the most likely culprits – inflaming anti-Muslim sentiment in the process. However, at this point it seem clear that the bombing was linked to one or more persons known for their extreme right-wing views and hatred of the federal government, fueled in part by the disastrous fire at the Branch Davidian compound in Waco, Texas, on the same day two years earlier. Clearly, the authorities had no sense that there could be a serious incident by members of the extreme right directly connected to Waco even though the public literature from that part of the spectrum had made Waco a critically important matter. A central element in the extreme right's belief system is that the US federal government is in the hands of hostile and alien forces bent on depriving the American people of their constitutional rights – particularly the right to bear arms.

Although the contributions to this volume on *Terror from the Extreme Right* were completed several months before the Oklahoma City bombing, many of the issues raised and discussed are highly relevant to an understanding of how it could happen. Two themes recurring throughout this volume may be mentioned in particular: Changes in enemy images and targets for hostility and violence; and the radicalization process.

Traditionally, most forms of right-wing extremist movements have directed their hatred and violence against non-governmental targets, such as ethnic minorities, immigrants, homosexuals or communists – groups considered inferior and alien. However, an increasing tendency among violent-prone groups on the extreme right in the US and elsewhere is to focus their hostility and terrorism against the state and the Establishment – whether that be called 'the Zionist Occupation Government' (ZOG) or 'the Federal Government's conspiracy with the United Nations to subjugate Americans under a New World Order'. The bombing of the federal office building in Oklahoma City appears to be an extreme expression of this trend.

A second theme where this volume may provide insights about the dynamics behind the Oklahoma City bombing concerns the process of delegitimization and radicalization through which radical groups may turn violent rhetoric into actual violence and terrorism. Most of these holding extreme views and ideologies stop short of going all the way into full-blown terrorism. However, certain events and developments may provide circumstances for radicalizing some groups and individuals to cross this threshold. The disproportionate use of force by US state agencies during the sieges of Waco and the Weaver family were two key events which have provided a basis for a radicalization of the American extreme right. This accelerated the strong growth of the anti-federal 'militia' movement. The contributors to the volume discuss thoroughly factors facilitating as well as inhibiting such radicalization.

The studies in this volume were originally presented and discussed at a workshop in Berlin 19–20 August 1994, made possible through economic support from the Norwegian Ministry of Foreign Affairs. I will also use the opportunity to thank professor David Rapoport, co-editor of the journal *Terrorism and Political Violence*, for his help and advice during the planning and editing of this volume. Thanks as well to our copy editor, Joan Witte, and the editor at Frank Cass Publishers, Randal Gray, for their generous assistance. And finally, thanks to the participants at the workshop for their contributions to the volume and constructive discussion.

TORE BJØRGO
May 1995

Introduction

TORE BJØRGO

In Mölln, Germany, one Turkish woman and two girls died and several others were wounded when two local skinheads firebombed their house during the night of 23 November 1992. This was one of more than 700 cases of arson with a presumed right-wing extremist motivation occurring in Germany that year.[1]

In Vienna, Austria, ten sophisticated letter bombs were mailed in December 1993 to politicians, journalists, human rights activists and other prominent personalities who had actively supported the rights of refugees. Four persons were badly injured, including a TV news editor, a priest, a lawyer's secretary, and the mayor of Vienna, whose hand was torn off when he opened the letter. Two leading activists of the neo-Nazi organization VAPO (*Volkstreue Ausserparlamentarische Opposition*) were arrested.[2]

In Boksburg, South Africa, the ANC leader Chris Hani, was gunned down outside his house on 10 April 1993. Two white right-wingers – linked to the extremist AWB (*Afrikaner Weerstandsbeweging*) and the Conservative Party – were convicted for the assassination. Hani was considered a likely successor of ANC leader Nelson Mandela, and a central figure in the transition process to give the former apartheid state a non-racial, democratic rule.[3]

In Denver, USA, the controversial Jewish radio talk show host Alan Berg was gunned down on 18 June 1984 by members of a terrorist organization which became known as The Order. This group was inspired by the anti-Semitic doctrine of Christian Identity theology and the novel *The Turner Diaries*. The organization collapsed after having carried out two murders and several robberies to finance their war against the 'Zionist Occupation Government' (ZOG). However, The Order remains a role model for other revolutionary racist groups, even abroad.[4]

In several parts of the world, terrorism and political violence of the late 1980s and early 1990s have gravitated increasingly towards the extreme right, in the direction of racism and extreme nationalism, and adopting slogans like 'ethnic cleansing and 'race war . On a lesser scale, this may resemble the situation between the First and Second World Wars, with its Fascist *Zeitgeist*.[5] After the Second World War, especially during the 1960s and 1970s, both

anti-colonialist movements, national liberation and ethnic secessionist movements, and youth protest movements alike generally found their ideological
inspiration and foreign allies on the left. They situated their local struggle
within the context of a global struggle against the forces of capitalism and
imperialism. Alternatively, such movements linked their cause to universalist
notions of human rights and democracy. Since the late 1980s, particularly
after the collapse of communism, both nationalist movements and rebellious
youth cultures have increasingly turned to more particularist notions of 'people, blood and soil' – notions commonly associated with right-wing and even
fascist ideologies. This shift in *Zeitgeist* has been particularly noticeable in
Europe. The trend is expressing itself through increasing electoral support for
xenophobic and radical right parties, through the growth of militant neo-Nazi
organizations and networks and xenophobic youth cultures, and through
increased violence against asylum seekers and other minorities.[6] A parallel
trend is represented by the increase of religious militancy and millenarian
movements, whose particularist world-views often combine well with right-
wing extremist politics and violence.[7]

The notion of 'extreme right' is problematic and somewhat elusive. Many
researchers in the field are uncomfortable with this label, due to its lack of
precision and the somewhat one-sided emphasis of the left-right dimension.
Part of the problem is that what are considered rightist and leftist issues
change from country to country and over time, and that some relevant issues
and traits transcend the left-right distinction. Even more complicating is the
fact that many of the groups and individuals who carry out acts of violence
perceived by others as 'right-wing' or 'racist', turn out to have no connections
with extreme political organizations, and often only rudimentary ideas of any
ideology. When researchers nevertheless continue to use the concept of right-
wing extremism, it is both for the lack of a better alternative, and because it
is sometimes useful to have a shorthand label which lumps together a relatively wide range of related phenomena in order to focus on both their similarities and differences. Most of the alternative labels, such as 'racism', 'fascism' or 'nationalism', are too narrow to encompass all the movements of relevance. One alternative is the concept of 'hate crime', commonly used in the
USA. One serious problem about this label is that it tends to isolate the criminal aspect of the phenomenon from its possible wider political context and
non-criminal activities. On the other hand, terms like 'right-wing extremism'
may sometimes have overly strong political and ideological implications to fit
criminal youth gangs and their violent acts. The notion of 'particularist
groups' is another promising alternative as a more general label, promoted by
Ehud Sprinzak in this volume (see below).

The basic elements of a right-wing extremist orientation have been described by Willem Heitmeyer[8] as an ideology of considering inequality between people as a nature-given principle, combined with an acceptance of violence as a legitimate way of acting. If we try to isolate the main issues and values promoted by movements commonly identified as extreme right, we may come up with a cluster of notions, of which some are shared by most of the groups: Authoritarianism, anti-communism/-socialism, anti-liberalism, militant nationalism, racism/xenophobia/anti-Semitism, intolerance towards minorities, Golden Age myths, a particularist (as opposed to universalist) morality, and the notion of violence as a creative and cleansing force – these are among the common basic issues and values of the extreme right. However, not all of these elements are shared by every group. Some groups put strong emphasis on special issues or values which may not be of any concern to most other groups of the extreme right. Many extreme right-wing groups, for instance, are strongly influenced by religious conceptions, often forms of millenarianism with strong elements of manichaean and chiliastic world views.[9] Other groups are non- (or even anti-) religious, although they may hold secular versions of some of the same apocalyptic world-views. Some groups explicitly link themselves to the historical 'grand traditions' of the extreme right – German National Socialism and Italian Fascism. Other groups vehemently deny – whether for tactical or factual reasons – that they have any connection with these traditions. Some groups normally considered as 'extreme right' may also promote certain issues which are often associated with the left, such as socialism or environmentalism.[10]

In any case – to try to define the 'essence' of right-wing extremism in terms of one single core issue, value or philosophical idea is a frustrating task. Such an approach will tend to be too narrow, excluding many of the movements which have many significant traits in common with the 'typical' extreme right.[11]

A more process-oriented approach for understanding political movements of the extreme right and their relation to the use of violence may be more rewarding. Such movements may be analyzed as forms of reactions to threatening changes at work in society, and as special styles of thinking about – and acting in relation to – these perceived threats.[12] The nature of the perceived threat may vary according to circumstances, but events tend to be interpreted as parts of conspiracies between two or more types of enemies (such as minorities and government, or external invaders and internal traitors). This perceived threat may take on apocalyptic proportions of a cosmic drama between the Forces of Good and the Forces of Evil. Although violence within such a frame of reference is seen as a normal and justifiable reaction to threat, actual violence and terrorism does not follow automatically from holding a right-wing extremist world-view. For that to happen, the group will normally have to go through a radicalization process whereby the enemies are progressively delegitimized and demonized, and the threat becomes perceived as acute.

In the following essay, which may be seen as a theoretical introduction to this volume, Ehud Sprinzak presents his general model for analyzing this process of delegitimization and radicalization into terrorism, with a special focus on right-wing or *particularist* groups. He argues that particularist groups are organized around the belief that the object of their intense opposition is *a priori* illegitimate. It does not belong to the same humanity as themselves, but should either be kept in an inferior legal status, expelled or even eliminated. As long as the situation is stable and tolerable, the group does not resort to violence. Violence, and gradually terrorism, emerge only when the group involved feels increasingly insecure or threatened. Although most of the violence is directed against the 'inferior' enemy group, at some point their violence may turn towards the political authorities, which are perceived as betraying their own people by assisting and protecting the threatening minorities. Sprinzak describes this as a process of 'split delegitimization' – an intense delegitimization of the main object of hostility, and a more diluted delegitimization of the authorities. He expands his model by introducing a typology of six main categories of right-wing terrorist groups: Revolutionary terrorism, reactive terrorism, vigilante terrorism, racist terrorism, millenarian terrorism, and youth counterculture terrorism. These types are not mutually exclusive, but can be distinguished on the basis of the *dominant* principles around which they are organized and on their various relations to minority and authority enemies within the dynamics of split delegitimation. Sprinzak does not claim, however, that the model of split delegitimization is universally applicable. It does not fit certain cases of reactive terrorism and its explanatory power for youth counterculture terrorism is limited.

On This Volume

The purpose of this volume is to bring together serious studies on various 'right-wing' terrorist groups and militant movements from different parts of the world. Such a collection of case studies may then provide the basis for a more general and comparative discussion of a complex set of phenomena, and serve as a test to the applicability of Sprinzak's model.

To our knowledge, this is the first volume which sets out to apply a comparative perspective on right-wing violence and terrorism on an international basis. There has recently been published several important volumes on right-wing politics and movements, but these do not incorporate a specific focus on the violent or terrorist dimension.[13] Various aspects of right-wing violence have also been the topic of several books, but these are generally limited to particular countries or regions, certain forms of right-wing violence, or on the judicial and political responses to it.[14] Those volumes with an international perspective on violence have tended to lack a clear comparative focus, addressing different aspects of the problem in each country – for instance by focusing on the characteristics of violent perpetrators in one country, police responses in another, or the role of the media in a third.[15] The present volume tries to address consistent series of questions and issues in different countries, with a special focus on the violent actors and their motivations, and the escalation process which may lead militant groups into terrorism.

The contributors, leading experts in the field of research on right-wing extremism and terrorism, convened at a workshop in Berlin during 19–20 August 1994, made possible by a grant from the Norwegian Ministry of Foreign Affairs. They were asked to focus their papers on how, under which circumstances, and for what motives, extremists turn from radical right politics – or from just harbouring racist or right-wing attitudes – to violent action. What is the relationship between ideology/rhetoric and actual violence? Does the widely held notion that violence is intrinsic to racist and right-wing extremist movements hold against empirical evidence? Although many right-wing groups propagate violence and hate, what can account for the often noticeable gap between their extremely violent rhetoric and their actual behaviour in terms of violent acts? (In fact, most of the racist violence is carried out by individuals and small groups *not* affiliated to political organizations, although often influenced by their propaganda.) Under what circumstances do such movements and groups cross the threshold into actual violence and even full-fledged terrorism? Which factors may keep groups that advocate violence from actually carrying out terrorist violence? Sprinzak's model on 'the process of delegitimization' (described briefly above, and presented in full in the following essay) was proposed to the contributors as a useful analytical approach.[16]

For comparative purposes, the contributors were asked to discuss the following aspects regarding the group/organization/movement in question:

- What are the sources, traditions and characteristics of its ideology?
- Who are 'the enemies', and what kinds of perceived threats do they represent?
- What are the militant activists' relations to the state, the established power structures, and wider political movements and parties?
- How, and under what circumstances, do ideology and rhetoric turn into actual violence and terrorism? What roles do non-political motives and processes play in this respect?

The primary focus of interest in this volume is on right-wing extremist *terrorism* – briefly defined as the systematic use (or threat) of violence to intimidate categories of people for political purposes. However, our analytical perspective on the radicalization process into terrorism means that non-terrorist or 'pre-terrorist' forms of political violence, such as assaults, riots, vandalism and threats, are also of great relevance.

Some Main Findings

Most of the contributors to this volume have applied or commented on aspects of Sprinzak's model of delegitimization or his typology. Others did not refer explicitly to Sprinzak's model, but all contributions explore points which are relevant to a discussion of its applicability. The cases analyzed in this volume generally provide empirical support to the main lines of Sprinzak's model on the emergence of right-wing terrorism – although with some important exceptions and deviations.

It should, however, be noted that some of the points of criticism raised in the contributions by Jeffrey Kaplan, Leonard Weinberg and Kenneth Szymkowiak and Patricia Steinhoff relate to Sprinzak's *original* formulation of his model in the Spring 1991 issue of the journal *Terrorism and Political Violence*. Some of these shortcomings were already resolved when Sprinzak presented a new and more elaborate version of his model at the Berlin Workshop – with a focus on right-wing extremist groups and a typology which related the model to different types of groups. Constructive discussions at the workshop made it possible to make further refinements for the final version presented in this volume. Some of these developments in Sprinzak's model are not reflected in the other chapters, as this would delay publication of the volume. However, where specific points of criticism raised in some contributions have been addressed in the new version of Sprinzak's paper, this is signalled by an 'editor's note' in the text.

Several authors question the applicability to their respective cases of Sprinzak's notion of 'split delegitimization' of enemies, which implies that the most intense delegitimization is directed towards non-governmental minorities, and that the government is subjected to a secondary and more diluted form of delegitimization. They argue that Sprinzak may underestimate the degree to which the political establishment in some cases serves as the main enemy and not merely as a secondary object of hostility. This is a point made by Szymkowiak and Steinhoff regarding Japanese right-wing extremists, who mainly direct their violence and harassment against establishment figures whom they consider to be betraying Japan's heritage. Bjørgo's study of the violent discourses of Scandinavian extreme nationalists point out that both (non-Nazi) anti-immigration activists and neo-Nazis increasingly tend to focus their hostility on the authorities, who are seen as traitors who let foreigners invade or occupy the country. Kaplan, in his discussion of US racist groups' theory of ZOG (the Zionist Occupation Government), argues that many on the violent fringes of the movement no longer distinguish between the government and 'the other'.

Thus, the notion of 'split delegitimization' may be too simplistic when it implies only two main sets of enemies. Sprinzak's model tends to lump together in the same 'non-governmental' enemy category both ethnic minorities (or 'foreigners') and political adversaries belonging to the same ethnic/national/racial collectivity as the right-wing militants, but who are outside the political establishment (such as communists, anti-racists or some liberals). It is also problematic to relate the alleged role of the Jews within the framework of ZOG conspiracy theories to either of the two categories of enemies: the Jews belong to a racial minority, but they are also allegedly controlling the government and the political establishment in general through their agents. The latter – 'racial traitors' – are often called 'spiritual Jews', effectively blurring enemy categories.

There are some important theoretical distinctions here which deserve to be worked out further. One possibility is to describe the constellations of enemy images along two dimensions: *Ethnicity* (including race, nationality and religion) and *power* (governmental/non-governmental or establishment/non-establishment). The table below provides an example of this.

TABLE 1
DIMENSIONS WITHIN RACISTS' IMAGES OF THEIR ENEMIES

	Governmental/ establishment enemies	Non-governmental/ non-establishment enemies
Ethnically in-group	Officials, politicians, journalists, experts, intellectuals, etc.	Communists, anti-racists, leftists, women activists, homosexuals, drug addicts, etc.
Ethnically out-group	Jews, 'Zionists'	Ethnic minorities, immigrants, asylum seekers, Muslims, 'foreigners', etc.

Comparative studies of enemy images between different right-wing extremist groups and over time might reveal interesting patterns and changes of emphasis along these dimensions. It would also elucidate patterns of alleged conspiracies between these various types of enemies. However, such a systematic comparative study of enemy images along these dimensions remains to be done.

Are all right-wing extremist movements 'particularist' in their value system? Weinberg argues that some important strands of Italian neo-Fascism hold ideas and values with some significant universalist dimensions (inspired by their favourite philosopher Giulio Cesare Evola). Thus, the label 'particularist' may not fit all right-wing extremist movements equally well – although this is probably a matter of degree more than of principle. The notion that right-wing extremist groups tend to hold particularist rather than universalist values is generally a valid observation.

Although right-wing extremist groups may be characterized as particularistic in values and goals, this collection of case studies demonstrates that many of the racist and extreme nationalist groups and movements are surprisingly 'internationalist' in sources of ideological inspiration and even in organizational networks. As one might expect, groups emphasizing the white race as their primary object of identification are more international in their orientation than narrow nationalist or ethnocentric groups. However, even the latter types of groups tend to be influenced by nationalist movements elsewhere.[17] Some right-wing and racist ideologies and symbols travel well – in spite of the fact that they have been developed in highly specific historical and local contexts. Such ideological elements and models of action are frequently borrowed from abroad, adapted to local circumstances and combined with other ideological elements and traditions into a form of ideological syncretism. Thus, American racists have taken over the belief system of British-Israelism (sometimes called Anglo-Israelism), transforming it to reinterpret Christian tradition into the radical anti-Semitic doctrine of Christian Identity (cf. Kaplan's contribution), and occasionally combining it with American Ku Klux Klan traditions or with German National Socialism. Young racists in Northern and Western Europe frequently adopt ideas, slogans and symbols from American racism[18] and combine these elements with local Fascist traditions, German National Socialism, and the style and music of the British skinhead movement. South African Apartheid ideology is also an important source of ideological inspiration to racist groups all over the world.

It may seem paradoxical that groups preaching mono-culturalism and racial purity are themselves practising a form of ideological syncretism and political multi-culturalism. Although notions of racial identity certainly may justify such constructions to the activists themselves, the contradiction between loyalty to race and loyalty to nation is a major source of tension within such racist movements.[19]

One of the striking differences between the various violence-prone racist and right-wing extremist traditions is seen in the role played by religion. In most Western and Northern European countries, racism, right-wing extremism and fascism are predominantly secular movements. Neither the historic 'grand traditions' of German National Socialism and Italian Fascism nor present-day neo-Nazism and xenophobic youth movements are much influenced by Christian religious conceptions – although Odinist symbols and mythology sometimes serve as an alternative.[20] This contrasts strongly with militant American racism, which is highly influenced by religious movements, in particular Christian Identity, an anti-semitic and rather unconventional (to say the least) reinterpretation of the Bible (see Kaplan's chapter). Also in Eastern and Southern Europe, South Africa, Israel and Japan, fundamentalist or conservative religious traditions are commonly tightly integrated with right-wing extremist ideologies. The Russian *Pamiat* movement, the Romanian (pre-war) Iron Guard and the post-communist *Vatra Romanesca*, General Franco's 'Catholic' version of Fascism in Spain, the *Afrikaner Weerstandsbeweging* (AWB) in South Africa, the late Rabbi Kahane's *Kach* movement in Israel and the Japanese extreme right's promotion of state Shintoism are all prime examples of this combination of right-wing extremism and fundamentalist or conservative religion. Millenarianism – the belief in a cataclysmic break in history and the emergence of a New World – is a common trait of many extreme right movements. Hitler's idea of the Thousand Years' *Reich* is a secular version of this religious theme.

Several of our case studies (Kaplan, Lööw, Willems and Szymkowiak and Steinhoff) have pointed out strong connections between criminality and right-wing extremism. This is not unique to right-wing terrorism.[21] There is nevertheless a surprisingly high proportion of activists within right-wing extremist groups and among perpetrators of right-wing violence who have substantial criminal records unconnected with their political or ideological views – in other words, 'ordinary crimes' such as theft, robbery, assault, murder, wife-beating, drunken driving or even drug-related crimes. As one might expect, Lööw's and Willem's studies both suggest that the proportion of those with non-political criminal records is higher among the less ideological groups, such as skinheads and xenophobic youth gangs, than among the more ideological groups. But even among ideological right-wing activists and leaders, non-political criminal records are fairly common.[22]

There are several possible explanations for this close connection between crime and right-wing extremism. One is that many individuals with 'negative careers' and a violent mentality tend to be attracted to such political movements, partly because right-wing extremism can offer scapegoats, and partly because these movements offer a context in which they can act out their violent tendencies.[23] Another explanation relates to the fact that many militant right-wing extremist movements organize prison ministries or special prison organizations with the double purpose of supporting their own 'prisoners of war' and recruiting new activists among inmates in prison. 'It is fearless and fanatical fighters with fanatical natures we need, which we can obtain by recruiting these jailbirds,' stated the Swedish neo-Nazi *Storm* magazine. It also emphasized that most of these hard-boiled 'white prisoners' have anything but a friendly attitude towards 'the system', and might therefore be useful.[24] A third factor relates to the tendency of many extremist groups (not only of the far right) to finance their activities and even support their members by carrying out robberies, theft or extortion. This often leads to a blurring of boundaries between political and non-political crimes, especially when they start to cut their ties to established society and go 'underground'. Such crimes are often justified as 'confiscating' resources from the enemy in order to 'fill the war coffers'. However, some of the robberies and other criminal activities carried out by right-wing activists may seem to be motivated as much by personal gain as by concern for a political cause.[25]

An interesting case of blurred boundaries between political and non-political crimes is presented by Szymkowiak and Steinhoff in their analysis of intimidation and violence by right-wing groups in Japan. They describe an emerging symbiosis among the Liberal Democratic Party, the ultra-right, and organized crime during the decades after the war. At a later stage, organized crime (*yakuza* and especially *sokaiya*) increasingly took on right-wing identities to perpetrate their racketeering enterprises. These pseudo right-wing organizations extorted money from corporations by exploiting issues espoused by the ideological right. A refusal to make a 'political contribution' could be tagged as unpatriotic and lead to intense harrassment. Committed to the principle of peace at any price, Japanese companies would normally pay to be left alone. Even 'genuine' right-wing groups sometimes used such methods. This practice leads to a confusing mixture of groups operating under the right-wing banner – including true ideological right-wing groups as well as criminal racketeers who were rightist in name only, argue Szymkowiak and Steinhoff. They criticize Sprinzak's model for paying too little attention to the dimension of economic motivation behind acts of violence and harassment carried out by (purportedly) right-wing extremist groups.

Stated more generally – the criminal dimension deserves more attention in the study of right-wing extremist harrassment, violence and terrorism. This aspect is also important in understanding recruitment patterns and activist careers.

Violent activists of the extreme right are almost exclusively males – a finding which seems to hold true for every country and group covered here.[26] In contrast to terrorist groups of the extreme left and some national liberation groups, where women often played important roles and were sometimes even the most uncompromising proponents of violence,[27] female activists in racist and other right-wing groups tend to be assigned to non-fighting and subordinate roles.[28] This contrast to leftist groups is related to ideological differences which assign men and women different roles in the respective struggles: women's emancipation from patriarchal structures vs. traditional notions of the sexual division of labour and women's task of raising (white) children. In many racist and extreme nationalist youth movements, being a warrior and displaying readiness for violence is also important components in their version of masculine identity. Especially among young perpetrators and activists, the connection between violent behaviour and construction of identity is very strong.[29]

Age is an important variable in right-wing extremist violence. Violent activists of right-wing extremist groups with a strong *ideological* profile are often adults or even middle-aged.[30] Most of the perpetrators of anti-foreigner violence in Europe are, on the other hand, very young, and their ideological commitment is often limited to a rather unreflected hostility to foreigners and the use of racist slogans and symbols. Helmut Willems reports in his contribution that more than 75 per cent of the perpetrators of xenophobic crimes in Germany were 20 or younger. Heléne Lööw found the average age of similar perpetrators in Sweden to be only slightly higher than in Germany. During the early 1990s, racism and extreme nationalism have in many countries increasingly taken the form of dynamic youth protest movements. The subcultures of skinheads and White Power movements are often seen as highly attractive to sections of the youth population. However, some of these more or less racist youth movements are gradually developing into more 'mature' political organizations and networks as their members grow older. The Swedish racist underground is a good example.[31]

One factor which gives right-wing extremism and violence a different direction and thrust in various countries is the presence or absence of immigration as a central political issue. In Western Europe in particular, the perceived threat represented by immigrants and asylum seekers is one of the few issues where movements of the extreme right can find a receptive audience among wider segments of the population. Sometimes with a considerable degree of success, nationalist or single-issue parties and organizations have launched political campaigns focusing on immigrants and asylum seekers as the cause of most social problems. Both militant racist groups and local xenophobic youth gangs, who were used to being marginalized due to their unpalatable politics or their criminal behaviour, suddenly found themselves hailed as local heroes when they directed their violence against unpopular foreigners.[32] Willems argues that in many communities in Germany, locals commonly experienced the arrival of numerous asylum seekers as a burden and source of conflict. This became a crystallization point for the development of corresponding attitudes and a disposition for violence. Right-wing and aggressive youths discovered that when their propensity to violence was directed against foreigners, it did not lead to social bans, stigmatizations and sanctions as before but, on the contrary, found understanding, sympathy and support from sections of the population. For the first time these groups could redefine their identity as being representative of general interest through the unspoken or open support of parts of the population (cf. Willems).

Peter Merkl demonstrates that anti-foreign violence is a phenomenon with long traditions in Europe, and the central theme in the reemergence of rightwing extremism in the early 1990s. But he also emphasizes that, although violence against foreigners gets most of the public attention, other categories of people are also targeted by the same violent groups. Lööw and Bjørgo also point out that the more ideological neo-Nazi groups tend to be more focused on enemies other than immigrants, although even they exploit the mobilization potential of the widespread dislike of 'foreigners'.

If immigrants and asylum seekers have for a long time served as the main scapegoats and issue of mobilization for the extreme right in Western Europe, this has not been the case in North America – at least until recently. In the USA and Canada, where most of the population is itself descended from immigrants, recent immigration has been only a minor issue to militant rightwing groups. Their aggression has generally been directed instead against other ethnic categories, primarily Jews and blacks, minorities which have histories in America as long as most whites. Increasingly, however, economically successful Asian immigrants and illegal (and poor) Hispanic immigrants have become objects of popular resentment, although such immigrant groups may not yet have been assigned an equally important role in the threat images and rhetoric of the extreme right as is the case with immigrants and asylum seekers in Western Europe. It is significant that the largest race riot in the USA during the early 1990s was carried out by blacks, who to a large extent directed their pent-up anger and frustrations against the businesses of successful Asian immigrants in Los Angeles. However, the immediate trigger of these April 1992 riots was the acquittal of several white policemen who had mistreated an African-American, Rodney King. There is nevertheless reason to expect that the American extreme right increasingly will try to exploit the mainstream anti-immigration backlash and get into line with their European fellow partisans.

Of the other countries discussed in depth here, South Africa is one region where immigration is not a central issue to the extreme right; there, the native black population is the main enemy (see Welsh). Neither is immigration a concern to the extreme right in Japan, where the influence of non-Japanese values rather than immigration of non-Japanese persons is perceived as the main threat (see Szymkowiak and Steinhoff). Traditionally, racism and xenophobia have not been important issues to the extreme right in Italy either (see Weinberg); but resentment against asylum seekers and illegal immigrants has increasingly become an issue, bringing the Italian far right more into line with the rest of Western Europe. There are indications of similar tendences in both Japan and some parts of the USA (California in particular), although local factors may give popular resentment against 'foreigners' a different political twist. In Japan, for instance, powerful pseudo right-wing criminal organizations have deep interests in illegal immigration due to their heavy involvement in the illegal labour market and prostitution.

It is my belief that the individual contributions in this volume – and the volume as a whole – advance our knowedge about the processes behind emergence of right-wing extremist violence and terrorism. We have not yet found satisfying answers to all of the questions we have asked, but we are closer to many of these answers. It is my hope that both the theoretical advances and the rich empirical material presented in this volume will encourage further systematic and comparative research in the field.

NOTES

1. Cf. *Verfassungsschutzbericht 1993* (Bonn: Bundesministerium des Innern, Aug. 1993), pp. 70–5. The total number of violent acts with a right-wing extremist motivation was put at 2,584.
2. *Neues Deutschland*, 6 Dec. 1993, *Die Welt*, 6 Dec. 1993, *Information*, 7 Dec. 1993.
3. The murder of Chris Hani is discussed in David Welsh's essay on South Africa in this volume.
4. The Order is described by the journalists Kevin Flynn and Gary Gerhard, *The Silent Brotherhood* (NY: Macmillan, 1989). *The Turner Diaries* was written by a leading US Nazi, William Pierce, under the pseudonym Andrew MacDonald.
5 Cf. Walter Laqueur, *The Age of Terrorism* (London: Weidenfeld, 1987), p.262.
6. See, e.g., the annual report of the German Office for the Protection of the Constitution, *Verfassungsschutzbericht 1993* (Bonn: Bundesministerium des Innern, 1994), which documents this shift from left to right, both in terms of membership in extremist organizations, and in terms of violent acts. For other countries, the increasing violence has also been documented in T. Bjørgo and R. Witte (eds.), *Racist Violence in Europe* (Basingstoke/NY: Macmillan/St. Andrew Press, 1993); F.J. Buijs and J. van Donselaar, *Extreem-rechts* (Leiden:

14   TERROR FROM THE EXTREME RIGHT

LISWO, 1994); and several reports from the Swedish Security Police (analyzed in Heléne Lööw's contribution in this volume). American 'hate crime' statistics produced by organizations like 'Klanwatch' show a similar increase since the late 1980s (e.g., presented in *Klanwatch Intelligence Report* No.65, Feb. 1993 and No.71, Feb. 1994; cf. Leonard Weinberg, 'The American Radical Right in Contemporary Perspective', Paper presented at IPSA Panel RC 6.2, 'The Revival of Right-Wing Extremism', IPSA World Congress, Berlin, Aug. 1994.

7. See, e.g., Prem Shankar Jha, 'The Fascist Impulse in Developing Countries: Two Case Studies', *Studies in Conflict and Terrorism* 17/3 (July–Sept. 1994).

8. These are the two basic elements in an elaborate definition of a right-wing extremist orientation as presented by Wilhelm Heitmeyer, *Rechtextremistische Orientierungen bei Jugendlichen* (Weinheim/München: Juventa Verlag, 4th ed. 1992), pp.13–16.

9. *Chiliastic* refers to the post-apocalyptic world order, a utopia of peace and plenty. *Manichaean* refers to an undifferentiated mode of thinking in terms of absolute good vs. absolute evil. See Jeffrey Kaplan's study in this volume.

10. The problem is illustrated by the fact that many National Socialists deny that they are part of the right, but insist that their socialism belongs to the left. Some strands of neo-Fascism claim that they are 'neither left nor right, but a Third Position' (Italian, *Terza Posizione*).

11. See Roger Eatwell's highly useful discussion of the concept of 'the right' in R. Eatwell and N. O'Sullivan (eds.), *The Nature of the Right: American and European Politics and Political Thought Since 1789* (London: Pinter Publishers, 1989), Chs.1–5. Eatwell dismisses the notion of isolating a single 'essentialist' philosophical core of right-wing thought, but rather sees the right-wing tradition as various styles of thought, and as a series of responses to the left, and more generally, responses to threatening changes at work in society. He makes a distinction between 'the reactionary right', 'the moderate right', 'the radical right', 'the new right', and 'the extreme right'.

12. Cf. Leonard Weinberg, 'Introduction' to P.M. Merkl and L. Weinberg (eds.), *Encounters With the Contemporary Radical Right* (Boulder, CO: Westview Press, 1993), p.7; Eatwell, 'Right as a Variety of Styles of Thought', in R. Eatwell and O'Sullivan (note 11), pp.62–76.

13. Among the most recent books are Peter H. Merkl and Leonard Weinberg (eds.), *Encounters With the Radical Right* (Boulder, CO: Westview Press, 1993); Paul Hainsworth (ed.), *The Extreme Right in Europe and the USA* (London: Pinter Publishers, 1992); Luciano Cheles, Ronnie Ferguson and Michalina Vaughan (eds.), *Neo-Fascism in Europe* (London and NY: Longman, 1991); and Eatwell and O'Sullivan (note 11).

14. See for instance Mark S. Hamm (ed.), *Hate Crime: International Perspectives on Causes and Control* (Cincinnati: Anderson Publishing/Academy of Criminal Justice Sciences, 1994); Tore Bjørgo and Rob Witte (eds.), *Racist Violence in Europe* (Basingstoke/NY: Macmillan/St. Martin's Press, 1993); Otto, Hans-Uwe; and Roland Merten (eds.), *Rechtsradikale Gewalt im vereinigten Deutschland: Jugend im gesellschaftlichen Umbruch* (Opladen: Leske + Budrich, 1993); Willems, Helmut *et al.*, *Fremdenfeindliche Gewalt: Einstellungen, Täter, Konflikteskalation* (Opladen: Leske + Budrich, 1993).

15. This is the case with T. Bjørgo and R. Witte (eds.), *Racist Violence in Europe*, as well as with, e.g., Mark Hamm's *Hate Crime: International Perspectives on Causes and Control* (note 14).

16. The contributors to this volume were in fact asked to refer to an earlier version of Ehud Sprinzak's model, which was published as 'The Process of Delegitimization: Towards a Linkage Theory of Political Terrorism', *Terrorism and Political Violence* 3/1 (Spring 1991), pp.50–68. This was a general model covering three different processes of delegitimization which may radicalize groups into terrorism (generally corresponding to left-wing, rightwing and liberation movements). His study here expands on one of the three main types, 'split delegitimization', covering 'particularist' groups such as racist, sectarian and right-wing extremist militants. Sprinzak's perspectives were applied in T. Bjørgo, 'Militant neo-Nazism in Sweden', *Terrorism and Political Violence* 5/3 (Autumn 1993), pp.28–57.

17. The French nationalist Jean-Marie Le Pen and his *Front National* are an important source of ideological inspiration to nationalist parties in other European countries. Anti-immigration

activists in Norway and Denmark have developed an identical form of discourse, linking their resistance against immigration to the resistance movement against German occupation during World War II (discussed in my chapter in this volume).

18. Ku Klux Klan rituals and slogans, anti-Semitic discourse about the 'Zionist Occupation Government' ('ZOG') and role models such as the terrorist group The Order are often adopted by European racists.

19. One example of this contradiction between loyalty to nation and loyalty to race is the way British 'nationalists' celebrate Adolf Hitler, Britain's arch enemy. The tension between nationalism and racism is explored in a Norwegian context by the historian Øystein Sørensen, *Hitler eller Quisling* (Oslo: Cappelen, 1989). This issue is also discussed in my own 'Extreme Nationalism in Scandinavia' in this volume.

20. Most of those displaying Odinist symbols probably use them less as an expressions of genuine religious sentiment than as elements in their construction of a masculine 'warrior' identity, and as a way of rejecting both Jewish-inspired Christianity (with its 'soft' values of turning the other cheek) and mainstream society. To some activists, however, a racist interpretation of Odinism and its notion of Ragnarok fit well with their apocalyptic world-view of a coming race war where only a small remnant of the Aryan race will survive to build a new world [cf. *Ung Front*, No. 3 (1994), p.7; and Andrew Macdonald, *The Turner Diaries* (Hillsboro, MD: National Vanguard Books, 1980)].

21. Left-wing groups like the German Red Army Fraction (RAF) carried out bank robberies; Latin-American leftists often kidnapped foreign business men or wealthy locals for ransom; ethnic and national liberation movements (e.g., some of the Palestinian and Kurdish groups) have sometimes been deeply involved in the drug trade. The Provisional IRA has financed some of its activities through extortion. For a general description, see James Adams, *The Financing of Terror* (London: NEL, 1986).

22. A number of names among leaders of German, Swedish, Danish and Norwegian neo-Nazi and anti-immigration groups come to mind.

23. See also H. Lööw, 'Från 'nassar'' til 'seriösa samlare av uniformer'', *Tvärsnit*, No.3 (Oct. 1991), describing a militant activist who was known by his peers to enjoy violence. An Italian study of personality patterns among left-wing and right-wing terrorists found that in contrast to terrorists of the extreme left, right-wing terrorists more frequently displayed a psychopathological personality structure. F. Ferracuti and F. Bruno: 'Psychiatric Aspects of Terrorism in Italy', in I.L. Barac-Glantz and C.R. Glantz (eds.), *The Mad, the Bad and the Different* (Lexington, KY: Univ. of Kentucky 1981), p.199.

24. Richard Scutari, 'Kampen bakom galler', *Storm*, No.7–8, Vol. 3 (1992), p. 17. Scutari is one of the imprisoned members of the US terrorist group The Order who regularly writes for *Storm* and similar racist magazines abroad and in the USA.

25. One example: an activist in the Norwegian *Nasjonalt Folkeparti* who had carried out several bombings against immigrant targets and other actions in the mid-1980s also committed several cases of fraud, armed robbery and theft for personal gain during the same period.

26. Referring to Sweden and Germany, respectively, both Lööw and Willems report that more than 95 per cent of xenophobic perpetrators were males.

27. See, e.g., Eileen MacDonald, *Shoot the Women First* (London: Arrow Books, 1991); Stefan Aust, *Der Baader Meinhof Komplex* (München: Knaur, 1989); Laqueur, *Age of Terrorism* (note 5), pp. 79–80.

28. See e.g. Heléne Lööw, 'Tant Brun: Män och kvinnor i vit makt värden och i de nationella-leden', *Historiskt tidsskrift*, No.4 (1992).

29. I have argued this point in, 'Terrorist Violence against Immigrants and Refugees in Scandinavia: Patterns and Motives' and 'Role of the Media in Racist Violence', Chs.3 and 7 in Bjørgo and Witte, *Racist Violence in Europe* (note 6); cf. my 'Militant neo-Nazism in Sweden' (note 16).

30. This is a characteristic of much of the right-wing violence in the USA. Many of the violent activists of groups such as 'The Order' and other Identity inspired groups as well as Klan groups were distinctly middle-aged. The main exception, of course, is skinhead and youth gang violence. See Leonard Weinberg, 'The American Radical Right: Exit, Voice and

Violence', in Merkl and Weinberg (note 12), pp.190–3.
31. See Lööw's chapter, and her article 'The Cult of Violence: The Swedish Racist Counterculture', in Bjørgo and Witte, *Racist* (note 29). See also Bjørgo, 'Militant Neo-Nazism in Sweden' (note 16).
32. See my 'Terrorist Violence' (note 29) and 'Militant Neo-Nazism' (note 16).

Right-Wing Terrorism in a Comparative Perspective: The Case of Split Delegitimization

EHUD SPRINZAK

The purpose of this article is to identify the distinctive features of right-wing terrorism and to develop an analytical typology of particularistic terrorist organizations. The article is based on the conceptual framework of the process of delegitimization developed earlier by this author. It argues that right-wing radicals usually reach terrorism through a trajectory of *split delegitimization*, which implies a primary conflict with an 'inferior' community and a secondary conflict with the government. Six sub-types of right-wing terrorism are identified: *revolutionary* terrorism, *reactive* terrorism, *vigilante* terrorism, *racist* terrorism, *millenarian* terrorism and *youth counterculture* terrorism.

The Case of Particularistic Terrorism

Insurgent terrorism usually evokes the association of an anti-regime terror and claims for a universal message. The atrocities involved are committed against an established regime that is charged with a flagrant violation of the fundamental human rights of either its citizens or subject nations. There is, however, one common form of insurgent terrorism which is not directed primarily against governments and is not committed in the name of universal values. The terror organizations involved, usually right wing collectivities, vigilante groups or racist organizations, do not speak in the name of humanity. They are particularistic by their very nature and respond often to perceptions of insecurity and threats. They fight private wars against hostile ethnic communities, 'illegitimate' religious denominations, classes of undesired people or 'inferior races'. The enemies they feel threaten them are, variably, Jews, Arabs, Catholics, Blacks, Communists, homosexuals, foreign workers or other classes of 'inferior' human beings 'who want to get more than they deserve'.

The most significant political difference between 'universalistic' terror organizations and 'particularistic' ones lies in their relationship to the prevailing authority. While left wing and nationalist radical movements are usually involved in a *direct* conflict with the ruling government and their terror campaign is directed against its emissaries, the conflict of many right wing, religious or vigilante groups with the regime is secondary. The government is rarely considered an opponent and in many cases is expected to cooperate or remain uninvolved. Conflict with the authorities or occasional anti-regimist violence, while likely to develop in such cases, emerges, and often greatly intensifies, only after these radicals do not obtain official help, political understanding or favorable silence.

The purpose of this essay is to develop an analytical typology of right-wing terrorist groups and to demonstrate its usefulness for the organization of the large amount of historical and current information already gathered about these movements. The study is based on the conceptual framework of the process of delegitimization developed earlier by this author.[1]

Terrorism and the Process of Delegitimization

The analytical affinity between terrorism and the process of delegitimization is based on the understanding of insurgent terrorism as a product of a lengthy political process of group radicalization *vis-à-vis* the regime. The essence of this process is a slowly evolving legitimacy crisis between an insurgent movement and the government. Terrorism is the peak of the process of delegitimization. The movement involved is so vehemently opposed to the regime's legitimacy that it is ready to challenge it by the use of unconventional violence. What terrorists do – and other radicals do not – is to bring their rejection of the regime's legitimacy to the utmost and express it by extranormal violence.

The importance of the understanding of terrorism in terms of a process of delegitimization is that terrorism is identified as a behavioral stage in the life history of an extremist movement, a phase in which the organization is ready and willing to use unconventional violence against government's agents. The idea of the process of delegitimization implies, therefore, the presence of *pre-terrorist* and less radical stages in the evolution of the movement involved. It also recognizes the possibility of *post-terrorist* stages in which the group involved is no longer ready or able to use terrorism. This approach allows us to talk about terrorism as the peak of a historical cycle – the rise and decline of a militant political opposition. Terrorism, according to this approach, is not a detached state of mind of crazy misfits but a type of political behavior which evolves (and declines) gradually under certain identifiable psycho-political conditions.

While processes of delegitimization vary greatly, the typical process implies a struggle of a challenge group against the government, and is made up of three consecutive stages: *Crisis of Confidence*, *Conflict of Legitimacy*, and *Crisis of Legitimacy*.[2] Each of these stages pertains to a political protest group composed of activists and followers who interact with the regime as well as among themselves and who obtain in the process a collective psycho-political identity. The group identity, which often changes rapidly as radicalization proceeds, contains a combination of political behavioral components, ideological and symbolic tenets and psychological traits. A short examination of the three ideal-typical stages of the delegitimization trajectory reveals the following features.

Crisis of Confidence is the earliest and most moderate stage of group radicalization and involves no violence. It is experienced by a movement, or a challenge group, whose confidence in the existing political government is greatly eroded. Crisis of confidence implies a conflict with specific rulers or policies. It does not presume a structural delegitimation because the foundations of the established political system are not questioned or challenged.

Crisis of confidence is marked by the rise of a distinct ideological challenge group, movement, or counterculture which refuses to play according to the established rules of the game. The group articulates its critique of the establishment in loaded ideological terms, dissents from mainstream politics and opts for protests, demonstrations, symbolic resistance and other forms of direct action. While not illegal, its behavior, group mentality and language are likely to be provocative. Early confrontations with the authorities and the police, including small scale and unplanned events of violence, may occur.[3]

Conflict of Legitimacy is the radicalized continuation of the crisis of confidence. It is the behavioral stage that evolves when a challenge group, previously confined to criticizing the government, is ready to question the very legitimacy of the regime. Conflict of legitimacy implies the emergence of an *alternative ideological and cultural system*, one that delegitimizes the prevailing regime and its code of social norms in the name of a better normative political order.

Conflict of legitimacy usually begins when the challenge group is greatly disappointed with its previous stage of radicalization. The former 'moderate' radicals become enraged and frustrated either by the government's hostile (sometimes excessively violent) response to their passionate critique, or by their own failure to reform the system. Mentally they now develop the need to channel their outrage into a more extreme form of protest. A proper course to follow seems to be the development of an *ideology of delegitimation* which communicates a complete chasm with the prevailing political order.

The evolution of the conflict of legitimacy is manifested by intense political action that ranges between angry protest (demonstrations, confrontations and vandalism) and the application of *intended low scale violence* against the regime. The challenge group now experiences considerable radicalization. The movement begins to solidify and closes rank. The individuals involved become revolutionary. Their jargon is slanderous and berates a totally discredited social order.[4]

Crisis of Legitimacy is the behavioral and symbolic culmination of the two preceding stages. Its essence lies in the extension of the previous delegitimation of the system to *every individual* person associated with it. Individuals who are identified with the 'rotten' and 'soon to be destroyed' social and political order are depersonalized and dehumanized. They are derogated into the ranks of the worst enemies or subhuman species. *Dehumanization* makes it possible for the radicals to disengage morally and to commit atrocities without remorse.[5]

The operational manifestation of the crisis of legitimacy is systematic terrorism. It usually amounts to the formation of a small terror underground, which is engaged in unconventional attacks on the regime and its affiliates, and which is capable of committing a wide range of atrocities. As a social unit, the terrorist underground is often isolated from the outside world. It constructs a reality of its own and a whole new set of behavioral and moral standards that are enforced in an authoritarian manner. The members of the group are so involved and entangled with each other that every individual act has a collective meaning of utmost importance. The psychodynamics of the whole unit, including its acts of terrorism against the outside society, assume a logic of its own and is, at many times, unrelated to any external factors.[6]

The three-stage process of delegitimization described above is the purest and most exhaustive form of insurgent terrorism. *It conveys the essence of the idea of terrorism, that is, the complete transformation of sane human beings into brutal and indiscriminate killers.* This is why I suggest calling it *transformational delegitimization.*[7] Terrorism reached through transformational delegitimization may represent the *ideal type* of terrorism, but is, of course, just one form of terrorism.

The Case of Split Delegitimization

The fact that particularistic terror organizations usually avoid confrontation with the authorities and start their career by directing the majority of their operations at non-ruling groups suggests a different pattern of delegitimization than the typical transformational model presented above. It indicates the possible presence of a *dual process of delegitimization*: an intense delegitimization *vis-à-vis* the unaccepted non-governmental collectivity and a *diluted* delegitimization towards the regime. Thus, while the Crisis of Confidence, Conflict of Legitimacy and Crisis of Legitimacy are all present, their sequential order and direction are not the same. The issue at stake is one of *split delegitimization*, namely, *a case where an uneven radicalization of a group of extremists develops against two separate entities.*

The distinguishing feature of the radicalization of most particularistic terror organizations is that it *begins* with a Conflict of Legitimacy. The majority of right-wing movements are organized around the belief that the object of their intense opposition is *a priori* illegitimate. It does not belong to the same humanity that they see themselves part of, and should either be kept in an inferior legal status, expelled or even be eliminated. Such a belief, which is usually the product of a long held tradition or cultural heritage, does not require immediate violent action. As long as the particularistic movement involved does not monopolize political power, is systematically delegitimized by the established culture or feels an immediate existential threat, it will not resort to violence. Instead, it will do its best to strengthen and perpetuate the existing social and cultural mechanisms of discrimination. Violence, and gradually terrorism, only emerge when the group involved feels increasingly insecure or threatened. For instance, the Jews may suddenly appear too strong, the Blacks too influential, the Arabs too treacherous and the Communists too close to a Marxist revolution. Severe measures must be taken to restrict their movement. These measures are likely to begin with campaigns of intimidation and escalate (under specific conditions) to terrorism. A comparative examination of occasional terrorist eruptions by groups such as the Ku Klux Klan, other white supremacist groups in America, neo-Fascists in Italy, neo-Nazis in Germany, vigilantes of Gush Emunim, and the followers of the late Rabbi Kahane in Israel, the AWB paramilitary formations in South Africa and others, shows the same pattern of radicalization: a constant – but largely non-violent – sense of delegitimation regarding the 'inferior' groups, a growing anxiety, efforts of low level intimidation and finally, outbursts of terrorism.

While much of the violence of particularistic terrorists is expected to involve non-ruling populations, at some point their violence may turn towards the political authorities. When vigilante movements, neo-fascists or neo-Nazis feel threatened by other groups, they often convince themselves that the government in charge is doing very little to protect their 'legitimate' community. The rulers, or the most unfriendly elements among them, are then portrayed as 'soft', 'internationalist' or 'leftist'. Such projection implies a sense of betrayal and *a Crisis of Confidence* with the regime. While the government itself may not be declared illegitimate, and be an object of their rejection, the group's respect for its authority is dramatically eroded. With this comes flagrant disobedience of the law. This atmosphere often produces splinter groups which break from the mainstream because they feel that the leaders of their movement are not doing enough.

The presence of *split delegitimization* may not, necessarily, be permanent. There are increasing indications that very extreme right-wing organizations tend to close the legitimacy gap between their different hate targets. This happens when the radical group in question perceives the government to be identical with the illegitimate minority group, and when both are accorded the same level of illegitimacy. The theory behind the 'disappearance of the split' is that the government has literally been taken over by the hated minority group and is no longer capable of reforming itself. It should therefore be destroyed with the same intensity as the original target group. The most significant example for the disappearance of split delegitimization is the recent rise of the imagery of ZOG (Zionist Occupation Government) in racist, neo-Nazi and millenarian circles, and the association of several Western governments with a Jewish-Zionist take over.[8] The ZOG imagery and its meaning will be discussed below in greater detail.

Unlike left-wing liberals, many particularistic terrorists, Fascists, Nazis, reactive vigilantes, racists and white supremacists do not feel remorse about their violence and the atrocities they cause. There is, in this case, no need to undergo a profound psycho-political transformation to become brutal killers. The desired world of most right-wing terrorists, with the notable exception of millenarian radicals, is not a reality of a non-violent universal humanity that is transformed temporarily – and for just reasons – into a bloody existence. Rather, it is a *Weltanschauung* which is predicated on conflict and dehumanization of specific classes of the population. From this perspective certain people just do not belong to the relevant community; they are outsiders and should be treated accordingly. Terrorism against these 'inferiors' is a control mechanism, a means of assuring that they do not multiply and prevail. This attitude is perhaps the reason why most particularistic terrorists never attempt to apologize for their brutal actions and why so few explanatory ideologies of terrorism exist in this cultural milieu.[9] Acts that are reasonable and natural do not require justification.

Right-Wing Terrorism: A Typology

The number of particularistic organizations which have resorted in the past century to terrorism is large, as are the variations among the respective organizations. Cultural and ethnic differences among nations increase this plurality significantly. This is why it appears useful to group them, for comparative purposes, into six general types: *revolutionary terrorism*, *reactive terrorism*, *vigilante terrorism*, *racist terrorism*, *millenarian terrorism* and *youth counterculture terrorism*. It is important to maintain that these six types of particularistic terrorism are not mutually exclusive. In reality we may find that reactive terrorism involves racism and that many racist and reactive terrorists see themselves as vigilantes, defenders of the normative order of society. Racist and reactive groups are often attracted to some type of fascist ideology as are youth countercultures. They are attracted not necessarily because of their fascination with fascist revolution. It may also be due to an emotional need to reject the normative order of liberal democracy and justify their violence. The following typology is based on the identification of the *dominant principle* around which the rightist group is organized and on its relation to the dynamics of split delegitimation.

A. Revolutionary Terrorism

The most influential particularistic terrorism in modern time has been produced by right-wing revolutionary movements belonging to the Fascist and Nazi schools. Fascist insurgent movements were intensely active across Europe between the 1920s and 1940s, and produced an enormous amount of violence and terrorism. Two movements in particular, the Italian Fascists and the German Nazis, even succeeded in taking power in their respective countries. Their insurgent violence was converted into massive state terrorism with horrendous consequences.

The historical process of delegitimization undergone by the fascist and Nazi movements was not short. Nor did it develop as a response to specific blunders of liberal democracy. It involved, instead, a lengthy trajectory of rejection of late nineteenth century bourgeois society and parliamentary democracy.[10] Part of the process was an early fascination with revolutionary socialism, which later developed into intense opposition. The Nazi variant of Fascism involved, in addition, rigid racist principles which added great impetus to the delegitimation of democratic culture. The radicalization of the European extreme right was enormously intensified by the violent experience of World War I and the post-1918 'culture of war'.[11]

It is important to stress that the violence of both Italian Fascists and German Nazis was neither a behavioral product of their war experience nor of their increasing conflict of legitimation with their rivals. Violence was an essential part of their original philosophy of government. Fascist and Nazi ideologues glorified the use of violence. They saw it as an essential ingredient to virtuous politics.[12] Very few Fascists worried about justifying their use of force.[13] Violence and terrorism were perceived as essential parts of the Fascist *Weltanschauung* and, consequently, did not require explanation or justification.

While the Fascist road to power in both Italy and Germany involved *split delegitimization*, a primary conflict with the socialists and communists and a secondary conflict with their respective governments, the distinction between the two was tactical. The Fascists despised parliamentary democracy just as they rejected socialism and communism and all three were considered equally illegitimate. Fascist leaders believed, however, that it was too risky for them to confront the government directly. Instead, they assumed that they could rise to power through the flawed mechanisms of democratic politics.

The overhaul of the system should come later. While postwar Italy was entangled in a virtual socio-political civil war, which allowed the *squadristi* to resort to terror and to the brutal killing of their direct enemies, the socialists and communists,[14] the Nazis were cautious not to alienate middle and higher class conservatives through the use of excessive terrorism. This required a 'legalistic' strategy to get to power and implied violent but non-terroristic types of action.[15] Although post-World War I right-wing radicalism evolved in an intensely violent atmosphere, thereby producing much terror, terrorism was, with few exceptions, an unintended by-product of violent intimidation, brutal street hooliganism and aggressive propaganda.[16] For tactical reasons, then, the Fascist and Nazi delegitimation of their respective regimes rarely crossed the threshold of *conflict of legitimacy*.

The most significant difference between revolutionary right-wing terrorism of pre- and post-World War II is the socio-political marginality of the latter and their relative lack of confidence. Prewar European Fascists and Nazis were part of the main struggle for the future of Western civilization. Along with the socialists, the communists and the liberal democrats, they attracted millions of supporters, including highly educated and wealthy elites. Even their rivals considered the Fascists serious contenders for the hegemony of Western world. Its defeat in World War II, as well as the horrors of the Holocaust, gave Fascism an enormous blow. Most Fascist organizations were either totally eliminated or remained at the very illegitimate fringes of Western society. Many of their leaders who survived the war were executed as war criminals, put in jail for life or went into hidden exile.

Fascism survived, however, and small movements and parties of neo-fascists and neo-Nazis resurfaced in Europe, maintaining a low profile and a considerable sense of inferiority.[17] At the extreme margins they also created, since the late 1940s, small and unstable violent groups such as the Italian *Fasci Azione Rivolutionaria, Ordine Nouvo, Squadre Azuione Mussolini, Avanguardia Nazionale, Nuclei Armati Rivoluzionari* and *Ordine Nero*, the French *Occident, Omega, Odessa, Charles Martel Club, French National Liberation Front, Ordre Nouveau*, the German *Deutsche Aktionsgruppe, Wehrsportgruppe Hoffman, Deutsche Alternative*, and *Nationale Offensive*, the Swedish *Nordiska Rikspartiet, Vitt Ariskt Motstand* (VAM), *Riksfronten*, the Dutch *Jongeren Front Nederland* and many others. While committed to the old dreams of creating a fascist civilization, most of these minuscule groups have been unable to bring to full use the old strategies of street violence, bloody intimidation and armed propaganda. They certainly were in a no position to directly challenge their respective governments. Their repertoire of violence and terrorism, which seems to have come in unsystematic waves, has included desecration of Jewish cemeteries and synagogues, vandalism and arson, violent attacks on foreign workers in Europe, fire bombing of shelters housing foreign asylum seekers, rare assassinations and occasional spectacular bombings of public places such as the 1980 Munich Oktoberfest, the Italicus Express in Bologna and a Jewish synagogue in Rue Copernic, Paris. Italian, French and German neo-fascists appeared in the streets in the late 1960s and 1970s, violently confronting new left demonstrators. Since the mid-1980s, however, there has been a dramatic increase in European neo-Nazi and radical rightist violent attacks on foreign workers and asylum seekers, especially in Germany.[18] There has also been a significant development of an international neo-Nazi and racist communication network. It appears that the growing resentment in Western Europe of Third World immigrants and anxiety regarding the job market have played a considerable role in the increasing appeal and confidence of the European radical right.[19]

Careful not to confront the governments in their respective countries directly, many neo-fascists and neo-Nazis have also been involved in *tactical* Split Delegitimization. While hostile to and critical of liberal democracy, they have reserved their sporadic violence and terrorism almost exclusively for political movements or communities they believed to be weak and vulnerable. Rarely have they attacked agents of the governments or symbols of authority. In Italy, which never really rid itself of Fascism, many neo-fascists have come to believe since the 1950s that the communist threat – which was taken seriously by many respectable and established politicians – would slowly lead to the erosion of the nation's chaotic democracy, thereby facilitating a return of Italy to Fascism. Tactical terrorism was consequently recommended in order to further destabilize the political system and produce calls for strong national power.[20] Part of the neo-fascist effort involved attempts to attract military and police officers worried about a communist takeover.

A significant development in recent times has been the intensification of the 'secondary' delegitimization processes of several European neo-Nazi organizations, that is, their radical confrontation with their respective governments. There are signs that the delegitimization of these organizations is not split any more. They are as negative about their respective governments as they are about the Jews, homosexuals, foreign workers and other 'inferior' groups. Some of them may even be ready to conduct terror operations against government agents and agencies. A case in point is the Swedish VAM (White Aryan Resistance). In the spring of 1991 leading members of the VAM network went underground. After stealing arms from a police station and conducting a bank robbery, they vowed to prepare for the 'Great Racial War', and made clear that their main target is none other than the government itself.[21] However, most were soon arrested and their declared war against ZOG has so far not got off the ground.

Why this development has taken place is not fully clear to me, but the rhetorical device that seems to have made it possible is identifiable. What is at stake is the rise to prominence of the ZOG (Zionist Occupation Government) language and imagery, and the increasing conviction among several European neo-Nazis that their governments have irreversibly been taken over by the Jews and their collaborators. If, in the past, there could be some hope of applying pressure on the respective governments to change their liberal policies towards the non-Aryan races, this is no longer the case. Governments that have been taken over by the Jews and their agents cannot be reformed. They must be brought down by force; and sabotage and terrorism are proper ways of starting the great struggle.[22]

One possible explanation for the radicalization of VAM and similar European neo-Nazis is the unprecedented growth of international neo-Nazi communication networks and the consequent feeling that the Nazi school is no longer small or isolated.[23] The very spread of the ZOG imagery is a good example. The discourse that the neo-Nazis have taken over was not invented in its present form in Europe. It was imported from the United States, where it had been developed and disseminated in the late 1970s and 1980s by several racist and Christian Identity organizations. For European right-wingers, just as for their American colleagues, it was an appealing post-communist answer to their quest for demons. The communist 'evil empire', which had long haunted the extreme right and served as its great Satanic enemy, may be gone, but the real demonic people, the Jews, are still around. Better organized than ever around their Zionist center in Israel and heavily represented in government, business, the media, and the dominant liberal culture, the Jews are again considered the real threat for the Aryan race. And as in past European history, an unmasked Jewish threat may make it possible to get wide public support. Another potential explanation for the rising neo-Nazi confidence is the dramatic increase in the public concern over East European immigrants, third world workers and asylum seekers. There is now, so it appears to the neo-Nazis, a much greater appeal for their racist interpretation of reality and for the ZOG conspiracy theory.

B. Reactive Terrorism

Particularistic terrorism is occasionally produced by status quo and conservative movements which react to real or perceived threats. This reactive terrorism is resorted to by organizations which have either lost their positions of power and social status or are fearful of such a development. The movements involved undergo an intense process of delegitimization *vis-à-vis* the forces that are out to take over. Terrorism is grasped as a means of last resort in order to restore the *status quo ante*, and is usually applied against organizations which themselves have reached power through the use of violence. The right-ist orientation of most reactive groups is normally a response to two circumstances, the first being left-wing terrorism which earlier on was in some way responsible for their expropriation. It may also be a response to a universalistic (i.e., 'leftist') frame of mind which threatens them by removing their privileged positions. While most reactive terrorists are not at first intensely preoccupied with right-wing ideology, they are often joined by old time fascists who hope to capitalize on their misery and recreate the glorious fascist past.

Reactive terrorists may be divided into two types: those who have already lost political power and are fighting an uphill battle to regain it, and those who have not yet been stripped of their power and privileges but are worried about such a development. Organizations which have lost political hegemony are usually weak and desperate. Their terrorism takes the form of sporadic revenge attacks and assassination attempts of government officials. This terrorism *does not involve split delegitimation* because the losers fight only the newly created government. In addition to the historical loss of power, which leaves them with few resources, they are vigorously pursued by the state's security apparatus. Members live either underground or in exile, and are usually ill-prepared for an effective campaign against the regime.

A historical example of an organization that seeks to regain lost power is provided by post-World War II Croat insurgents, who for years fought the communist regime of Yugoslavia. The Croats have a long history of right-wing violence and terrorism. In 1934 Croat assassins murdered Yugoslavia's King Alexander, together with French Minister of Foreign Affairs Louis Barthou. Throughout 1941–45 the Croat *Ustasha* collaborated with the Nazis, controlling Croatia and other Yugoslav areas. Ardently Roman Catholic with a fascist inclination, they hated the Orthodox Christian Serbs, accusing them of unduly dominating the other peoples of Yugoslavia.[24] Hitler's defeat and Yugoslavia's takeover by the Communists ended Croatia's independence. Members of the old regime, who managed to escape Tito's retribution, resurfaced in several remote countries, most notably in Australia and Latin America. They vowed to return, retake Croatia from Tito and use all means necessary. The international rise of modern terrorism in the late 1960s and early 1970s and the reinstitution of the myth of terrorism as an effective revolutionary strategy had a great impact on the Croat diaspora. They believed terrorism could be used to publicize their cause among Croats to such an extent that it would make an invasion of Yugoslavia possible. Beginning in March 1971, when they blew up the Yugoslav consulate in Milan, the organization conducted several spectacular operations, including the successful hijacking of a Swedish airplane, of a TWA aircraft bound to Chicago and the planting of a bomb in Grand Central Station in New York.[25] In June 1972 the

Ustasha attempted and failed at a raid into Yugoslavia.[26]

The desperate terrorism exercised by former *Ustasha* and several other groups of Croat emigres did not help them politically. The Croat reactive struggle greatly declined in the 1980s. However, it did help reinvigorate Serb hatred which appeared in full force following the 1989 dissolution of Yugoslavia. The Civil War in that troubled country, launched in June 1991 among the Serbs, Croats, and Muslims of Bosnia and Kosovo, was not waged over the legacy of the emigres, many of whom came back to retake Croatia. However, the historical memories of their reactive violence contributed to the easy passage to violence, terrorism and ethnic cleansing that continue to plague the region.

An example of reactive terrorism which started before the final loss of power is provided by the *Organization Armée Secret* (OAS), the terror organization established in 1961 by the French *Colons* in Algeria, in a last minute effort to stop the French retreat from the colony. In spite of their large concentration, the former French fascists in Algeria felt no desire to conduct a fascist revolution: the privileged French *pieds noirs* led a good colonial life in Algeria, and wanted to keep it that way. Full of contempt for the local population, they were consistently opposed to equal rights for the 'natives'.[27] An intense conflict of legitimation between these two populations was long in the making. The civil war which began in 1954 in Algeria triggered an intense radicalization between the *colons* and the local population. It also started a secondary process of delegitimization between the *colons* and the French government, which was seen as 'too soft' on the Algerians.[28] In that context, the *ultras*, the most extreme among the settlers, even established small terror hit teams which 'helped' the French Army launch counter strikes against the Algerians.[29] The situation deteriorated significantly between 1959 and 1960 when the *colons* found out that President Charles de Gaulle was ready to compromise with the FLN. Their process of delegitimization with the French government intensified dramatically.

The subtler sense of betrayal by France's historical hero was shared by several of the nation's most decorated generals, who vowed to keep Algeria French. By 1961, when de Gaulle's intentions to leave Algeria became a fact, the recently started process of delegitimization reached its peak. The disgruntled *pieds noirs* and the embittered generals established the OAS. Moving fast from conflict to crisis of legitimation with the French government, they launched a dual terror campaign. While applying vengeance terrorism against the Algerians in an effort to destroy the peace talks and accentuate the situation,[30] they also engaged in a massive terror campaign against the government. This they did in Algeria, in France and in Europe. OAS terrorism tragically backfired, however. In addition to its failure to stop the 1962 French retreat from Algeria, it destroyed the conditions for any kind of European-Algerian co-existence in the newly created Algerian republic. A massive exodus took place, which in a short time brought to France over one million former Algerian settlers.

Reactive terrorism, to conclude, usually starts with the terrorization of many non-governmental groups and communities. However, it is almost always transformed into an intense process of delegitimization with the government and anti-regimist terrorism.

C. Vigilante Terrorism

A special variant of reactive terrorism is *vigilante terrorism*. Vigilante terror is used by individuals and groups who believe that the government does not adequately protect them from violent groups or individuals and that they must protect themselves. Vigilante movements rarely perceive themselves involved in conflict with the government and the prevailing concept of law. They are neither revolutionary nor interested in the destruction of authority. Rather, what characterizes the vigilante mind is the profound conviction that the government and its agencies have failed to enforce the law or establish order in a particular area.[31] Backed by the fundamental norm of self-defense and speaking in the name of the law of the land, vigilantes see themselves as enforcing the law and executing justice. Vigilantes are, therefore, particularistic supporters of the status quo and have no alternative political system in mind. They believe that they are acting legally against criminal elements because the authorities are either too weak to enforce the law or negligent in their duties.[32]

Vigilantism, it should be stressed, is by no means synonymous with terrorism. In reality, the majority of vigilantes rarely resort to atrocities in order to uphold the law. However, under circumstances of serious pressure, often involving violence against them, vigilantes undergo a process of delegitimization which pushes them toward the use of terror. Like most other particularistic terrorists, the primary process of delegitimization of the vigilante movement involves a non-governmental group or individuals who are believed to have broken the law. But vigilante terrorism, unless tacitly supported by the regime, is likely to trigger conflict with the government's agents. Most effective governments cannot tolerate systematic vigilantism and try to curtail its activity. If the stakes and the level of vigilante terror are high, this could lead to intense radicalization and serious conflict with the government. Two situations are particularly prone to the evolution of vigilante terrorism:

- lawlessness in border areas where the military and police are unable to fully protect the pioneering settlers;
- the presence of intense insurgent terrorism which cannot be effectively contained by the authorities.

Vigilante terrorism has developed, for example, in the occupied territories of Israel as a direct result of the rise of Palestinian violence and the inability of the Israeli Army to provide the settlers with complete protection. A group that was called the Jewish Underground by the Israeli press conducted several terror operations in the early 1980s in an attempt to restrain the Palestinians and maintain a system of control through terrorism. The most spectacular operation of the Jewish Underground was the blowing up of the cars of two Arab mayors believed by the group to be the major coordinators of PLO operations in the area. The vigilantes of Gush Emunim, a religious and messianic Israeli movement, believed they were upholding the law. They obtained rabbinical approval of the act based on the Jewish Halachic rule that, 'he who comes to kill you, you kill him first', and argued in court that this was also the spirit of Israel's positive law.[33] Members of the Jewish Underground also convinced themselves that the military government of the area was tacitly behind them, and that several of the military officers involved, who knew the political constraints of the government, secretly encouraged them to carry out their plans. The decision of the Jewish underground to attack the mayors was exceptional and unprecedented in Jewish and Israeli contexts. It implied a serious secondary process of delegitimization with the government of Israel which was previously considered holy. However, the underground's conflict with the Israeli government never reached the point of a crisis of legitimacy and anti-Jewish terrorism.

Since the 1960s, vigilante killing of 'subversive' elements has played an unprecedented role in Latin America, where the practice is long known and associated with the military and the police.[34] Following a wave of left-wing insurgent terror in the 1960s, a period which greatly destabilized countries such as Argentina, Brazil, El Salvador and Guatemala, a counterstrike was launched, with even worse human and political consequences. Unable to suppress terrorism through the ordinary legal system, police and military officers decided to take the law into their hands and to eliminate the leftist threat privately. They did this through the establishment of death squads which swept through the respective countries killing scores of suspected terrorists or alleged collaborators. What was unique about these vigilantes is that many of them were military officers acting in their free time. There is, in fact, a large body of information which shows that these operations were conducted with the full cooperation of the armies and governments involved, and that the whole idea was to free the officers from the legal constraints of due process.[35]

An early case in Argentina is that of President Isabella Peron's Minister of Social Welfare, José Lopez Rega, who established the Anti-Communist Alliance (Triple A). Rega recruited for the job federal and provincial policemen and armed them with weapons bought by state funds. Responding to the terror campaign of the *Ejército Revolutionario del Pueblo* and the *Montoneros* – organizations which had destabilized Argentina since the late 1960s – the Triple A assassinated over 200 people and intimidated many more in 1974–75. In August 1976 Triple A killed 46 suspected terrorists.[36] Similar quasi-official vigilante groups operated in the 1960s and 1970s in Mexico, Brazil and El Salvador. In Guatemala, which between the mid-1950s and the mid-1980s witnessed a virtual civil war with three waves of intense terrorism, the right was represented by nearly 20 vigilante groups. These paramilitary organizations with such names as the New Anti-Communist Organization, the Purple Rose, and the White Hand, comprised supporters of the status quo such as landowners, police and military officers.[37] What marks the Guatemalan as well as many other Latin American vigilantes, is the nearly automatic support they receive from the government and the security forces. What is really occurring is state terrorism in disguise. Vigilantism in Guatemala, just as leftist insurgent terrorism, has become a way of life, a part of a 'culture and counterculture of terror', which in the last 40 years took the lives of over 150,000 people.[38]

Vigilante terrorism often involves split delegitimization, but the secondary process of delegitimization rarely reaches terroristic maturation. People who believe they uphold the law of the land may get angry at the small support they receive from the authorities, but rarely, if ever, confront the government. Unless intensely abused and mistreated by government agents in jail, they are likely to restrict their occasional terrorism to the 'law breakers'.

D. Racist Terrorism

Most particularistic terror organizations display some kind of racism, that is, a belief that race is an important organizing principle in society and that certain groups of 'colored' people are inherently inferior. Several organizations, however, see race as the *main* organizational principle that counts, and devote all their energy to the struggle for racist supremacy. In contrast to revolutionary terrorists who dream about a total transformation of the social, cultural and political system and the creation of a fascist civilization, racist terrorists are usually political conservatives. Their sole desire is a social system which will either recognize their racial superiority officially or informally guarantee its perpetuation. Racist movements go into conflict with the prevailing government, namely, *engage in split delegitimization*, only after the regime involved has failed to support their platforms or has been actively engaged in their containment. Terrorism is often resorted to by these racists as a *control mechanism*, an effort to restore the previous caste structure of society in which the inferior race must remain, permanently, an underprivileged second class. In extreme cases racist terrorism is also utilized against government agencies or agents who are especially involved in law enforcement against the perpetrators of terror.

Racist terrorism has been almost synonymous with the American Ku Klux Klan, an umbrella secret society established in 1865, following the defeat of the Confederacy in the Civil War. The Klan underwent several historical transformations, and recently has been in a steady decline. Over the years, it has added to its original anti-Black platform new ideological concerns such as anti-Semitism, anti-Catholicism, anti-Communism and the idea of '100 per cent Americanism'. Rarely as monolithic and centralized as its public image wants the average person to believe, the Klan has existed locally under a variety of names and titles. Since its foundation, however, the Ku Klux Klan *as an idea* has been the inspiration for many similar organizations.[39]

The 'classic' KKK terror operation, a pattern developed in the late 1860s and maintained for generations, involved a small group of masked and hooded night raiders. A typical target was a black individual suspected of violating some 'white man's values'. Klansmen had all the advantages – darkness, disguise, superior numbers and armaments. Victims had an ingrained fear of the Klan and little or no military skills. In one given night, the Klan group might visit several black cabins to inflict 'lessons' and punishment. Black suspects were often taken to a wooden area for a mock trial. Their homes were usually set on fire. Many trials were concluded by lynching the suspects, shooting them, or severely injuring them. An individual allowed to live was warned that there would be no second chance, and was sent to transmit the message to his peers and colleagues.[40]

The Ku Klux Klan and Klan-like organizations rarely attacked the Federal government or its agents directly, but have almost always been involved in a secondary process of *delegitimization* with Washington. In that respect, the Klan is a direct descendent of the influential American traditions of *populism* and *nativism*.[41] The role of the Federal government in the Civil War and the First Reconstruction, and its increasing involvement in public affairs in the post-1929 Franklin Roosevelt era, had constantly haunted the organization. KKK-like organizations argued persistently that the movement had been loyal to the Constitution of the United States, and that the original Constitution never intended to give the Federal government and Congress the degree of authority they came to possess. KKK's America grew up from individual settlers and independent local communities and was intended to remain that way.

The increased isolation of the Ku Klux Klan in America during the 1960s, the greater commitment of the Federal government to take anti-Klan action and the successful penetration of the organization by federal agents led to the organization's significant decline. The KKK lost its hold on the deep South and its followers became increasingly marginal. A resurgence attempt in the 1970s did not last long.[42]

Racist and white supremacist groups have not vanished from the American landscape, however, and several anti-communist paramilitary and survivalist groups gained some public notoriety between the 1960s and 1970s. The traumatic experience of the Vietnam War and the perception of an imminent communist threat were responsible for the rise of several paramilitary organizations and for the occasional resort of some of their members to violence.[43] Since the 1970s there has, furthermore, been a dramatic increase in the number and interaction of white supremacist groups with strong religious and millenarian inclinations. While marginalized and delegitimized by mainstream American culture, these groups and organizations seem to have been successful in the creation of a rather wide and self-supporting racist counterculture.

E. Millenarian Terrorism[44]

The fifth type of particularistic terrorism is millenarian terrorism, terrorism resorted to by religious groups which believe that the end of the world is imminent and that if spiritually prepared, they will be saved.[45] Terrorism and millenarianism, it must be stated at the outset, are by no means synonymous or even behaviorally interconnected. The majority of the millenarian sects are not terroristic. A typical feature of millenarianism is a peaceful withdrawal from the world.[46] The spiritual leaders of the group believe that only in a state of isolation and seclusion can they properly prepare themselves for the demise of the sinning world and for their own salvation. The millenarian separation from the rest of society implies either a simple conviction that God will punish the sinning people and that the group should mind its own spiritual business, or an admission of weakness and inability to struggle against the evil forces of society.

Millenarian sects that commit terrorist acts usually do so for reasons which are not directly related to their spiritual and chiliastic dreams. They resort to terrorism either because of the presence of individual leaders who are violence-prone, or because the external society or some of its agencies push them aggressively into a corner. So much hate, alienation and desperation are experienced by the group that on occasions, and after specific incentives have been created, it will resort to terrorism.[47] The occasional shift to terrorism implies the group's inability to fully seclude itself and sever all contacts with organized society.

Millenarian terrorists differ from most particularistic terrorists in their vision of the future. It was mentioned earlier that unlike left-wing terrorists, whose desired society is non-violent, many particularistic terrorists are convinced that violence and conflict are essential ingredients of the good society or are at least necessary for the preservation of their desired world. This is, however, not the case with millenarian terrorists. The ideal society of the millenarians is peaceful, harmonious and non-violent.[48] It is peaceful because the post-apocalyptic vision of the group leaves no room for conflict. The sinning world is expected to be destroyed and the future community will consist only of loyal believers. The terrorism committed by most millenarian groups is, thus, a necessary evil. It is often projected by the organization leaders as an act of self-defense against an aggressive and merciless external society. Bank robbery is not virtuous but may be justified by the legitimate financial needs of the group. An attack on a representative of the 'Zionist controlled government' may, in the same spirit, be legitimate if that individual is perceived as an immediate threat to the organization. Terrorism may also help group members obtain the military experience that will be needed at the time of Armageddon.

Millenarian terrorism has occasionally been produced in the 1980s by several Christian Identity groups, an American umbrella subculture espousing a variety of racist, anti-Semitic, Christian-fundamentalist and anti-Federalist beliefs. The Christian Identity Movement seems to have grown up from the racist periphery of American fundamentalism and the extreme right, which in the last two decades has undergone a noteworthy revival. More radical and revolutionary than the Ku Klux Klan ever was, this plethora of millenarian sects, churches and small paramilitary organizations views the American political and cultural system as entirely illegitimate.[49] It is a decadent society hopelessly polluted by racially or ideologically inferior people such as Jews, Blacks, communists, homosexuals and liberals of all sorts. While many followers of the Identity schools are not full-time political revolutionaries, and may just be interested in a peaceful withdrawal from the world, their ideotheology indicates a profound Crisis of Legitimacy with the American system. It further implies considerable violent potential. The American government, according to the new movement, as well as the nation's most important institutions, have been totally taken over by the Zionist Occupation Government (ZOG) and are beyond repair. The Jews and their collaborators are all over the place. Not only are they in control of the nation's many established institutions such as government and mass media, but their organizations have intensely marginalized and delegitimized the entire patriotic American radical right.[50]

Much of the Christian Identity Movement's hopes for a better future relies on their messianic belief in the imminent Second Coming of a White Aryan Christ. This will occur after a seven year period of tribulation, a modern-day Armageddon, when the entire world will change dramatically. Jews and other 'mud people' will be eliminated and genuine Anglo-Saxons will finally take over. For this reason, many Identity preachers recommend that their followers live in isolated encampments, mostly in the racially homogenous North-West, and arm themselves in preparation for the great moment.[51] While most of the arms are kept for the final struggle, it is legitimate also to use them, occasionally, against representatives and symbols of ZOG, which is presently in control of Washington. Bank robberies and other crimes aimed at strengthening the movements are also fully legitimate.[52]

Their ideo-theological rejection of the American system at nearly all levels, which is no longer different from their rejection of the original target communities such as Jews or Blacks, puts many Christian Identity groups at a very advanced position on both wings of the split delegitimization. While some of them express it by self-seclusion and withdrawal, others resort occasionally to terrorism, including direct attacks on government installations and symbols of authority. It appears, in fact, that if not for the persistent pressure and crackdowns of the Justice Department and the Federal Bureau of Investigation on white supremacist groups, several of them would have very likely resorted to intense anti-establishment terrorism in the 1980s.

F. Youth Counterculture Terrorism

A special type of particularistic terrorism which has grown since the mid-1970s, attracting increasing public attention, is right-wing terrorism conducted by alienated and isolated youth gangs. Many of these are shaven-headed and have come to be known as Skinheads or 'Skins'. Others are soccer rowdies involved in 'spontaneous violence'. The majority of them are very young and are more involved in a cultural than political crisis of legitimation with the democratic culture. Music is a key element in the Skinhead counterculture and serves as a recruiting tool, a propaganda weapon, a celebration of the gang ethic and a call for violence. The Skinhead 'white power' music is aggressive, loud, and radiates a message of violent cultural revolt.[53] Just as their music expresses a rebellion against middle-class pop music, Skinhead behavior implies a rejection of the entire normative order of bourgeois society. The political essence of Skinheadism focuses on the glorification and perpetration of brute violence against racial and ethnic minorities, homosexuals, leftists, and Jews. The adoption and glorification of racist and anti-Semitic violence seems to be less a logical conclusion of a certain political thinking and more of an emotional consequence of a youthful cultural rebellion and a denial of the normative status quo.[54]

The Skinheads, just as many other right-wing extremists, are by no means systematic terrorists and terrorism is only a small part of what a few of them do. Skinhead terrorism seems to be an unintended extension of non-political glorification of brutal physical force and symbolic excitement about violence. Many Skins come to their concerts armed with knives, axes, baseball bats and material for manufacturing firebombs. After several hours of listening to the throbbing beat of their wild bands and augmented by a flood of alcohol, they strike and occasionally kill. In the last decade Skinheads have been involved in fire bombings and murderous assaults which took the life of numerous innocent civilians in several Western countries. Moreover, these assaults left many more members of the targeted communities terrorized. The most notorious youth counterculture assault took place on 23 November 1992, in the German town of Mölln, where three Turkish women and girls were killed in a fire-bomb attack.

The Skinhead subculture, whose German annex has recently attracted much attention, originated in the 1970s in Great Britain and spread to several Western countries, including the United States. The shaven-headed Skinheads began to be seen in the streets in the early 1970s. Tattooed and wearing Doc Martens boots, they were reminiscent of the young thugs portrayed in the famous movie, *A Clockwork Orange*. Their style was aimed to stand in symbolic contrast to the liberal, pacifist, middle class values of the long hairs, and to stress patriotic, bellicose, anti-immigrant, working class attitudes. Skinheads can now be found in Germany, Hungary, Poland, Czechoslovakia, Italy, Sweden, Norway, Denmark, the Netherlands, Spain and the USA. The dislocation created by the unification of Germany and the demise of the GDR has led among other things to significant growth of a rather large Skinhead subculture in East Germany. In parts of East Berlin and in several border towns close to Poland, Skinhead gangs have virtually taken over, terrorizing both the opposition and local authorities into silence. Youth centers established by the government to provide housing and social care have been taken over by the Skins and turned into aggressive counterculture centers with strong neo-Nazi overtones. The nearby neighborhoods as well as bars have been terrorized into silence and acceptance of the Skinhead lifestyle. Much of the aggression of the gangs is directed against the huge number of immigrants, guest workers and asylum seekers in Germany, who are believed to have taken away jobs and opportunities.

As alarming as the rise of the violent right-wing youth counterculture may be, it appears that its real danger involves the interaction between these youngsters, other youth gangs and older and more experienced neo-Nazis. Even though Skins are not easy to organize, there are increasing indications that inexperienced Skins are occasionally mobilized for radical action and being used by several more experienced right-wing extremists.[55] The social marginality of the Skinheads and other youth gangs, their young age and their socio-economic detachment from organized society make some of them potential front-line 'soldiers' for neo-fascist and neo-Nazi movements whose elderly members either cannot afford to get directly involved in extralegal activities or constantly suffer from manpower shortage. Most of the American Skinheads, for example, are affiliated with neo-Nazi organizations or the Aryan Nation and go by such names as Northern Hammerskins, SS of America and Aryan Resistance League. According to the American ADL, which has been carefully monitoring these groups, they have been put into destructive action by more experienced neo-Nazis. From 1987 to June 1990 there was a total of six cases of killing; but in the three years since, 22 murders were committed by Skinheads.[56] Most of the victims have been members of minority groups: Blacks, Hispanics, Asians, homosexuals and homeless persons. In addition, Skinheads had been involved in thousands of lesser crimes: stabbings, shootings, beatings, thefts and synagogue desecrations. The ADL has concluded that 'Skinheads are today the most violent of all white supremacy groups. Not even the Ku Klux Klan, so notorious for their use of the rope and the gun, come close to the Skinheads in the number and severity of crimes committed in recent years.'[57]

It appears that the conceptual framework of the process of delegitimization has almost no explanatory power for the terror produced by the youth counter-culture of the Skinheads, the soccer hooligans and other musical punks and youth gangs. What is involved is not a lengthy process of political delegitimization but a cultural rebellion of marginal youth groups who are in conflict with the demanding post-industrial society as well as with their parents, and who wish to provoke both. They are relevant to the present study because much of their cultural and experiential world is shaped by neo-fascist and neo-Nazi symbols and because their outrage is directed at enemies of the racist right. While much of this violence remains symbolic, criminal and non-political,[58] there is in the United States and certain European countries a feeling that a racist and neo-Nazi subculture has slowly been evolving at the margins of society since the 1980s, and that its effects are likely to be felt for a long time.

The Modus Operandi of Right-Wing Terrorism: A Part-Time Job

The huge political, historical and cultural variation among right-wing extremist groups makes it difficult to generalize about their behavioral dynamics. And yet it appears that there is a major difference in the *modus operandi* of universalistic and particularistic terror-producing organizations. While the former – usually extreme left, nationalist or anti-authoritarian terrorists – often operate in secret undergrounds, which presuppose full-time revolutionaries pursued by the law, the majority of right-wing terrorists do not devote their entire lives to the terrorist cause and rarely go underground. Many of them live almost a normal life, sustain families and perceive of themselves as distinguished members of the community. Their terrorism is, in most cases, a side function carried out after 'working hours'. As we shall see below, however, there are several exceptions to this rule.

The explanation for the part-time character of right-wing terrorism involves the nature of the delegitimization process undergone by particularistic terrorists and the target of their atrocities. Unlike universalistic terrorists who mostly fight repressive rulers and governments, the majority of particularistic terrorists do not directly challenge the structure of authority. The target of their outrage is a specific 'inferior' community or individuals whom they wish to discriminate against and intimidate. In most cases they expect the government to fulfill this task and react only when government leaders are unwilling to cooperate or follow 'their advice'. This rule also applies, as was mentioned earlier, to revolutionary right-wing terrorists, whose ultimate goal is a structural change but who opt, for tactical reasons, for legalistic strategy. It goes without saying that legality does not preclude secrecy, and that most organizations involved in violence are extremely secretive about their terror plans. But in the majority of right-wing cases, the proponents of terrorism do not hide and are usually registered in the local telephone directory.

There are three exceptions to the part-time nature of right-wing terrorism: religious millenarian sects, youth counterculture groups and very extreme neo-Nazi organizations. Membership in these collectivities usually presupposes alienation from the community and rejection of its cultural and political norms. It further implies many fewer commitments to bourgeois society, including orderly family life and property ownership. The American millenarian organization of Robert Mathews, the Order, or the Swedish VAM network, as well as several Skinhead groups can serve as examples for groups whose alienation and separation from organized society are almost total. But as we have seen, terrorism is not the main concern of these collectivities. Most millenarian groups withdraw from ordinary life and peacefully prepare themselves for the Second Coming of Christ. And the neo-Nazis and Skinhead counterculture is very much into noisy music, racist camaraderie, hostility to organized society and a culturally provocative lifestyle.

The legal status of most particularistic organizations involved in terrorism is also responsible for the low frequency of their terror operations. An organization which fulfills other social functions and is likely to be suspected of extremist operations is probably under constant surveillance by the security services of the regime. It must, therefore, keep a low profile. Its leaders, who are often much older than most active warriors in universalistic insurgency, wish to maintain their respectable community status, and simply cannot afford to be caught. One may also add that the kind of terrorism applied against 'inferior' communities does not require great military skill or a highly sophisticated underground. Bruce Hoffman noticed back in 1984 that the favorite right-wing weapon is the bomb, the use of which does not require a sophisticated and well-organized conspiracy.[59]

Since the majority of present day right-wingers do not fundamentally challenge the structure of authority, their unsystematic terrorism is merely an additional method of coping with the socio-cultural anxieties they face. Four sets of circumstances seem to increase the likelihood that right-wing true believers will move from conflict to crisis of legitimation and resort to terrorism: (a) a sudden and intense sense of insecurity which produces emotional extremist action; (b) a conviction of right-wing leaders that they can rationally benefit from terrorism ; (c) a sense of increasing public support for radical action against 'undesirable people'; (d) the imposing presence of violent personalities whose resort to terrorism is made for purely personal-psychological reasons.

Small, isolated and poorly organized particularistic extremist groups are likely to respond to perceived threats without much calculation. A sudden anxiety, a decline in the group's sense of political control, a socio-economic recession, a fear of imminent leftist aggression or a profound outrage with certain acts of the authorities may drive members of such groups to occasional atrocities. Terrorism is resorted to emotionally in a desperate effort to restore the *status quo ante*. Many Ku Klux Klan and white supremacy organizations, small European neo-fascist cells in the 1970s and some Israeli right-wing extremists have acted in this fashion. Their terrorism has been an unplanned and unsystematic mechanism for the temporary release of group anxiety and tension.

More sophisticated and well-organized right-wing movements try not to act emotionally. Aware of their weakness and of the effectiveness of law enforcement agencies, their leaders order strikes only when convenient and when the government is seen to be in disarray. The presence of intense extralegal left-wing activity, which can be blamed for much of the violence, may be helpful, as was the case in Italy and France in the late 1960s and early 1970s. A special case in point is the 'strategy of tension' of Italian neo-fascists since the 1950s. Responding to significant socio-economic strains, the rise in left-wing radicalism and a perception of potential support by the armed forces and police, group leaders like Pino Rauti recommended violent confrontation with the left and even terrorism.[60] Prudent leaders of reactive and vigilante groups may also use terrorism to attract public attention and place issues that trouble them on the public agenda.

Concluding Remarks

Students of political violence have long been familiar with the positive correlation between the radical group's sense of public support and the likelihood
that it will resort to violence.[61] This correlation appears to be holding for right-
wing terror groups. A case in point is the enormous rise in the aggression and
violence of Israel's Kach movement in the early 1980s. A strong anti-Arab
sentiment which swept the country made Rabbi Meir Kahane, who for years
was the isolated leader of the movement, a legitimate actor in Israeli politics.[62]
The unexpected 1984 election of the rabbi to parliament, surprisingly did not
reduce the level of Kach's violence. On the contrary, their attacks on Arabs
increased. In the same fashion it appears that the steady decline in violent
operations of the Ku Klux Klan since the 1960s has had to do with, among
other things, the dramatic decrease of public support. The rule seems to be
holding currently in Germany where neo-Nazi violence has reached crisis
proportions in the 1990s. The increasing confidence of the neo-Nazis in the
rising anti-alien sentiment in Germany and several other European countries
seems to have contributed to their daring activities.[63]

Psychologists and students of political violence have so far failed to fully
explain the violent personality. We just know that the evolution and activity
of certain violent groups, especially those that are small and poorly organized,
cannot be reduced to socio-political factors. The heads of such groups just
happen to be more violent than others, more excited with weapons, angrier at
society or at its established leaders, or more moved by romantic dreams of
virility and glorious violence. Such groups are almost always products of a
single man. The leader's personality, more than the group's ideology or socio-
political conditions, determines the level, repertoire and timing of violence.
Unless developed into a larger and more broadly appealing movement, the
death or arrest of the leader is often the end of the group. This seems to have
been the case with neo-Nazi activists such as the German Karl Heinz Hoffman
and his *Wehrsportgruppe Hoffman*, Robert Mathews of the American Order
and to some extent even with Israel's Rabbi Kahane and several of his successors.[64]

NOTES

1. Ehud Sprinzak, 'The Process of Delegitimization: Towards a Linkage Theory of Political
    Terrorism', *Terrorism and Political Violence* [hereafter *TPV*] 3/1 (Spring 1991) pp.50–68. To
    clarify any possible confusion: I use the term 'delegitimization' whenever I am talking about
    a behavioral process over time. The term 'delegitimation' I use to denote an attitude.
    However, this distinction is of linguistic rather than theoretical significance, and I do not
    expect others to follow my usage.

2. Ehud Sprinzak, 'The Psycho-political Formation of Extreme Left Terrorism in a Democracy: The Case of the Weathermen', in Walter Reich (ed.), *Origins of Terrorism* (NY: CUP, 1990), p.79.
3. Sprinzak (note 1), pp.54–5.
4. Ibid., pp.55–6.
5. Albert Bandura, 'Mechanisms of Moral Disengagement', in Reich, *Origins of Terrorism* (note 2), pp.180–2.
6. Jeanne N. Knutson, 'Social and Psychodynamic Pressures Towards a Negative Identity: The Case of an American Revolutionary Terrorist', in Yonah Alexander and John M. Glison (eds.), *Behavioral and Quantitative Perspectives on Terrorism* (NY: Pergamon Press, 1981), pp.211–15; Jerold M. Post, 'Notes on a Psychodynamic Theory of Terrorist Behavior', *Terrorism: An International Journal* 7/3 (1984), pp.250–3.
7. Sprinzak (note 1), p.53. In addition to 'transformational delegitimization', the article also identifies as a type 'extensional delegitimization', which is more suitable for terrorism of national liberation movements. Extensional delegitimization implies a process which starts with long held cultural hostility towards a foreign ruler. The terrorism that develops does not represent a psycho-political transformation from early agreement to a bitter disagreement, but a rather radicalized and bloody extension of an already existing hostility and conflict.
8. This tendency within the ZOG discourse and related ideologies towards a complete identification of the hated minority with the government has been pointed out to me by Jeffrey Kaplan and Tore Bjørgo, cf. their chapters in this volume.
9. Walter Laqueur, *The Age of Terrorism* (London: Weidenfeld, 1987) p.67.
10. Zeev Sternhell, 'Fascist Ideology', in Walter Laqueur (ed.), *Fascism: A Reader's Guide* (Berkeley, CA: Univ. of California Press, 1976), pp.320–37.
11. Adrian Lyttelton, 'Fascism and Violence in Post-War Italy: Political Strategy and Social Conflict', in W.J. Mommsen and Gerhard Hirshfeld (eds.), *Social Protest, Violence, and Terror in Nineteenth and Twentieth-Century Europe* (NY: St. Martin's Press, 1982); Peter Merkl, *The Making of a Stormtrooper* (Boulder, CO: Westview Press, 1987), pp.15–18; Jens Petersen, 'Violence in Italian Fascism', in Mommsen and Hirshfeld cited above.
12. Merkl (note 11), pp.299–305; Ernst Nolte, *Three Faces of Fascism* (NY: Mentor Books, 1965), pp.260–3.
13. James A. Gregor, 'Fascism: Philosophy of Violence and the Concept of Terror', in David C. Rapoport and Yona Alexander (eds.), *The Morality of Terrorism* (NY: Pergamon Press, 1982).
14. Petersen (note 11).
15. Jeremy Noakes, 'The Origins, Structure and Functions of Nazi Terror', in Noel O'Sullivan (ed.), *Terrorism, Ideology and Revolution* (Boulder, CO: Westview, 1986).
16. Laqueur (note 9), pp.76–7.
17. Paul Wilkinson, *The New Fascists* (London: Grant McIntyre, 1981), Ch.3.
18. Anti-Defamation League, *The German Neo-Nazis: An ADL Investigative Report* (NY: ADL, 1993).
19. Tore Bjørgo and Robb Witte, *Racist Violence in Europe* (NY: St. Martin's Press, 1993).
20. Leonard Weinberg, 'Italian Neo-Fascist Terrorism: A Comparative Perspective', in this volume.
21. Tore Bjørgo, 'Militant Neo-Nazism in Sweden', *TVP* 5/3 (Autumn 1993).
22. Heléne Lööw, 'The Cult of Violence: The Swedish Racist Counterculture', in Bjørgo and Witte (note 19), pp.67–70.
23. Erik Jensen, 'International Nazi Cooperation: A Terrorist Oriented Network', in Bjørgo and Witte (note 19).
24. Albert Parry, *Terrorism: From Robespierre to Arafat* (NY: The Vanguard Press, 1976), p.496.
25. Knutson (note 6), p.116.
26. Parry (note 24), p.498.
27. Alistaire Horne, *A Savage War Peace: Algeria 1954–1962* (London: Macmillan, 1977), pp.36–7.

28. Ibid., pp.148–50.
29. Ibid., pp.349–50.
30. Martha Hutchinson (Crenshaw), *Revolutionary Terrorism: The FLN in Algeria 1954-1962* (Stanford, CA: Hoover Inst. Press, 1978), pp.58–9.
31. Jon H. Rosenbaum and Peter C. Sederberg, 'Vigilantism: Analysis of Establishment Violence', *Comparative Politics*, Vol. 6 (July 1974).
32. Richard Maxwell Brown, 'The American Vigilante Tradition', in Hugh Graham and Ted Robert Gurr, *Violence in America* (NY: Signet Books, 1969), pp.176–7.
33. Ehud Sprinzak, 'From Messianic Pioneering to Vigilante Terrorism: The Case of Gush Emunim Underground', in David C. Rapoport (ed.), *Inside Terrorist Organizations* (London: Frank Cass, 1987), pp.210–14.
34. Martha K. Huggins, 'Introduction: Vigilantism and the State – A Look at South and North', in Martha K. Huggins (ed.), *Vigilantism and the State in Modern Latin America: Essays on Extralegal Violence* (NY: Praeger, 1991), pp.1–4.
35. Ibid.
36. John Sloan, 'Terrorism in Latin America', in Michael Stohl (ed.), *The Politics of Terrorism* (NY: Marcel Dekker, 1979), pp.389–90.
37. Ibid., pp.392–4.
38. Carlos F. Ibara, 'Guatemala: The Recourse of Fear', in Huggins (note 34), pp.73–80.
39. David M. Chalmers, *Hooded Americanism* (Chicago: Quadrangle Paperbacks, 1968).
40. A. W. Trelease, *White Terror: The Ku Klux Klan Conspiracy and the Southern Reconstruction* (NY: Harper Torchbooks, 1971), pp.29–46.
41. Seymour Martin Lipset and Earl Raab, *The Politics of Unreason: Right-Wing Extremism in America 1790–1970* (New York: Harper and Row, 1970), pp.165–9.
42. Anti Defamation League, *Extremism on the Right: A Handbook* (NY: ADL, 1988), p.26.
43. Jerome H. Skolnick, *The Politics of Protest* (NY: Ballantine Books, 1969), pp.231–9.
44. I owe the inclusion of this category in the typology to Jeffrey Kaplan's constructive critique of an earlier version of my model (cf. his essay in this volume).
45. Michael Barkun, 'Millenarian Aspects of "White Supremacist" Movements', *TPV* 1/4 (Oct. 1989), pp.410–3.
46. Jeffrey Kaplan, 'The Context of American Millenarian Revolutionary Theology: The Case of the "Identity Christian" Church of Israel', *TPV* 5/1 (Spring 1993), pp.30–1.
47. Ibid., pp.54–6
48. Ibid., pp.31–2.
49. Ibid.
50. Leonard Weinberg, 'The American Radical Right: Exit, Voice and Violence', in Peter H. Merkl and Leonard Weinberg (eds.), *Encounters with the Contemporary Radical Right* (Boulder, CO.; Westview, 1993), pp.186, 201.
51. Ibid, p.14.
52. Kevin Flynn and Gary Gerhardt, *The Silent Brotherhood: Inside America's Racist Underground* (NY: The Free Press, 1989), Ch.4.
53. Anti-Defamation League, *Sounds of Hate, Neo-Nazi Rock Music from Germany; An ADL Special Report* (NY: ADL, 1992).
54. Peter Merkl, 'Conclusion: A New Lease on Life for the Radical Right?' in P. Merkl and L. Weinberg (note 50), pp.208–9.
55. Tore Bjørgo, 'Terrorist Violence Against Immigrants and Refugees in Scandinavia: Patterns and Motives', in Bjørgo and Witte (note 19), p.30.
56. Anti Defamation League, *Young Nazi Killers, The Rising Skinhead Danger: An ADL Special Report* (NY: ADL, 1993), p.3.
57. Ibid.
58. Peter Merkl, 'Conclusion: A New Lease on Life for the Radical Right', in Merkl and Weinberg (note 50), pp.212–14.
59. Bruce Hoffman, 'Right-Wing Terrorism in Europe', *Conflict* 5/3 (1984).
60. Paul Furlong, 'Political Terrorism in Italy: Responses, Reactions and Immobilism', in Juliet Lodge (ed.), *Terrorism: A Challenge to the State* (Oxford: Martin Robertson, 1981), p.70;

Piero Ignazi, 'The Changing Profile of the Italian Social Movement', in Merkl and Weinberg (note 50), pp.80–2.

61. William Gamson, *The Strategy of Social Protest* (Homewood, IL: Dorsey Press, 1975), pp.81–2.

62. Ehud Sprinzak, 'Violence and Catastrophe in the Theology of Rabbi Meir Kahane; The Ideologization of the Mimetic Desire', *TPV* 3/3 (Autumn 1991), pp.48–70.

63. Graeme Atkinson, 'Germany: Nationalism, Nazism and Violence', in Bjørgo and Witte (note 19).

64. Peter Merkl, 'Rollerball or neo-Nazi Violence', in Peter Merkl (ed.), *Political Violence and Terror: Motifs and Motivations* (Los Angeles: Univ. of California Press, 1986), pp.240–4; Flynn and Gerhardt, *Silent Brotherhood* (note 52); Robert I. Friedman, *The False Prophet: Rabbi Meir Kahane – From FBI Informant to Knesset Member* (NY: Lawrence Hill Books, 1990); Ehud Sprinzak, *The Ascendance of Israel's Radical Right* (NY: OUP, 1991), pp.211–14.

Right Wing Violence in North America

JEFFREY KAPLAN

This article offers a typology of radical right wing movements which emphasizes their roles in what may be termed an oppositional community. The examination stresses both their interdependence through the application of Colin Campbell's theory of the cultic milieu and the movements' isolation from the American cultural mainstream, a graphic picture of which is provided via Martin Marty's mapping theory. Secondarily, the article offers some suggestions for the further refinement of Ehud Sprinzak's theory of split delegitimization.

> *Even if we were to link up all the Klan groups, all Identity, Nazis or whatever, then so what? We still don't amount to anything.* [Arkansas Klan leader Thom Robb, 1991][1]

On 9 December 1984 Robert Mathews, founder of the *Bruders Schweigen* or Silent Brotherhood, more popularly known as the Order, died in a hail of FBI gunfire on Whidby Island off the coast of Washington state. The long-cherished dream of many denizens of the American radical right – that the nation might awaken to the truth of its 'subjugation' at the hands of an alien conspiracy and purify itself through the cleansing violence of a popularly-based revolution – died with him.

The demise of the Order was only the latest in a series of disappointments to which the radical right has experienced in recent years. The Ku Klux Klan, the post-Civil War organization synonymous with racial violence, was by the mid-1980s a fragmented, divisive, and dwindling cadre of true believers thoroughly infiltrated – and occasionally led – by agents of the FBI. Yet even the Ku Klux Klan held out greater promise than such pretenders to revolutionary activism as the Posse Comitatus or the Phineas Priesthood. The Posse, it turned out, was composed of a small group of high profile 'leaders' backed by a membership no more substantial than a mailing list peopled by an anonymous group of correspondents who, for the cost of a stamp and perhaps a contribution of a few dollars, could become the proud owners of a Posse Comitatus membership card and a stack of literature which the putative new local Posse leader was invited to reproduce and distribute at will.

The Phineas Priesthood is a case in point to illustrate both the fervent hopes of the believers and the credulity of those whose mission it is to serve as 'watchdogs' over the machinations of the radical right. The literary invention of one Richard Kelly Hoskins, the Phineas Priests were embraced as a kind of an Illuminati-like order of assassins from the very dawn of time whose self-imposed mission is to slay the enemies of God. Once again, the credulous on both extremes of the American political spectrum seized on the Phineas Priests as a source of either chiliastic hope or of dread danger to the republic, until at last the Phineas Priests did come to enjoy a form of quasi-existence as a mail order Order along much the same lines as the Posse Comitatus. That is, a group of entrepreneurs created a line of Phineas apparel and accessories suitable for framing or as conversational fodder for an otherwise monotonous hunting trip.

If the dream of revolutionary violence under the direction of a vanguard movement is no longer credible, however, the same cannot be said of random acts of violence initiated by adherents of right wing ideologies on an individual or small group basis. Such acts of violence are most often directed against members of other racial or ethnic groups or, increasingly, members of the homosexual community in North America. The forms which this violence takes most often involves physical assaults, often though not invariably with weapons ranging from blunt objects to firearms. Bombings and arson occur as well, although with far less frequency.

Part I of this article will offer a brief typology of the organizations and ideologies represented among North American radical right wing movements. Part II will utilize Ehud Sprinzak's theory of split delegitimization as a vehicle to explore the factors which may be responsible for catalyzing right wing violence, and will present a comparative framework which will examine in some depth movements which have turned to violence. This examination will take into account such variables as the group's ideology, identification of 'enemies' and perception of threat stemming from these perceived foes, and the reaction of both state and non-state interest groups to radical right wing activities.

I. The Right Wing Constellation

In a 1993 article in the journal *Terrorism and Political Violence*, I suggested a typology of far right wing groups. What follows is a brief updated review of that typology which, while concentrating on the susceptibility of a particular ideological appeal to calls to violence, emphasizes the difficulty of differentiating ideological appeals which have many common beliefs yet at the same time are bitterly divisive and competitive for the allegiance of a limited pool of adherents. Informing this presentation are theoretical constructs of countercultural communities such as that of the cultic milieu suggested by Colin Campbell and religious mapping championed by, among others, Martin

Marty.[2] Both systems posit deviance from the beliefs of mainstream society as
the key analytical factor, with mapping theory seeking to locate a particular
belief system in relation to the dominant culture and Campbell's cultic milieu
documenting the close interactions of members of this oppositional community. Campbell's description of the cultic milieu is particularly relevant to a
discussion of the constituent elements of the radical right wing:

> ...cults must exist within a milieu which, if not conducive to the main-
> tenance of individual cults, is clearly highly conducive to the spawning
> of cults in general. Such a generally supportive cultic milieu is continu-
> ally giving birth to new cults, absorbing the debris of the dead ones and
> creating new generations of cult-prone individuals to maintain the high
> level of membership turnover. Thus, whereas cults are by definition a
> transitory phenomenon, the cultic milieu is, by contrast, a permanent
> feature of society.[3]

Given the close association of the adherents of the radical right wing within this oppositional milieu, it is extraordinarily difficult to separate appeals
which share such primary characteristics as a Golden Age Myth, the perception of a 'Theft of Culture'; scripturalism, a manichaean world view, a conspiratorial view of history, a vision of the group as an 'elect' or, in religious
terms, as a 'righteous remnant', and finally, an apocalyptic or chiliastic analysis of society.[4] This difficulty is compounded by the pronounced tendency of
the adherents of radical right wing ideologies toward serial or simultaneous
membership in more than one group or belief system. Indeed, a researcher
would be hard pressed to point to a single individual in the constellation of
right wing movements who has not already passed through several ideological way stations, and who no doubt has stops yet to make during his or her
life. Yet it is important to make these distinctions. Some groups do tend to be
more susceptible to appeals for violent confrontations than others. Moreover,
in terms of mapping theory, the more distant a particular group tends to be
from the values and beliefs of the mainstream society, the more difficult it
becomes for an adherent to moderate or give up the belief system altogether.
Association with a highly stigmatized ideological appeal, say Nazism or holocaust denial in contemporary North America, may well brand someone as
beyond the pale of the society's acceptable discourse, and thus not only
socially unacceptable, but in fact, literally unemployable.[5]

Given these qualifications then, the primary constituents of the radical
right wing in North America are: Ku Klux Klan groups, Christian Identity
believers, Neo-Nazi groups, Reconstructed Traditions, Idiosyncratic sectarians, and the catch-all category of Single Issue Constituencies and the inchoate
hope seeking a means of fulfillment (or less elegantly, the young toughs or

knuckle draggers of the movement).

Ku Klux Klan Groups

> *Throughout the millenniums of warfare between the Aryan and the Jew, neither we nor they have ever 'won'. The victories each has in turn known, when spread over the centuries, equal stalemate. However, Aryan technology has shrunk the whole earth to the size of one battlefield. The eternal war, which can most properly be called a Conflict Of The Ages, has taken a final turn. The age-long conflict approaches the last battle – Ragnarök, Armageddon – is about to be fought, and there will be only one survivor of this struggle.*[6] [Louis Beam, 1984]

In the contemporary demonology of American culture, no organization elicits a more negative reaction than does the Ku Klux Klan. Fear of the Klan, and perhaps a shared collective shame for the power which the movement accrued in both the Reconstruction-era American South (c.1865–76) and in several Northern states in the 1920s, is deeply rooted in the collective American consciousness. It is a fear which at once attracts and bedevils Klan recruits who often find that their initial attraction to the Klan's mystique of secrecy and popular fear wanes with the realization that virtually any public activity undertaken by the Klan is certain to be met by a far greater crowd of counterdemonstrators. Worse, covert Klan operations appear to be undertaken at the sufferance if not the outright invitation of government authorities, given the success of federal agencies at infiltrating Klan ranks and inducing Klan leaders to cooperate in federal investigations. Thus, for a Klan group to undertake or even seriously contemplate violent action is tantamount to organizational suicide. On the one hand, members face indictment not only for whatever criminal acts may occur, but through the imaginative utilization of standing conspiracy statutes and the newly adopted hate crime sentence enhancement provisions available in many states, lengthy incarceration. Moreover, the successful use of civil litigation initiated by such watchdog organizations as the Klanwatch Project of the Southern Poverty Law Center on behalf of victims of Klan violence has the intended effect of putting those Klan organizations which do perpetrate acts of violence out of business.[7]

Given these powerful disincentives to violence, it is not surprising that the already fragmented Klans in North America would enter into a bitter battle of polemics over the tactics of non-violence vs. the Klan's tradition of violent activism. Emerging from this internecine debate are two very different approaches: the call to violence championed by such firebrands as Louis Beam of Texas and Dennis Mahon of Oklahoma as opposed to the mediagenic call to non-violence, best embodied by Arkansas based Thomas Robb.[8]

Louis Beam, the author of the manichaean and apocalyptic analysis of contemporary history which opened this section, is a rarity among Klansmen.

Undeniably intelligent, articulate and widely read – the driving force behind the dreaded right-wing computer bulletin boards of the late 1980s – Louis Beam has lived the life that many Klansmen and would-be Klansmen fantasize over. A Vietnam veteran, Beam preaches the dream of revolutionary violence and has himself not been loath to take up the dangerous existence of the underground fugitive. The most celebrated of Beam's exploits may well be the shoot-out in which Mexican federal officers attempted to take Beam and his wife into custody. In the ensuing confrontation, Beam's wife managed to pin down the arresting officers, allowing her husband to make good his escape. Beam's charmed life did not end with his return to the United States and his role in the ill-starred sedition trial held at Fort Smith, Arkansas, in 1989. Here too he was acquitted, and he remains free at this writing.

Beam's successes should not, however, obscure the essential futility of his primary quest: to modernize the Ku Klux Klan by unifying its many disparate factions and forging the organization into an effective vanguard revolutionary force. The theory, put together with the help of the late Robert Miles and others, was called the 'Fifth Era Klan'; a Klan capable of a clear-eyed analysis of the incompetence and, indeed, treason, which has been the history of the Klan since the original movement was disbanded in 1869, as well as an honest appraisal of the remarkably poor quality of recruits the present day Klan organizations have managed to attract.

Only when these difficulties are addressed and rectified will Beam's ecumenical calls to take up arms, overthrow the current socio-political order, and ruthlessly take vengeance on 'lying politicians, criminal bureaucrats, racial traitors, communists, assorted degenerates, culture distorters, and those who resist the implementation of lawful constitutional government'[9] be more than a pipe dream. In the meantime, Beam's ecumenism is aptly demonstrated in his extra-Klan contacts, ranging from his close association with Richard Butler's Christian Identity Aryan Nations compound in Idaho to the sort of generic Odinism alluded to in his equating of the Christian Apocalypse with the Norse end-time scenario of Ragnarök in the quotation above.

Dennis Mahon is no Louis Beam, but he too has come to represent a revolutionary voice in Klan circles – so much so in fact that, having come to much the same analysis of the Klan's current status as Louis Beam, he amicably left the Klan in 1992 for Tom Metzger's White Aryan Resistance (WAR). Prior to his defection to WAR, Mahon was best known for his association with Terry Boyce's Confederate Knights of America Klan chapter and for his calls to arms in the Knight's journal, the *White Beret*, as well as for his occasional forays to Europe and Canada on behalf of the Klan.[10] Mahon's drift from the KKK to WAR speaks volumes to the applicability of Campbell's cultic milieu to the radical right, but of greater interest is his frank analysis of the

Klan. Interspersed between intemperate attacks on Thom Robb ('the Grand
Lizard') and Robb's attempts to remake the image of the Klan from a revolutionary force to, in effect, a civil rights group, is a telling appraisal of the current state of the Klan:

> ...after 12 years of proudly wearing the robe of the Invisible Order, I feel
> that Tom Metzger's leadership and personal strategies fit my personali-
> ty and mindset better at this time of my life. Also, I just got tired of see-
> ing so many mistakes in tactics and ideology of the leaders of the other
> 25 or so Klan groups in Zoglandia. So many of these mini-führers of
> these other Klans have embarrassed me with these displays of weakness
> and idiotic statements of 'Niggers are the cause of all our problems – we
> got to kill the niggers – nigger this, nigger that'. It's like a broken
> record.
> The Jewsmedia always link the Klan with 'lynching niggers'. The
> average 'Joe Six-pack' out there, whenever he thinks of a Klansman,
> pictures an uneducated hick half drunk, in bib overalls, with tobacco
> juice dripping down his chin, burning a cross on some poor Blacks (sic)
> lawn, and the Klansman stating how he 'put the nigger in his place'.
> Unfortunately, many Klansmen knowingly fit the media stereotype.[11]

Mahon continues his analysis throughout the premier issue of his post-Klan
vehicle, *The Oklahoma Excalibur*. The effortless penetration of Klan leadership ranks by government agents as well as by informants reporting for private watchdog groups is decried, as are the tactics of non-violence and staged
events in which Klan groups are seen as demonstrating peacefully until they
are attacked by anti-Klan demonstrators which is the forte of Thom Robb. For
Mahon, the contradictions of the modern Klan became intolerable, and thus
the switch to WAR.

During of an interview with this writer in Chicago in 1991, Identity minister and Klan leader Thom Robb made the surprising declaration that, virtually alone among members of the radical right in America, he was pleased
with media coverage of his Knights of the Ku Klux Klan. Indeed, in as much
as the Ku Klux Klan could get positive media coverage, Robb's message of
love for the White race while eschewing any (public) negative comments on
any other race has dovetailed nicely with a certain trend in American society
toward the reinforcement of ethnic as opposed to national identity.[12] Robb's
kinder, gentler Klan is unlikely to do much to erase the intensely negative
associations which the organization engenders in Americans, and, as Dennis
Mahon's writing amply demonstrates, it has done much to further divide an
already disintegrating movement.

How low the Ku Klux Klan's fortunes have ebbed in recent years is clearly documented by the watchdog community. According to Anti-Defamation League figures, total Klan membership had by 1988 hit a record low of between 4,500 and 5,000 members. These figures represent the lowest Klan membership total in 15 years according to the ADL, and Klanwatch's 1990 estimate of 5,000 shows little hope of upward growth.[13] So dire are the Klan's current fortunes that in its 1991 report on the KKK, the ADL was moved to write:

> Although the Klan's decade-long decline has stopped, and it may begin to grow again – especially if the current recession becomes lengthy and severe – there is little prospect of the hooded order once again becoming a significant force in the land.... As long as it continues to exist, it poses a danger to the communities in which it operates. The danger consists specifically of violence and terrorism. The Klan's very presence in a community constitutes a source of anxiety to members of minority groups and a standing threat to peaceful and friendly relations among the citizens....Nevertheless, considered from the standpoint of the nation as a whole, the KKK has only limited present and potential significance.[14]

Christian Identity

Perhaps no single constituency of the North American radical right has met with such fervent organized opposition as has the heterodox theology of Christian Identity. This state of affairs is hardly surprising in light of the adherence to Identity doctrine of leaders such as Robert Mathews of the Order and Richard Butler of the Aryan Nations. Yet for all of the current interest in the movement, Identity's origins and its widespread appeal have been something of a mystery. This section is a brief history of the movement, followed by an introduction to several of the more influential Identity churches in North America.

The movement which has come to be known as Christian Identity evolved out of the no less heterodox theology of British-Israelism. British-Israelism may have been inspired by the eighteenth century writings of Richard Brothers (1757–1824), an eccentric Englishman born in Newfoundland who spent several of his years incarcerated in London madhouses. However, the central tenet of Brothers' teachings – the belief that Anglo-Saxons are in fact the direct descendants of the Lost Tribes of Israel – had considerable appeal in nineteenth century imperial Britain. Adherents of British-Israelism in the last century represented the elite of British society, and it was via these social circles that the movement was disseminated throughout the Commonwealth. British-Israelism was introduced to North America primarily through the

work of a Canadian, W. H. Poole. This is of considerable significance, for –
unlike the uniquely American genesis of the Ku Klux Klan – Canada, and in
particular British Columbia, would play a vital role both in introducing
British-Israel beliefs to the United States and in the transformation of the
rather philo-Semitic British-Israel movement into the virulently anti-Semitic
theology of Christian Identity.[15]

This transformation occurred in the 1930s, the product of the interaction
of the tireless British-Israel evangelist Howard Rand and the anti-Semitism of
his associate, William J. Cameron. The Canadian-born Cameron would come
to fame as the chief spokesman for Henry Ford and, of greater import, as editor of Ford's newspaper, the *Dearborn Independent*. It was the *Independent*'s
1920s series, collectively titled 'The International Jew', which would provide
an entry for many to the world of anti-Semitism. Cameron would leave
British-Israelism in the 1930s, and Howard Rand would distance himself from
the movement in the same period, but the groundwork for the emergence of
modern Christian Identity had been laid.

Modern Christian Identity emerged in the 1940s. Doctrinally, the movement placed its primary stress in the so-called two-seeds doctrine. That is, the
Bible was held to be the history of only one people, the descendants of the
race of Adam, the true Israelites who are in reality the White race. The Jews
represent a separate creation – the result of the seduction of Eve by Satan –
with the issue of the union, Cain, as the carrier of the seed of Lucifer. Put
under a curse of eternal enmity from the seed line of Adam, the two seed lines,
that of White Adamic man and that of the children of Satan, the Jews, 'have
been locked in conflict for the last six thousand years upon this earth'.[16] The
Jews in this view are not truly Israelites; they are the synagogue of Satan
(Revelations 2:9 and 3:9), who are believed to have dispossessed the true
Israelites, the White race, from their identity, although the Jews have failed to
wrest from them the covenant relationship with God.[17] Other races are identified with the 'beasts of the field' (Genesis 1:25) who took human form as a
result of illicit mating with the nefarious Jews.

The process by which this doctrine came to be held as a sort of Identity
Orthodoxy is complex. William Cameron may have been a primary influence,
but the key events involved the extensive contacts between such anti-Semitic
British-Israel figures as C. F. Parker and Clem Davies in Vancouver and such
West Coast American adherents as the core of influential Identity figures
associated with Gerald L. K. Smith. The most influential of these California
figures were Wesley Swift, Bertrand Comperet and William Potter Gale. The
actual medium of exchange was a series of conferences, with the first in 1937
attended by no lesser lights than Howard Rand and Reuben Sawyer, whose
primary claim to fame lies in his being the first to combine Identity theology

with Ku Klux Klan leadership. By the end of World War II, however, the development of Christian Identity doctrine shifted to the United States, with the coterie surrounding Gerald L. K. Smith as the key figures.[18]

The newly energized doctrine of Christian Identity was soon to gain wide currency in the world of the American radical right. Adherents seem to have been drawn primarily from the ranks of conservative Protestant churches – particularly from Protestant fundamentalism where belief in anti-Semitism or conspiritorialism alienated many from the pro-Zionist stance of the fundamentalist churches. Jack Mohr and John Harrell are typical of this evolution. More, the apocalypticism characteristic of Christian Identity is little different from that which is found in Protestant fundamentalism in all but one key element: where fundamentalists can await the eschatological 'End of Days' secure in the knowledge that in the dreaded seven-year period of the Tribulation when war and famine and disease engulf the earth they will be raptured into the air to await the inevitable conclusion of history at Jesus' side, the Identity believer has no such hope of supernatural rescue. Rather, the Christian Identity believer is secure only in his ability to persevere – to survive by the grace of God, by virtue of his own wits and through recourse to his own food stores and weapons.

Why did Christian Identity appeal to these alienated seekers? It appears that the primary explanation lies in Identity's unique ability to meet the need of many members of the racialist right for spirituality, fellowship and ritual in a Christianity shorn of its Jewish roots. Identity in this view provides the hermeneutical key to unlocking the mysteries of past, present and future while offering the faithful an explanation for their current perception of dispossession. Identity apprises them of their golden past before the machinations of the satanic Jews robbed them of the knowledge of their covenantel birthright, and it assures them of their promised future of happiness and terrestrial power. Perhaps of greatest import of all, Identity doctrine gives shape and substance to the conspiratorial suspicions of the faithful remnant. In this respect, the efficacy of the two-seed theory centers on its ability to demonstrate to the faithful the truth of what to the uninitiated is the weakest link in the extravagant conspiracy scenarios which it is the passion of the far right wing to unravel. That is, how is it that the Jews have succeeded in keeping alive a centrally directed conspiracy against Christianity over the course of two millennia? Identity's explanation is as simple as it is elegant. This conspiracy is genetic,[19] for as the Book says, 'Ye are of your father the devil; and it is your will to practice the lusts and gratify the desires of your father. He was a murderer from the beginning, and does not stand in the truth, because there is no truth in him. When he speaks a falsehood, he speaks what is natural to him; for he is a liar and the father of lies and of all that is false' (Rev. 3:9).

Identity theology today is highly decentralized. There is no center of orthodoxy, and in the post-Wesley Swift era, no preeminent figure to tie together the fractious world of independent Identity churches. The three Identity leaders discussed below were therefore selected to illustrate the diversity characteristic of the Identity world.

Perhaps the Identity minister who has become synonymous with the construction of Christian Identity as the 'Theology of Hate' is Richard Butler and his Aryan Nations compound at Hayden Lake, Idaho.[20] Butler, a disciple of Wesley Swift in California who moved to Idaho in 1973, probably possessed the strongest claim to be the Swift's spiritual heir. In the late 1970s and early 1980s, Butler's star did indeed appear to be in the ascendant. His Aryan Nations compound became a mecca for the radical right and his annual 'open house' attracted adherents of a wide variety of far-right belief systems. A central attraction of this carnival was the weapons and survivalist training offered by Aryan Nations 'experts' who, in their snappy brown imitation-Third Reich uniforms, veered as close to neo-Nazism as Christian Identity in North America has come. Of greatest import, the Aryan Nations' prison ministry appears to have been highly influential in the formation of the Aryan Brotherhood movement among white prisoners.[21]

Reverend Butler was one of the star defendants at the 1989 Fort Smith conspiracy trial. His legal position at that point was precarious. The Order emerged from the area around Hayden Lake, and several founding Order members were Aryan Nations residents. Worse, the printing press used in the Order's counterfeiting operation belonged to the Aryan Nations. Finally, when Robert West, one of the residents of Butler's compound, was found to be unable to drink and keep quiet at the same time, he was murdered at the direction of Order founder Robert Mathews. His body has never been found.[22]

Yet Richard Butler was acquitted of all charges at Fort Smith, and indeed, he has been remarkably successful at skirting the law without actually crossing the line. This innate caution does much to explain the precipitous decline in Reverend Butler's fortunes in the 1990s. In a word, he preached a violent message while refusing to sanction – or even discuss – the possibility of acting on his words. Thus, while Robert Mathews and the Order were at the zenith of their fortunes and donating large sums of cash to several far right wing movements, Richard Butler, whose Aryan Nations compound supplied the Order with much of its manpower, saw little if any of this largess. Mathews seems to have held Butler in some contempt.[23] And, as an aging Butler casts about for a successor, the Aryan Nations movement appears to be fragmenting. Security chief and leading candidate for the succession Floyd Cochrane left the movement and publicly renounced his racist views. Louis Beam tried to shore up the group, but seems to have little interest in replacing

Butler. Indeed, so low have Richard Butler's fortunes sunk that at the last Aryan Nations Congress in 1993, fewer than one hundred people made the trek to Hayden Lake.[24] There appear to be few realistic prospects for the movement to long survive Butler's demise.

Younger, more outspoken and also peripherally connected to the Order is Pete Peters, an Identity minister based in northern Colorado. Peters, a well known figure in the world of Christian Identity, first came to public notice during the investigation of the Order's connection with the murder of Denver radio talk show host Alan Berg with the revelation that several members of the Order attended services at Peters' Laporte, Colorado, church. He has more recently been vilified for his authorship of a booklet which owes as much to Christian Reconstructionism as to Christian Identity. The title succinctly states the message of the tract: *Death Penalty for Homosexuals.*[25]

Pastor Peters' efforts to step into the vacuum of Identity leadership brought on by the decline of Richard Butler's influence and the further splintering of the movement in the wake of the Fort Smith fiasco have, at this writing, brought him little more than increasing difficulties with Colorado authorities. An opportunity to assert this claim to influence presented itself in August 1992. This occasion followed the events which took place near Naples, Idaho, on 21–22 August 1992. There, in an event that would eerily resemble a small-scale version of the federal action at the Branch Davidian compound in Waco, Texas (1993), an 18-month stakeout of the cabin of Identity adherent Randy Weaver culminated with the deaths of a federal marshal, Weaver's 14-year-old son and his wife – shot in the head while holding her infant daughter in her arms. The battle electrified the world of Christian Identity. By chance, this drama was played out during the 22–28 August Scriptures for America Bible Camp conducted in Colorado by Peters.[26]

Following the camp, Peters attempted with limited success to channel the outrage felt throughout the far right wing into an organized movement which would seek to prevent such an event from happening again, either through legitimate political action or, if no other recourse were possible, by fighting back rather than allowing the federal government to eliminate Christian Patriots one by one.[27]

So fractious is the world of Christian Identity that it almost goes without saying that Pete Peters has had little success in his quest to unite the small, far-flung kingdoms that are the Identity ministries in North America. Worse, the authoritarian personality documented by Lipset in regard to those susceptible to right wing ideologies, while overstated, does seem to have come home to roost in the case of Pete Peters. A stubborn man, convinced of his own basic 'rightness', Peters held fast to his principles for over two years of complicated legal wrangling with the state of Colorado over a minor election law violation which carried a small fine. By refusing all efforts at compromise, Peters at this writing had amassed fines plus interest of over $10,000. On 26 February 1993 the state of Colorado seized his church and froze his bank accounts in an effort to make good on the debt.[28]

Pastor Dan Gayman of Schell City, Missouri, represents the opposite end of the Identity spectrum. Where a Richard Butler could gather a group of the disaffected and dream of revolution, and a Pete Peters could urge the Identity community to unite for self-defense against a government seen as bent on the destruction of the 'righteous remnant', Dan Gayman would urge the faithful to withdraw to the greatest possible degree from the surrounding society and prepare as best they can for the imminent End of Days. This is not to say that Pastor Gayman is a pacifist. A student of Gerald L. K. Smith acolyte Kenneth Goff, Gayman in his younger years was closely identified with the most radical wing of Identity believers. More, Gayman apparently received at least $10,000 from the Order, although at FBI insistence at the time of the Fort Smith trial, this money was returned.[29]

Yet in the wake of the Fort Smith trial, Pastor Gayman's evolution from confrontation to accommodation with government authority was greatly accelerated. These new found principles of non-violence were announced in a 15 January 1987 resolution adopted by the congregation of Pastor Gayman's Church of Israel:

> ... be it hereby known that the CHURCH ...and the Board of Trustees, the Pastor, and the congregation of the same in America and throughout the world do not offer this Church as a sanctuary, cover, or 'safe house' for any person or persons, organizations or groups, that teach civil disobedience, violence, militant armed might, gun-running, paramilitary training, hatred of blacks, reprisals against the Jews, posse Comitatus, dualist, odinist (sic), Ku Klux Klan, Neo-Nazi, national socialism (sic), Hitler cult, stealing, welfare fraud, murder, war against the government of the United States, polygamy, driving unlicensed vehicles, hunting game without proper licenses, etc.[30]

This declaration was followed by a series of scriptural teachings based on Romans 13 mandating submission to all but the most unjust of secular authorities and culminated with a stern denunciation of the fictional commandos from the dawn of time, the Phineas Priesthood.[31]

The future of Christian Identity is difficult to gauge. The movement is in constant flux with adherents taking up the cause only to abandon the belief system months or years later. The decentralized nature of Identity combined with a largely mail order congregation precludes reliable estimates of the size of the Identity flock at any given time. Yet Identity has proven to be as resilient as was its British-Israel predecessor, and the ability of Identity pastors to combine Identity doctrines with other right wing appeals – Thom Robb's mix of Identity and the Ku Klux Klan comes immediately to mind – suggests that Christian Identity will be a feature of the North American racialist right for some time to come.

Neo-Nazi Groups

> *Right now this movement is plagued with little self-appointed SS groups who spend huge bucks in assembling SS paraphernalia and putting it on for secret photographic sessions that almost smack of queers coming out of the closet – indeed, in some cases, that is what it is. The fact is (and we had better start admitting some of these unpleasant facts) that this movement has a distinct tendency to attract faggots because of the leather-macho image that the System Jew media imparts to the SS uniform...*
>
> *...in the past year we have had here in North Carolina as 'house guests'...:*
>
> *A 32-year-old 300 pound psychotic who tried to play junior Martin Bormann, spent his time here insulting, threatening, and spreading rumors about other Party members, and would throw screaming tantrums like those of a four-year-old child when opposed. One person described these fits as 'a bearded Gerber baby on a rampage'....*
>
> *And this is in Carolina, admittedly the best and most selective unit in the Party! The other units are even worse...drug addicts, tattooed women, total bums and losers, police informers, the dregs of urban life....*[32] [Harold Covington]

More a study in political pathology than a viable political movement, the highly disparate world of explicitly neo-Nazi groups in North America is notable both for its high profile activism – they are a highly visible feature of the landscape of every right wing march – and for its minuscule size. This is not to say that National Socialist groups are without influence – quite the opposite is true – but if Christian Identity is fractious, National Socialism is fratricidal! The movement in fact has been preoccupied with its internecine rivalries since 1967 when Commander George Lincoln Rockwell was assassinated in Arlington, Virginia. Matthias Koehl inherited Rockwell's American Nazi Party, changing its name to the National Socialist White People's Party and beginning what would be an ongoing feature of the movement since then: a seemingly unending round of purges and angry resignations. Such high-profile Christian Identity figures as James Warner and Ralph Forbes began their careers in the radical right in the ANP only to be harried into other appeals in the cultic milieu through this process of Koehl-era fragmentation. Dr William Pierce, whose visionary novel *The Turner Diaries* had such a strong influence on the tactical approach of the Order, and Harold Covington, whose widely shared observations of the quality of adherents that neo-Nazi movements in North America manage to attract opened this section, were both purge victims as well.[33]

Today, National Socialism, in the widely shared observation of West Virginia Nazi figure George Dietz, is a movement boasting 'a lot of little führers with no brains and lots of guts'.[34] In other words, it is a highly idiosyncratic collection of 'leaders' scattered around the country whose unenviable task it is to lead a tiny and unsavory band of followers toward the dream of revolution and the institution of a New Order. Here too, the movement is bitterly divided between the conservative majority of party activists who favor the theory of mass action which calls for carefully building a broad, revolutionary coalition, and those few who favor immediate revolutionary violence on the model of 1960s era left wing guerrilla movements.[35] In either case, the dream is frankly millennial, and thus, admittedly, ahistorical. But it is a dream which is, to the faithful, very much worth fighting for.[36]

As the introduction to this section indicates, it is no easy task to find an influential leader in National Socialist ranks today. Many have passed through the movement, but almost all have gravitated to other racialist appeals less stigmatized by the negative public image of Nazism and less prone to attract the sort of adherents decried by Harold Covington in the quotes presented above. What remains are a small group of true believers – Hitler cultists in every sense of the term – and a relative few for whom veneration of the Third Reich does not stand in the way of an objective analysis of the current condition of the movement and the flexibility to adapt National Socialist doctrine to the exigencies of contemporary North America. This section will examine several of the more influential of these modernist 'little fuehrers' and consider how a movement with so few adherents – and those held in contempt by their own leaders no less than by the far right wing generally – could enjoy as much influence as it does.

There is little question that the single most influential neo-Nazi in North America is National Alliance leader William Pierce. It was Pierce, writing under the pseudonym of Andrew Macdonald, who authored *The Turner Diaries* which strongly influenced the founder of the Order, Robert Mathews. Indeed, Mathews was once a member of the National Alliance before his discovery of Christian Identity, as was Tom Martinez, the man whose betrayal would cost Mathews his life. Pierce's career considerably predated the *Turner Diaries*, however. A PhD physicist who resigned a professorship at Oregon State University to become a core member of Rockwell's American Nazi

Party, Pierce edited the ANP's quarterly journal, *National Socialist World*. Pierce remained with the ANP for three years after Commander Rockwell's assassination in 1967 before that organization's internal upheavals forced him into the arms of veteran racist Willis Carto and his National Youth Alliance. Like every associate of Carto, this affiliation was short lived and the National Alliance was born. After 1978 the National Alliance was joined by a new Pierce creation, the Cosmotheist Church, whose primary tenet of faith appears to be that 'Thou shalt not deny Dr Pierce tax exempt status' as had the Internal Revenue Service in that year.[37]

Prior to producing *The Turner Diaries*, Dr Pierce's influence in the world of the radical right was based less on his Rockwellian pedigree than on his own ecumenical approach to National Socialism. No mere Hitler cultist, Pierce has consistently eschewed the swastika or other overt displays of Third Reich nostalgia. Instead, his journals (*Attack!* and its successor *National Vanguard*, and the internal *Action* and its successor *National Alliance Bulletin*) have consistently been not only literate but also intellectually challenging. This is no mean feat in this milieu! More, with the unremarkable exception of Willis Carto, Dr Pierce has managed to remain on good terms with a considerable number of radical right figures.[38] But it is the *Turner Diaries*, and perhaps its successor, *Hunter*, for which Pierce will best be remembered. The *Turner Diaries* best captures the seductiveness of the chiliastic dream that allowed a certain segment of the radical right to ignore the glaring disparity between the forces of ZOG (Zionist Occupation Government) and those of the 'revolution' and to enlist in Robert Mathews' quixotic Order. With the Order crushed and the dream of the 'revolutionary majority' in tatters, Pierce launched *Hunter* into the post-Fort Smith void to suggest to the dispirited movement that all was not lost. Rather, a change in tactics was in order, with the lone wolf assassin providing for the moment the only realistic outlet for revolutionary violence.[39]

Rick Cooper and Gerhard (Gary) Lauck do not approach the status of William Pierce in the world of the radical right. Both head National Socialist organizations which have no members. Yet both do enjoy a certain degree of influence in National Socialist circles; Cooper in North America and Lauck abroad, most notably in Germany. Their approaches to NS doctrine are polar opposites. Where Cooper seeks to adapt NS principles to the creation of a small, separatist utopian communalism, Lauck unabashedly dreams of world revolution and pledges explicit obeisance to the ghost of Hitler.

Lauck's name is perhaps better known to an international audience. Through translations of its newspaper *New Order*, the NSDAP/AO reaches an audience throughout Europe, the Americas and South Africa, with its primary appeal directed to skinheads. *New Order* in America is published and distributed from a post office box in Lincoln, Nebraska. The NSDAP/NO was founded in 1974 following Lauck's expulsion from West Germany for giving a speech on American National Socialism. Undaunted, Lauck tried again in 1976 and was arrested, briefly incarcerated and banned from entering the country for life.[40]

Ricky Cooper's National Socialist biography is less colorful than Gary Lauck's. A former member of Matt Koehl's NSWPP, Cooper and co-founders Don Stewart and Fred Surber, both NSWPP veterans, made a virtue of necessity in stating at the inception of their National Socialist Vanguard (NSV) that the organization neither had nor would they accept followers. Rather, the NSV would work to create a separatist enclave which they called Wolf Stadt which would ultimately provide a refuge for the 'righteous remnant' of the racialist right. Wolf Stadt would be built from the proceeds of a group of private business established by the trio in Salinas, California. The NSV migrated from Salinas to Oregon and then Washington, with the service companies reportedly doing worse at each location. Nonetheless, the NSV could hardly be accused of obfuscation. Among its ventures were: Nordic Carpet and Upholstery Cleaning; Hessian Janitorial Service, Quartermaster Laundry, and the memorable Galactic Storm Troop Amusement Center![41]

Cooper's influence in National Socialist circles stems from his affability – he never met a racialist ideology in which he could not find at least some positive points – and from the role of the *NSV Report* which provides something of a friendly tabloid documenting the recent doings of the radical right and reviewing the latest books, television programs and films which might be of interest to what the NSV calls the White Nationalist community. Cooper is of particular note for making himself available for class room appearances (there seem to be no shortage of these opportunities) and for his innovative mass mailings to high school students in selected cities in the United States.[42]

Cooper's willingness to forge alliances across ideological chasms, like that of William Pierce, is the key to the riddle of how so tiny a movement as National Socialism could exercise such a considerable influence on the radical right wing. The minuscule number of literate, intelligent propagandists that North American National Socialism has managed to produce in the wake of George Lincoln Rockwell's assassination have proven to be a valuable resource for a broad spectrum of appeals across the spectrum of the radical right wing.

Reconstructed Traditions: Odinism
  Brothers will fight
  and kill each other,
  siblings do incest;

men will know misery,
adulteries be multiplied,
an axe-age, a sword-age,
shields will be cloven,
a wind-age, a wolf-age...
[Odin's description of Ragnarök, Prose Edda, 12th century][43]

Reconstructed traditions are belief systems which are consciously modeled on idealized traditions of the past and are adopted by adherents attempting to reconstruct in the modern world the spirit if not the substance of that past Golden Age. In the world of the radical right, two reconstructed traditions have played important roles. Dualism, an elaborate construct based on Mountain Kirk impresario Robert Miles' Francophile fascination for the medieval dualist sect, the Cathars, died with pastor Miles in 1992. The other, Odinism, remains vibrant and shows considerable potential for growth in the foreseeable future.

Odinism, a reconstruction of the Viking-era Norse pantheon, plays a vital role in the world of the radical right and in the wider universe of the cultic milieu.[44] In terms of mapping theory, Odinism is located at the spiritual cross-roads linking the racialist appeals of the radical right with the occult/magical community of Wiccan witchcraft and neo-paganism. As denizens of the cultic milieu, Odinists practice an imaginative blend of ritual magic, ceremonial forms of fraternal fellowship, and an ideological flexibility which allows for a remarkable degree of syncretism in adopting elements of other white supremacist appeals – Nazism and, remarkably, Christian Identity in particular. More, as the above text indicates, Odinists tend to subscribe to beliefs which are explicitly Christian. Anti-Semitism, for example, would have puzzled the pagan era Norse, as would the various conspiratorial fantasies which are ubiquitous in the radical right.

Contemporary Odinism originated in the fanciful revival of the cult of Odin among certain elements of the Weimar era 'German Youth Movement'. This cultic activity would flourish in Nazi Germany, and would find resonance with sympathizers abroad whose anti-Semitic beliefs would lead them to conclude that, as Christianity is built on a Jewish foundation, it too must be swept away in the construction of a chiliastic 'New Order'. Alexander Rud Mills, an eccentric Australian, was one such, and it is his writings that inspired the first generation of Odinist adherents in the postwar Americas.[45]

Mills' work disappeared for a time, only to be resurrected in the late 1960s by Else and Alex Christensen in Florida as the culmination of their search for 'the answer' to society's ills. The Christensens' quest, which is typical of the right wing milieu, took them from Spengler to Yokey before quite by accident coming across Mills.[46] The formation of the widowed Else Christensen's Odinist Fellowship and the publication of the first issue of *The Odinist* in

1971 coincided with the discovery of the Norse pantheon by other seekers, most notably Steve McNallen who would at virtually the same time found the Ásatrú Free Assembly.

Although Christensen's Odinism and McNallen's Ásatrú were at their inception difficult to distinguish, by the late 1970s the two movements would come to differ considerably, with the primacy of racialism in Odinism at the heart of this division. At that time, the inherent tensions within the Ásatrú Free Assembly shattered the movement, race being a primary but not sole source of this tension. How difficult the issue of race – and of National Socialism – would be for the fledgling Odinist/Ásatrú movement was illustrated in 1978 when the tiny National Socialist White Workers Party led by ANP veteran Allen Vincent obtained a meeting room in San Francisco by claiming to be 'The Odinist Society'. McNallen's reaction marks a decisive and painful break with the racialist roots of the modern Odinist revival:

> [this] Nazi-Odinist identification has persisted down to this day [1978], but most of us either learned to live with it or simply hoped it would go away if we ignored it. The Ásatrú Free Assembly announces the end of that tolerance.
>
> We...sympathize with the legitimate frustrations of white men who are concerned for their kind and for their culture. These concerns are fully justified. It is a tragedy that these men are driven to radical groups such as the NSWWP because there is no well-known, responsible organization working for white ethnic awareness and identity.[47]

Two successor organizations filled the void left by the AFA's demise; the Ásatrú Alliance headed by Mike Murray of the Arizona Kindred and the Ring of Troth founded by Edred Thorsson. The latter group eschewed race and concentrated instead on revitalizing the magical traditions of the pagan Norse-Germanic peoples while at the same time aspiring to create an Ásatrú 'priesthood' modeled closely on that of the early Church. But the Alliance – whose leader was himself a graduate of the NSWPP's odd Nazi Motorcycle Club headed by James Warner and who in those days signed his letters with a hearty 'Heil Hitler' – presented a more complex case. Faced with a conflict between those whose primary quest was spiritual and those who sought to use Ásatrú as a primarily racialist vehicle, the Alliance adopted a Steve McNallen/AFA policy banning its organization from espousing any political line while allowing its constituents to follow any path they wished so long as they made no attempt to involve the national organization in their activities.

Else Christensen's Odinist Fellowship (OF) followed quite a different path in these years. Primarily a mail order kindred, Mrs Christensen began to fashion the OF into an influential prison ministry, offering (according to her version of events) an educational vehicle providing white prisoners with a message of racial pride, self-respect, and a way to transcend violence and anger so as to emerge from prison a new man. That this transformation of criminals into productive citizens was not always efficacious is amply demonstrated by the octogenarian Mrs Christensen's arrest and current incarceration on a marijuana charge – the result of her loyalty to her 'boys' upon their release![48] Nonetheless, Mrs Christensen's influence should not be underestimated. She remains the most recognizable figure in contemporary Odinism, and her American vehicle, *The Odinist*, as well as the Toronto-based *Sunwheel* (for which she was listed in an apparently honorary capacity as managing editor) has had a remarkable impact on a generation of Odinists.[49]

The current constituency of North American Odinism is, to put it mildly, diverse. Best known are David Lane and other Odinist members of the Order,[50] although a variety of skinhead groups and bikers, as well as more than a smattering of National Socialists profess to be followers of Odinism. Too, Odinism travels well, linking racialist adherents in North America with like minded groups in Germany, southern Africa and Scandinavia. For example, Ásatrúarmenn in Iceland was formed by the late Sveinbjørn Beinteinsson in 1973,[51] and in the same year, the Committee for the Restoration of the Odinic Rite was founded by John Yeowell in England. Indeed, the primary challenge faced by Odinism today may be less the related appeals of other ideologies in the constellation of white supremacist groups than with competition from the non-racialist Ásatrú community.

Idiosyncratic Sectarians: Church of the Creator and Assorted Survivalists

Idiosyncratic sectarians were described in my Spring 1993 article in *Terrorism and Political Violence* as groups whose structures more nearly approximate a religious cult than a political movement. These groups may have started out in a particular camp, principally the Klan or Christian Identity, but during their development there occurred a marked change in the group's structural dynamic. This change often followed a withdrawal from the surrounding society into isolated compounds where increasing psychological and physical isolation, a shared sense of persecution, and the increasing dominance of the group by a single charismatic, authoritarian leader may have led to a powerful strain of antinomianism. Where the earlier essay concentrated on isolated compounds, this section will examine individual survivalists through the microcosm of the Randy Weaver incident and the broader universe of idiosyncratic appeals through the uncertain fate of the Church of the Creator in the wake of the 1993 suicide of its leader, Ben Klassen.

The individual survivalist and the 'creators', as the adherents of the Church of the Creator like to be called, have more in common than it might seem at first glance. Both are composed of highly idiosyncratic individuals who profess fealty to no one. This might seem odd in the case of the creators, given their affiliation with an appeal which styles itself as a 'church' and which was headed by a charismatic and highly authoritarian leader. However, despite these organizational trappings, the Church of the Creator remains a mail order ministry in every sense of the word. Beyond an ever changing core of would be successors to the late 'Pontifex Maximus' Ben Klassen, the COC membership is diffuse and no more substantial than a name on an application form, a check to pay dues and buy literature, and in the case of the most committed adherents, an avocation for passing out the COC newspaper *Racial Loyalty* to anyone willing to buy or accept a copy. This diffuse organizational structure combined with the COC's histrionic racialist appeal brought the COC a scattered group of adherents worldwide. Yet despite the fact that 'creativity' tends to be an urban phenomenon, creators in reality are every bit as alienated and alone as are the rural survivalists. Moreover, whereas the geographic isolation of the survivalist makes him a rather unlikely candidate to commit an act of violence against anyone, the urban creators have been implicated in invariably random acts of racially motivated street violence. This violence is at once encouraged by the tone of COC literature and overtly discouraged by the cautious Klassen's practice of framing the most violently racialist prose with disavowals of any intent to foment violent behavior among his church's 'ministers'.

The COC centers on the belief that Christian Identity's quest to wrest back the divine covenant from the Jews is misguided. Rather, the COC holds that the nearly universal perception that Christianity is built upon the foundation of Judaism, and that Jesus himself was a Jew, is in fact correct. Thus, Christianity itself is Jewish and therefore anathema – as is the society which would embrace such a Jewish religion (styled JOG or Jewish Occupation Government). Following this line of reasoning, the Pontifex Maximus deduced that as Christianity is built on a lie, so then must all religions be false. More, as the Jews are the font of all of the lies of this world, it therefore stands to reason that all religions are Jewish creations constructed to mislead and thus enslave the world.[52]

Having rejected the existence of God or any other supernatural being, the COC has erected in His place a religion it calls Creativity, an odd blend of rewritten Christianity, health faddism, and scabrous racism. Theologically, the COC's program is primarily negative. That is, literally thousands of pages are devoted to debunking religious belief, especially those religions seen as appealing to potential COC adherents. Thus, COC publications attack every belief system from Mormonism to Odinism, but it is Christianity that comes in for particular vilification:

Where did the idea of Christianity come from? As we have shown...the Jews, who were scattered throughout the Roman Empire, have been *Master Mind-manipulators* of other peoples from the earliest beginnings of their history. They have *always been at war* with the host peoples they have infested like a parasite....They had tried military opposition and failed miserably, being no match for the superlative Romans. They looked for an *alternative – mind-manipulation through religion –* and they found the right creed in a relatively unimportant *religious sect called the Essenes...*

So let us proceed further in first of all exposing the ridiculous Jewish story known as Christianity, which I prefer to call the 'spooks in the sky' swindle, the greatest swindle in history.[53]

With so much time devoted to attacking other religious faiths, it is hardly a revelation that Creativity would provide little in the way of a creed of its own. What passes for a COC credal statement is contained in the Sixteen Commandments of Creativity and a number of 'credos' which do little more than recycle the aphorisms which abound in Klassen's writings. So important are these Commandments – the COC asks little more of ministers than an adherence to these basic doctrines – that a comprehensive listing is included below:

The Sixteen Commandments

1. It is the avowed duty and the holy responsibility of each generation to assure and secure for all time the existence of the White Race upon the face of this planet.
2. Be fruitful and multiply. Do your part in helping to populate the world with your own kind. It is our sacred goal to populate the lands of this earth with White people exclusively.
3. Remember that the inferior colored races are our deadly enemies, and the most dangerous of all is the Jewish race. It is our immediate objective to relentlessly expand the White race, and keep shrinking our enemies.
4. The guiding principle of all your actions shall be: What is best for the White Race?
5. You shall keep your race pure. Pollution of the White Race is a heinous crime against Nature and against your own race.
6. Your first loyalty belongs to the White Race.
7. Show your preferential treatment in business dealings to members of your own race. Phase out all dealings with Jews as soon as possible. Do not employ niggers or other coloreds. Have social contact only with members of your own racial family.

8. Destroy and banish all Jewish thought and influence from society. Work hard to bring about a White world as soon as possible.
9. Work and creativity are our genius. We regard work as a noble pursuit and our willingness to work a blessing to our race.
10. Decide in early youth that during your lifetime you will make at least one major lasting contribution to the White Race.
11. Uphold the honor of your race at all times.
12. It is our duty and privilege to further Nature's plan by striving towards the advancement and improvement of our future generations.
13. You shall honor, protect and venerate the sanctity of the family unit, and hold it sacred. It is the present link in the long golden chain of our White Race.
14. Throughout your life you shall faithfully uphold our pivotal creed of Blood, Soil and Honor. Practice it diligently, for it is the heart of our faith.
15. Be a proud member of the White Race, think and act positively. Be courageous, confident and aggressive. Utilize constructively your creative ability.
16. We, the Racial Comrades of the White Race, are determined to regain complete and unconditional control of our own destiny.[54]

The themes presented in the Sixteen Commandments – and the tone in which they are presented – are archetypical Ben Klassen. Calls to racial pride and group solidarity are interspersed with Klassen's fascination for eugenics and National Socialist imagery. More intriguing, however, are the ambiguous suggestions of violence contained in commandments 2, 3, 8 and 10. Here, the earth is posited as the exclusive domain of the White Race (2), but no suggestion is offered as to how this felicitous denouement is to take place. In commandment 3, Klassen calls for *lebensraum* by 'expand(ing) the White race...shrinking our enemies'. Commandment 8 mandates the purging of 'Jewish thought and influence' in an effort to cleanse the earth of all but the White race, while commandment 10 urges the faithful to undertake at least one act that will make a lasting difference to the status of the 'White Race'. Are these calls for a 'final solution', or merely a chiliastic dream? Klassen's writings could easily support either interpretation.

The fate of the Church of the Creator in the post-Klassen era remains, at this writing, uncertain. Klassen's apparent suicide in 1993 capped a chaotic period in the existence of Creativity. Formed in 1973 as either the fruition of a burst of religious illumination or a tax dodge, the Church of the Creator came to appeal to an audience made up increasingly of skinheads and prisoners. The COC by the late 1980s enjoyed considerable growth while in the process gathering more than its share of enemies in the competing camps of the 'right wing synthesis'. By 1992, however, the COC began to falter. Klassen's advanced age and failing health – and at the end perhaps the death of his wife of many years – necessitated a search for a new Pontifex Maximus. In rapid succession, Rudy Stanko, Charles Altvatar, Mark Wilson and Dr. Rick McCarty were named as Klassen's successor. Attacks on Klassen mounted, with National Socialist figure Harold Covington following long-standing precedent in far right wing circles and publicly accusing Klassen of being a homosexual and a Jew. Finally, on 6 August 1993, Klassen took some boxes of documents to a local recycling center, returned to his home and ingested the contents of four bottles of sleeping pills. He reportedly left behind a suicide note which referred to a passage in *The White Man's Bible* which asserted suicide to be an honorable way to end a life that was no longer worth living.[55]

To paraphrase an American aphorism, for some men survivalism comes naturally, for others, it is thrust upon them. The latter describes the case of Randy Weaver, a young Christian Identity adherent loosely tied to Richard Butler's Aryan Nations, who, as a result of government conduct which would ultimately be found to be beyond the pale in an American courtroom, would be forced to live for over two years the subsistence existence of the survivalist. The Weaver case, however, would be substantially different from other post-Order instances of violent conflict involving agents of the Bureau of Alcohol, Tobacco and Firearms (BATF) and the Federal Bureau of Investigation. The case of Randy Weaver became national news, and for once the White supremacist beliefs of the suspect were considered to be less important than either the force utilized by government agents in the effort to apprehend him or the fanciful explanations offered for government conduct at the ensuing trial.

Weaver's story is straightforward enough. An Identity believer of no particular distinction, Weaver was entrapped into selling undercover agents a sawed-off shotgun with a barrel slightly under the legal length. Offered an opportunity to avoid prosecution by becoming an informer, Weaver refused and a trial date was set. At this point the tale becomes murky. What appears to have happened is that Weaver was given the wrong trial date – not an unusual occurrence in the chaotic American court system – and when he failed to appear at the correct time, a bench warrant was issued for his arrest. Fearing that a ZOG plot was afoot, Weaver fled with his family to a cabin in the Idaho hills where federal agents soon materialized and placed the site under surveillance. For 20 months! Finally, in August 1993, the Weavers' dog rushed at one of the agents who panicked and shot it. Weaver's 14-year-old son, Samuel, was shot in the back and killed at this point, as was Federal Marshal William Degan, and what had been a low-level surveillance was transformed into a siege. For 11 days the Weavers and a family friend, Kevin Harris, held out. Finally, either a federal agent using a high powered rifle or an automated robot equipped with such a weapon fired a bullet which penetrated the cabin's wall and entered the skull of Vicki Weaver as she sat at the kitchen table holding their 10-month old baby. She was killed instantly.

At last, Populist Party candidate Bo Gritz negotiated Weaver's surrender. Weaver and Harris were charged with murder in the killing of William Degan, and Weaver was further charged with the original weapons violation and unlawful flight to avoid prosecution. And there it should have ended, had precedent held true. This time, however, popular indignation spread beyond the insular world of the radical right. Part of this may be explained by the way in which Vicki Weaver died while cradling her baby in her arms, part of it with the killing of a 14-year-old boy whose primary sin seems to have been in investigating the death of his dog and firing back when shot at by men concealed in dense underbrush and firing high powered weapons. Part of it too had to do with timing. Weaver's trial coincided with the Branch Davidian siege at Waco, and the similarity of the two events was lost on no one. In any case, Gary Spence, a flamboyant defense attorney from Wyoming took the Weaver case on a *pro bono* basis and proceeded to put the government on trial for its actions. In a classic defense which would be imitated with nearly as much success by the attorneys representing the Branch Davidians, the government's often contradictory explanations for the events surrounding the Weaver case were held up to ridicule. More seriously, Spence's warnings that what the government did to Randy Weaver it could easily one day do to any other citizen was suddenly credible to a white, middle class American jury with the cataclysmic denouement of the Waco siege fresh in mind. Ultimately, to the surprise of one and all, the jury voted to acquit both Weaver and Harris of all charges against them.[56]

Single Issue Constituencies

Given the applicability of the theory of the cultic milieu, the true single-issue constituency is a rarity in the world of the radical right. It appears that for most adherents there exists an interlocking composite of beliefs which allow the seeker to subscribe to several ideological appeals either serially or simultaneously. The primary cases of single issue zealotry in the world of the radical right are significant for their intellectual rigor. The tax protest movement, for example, has provided a frequently used port of entry for the neophyte right wing extremist. It has held the attentions, however fleeting, of such stalwarts of the violent fringe of the radical right as Identity minister and Posse

Comitatus founder William Potter Gale and Robert Mathews, founder of the Order. Few however, remain exclusively in the tax movement.

For most of these neophyte enthusiasts, tax protests hold little lasting appeal. The reasons for this fleeting attraction are not difficult to discern. First, the literature of the tax protest movement is arcane, laden with questions of constitutionality, conspiratorialism (with the Federal Reserve system as prime suspect), law, and the incomprehensible body of the tax code itself. Unraveling these mysteries is a task for which few in this milieu are intellectually or temperamentally equipped. Second, as though peeling the layers of an onion, the newly initiated tax protester will find that the pursuit of 'truth' behind the federal government's taxation policies will lead to other, more interesting revelations. Who in this view stands behind the bankers who profit from the 'illegal' Federal Reserve system? Naturally, it can only be those masters of financial chicanery, the Jews.

Having made this deduction, the theorist is then faced with a conspiracy of considerably greater antiquity than the paltry 80 years since the Federal Reserve Act was passed in 1913 or the mere 219 years of American statehood. More, should he or she have the stamina to persevere, the radical right wing provides a banquet of conspiratorial scenarios from which to choose. Finally, there is a more immediate disincentive to lasting affiliation with the tax movement: the aggressiveness of the Internal Revenue Service in combating anything which smacks of tax resistance. Robert Mathews' experience is perhaps exaggerated, but it is not terribly atypical of the experiences which tax resistance survivors have related during this research. In a letter which was widely republished in movement journals, Mathews describes a pattern of harassment by IRS agents which drove him ever deeper into the milieu of the radical right:

> This campaign of harassment and intimidation began because of my involvement in the Tax Rebellion Movement from the time I was fifteen to twenty years old. The government was on me so much in Arizona that during one incident when I was eighteen, IRS agents shot at me for nothing more than a misdemeanor tax violation.
>
> I left Arizona and the Tax Rebellion when I was 20. I left not out of fear of the IRS or because of submission to their tyranny, but because I was thoroughly disgusted with the American people...our people have devolved into some of the most cowardly, sheepish degenerates that ever littered the face of the planet.[57]

Despite the tribulations of the tax movement, there are few such as Colorado's Arch Roberts who adhere to tax protests as a single issue crusade. More to the point are tax protest groups who have turned to paramilitary activity. The most significant of these was the Committee of the States, founded in 1984 by William Potter Gale. Another Gale vehicle, the Posse Comitatus, too was primarily a tax protest organization which came to have considerably wider aspirations.[58]

While the tax protest movement has been of considerable concern to the US government, the activities of a small but dedicated band of Holocaust revisionists have been a far greater source of concern to the organized Jewish community in the United States and Canada. Holocaust revisionism, like tax protest, requires a cadre of single minded specialists willing and able to comb the vast literature emanating from World War II for evidence to disprove the allegation that the Nazi regime systematically exterminated six million Jews. In their view, this was a lie perpetrated by Zionist Jews and their elite western co-conspirators in their quest to make the dream of a Jewish homeland a reality, to extort financial support for that homeland, and to discredit German National Socialism.

Both the United States and Canada have produced a core of high-profile holocaust revisionists. There is considerable contact between these sets of pseudo-scholars, although there are distinct differences in their organization and approaches. In the United States, the epicenter of holocaust revisionism may be found in Newport Beach, California, at the Institute for Historical Review and in the pages of that organization's glossy periodical, *The Journal of Historical Review*. The activities of the IHR consciously mirror those of the academic think tank, producing studies with all of the trappings of rigorous scholarship, holding annual conferences, placing archives of revisionist documents in the public domain through easily accessed computer archives known as FTP (File Transfer Protocol) sites, and serving as a resource for such independents as Bradley Smith. Despite the IHR's tireless efforts to bring Holocaust revisionism to the center of American public discourse, it is arguably Smith's tactic of placing advertisements in college newspapers throughout the country which has brought revisionism the greatest media exposure. Whether the advertisement is published or censored, the ensuing debate provides publicity of which the IHR could only dream.[59]

Canada's more draconian approach to the challenge to public amity posed by right wing extremists is less conducive to the formation of Holocaust revisionist organizations. For this reason, the best known figures associated with the revisionist movement in Canada tend to do so as loosely associated individuals: men such as Ernst Zundel, Malcolm Ross and James Keegstra. All have had legal proceedings brought against them, and Zundel's legal tribulations in particular have made headlines on both sides of the border. Zundel's legal problems began with the efforts of the Canadian Holocaust Remembrance Association to have his postal privileges revoked to stop the dissemination of his publications, 'The West, War and Islam' and 'Backlash' in 1981. When this effort failed, the same Jewish organization – despite a considerable split in the ranks of organized Jewry in Canada over the advisability of the CHRA's tactics – managed to have Zundel indicted under a little known 1920s era law prohibiting the publication of false news. The tracts at issue this time were the same 'The West, War and Islam' and 'Did Six Million Really Die?' Zundel was convicted of these charges in 1985 in regard to the latter tract, but this verdict was ultimately overturned by the Canadian Court of Appeals.[60] Indeed, convictions against Keegstra and Ross for similar offenses were eventually overturned as well.

It is hardly a revelation that it is primarily anti-Semitism packaged as more fashionable anti-Zionism which motivates most Holocaust revisionists. Despite the scholarly accoutrements of revisionism, Holocaust revisionists make little secret of their methodology; that is, an obsessive search for random, often 'long suppressed' facts which will collectively work to undermine what they see as the weakest link of the Jewish claim to the conscience of the world. This weakness centers on the mantra-like number of six million Jews murdered by the Nazi regime which revisionists see as impossible to substantiate. If the actual number of victims could be shown to be fewer than six million, would that not plant a seed of doubt that perhaps other holocaust claims are specious as well? If only respectable historians could be convinced that claims of Nazi genocide directed at Jews were exaggerated, or in movement terms, if they could be freed to speak a truth which they currently dare not utter 'for fear of the Jews', then and only then would the 'seamless garment' of Jewish claims unravel and the public would at last see the Jew as does the revisionist: a master conspirator engaged in an age-old manichaean battle with the beleaguered forces of righteousness. At a stroke, perceived Jewish control of the US government would be sundered. More, then and only then could a primary target of revisionist activity, the state of Israel, be shown to be illegitimate, built as it was in this view on world sympathy for the Jews arising from fabricated revelations of the activities of the Nazi concentration camps.

Holocaust revisionism is, in short, an ambitious and intellectually demanding undertaking. Revisionist claims, remarkably enough, have found some fertile ground in North America where the historical memory of the World War II generation has begun to fade and where such ill-considered efforts to revive these memories as the fiasco that was the deportation and trial in Israel of John Damjanjuck on false charges of being a notorious concentration camp guard known as 'Ivan the Terrible' have given new credibility to those casting doubt on all Jewish claims. Indeed, it may well have been the inroads made by revisionist activities which motivated *Stephen Spielberg* to take the considerable financial gamble which ultimately produced the effective film *Schindler's List* in an effort to present the holocaust to a generation of viewers far removed from the memory of Hitler or of Nuremberg.

Hope Seeking a Means to Fulfillment (or knuckle draggers galore?)

West Coast Bomb And Assassination Plots Spearheaded by Racist Skinheads: Young White Supremacists Eager to Act on Violent Race War Fantasies of the Movement's Elders [Klanwatch Intelligence Report headline][61]

The 1993 headline encapsulated the fears of observers that groups of young, neo-Nazi skinheads would place themselves under the command of veteran racist leaders in a terrorist campaign aimed at bringing to life Charles Manson's fondest dream: igniting a race war in America. The plot allegedly centered on a planned bombing of a Los Angeles church whose parishioners included such well known Black celebrities as Arsenio Hall and Dionne Warwick. Implicated in the plot were skinheads affiliated with the racist skinhead organizations American Front and Fourth Reich Skins. Adding tantalizing hints of bigger game to be caught were the connections of members of the conspiracy to Tom Metzger's WAR and the Church of the Creator. The charges, if true, are of some note, for heretofore skinhead violence had always been impulsive and sporadic, selecting targets of opportunity on the streets of America and never initiating an attack unless even the most seemingly helpless target could be surrounded by skins. Skinheads always hunt in packs.

From the perspective of such movement leaders as Tom Metzger too, the alleged plot, if proven, would indicate a reckless disregard for the difficulties which he has already encountered as a result of his courtship of skinhead groups. This flirtation became risky in the wake of the successful Southern Poverty Law Center's (SPLC) civil suit holding Metzger responsible for the murder of a black Ethiopian immigrant in Portland, Oregon. The plaintiffs asked for an award of $10m (they ultimately received $12.5m) in an action to, quoting SPLC founder Morris Dees, 'Build a fence $10 million high' to keep the Metzgers out of Oregon. Tom Metzger and his son acted in their own defense, contending that 'skins can't be organized'. They in fact did more to lose the case than the plaintiffs did to win it.

The trial graphically demonstrated the interconnections between skinheads and racialist leaders when Dees played a videotape of Metzger in Tequila, Oklahoma, talking to a group of skins and suggesting that they 'kick a little ass'. Dees then played a tape of Metzger's telephone bulletin board which justified the killings after the fact, claiming that these 'beautiful Blacks' (the victims) were 'high on crack' and that the killers were doing 'a civic duty'. Another tape claimed that 'One young fighter, Ken Mieske, received life', and that the victims should 'get their Ethiopian ass (sic) out of this country'. The success of the SPLC suit temporarily closed down Metzger's operation, as well as making him technically homeless and garnishing 40 per cent of any future moneys he may manage to earn.[62]

Beyond the very real instances of skinhead violence in North America, it is difficult to assess with any accuracy precisely how great a threat the skinhead movement represents. No accurate estimate of skinhead numbers exists, and even the rather dubious numbers which are offered are unable to account for the relative numbers of non-racist and anti-racist as opposed to racist skinheads. The most comprehensive publicly disseminated estimate is provided by the ADL, and while this research has received various indications that the ADL's figures are exaggerated, they are worth some consideration both for their indications of the skinhead movement's scant appeal on these shores and for the movement's clearly static growth curve.[63]

TABLE 2
ESTIMATED SKINHEAD MEMBERSHIP IN THE USA

Date	Members	States
February 1988	1,000 to 1,500	12
October 1988	2,000	21
June 1989	3,000	31
June 1990	3,000	34
June 1993	3,000–3,500	40

Even if the ADL's worst case scenario were to be accepted with 3,500 'Neo Nazi Skinheads' (or more recently 'Young Nazi Killers'), none of whom being non-racist or anti-racist, precisely what does this mean in a crime ridden nation of more than 260 million? While there is as yet little academic data on the movement in North America,[64] there are some sources of insight. On the computer literate fringe of the movement, the battle of polemics between racist and anti-racist skins can be observed in all its vacuity on the alt.skinheads news group. Of greater interest are the writings of some of the most determinedly racist skinheads in America – those currently incarcerated for involvement in violent hate crimes. A portion of one such letter was offered in my previous article in *Terrorism and Political Violence*.[65] What follows however, is a narrative put together from three letters written by another skinhead inmate in Crescent City, California, during the summer of 1990. The text is presented as it was written, errors and all. This review of the current state of the milieu of the radical right wing in North America could have no better conclusion.

So I am the first skinhead you've met. Well this isn't the first time I've been in this spot so I'll tell you a little about skinheads. There are a few different fractions of our movement. Nazi Skins? Well a lot of us look toward National Socialism as a great form of government compared to the one we are stuck with right now. But skins are pretty split up right now. There are COTC skins....And there are Odinist skins and there are Atheist skins. And then comes the two fractions that I really don't agree with. I don't consider these two as anything but confused. Identity skins, they are contradictive idiots that don't deserve to wear our clothing or haircuts....And then my biggest enemy under the code of skins. SHARP (Skinheads Against Racial Pregudest [Prejudice]). They dress a little different than we do though. We wear Black jackets, they wear Green ones.

I guess that one thing I could tell you about skinheads is that our primary concern is for the future of our race. That is our reasoning for being out front. It is to show that we are not a part of the mainstream sheepish society running around kissing up to the Jews. We are proud of our race and unafraid to fight to defend it....But that does scare some Racists off. Most of the Klan hates us. They say we are too violent and act like pagan Vandals. That's ok though they are not what they used to be. And the whole idea of wearing hoods is a sign of fear to be known as a racist.

Anyway I'm starting to get the drift that some of the Odinist groups are starting to do like the Klan and don't want anything to do with us because we are too radical...How can a person be too dedicated to securing the future for our children. We are just sick of seeing what's going on in this country. Hell even in this prison I can see it. They have a Racist Black TV station that is called Black Entertainment Television but if [Tom Metzger's] Race and Reason was on they would be outraged and claim the state was racist. I can see this only getting worse in the future and I personally want what is Rightfully ours back. This is our country and we want it back.

...When a White is proud of his heritage and wants to help and be with people that are of his ethnic background he's an evil racist. But if a nigger or anyone non-white is proud then they are just making up for all that torment that Whites have given them. All the sweat and toil our Race has given and we are left with this. So I put race first in my fight. That's what 99 per cent of the skins also feel. We are the youth that has been left with the mess...I know that it will be even worse for my kids when I have 'em. That scares me...

You know one thing that pisses me off about the Skinhead Movement in the last few years is that my comrades are all sucking up to these 'Movement Politicians'. I'm talking about people like Metzger, Butler,

Miles, etc...! That is causing alot of stupid turmoil between Skins because of influence from these older Racists who have been fighting each other over stupid reasons for years...[66]

II. The Question of Terrorist Violence

In the introduction it was suggested that despite the fondest wishes of some of the most radical adherents of right-wing appeals in North America, actual instances of revolutionary violence in the wake of the Order's demise have been few and far between. Random acts of street violence directed at targets of opportunity have been much more the norm. Indeed, the pattern of violence manifested by right wing groups in North America is sufficiently reminiscent of Ehud Sprinzak's theory of delegitimization as to make an application of that theory to the cases presented here a valuable exercise.[67]

Sprinzak's theory of delegitimization is a promising step toward the creation of a predictive instrument which may be applied to conditions that appear conducive to the formation of a terrorist movement. In the present context, split delegitimization offers valuable insights into the uniqueness of the phenomenon of right wing terrorism occurring in Western democracies. The following criticisms are, therefore, offered to suggest further refinement of the theory rather than to question the fundamental tenets of Sprinzak's work. [Editor's comment: The critical comments relate primarily to Sprinzak's original 1991 formulation of his model. Several points raised here by Kaplan are incorporated into Sprinzak's revised model presented in this volume.]

The four areas of concern to be addressed below are: (1) delegitimization in the case of right wing movements in North America appears to be a reciprocal rather than a unilateral process; (2) the theory's concentration on violence directed primarily at the 'other' rather than the state underestimates the degree to which the state has lately come to be identified with the 'other'; (3) Sprinzak's vision of the adherents' 'desired world' underestimates the religiosity of the radical right in North America, and thus the distinctive chiliasm of the movement's ultimate vision; and (4) the theory may underestimate how far even a democratic state is prepared to go in suppressing right wing movements when subjected to sufficient pressure to 'do something' about an unpopular subculture.

Delegitimization as a Mutual and Reciprocal Process

A central tenet of the theory of split delegitimization holds that, when the right wing oppositional group deduces that the government is unwilling or unable to act in the interests of its 'true citizenry', the resulting sense of betrayal may create a crisis of confidence in the regime. This crisis of confidence is an important precondition for the transformation of a heretofore generally law abiding dissident group into a movement increasingly disrespectful of legal norms, and therefore less resistant to adopting violence. This observation is undoubtedly correct, but could profitably be expanded to include a process which might be called mutual delegitimization. That is, not only is the nascent dissident group engaged in a process of stripping the regime of its claim to legitimacy, but either simultaneously or more often as a precondition for the radicalization of the right wing group, the dominant culture on both state and non-state levels have anathematized the discourse of the radical right. The resulting marginalization of right wing discourse leaves the adherent with only two options: to withdraw into the milieu of the radical right, or to resort to the 'propaganda of the deed' to make his beliefs felt. Here, Marty's mapping theory is of value, for it suggests in graphic terms the considerable distance from the borders of the North American cultural heartland to which the milieu of the radical right has been banished.

This virtual demonization of radical right wing discourse in America is of comparatively recent vintage. As recently as the 1920s, the Ku Klux Klan held considerable sway in American politics, and in fact held the reigns of government in several northern states and municipal governments.[68] This tolerance for the rhetoric of the radical right came to an end in the era of Gerald L. K. Smith and his Christian Nationalist Crusade. How this came about provides some insight into the process of reciprocal delegitimization.

Gerald L. K. Smith was, in the years before World War II, a populist orator of the first magnitude and, as opposition to his message grew – an opposition which he identified as emanating primarily from the American Jewish community – was alongside Father Charles E. Coughlin among the leading anti-Semites in the nation. More, Smith's crusade brought together the adherents of several radical right wing appeals in a coalition which, given its fractious nature, is unlikely to occur again in the Americas. At first, the organized Jewish community in the form of the American Jewish Committee (AJC) and the Anti-Defamation League of the B'nai B'rith (ADL) did little to combat the Smith phenomenon. This would soon change. War was looming in Europe and the Depression era flourishing of populist appeals of the left and the right had yet to fade. More, Nazi Germany had strong regional pockets of North American admirers and a core of high profile propagandists in both the United States and Canada. With American engagement in the war on the side of the Great Britain and Stalin's Russia, the interests of the American government and the Jewish organizations converged on the necessity of neutralizing the still influential voices of the radical right for whom distrust of Britain was only marginally less acute than hatred of Soviet communism. One symptom of this sensitivity to the voices of the radical right was the great sedition trial of 1944 in which Gerald L. K. Smith was fortunate to escape indictment.[69] Another symptom was the evolution of resolve in the Jewish community to make an example of Smith to any would-be successor to his mantle as the doyen of the racialist right.

The American Jewish Committee first focused on the activities of Gerald L. K. Smith on a formal level in May 1947 when, alarmed at the apparent success of Smith and other right wingers at linking Jews to Soviet communism, the AJC executive committee met to form a plan of attack against the Smith crusade.[70] This and subsequent meetings failed to come to an agreement on a coherent strategy, due primarily to the delicate balance of the body politic in this, the first flush of the Cold War. Soviet Jews were simply too deeply involved in the Soviet state, and with the international communist movement as well, to risk involving a Jewish organization in the controversy.[71] Making a virtue of indecision, the strategy which both the ADL and AJC eventually arrived at was termed at the time 'dynamic silence'. Championed by Rabbi S. A. Fineberg of the AJC, the idea was to close off all access to the public media – and thus the larger culture – to 'rabble rousers' such as Smith.[72] This decision would mark the moment in time when the radical right would gradually fade from direct access to the popular media, and thus the public consciousness, leaving the 'watchdog' organizations such as the ADL and AJC in a position to assume stewardship of the public exposure of the movement.

It was not until the attempt by Smith and others to block the appointment of Anna M. Rosenberg as an Assistant Secretary of Defense in 1950 that both the American Jewish Committee and the ADL opened a full-fledged attack on Gerald L. K. Smith by bringing charges of anti-Semitism before the US Senate. By then, the tactics employed by the ADL and the AJC were well honed: to identify potential anti-Semites and to seek to preempt if possible, to halt if not, their activities by putting pressure on elected officials and on local and national newspapers, by printing the names of suspected anti-Semites, and by distributing 'educational' materials intended to neutralize criticism of the Jewish community. It is an interpretive role that today continues to be performed by the 'watchdog' groups of which the ADL is the most influential.

Acting in a role which is strikingly reminiscent of a 'high priesthood' whose self-appointed task it is to interpret the distant rumblings of the radical right wing milieu, the ADL and its numerous imitators have, through carefully nurtured connections with Congress, government agencies and the media, succeeded to a remarkable degree in banishing the adherents of right wing appeals to the margins of society. What is more, the ADL, once fastened on a target, is tenacious in its endeavors to isolate the target movement from the mainstream culture. No better example could be given of an attempt physically to isolate a perceived enemy than the 1969 effort by the ADL to prevent the building of a road at public expense linking an aging Gerald L. K. Smith's biblical theme park and annual passion play in Eureka Springs, Arkansas, with the main highway.[73]

Using tactics perfected in the 1950s, the ADL acted along two tracks: a somewhat covert press campaign which attempted to influence local and national newspapers to write in opposition to the road building effort, and a high profile campaign headed by ADL National Chairman Don Schary to appeal to government officials to intervene. Included in this latter campaign were President Richard Nixon, Secretary of Commerce Maurice Stans and Secretary of Transportation John Volpe. Smith's theme park did in the end get its road, but not before the ADL set out to punish any individual or company having any connection with the project.[74] Smith himself ended his career in virtual obscurity, publishing his *Cross and the Flag* newsletter and putting out ever more inconsequential tracts purporting to contain 'revelations' of the Jewish hand behind sex education, Capital Hill debauchery, and ad *infinitum*.[75]

The tactics pioneered against Smith proved so efficacious that even before the onset of the 1980s language rectification movement known somewhat derisively as 'political correctness', the radical right had been all but silenced in the American public square. In Canada, the process has gone further with active prosecutions of right wing figures; holocaust revisionists in particular have fallen afoul of Canadian prosecutors if not courts of appeal. Examples of this dearth of media access were noted in the context of Christian Identity in my previous *Terrorism and Political Violence* article, and efforts to break through to the mainstream culture have been just as unavailing for other radical right wing ideologies. Recently, however, through the medium of popular afternoon 'talk shows', this wall of media silence has begun to crumble. This allows radical right wing ideologues uncensored access to a segment of the North American public for the first time in years, albeit at the cost of the trivialization of their message.

The importance of this media breakthrough must not be underestimated, although what its long term implications might be are as yet unclear. The appearance of radical right wing figures on television and radio talk shows was not unprecedented, however. Suitably packaged spokesmen for far right causes have occasionally been featured on late night network television. David Duke, for example, attracted the interest of right wingers beyond the borders of Louisiana through an appearance on Tom Snyder's late night show on the National Broadcasting Company.[76] The treatment meted out to some guests on these programs by such as Denver radio talk show host Alan Berg has often been less than civil, however, and Berg's particularly censorious behavior made him an early assassination victim of the Order.

This near invisibility changed when the ratings competition among network and syndicated cable talk show hosts brought into millions of homes across America tales of private pathology, horror stories of dysfunctional families, revelations of rampant Satanism, and at last, the political 'monsters' lurking in the outlands of the radical right. One such panel, composed of adherents of the racialist right and equally unrepresentative Black nationalists, made national news by erupting in a chair swinging fight which broke the nose of the sleaziest of this new breed of talk show hosts, Geraldo Rivera, and thus demonstrated the marketability of these prepackaged confrontations.

How manipulative these televised spectacles can be was graphically demonstrated in an edition of the Jerry Springer Show, filmed in Chicago and televised on 11 May 1993. Here too, a brief scuffle erupted among participants, although the expected ratings bonanza did not appear to materialize. The panel was composed of such radical right stalwarts as Tom and John Metzger and such self-promoting non-entities as the Nazi uniformed Art Jones, National Chairman of the America First Committee, who was accompanied by both of the members of that organization, similarly garbed and prominently displayed in the front row of the audience. On the other side stood Black nationalists Michael McGee and Doris Green. There was less to the confrontation than met the eye, however. Jones, a last-minute addition to the spectacle, was assured a place on the panel by his willingness to follow the suggestions of the producers and 'say something outrageous'. When Jones protested that to do so could start a fight, he was assured that there was nothing to worry about on that score, the show would have plenty of security. Still dubious, Jones was not sufficiently incendiary on a first run through, causing the host to call a halt to filming and start again. Jones responded with a recitation of FBI crime statistics which Commander of the Black Panther Militia McGee took to imply that Black women and prostitution were synonymous and the tussle was on. This epiphany was short lived. Jones immediately apologized for the misunderstanding and shook hands with McGee. Worse, as the discussion wore tediously on, it became clear that the panel had more areas of agreement than disagreement, and indeed, the Metzgers were ultimately invited to address McGee's group – a meeting that went well according to all concerned. The duplicitous host was left to end the show with a platitudinous soliloquy to the effect that none of the guests were nice people while the mailing addresses of each participating group were flashed on the screen.[77]

The dramatic descent from the vast audiences commanded by a prewar Gerald L. K. Smith or a Fr. Coughlin to the tawdry carnival side show that is the Jerry Springer Show speaks volumes on the reciprocal nature of delegitimization. Long before the milieu of the radical right came to despair of redeeming the American government from the perceived influence of the 'other', the dominant culture – and thus the state itself – had determined that the views of the radical right were beyond the bounds of legitimate discourse in the American public square. Deprived of mainstream outlets through which to disseminate its views, banished to the margins of American culture, the racialist right had by the late 1950s turned in on itself, contriving ever more fantastic conspiratorial scenarios to explain its marginalization. From this period of isolation and savage infighting came the view that today defines the movement: that the US government has been irretrievably lost as the malign 'other' has come to control the apparatus of the state. This observation leads to the second criticism of Sprinzak's theory: that the conception of split dele-gitimization underestimates the degree to which the contemporary discourse of the radical right identifies the 'other' with the state.

The Omnipresence of ZOG

> In the past, despising the evil that was around me and yet not wanting to be a martyr, I deceived myself into believing that merely by refusing to aid my ene-mies in their machinations would be sufficient to salve my conscience and yet not jeopardize my life. In keeping with that delusion, I tried hard to separate myself from the system so I would not be a party to its crimes. I wanted to be left alone and not forced to participate in my own destruction. Now, of course, I know better. I no longer suffer from any delusions regarding the motives, means and dedication of our enemies.
>
> For though I stopped paying my tithes (income tax) to the satanic system, revoked my slave number (social security number), stopped working for corporations or other system creations, canceled my bank accounts and stopped accepting checks, working for cash or for barter only...I was not left alone. I was 'criminally' investigated by the IRS in 1982-1983. Several of my friends and associates were subpoenaed (without due process or grand jury investigation) to give information about my private, personal affairs (source of livelihood, political beliefs, etc.). This came, no doubt, from my public efforts to expose the criminal acts of the Jewish-owned Federal reserve system and its collection agency, the IRS...
>
> Thus I...have declared war on ZOG...
>
> I know that most of my people will not understand my motives nor my actions...yet they remain immutably worthy, necessary, and in the final analysis, inevitable. To watch my people devoured by Judaism and not resist would destroy me just as surely as ZOG's bullets and jails...
>
> I KNOW NOT WHEN I WILL DEPART FROM THIS EARTH, ONLY THAT IT WILL BE SOON. I leave with no regrets. There is nothing here to hold me. I am a stranger in my own land and to my people. Alienated from the dominate (sic) trends of judaized culture, disgusted by its commercialism, its art, its music, its politics, and above all, its hypocrisy.[78] [David J. Moran, 1986]

The extended quotation above is taken from the Last Will and Testament of David J. Moran, a founding member of the Committee of the States. Moran died in a shoot-out with police on a lonely highway in rural California on 8

December 1986. Ironically, his death occurred on the second anniversary of the day in which Moran's hero, Robert Mathews, met a similar fate. Both died at precisely 9:00 p.m. The letter is unremarkable in the internal discourse of the radical right wing today, and was chosen for inclusion here primarily for its accessibility in a published work. Moran's themes of alienation and isolation are ubiquitous in the milieu of the contemporary radical right, but what interests us here is how complete is the identification of the state and the dominant culture with the 'other'. In this manichaean conception, the Zionist Occupation Government epithet is no mere rhetorical device. Like its Church of the Creator equivalent JOG (Jewish Occupation Government) or the recent contribution of Identity pastor Paul Hall, BOG (Babylonian Occupation Government), the term is evocative of the despair felt by adherents of ever being able to reverse this latest example of the Jewish theft of culture. This belief strongly conditions the forms which violence will take, once the conclusion is reached that no other alternative is possible.

It is important to note, however, that Sprinzak's observations of the rarity of violence in this milieu is borne out in North America. As in Sprinzak's theory, violence is undertaken only by splinter elements of a movement. More, the resultant terrorist groups tend to be small, autonomous, and composed of part-time revolutionaries who continue to maintain jobs and families. Operations tend to be largely focused on targets of opportunity arrived at as a result more of an emotional outburst than a process of rational planning. Only a minority of these groups are more sophisticated, employing a rational calculus of risk to potential benefit before undertaking an operation.

There is some difficulty, however, with the conception of split targeting.[79] That is, as a result of 'two contemporaneous processes of delegitimization: an intense delegitimization *vis-à-vis* the hated non-governmental collectivity and a diluted delegitimization towards the regime', 'the main violence...is expected to involve non-ruling populations, [while only] some of the heat is likely to reach political authorities'. This observation certainly describes the random street attacks perpetrated by racist skinhead groups and the increasingly rare instances of Ku Klux Klan acts of local vigilantism. Yet as David Moran's statement indicates, many on the violent fringes of the movement no longer make a distinction between the government, the dominant culture, and the 'other'. They have in recent years become inextricably interconnected, and thus to strike at one is to strike at them all.

This powerful strain of manichaeism has led to forms of violence beyond the vigilantism noted above. At one extreme are the confrontations between state authority and the inhabitants of isolated compounds or individual survivalists. Here, despairing of the dominant culture, groups of adherents seek to withdraw completely from the 'system' and move beyond the reach of its minions. The motivations for this course of action are primarily millenarian, and by situating themselves in the most isolated pockets of rural America, there is obviously little opportunity for acts of vigilante violence directed at the now distant 'other'.

Apocalyptic millenarians all, bereft of the hope of supernatural rescue through the doctrine of rapture in the 'soon coming' Last Days, these isolated compounds in the 1970s and 1980s were armed camps. They were isolated only in a geographic sense, however. They maintained contacts with each other and with other appeals in the right-wing milieu. Eventually, a kind of specialization evolved with on the one hand Richard Butler's Aryan Nations compound serving as both the annual mecca for movement gatherings and the public face of the movement, and on the other, James Ellison's Covenant, Sword and the Arm (CSA) of the Lord becoming the movement's armorer and preferred location for training in weapons and non-conventional warfare tactics for the 'serious' adventurer.

Ellison's compound provides an interesting case study in the effects of physical isolation and complete alienation from the surrounding culture. Ellison, already unstable, came to take on regal pretensions while a marked strain of antinomianism developed at the CSA compound. Violence too was not long in coming. Here, two distinct patterns emerged. On the one hand, some Order-inspired CSA adherents did undertake a spree of revolutionary violence. The most notorious of these, Richard Snell, is currently on death row in Texarkana, Texas, for the murder of a Black Arkansas state trooper during a routine traffic stop. Previous to this murder, Snell was involved in a series of terrorist acts, culminating in the murder of a pawnshop owner believed by Snell to be Jewish. Yet Snell and his confederates were by then acting outside of the aegis of CSA, and the pattern of their activities suggests an ultimate dream far beyond vigilantism's aim to preserve the status quo.

The primary confrontation involving the organization was not with random targets of opportunity, but rather with the state itself. It was a hopeless battle, and in April 1985 the CSA compound was surrounded and Ellison and others arrested. This pattern of withdrawal, siege by government forces and a forced decision to resist or surrender is by far the dominant pattern of violence in the movement's survivalist fringe. This pattern holds true for targets as disparate as the idiosyncratic CSA or the lone figure of a Randy Weaver. In this milieu, the outside world is perceived as literally demonic, and to strike out at a Jew, a Black policeman or an FBI agent is essentially to resist the devil himself.[80]

Closer to home are instances of revolutionary violence aimed directly at the 'system'. IRS buildings and agents are fair game here, as are softer targets such as judges or other government officials. Here lie the dreams of Robert

Mathews of the Order, whose revolutionary tactics were honed as a tax resister in the Arizona Patriots. Here too rests the core charge behind the Fort Smith conspiracy trial featuring the hapless Ellison as the star witness; conspiracy to overthrow the government of the United States! And here as well are the acts – or more precisely, threats – issued by the Committee of the States and adherents of the amorphous Posse Comitatus.

The objectives here are clearly not vigilante violence. Blacks are not attacked – they are seen as having too little intelligence or initiative to be perceived as a threat. Indeed, an early Robert Mathews directive to the Order was to eschew any racist remarks in public. Jews conversely, are seen as a threat – the hidden hand behind everything from the Civil Rights Movement to the tyranny of the state. But with the exception of a few high-profile figures, individual Jews were rarely marked for death, and attacks on synagogues were seen as both futile and counter-productive. Indeed, the Order's assassination of Alan Berg appears to have been the result of a last minute substitution for the less accessible Baron de Rothschild, Henry Kissinger, Norman Lear and the non-Jewish Morris Dees.[81]

The target here is in fact the state itself, and the tactics are indirectly borrowed from European leftist terrorists as distilled by such American imitators as the Symbionese Liberation Army and the Weather Underground. Robberies of 'system targets' such as banks (and armored cars) are undertaken to finance the revolution until such time as the less risky method of counterfeiting currency can be perfected. The money is then recycled to finance other appeals in the radical right wing with the immediate objective of forging alliances and demonstrating through the 'propaganda of the deed' that revolution is possible and that ZOG is not as all powerful as the manichaean *Zeitgeist* of the radical right imagines. Assassination in this conception is no mere act of impulsive vigilante enforcement of threatened norms, but is rather a form of armed propaganda aimed at instilling the maximum hope in the faithful by demonstrating the vulnerability of the hated 'system'.

How susceptible the milieu of the radical right is to propaganda, be it of the deed or of the pen, is of considerable interest here. Clearly, the denizens of this milieu thrilled to the Order's exploits once they could be convinced that Mathews and company were genuine revolutionaries rather than part of an elaborate government entrapment scheme. But in line with Sprinzak's observation, few were prepared to place their own lives on the line to join the revolution, and the government did not lack for self-serving prosecution witnesses at Fort Smith! More, the fictional *Turner Diaries* and the imaginary enforcers of the *Vigilantes of Christendom* would become ubiquitous on the book shelves of the faithful, but few would take the dream beyond the unfashionable literary circle which is the world of right-wing newsletters into the streets of America. Thus the Turner Diaries' bitter sequel, *Hunter*, suggesting a return to lone wolf attacks on 'system' targets.

For the considerable population of the faithful whose apocalyptic perception of contemporary American culture forces them to action but whose innate caution rules out such lone wolf adventures, other options remain. One of the more popular of these in the early 1990s is the militia movement. These growing citizen militias are strongest in several midwestern and western states. Based closely on the dreams of Robert DePugh's 1950s era Minuteman group and on the early models of William Potter Gale's California Rangers, John Harrell's Illinois-based Christian Patriots Defense League, and the Arizona Patriot group that was Robert Mathews' gateway to the revolutionary right, the citizen militias are composed of a diverse band of weekend warriors. Taking to the hills and the forests, clad in camouflage fatigues and armed with a variety of weapons, the militias diligently prepare for the day in the not too distant future when, they are certain, the government will descend to wrest from this beleaguered remnant of the last of their cherished constitutional freedoms as a aprelude to the imposition of an international dictatorship under the United Nations.

The various militia groups have studiously eschewed violence. Theirs is a call to vigilance and preparation for the coming time of tribulation. Yet the militia groups themselves are at best ad hoc collections of part-time enthusiasts whose backgrounds and opinions are startingly diverse. Women, a few Jews, and members of racial and ethnic minorities can be counted among their number.

The loosely organized state militias communicate with each other in a variety of ways: journals and newsletters, meetings, travels of militia members from state to state, a fax network, and, most recently, a proliferation of computer BBS and mailing groups. This rapid exchange of ideas further facilitates the already marked tendency toward serial and simultaneous cross-smemberships in which militia members can be affiliated with a variety of other ideological appeals across the spectrum of the radical right wing.

The militias themselves are organized on local and state levels and are structured around a core of local leaders with a fluctuating band of followers. However diverse the membership may be, there does appear to be a core of beliefs that are in keeping with the radical right's accepted orthodoxy: apocalypticism, manichaeism, and a view that the Federal government has fallen under the control of a hostile conspiracy bent on seizing from the dwindling ranks of true Americans the last vestiges of their constitutional liberties.

Typical of the militias' appeal is an undated pamphlet issued by the Militia of Montana (MOM) led by Randy Trochman of Noxon, Montana. In an undated pamphlet titled 'Executive Orders for a New World Order', Trochman presents in reasoned tones the outlines of the evolving orthodoxy of the radical right wing in the 1990s. Adopting as MOM's slogan the Robert Mathews-coinced termed 'sheeple' 'Refuse to be "Sheeple" Become Informed'), the brief text sets out the importance of executive orders in what the radical right wing firmly believes to be the culmination of a conspiracy to subvert American sovereignty in favor of membership in a UN-inspired New World Order whose dictates are to be enforced by UN troops;

> All other forms of government throughout the world must cease to function...Because the Constitution is a document that safeguards [our] sovereignty it must be destroyed. Because of the genuine threat of the American militia, the American people must be disarmed, and become addicted to the government hand-outs and thus become 'sheeple'.[82]

Yet as Sprinzak correctly suggests, violence resulting from split delegitimization is the province of the few rather than the many. And here, the relationship of propaganda to violence is more complex. Robert Mathews was influenced by the *Turner Diaries*, and in the Order's formative stages he pressed a copy on each potential recruit. He was in fact an early disciple of the author of the *Turner Diaries*, Dr William Pierce. Yet much of the tactical advice contained in the book had already been employed, albeit on a less systematic basis, in the world of radical tax protests, among which were Mathews' own Arizona Patriots. More, the *Turner Diaries* got a markedly mixed reception within the Order itself.[83] Similarly, the popularity of the *Vigilantes of Christendom*'s Phineas Priesthood appears to have motivated but a few of the most gullible denizens of the milieu to style themselves Phineas Priests. More commonly, however, the Phineas Priesthood became more a fashion statement than a serious call to arms.

The resistance of the milieu of the radical right to such overtures to violence as the *Turner Diaries* or the *Vigilantes of Christendom* may speak to the most fundamental criticism of the theory of split delegitimization; that it seriously underestimates the religiosity, and thus the millenarianism and concomitant chiliasm, inherent in the radical right wing in North America.

The Millenarian Ethos of the North American Radical Right

What dream could be so alluring as to induce a man to risk all in a lonely battle against a foe whom he perceives to be immensely greater than himself? More, having won through to victory against impossible odds, what will the world which he sacrificed so much to bring into being look like? According to Sprinzak:

Their desired world is not a reality of some non-violent universal humanity that is transformed temporarily – and for just reasons – into a bloody existence. Rather, it is a reality, and an implied Weltanschauung, which is predicated on conflict, permanent discrimination against certain classes of people and their dehumanization.... Terrorism against these 'aliens' or 'subhumans' is just another means of making sure they do not multiply or prevail.[84]

In other words, the prize is a continuation of the hated status quo, albeit with the significant difference that those who would challenge this 'natural order' have with difficulty been put in their place. Such visions were indeed once features of the literature of the racialist right – particularly in Ku Klux Klan circles – but in recent years these appeals for a restored status quo have been abandoned in favor of visions which are frankly chiliastic. In these felicitous scenarios, the 'other' have not been 'put in their place', but rather, they have been banished altogether. What is striking about these scenarios is how reminiscent they are of the Christian apocalyptic tradition. This would hardly be surprising in an appeal as strongly biblical as Christian Identity, but the dream is articulated in nearly identical terms in the avowedly secular world of National Socialism, in the neo-pagan world of Odinism, and in the demand for a 'whiter brighter world' from the stridently anti-religious Church of the Creator!

It was not always so. In the 1950s the movement's vision was indeed more reformist than revolutionary. This contrast could not be better seen than in a comparison of the respective denouements of the radical right's visionary novel of the 1950s, *The John Franklin Letters*,[85] and that of the 1980s, the *Turner Diaries*. In the former, the apocalyptic confrontation between the forces of good and true Americanism and the 'enemy within' of international communism eventuates in a reconstituted American state in which constitutional government is restored. In this resurrected *status quo ante*, the constitutional line of succession to the presidency is followed with such meticulous care that the novel ends with the swearing in of a Black president! The *Turner Diaries* offers no such heart warming prognostications. Rather, the planet is devastated by 'chemical, biological and radiological' means in a war of extermination against Jews and non-Whites conducted on a global scale. The chiliastic dream is of an elite band of survivors inhabiting truly 'a new heaven and a new earth'.

The chiliastic visions current in the milieu of the radical right all appear to contain three distinct stages. First, there is a preliminary demand for separation. This may be articulated in the discourse of White nationalism such as the call for a home for the 'remnant' peoples to be created in several northwestern states. Robert Miles came to this view in his later years, and this too was an early dream of Robert Mathews. For many who took up residence in rural compounds, this withdrawal motif was seen in these terms as well. In all cases, however, withdrawal from the contamination inherent in any dealings with ZOG or the culture that could give rise to such a demonic entity was seen as but a preliminary step. The goal was to prepare for the coming Tribulation, and it is precisely this intermediate stage which is described by Sprinzak in the quotation offered above.

To discern precisely when that Tribulation may begin (or may have begun) is no easy task. In its literal Christian form, the Tribulation is seen as a seven year period in which the Antichrist will peacefully gather together a world coalition for 3½ years which will be followed by 3½ years of apocalyptic violence. Jesus will then return to defeat the Antichrist and create a millennium of peace and plenty for the faithful remnant. The difficulty is to discern by means of signs and portents – the Bible and CNN in modern terms – that the time of the End is nigh. Christian Identity does not lack for interpreters of the signs of the End. Earl Jones and Dan Gayman are but two of the most important Identity figures involved in this complex task of hermeneutics. Yet as the examples quoted throughout this study indicate, the literature of Odinism, National Socialism and Creativity no less than that of Christian Identity are deeply apocalyptic, and each foresees a period of tribulation as the necessary birth pangs of the desired new world.

What that new world may look like differs according to the dreamer. Klansmen such as Thom Robb and Louis Beam see a pristine, all White America on the lines of what they imagine the colonial period to have been like. This may be accomplished in Robb's view by a peaceful decision to separate with passage for Blacks and Jews to wherever they came from cheerfully supplied by White Americans. Beam sees the world in less rosy hues, and with Fanon sees the violence needed to rid the nation of the Jew and the Black and the alien liberating in and of itself. National Socialist chiliasm tends more towards Beam's eagerness to engage in battle, as does Creativity, but the end is the same; a whiter brighter world from which the pollution of the 'other' is eradicated and a uniracial, unicultural paradise of peace and mutual cooperation is born. The Odinist Ragnarök too envisions a world without the 'other', but with the significant difference that the new world is 'remagicalized', the old gods returning as Christianity is defeated. These fantasies appear to be drawn along the lines of Norse mythology as rendered through the medium of sword and sorcery novels and movies. Identity chiliasm is not greatly different from other appeals in that the new world of peace and plenty will be one in which the 'Israelite', that is, the White man, will be allowed to live in peace and happiness among his own kind under the benevolent rule of the returned Jesus. What distinguishes it, however, is a marked pre-Adamistic schematic in which the races are separated and each lives in the place assigned to it by the Creator as determined by Identity's exegesis of Genesis.

The idealism of the 1950s was reflected in the milieu of the radical right wing in a decidedly reformist vision which saw America as imperiled but intrinsically good. While it was true that America's enemies would be defeated in an apocalyptic conflagration, the new world which would emerge would be nothing but a purified version of the contemporary American state. However, as the voice of the radical right was increasingly banished from the public square, and as the processes of immigration, integration and eventually multiculturalism gained momentum and the state was seen as irrevocably hostile to the 'remnant' of 'real Americans', this reformist vision would change. The state, ZOG, was increasingly seen as not worth reclaiming, and with this conclusion, the movement's dreams became increasingly chiliastic. With this, too, the pattern of violence emanating from the fringes of the movement began to shift from vigilantism to anti-state terrorism.

This latter development was not unexpected and the resort to deadly force was, again, not unilateral. This is the fourth suggestion for the further development of Sprinzak's theory; some account must be made of the effect of violence directed at the radical right by state agencies.

An Incipient Martyrology

Gordon Kahl, Arthur Kirk, Robert Mathews, David Moran, Vickie and Samuel Weaver. With the exception of Kahl, about whom a television movie was made, these names and many more are largely unknown to the American cultural heartland but are instantly familiar throughout the milieu of the radical right. From the sieges of the Covenant, Sword and the Arm of the Lord's compound, Randy Weaver's cabin, and ultimately, to that at Waco, there has in recent years been an escalation in the use of force against inhabitants of the cultic milieu across the board in America. The reasons for this increase in violence are complex, necessitating a study in itself. What concerns us here, however, is the effect that this resort to force may have on the movement's own recourse to terrorist violence. It is a question that the current internal literature of the movement is wrestling with, and one for which it is as yet impossible to offer much illumination.

What is certain is that in the more sophisticated reaches of the radical right wing, the view that the US government has become the agent of a triumphant Jewish conspiracy has become accepted orthodoxy. The occasional armed skirmishes which began with the effort to suppress the anti-tax movement have come to involve adherents of other appeals in the milieu of the radical right. The key event here may in retrospect prove to be the siege of Randy Weaver's cabin and the subsequent acquittal of Weaver and Kevin Harris of all charges resulting from a confrontation which resulted in the death of a federal agent. That this was followed so quickly with a similar verdict in the case of the Branch Davidians in a trial that involved the death of four federal agents may well prove to be a turning point for both sides. The manichaean 'us against them' ethos which characterizes the radical right could well engulf those whose task it is to enforce the law. Add to this a budgetary environment which pits agency against agency in the suddenly competitive national security community – a widespread suspicion regarding the Bureau of Alcohol, Tobacco and Firearms' actions at Waco scarcely two weeks before the agency's congressional budget hearings were due to convene – and the barriers to a too rapid resort to force in executing warrants could be ever smaller.

While it is true that most Americans would shed few tears were there to be fewer denizens of the milieu of the radical right to remind us all of the darker side of our history and culture, it is also true that, as the siege of the Branch Davidian compound demonstrates, state violence once unleashed can acquire a momentum of its own. The consequences of this are surely considerably more deleterious than the disquieting views espoused by the radical right.

NOTES

1. Author's interview with the Grand Dragon of the Knights of the Ku Klux Klan, Thomas Robb, 24 Aug. 1991.
2. Jeffrey Kaplan, 'The Context of American Millenarian Revolutionary Theology: The Case of the "Identity Christian" Church of Israel', *Terrorism and Political Violence* [hereafter *TPV*] 5/1 (Spring 1993) pp.30–82; Colin Campbell, 'The Cult, the Cultic Milieu and Secularization', in *A Sociological Yearbook of Religion in Britain* 5, (1972), pp.119–36; and Martin E. Marty, *A Nation Of Believers* (Chicago, IL: Univ. of Chicago Press, 1976).
3. Campbell (note 2), pp.121–2.
4. *Manichaean* refers to an undifferentiated *zeitgeist* of absolute good vs. absolute evil. *Chiliastic* refers to the post-apocalyptic world order, i.e., the Kingdom in Christian terms. The connotation is of a utopia of peace and plenty.
5. This research has indicated cases in which right wing extremists have been dismissed from their jobs following visits from representatives of watchdog groups. Klansman Dennis Mahon's loss of his employment at an aircraft manufacturing plant is typical of these anecdotes.
6. John C. Calhoun and Louis R. Beam, 'The Perfected Order of the Klan', *Inter-Klan Newsletter and Survival Alert* 5 (1984), p.3.
7. 'The Ku Klux Klan: A History of Racism and Violence', *Klanwatch Special Report*, 4th ed. (1991), pp.30–1. The model for this strategy is based on a successful case brought by Klanwatch on behalf of Beulah May Donald whose son Michael was murdered in 1981 by three members of the United Klans of America. The killers were caught and convicted of criminal charges. The Klanwatch civil action, however, was taken against the United Klans of America and the organization's Imperial Wizard, Robert Shelton. The jury found that although Shelton knew nothing of the killing in advance, the UKA was responsible for the acts of its members. Thus in 1987, Mrs Donald was awarded control of the group's

Tuscaloosa headquarters, including its printing equipment, effectively putting the United Klans of America out of business. This case is recounted in considerable detail in Bill Stanton, *Klanwatch: Bringing the Ku Klux Klan to Justice* (NY: Grove Weidenfeld, 1991). Cf. 'Invisible Empire Turns Over Assets to the NAACP', *Klanwatch Intelligence Report* 69 (Oct. 1993), p.1, detailing the demise of Imperial Wizard James W. Ferrands' NC-based Klan group.

8. The split by 1992 had come to the attention of the watchdog groups as well. See 'Hate Groups in Bitter Struggle Over Public Image: Militants Call for Violence; Old Style Groups Claim to Condemn It', *Klanwatch Intelligence Report* 59 (1992), pp.3–4. Perhaps the best introduction to Beam's vision for the Klan and the country is Louis Beam, 'On Revolutionary Majorities', *Inter-Klan Newsletter and Survival Alert* 4 (1984), p.1. Finally, for Beam at his most vociferous, promising to one day 'round up those guilty of heinous crimes like the mad dogs they are and execute the ones guilty, hang 'um', deport them or otherwise rid our Nation of their miserable presence', see Louis Beam, 'We Are At War', *The Seditionist* 10 (Summer 1991), p.1.

9. Louis Beam, 'On Revolutionary Majorities' (note 8), p.7.

10. On the less than hospitable reception Mahon received on one of these forays, see 'White Supremacist Nabbed in Toronto', *Kitchener-Waterloo Record*, 23 Jan. 1993, p.A3.

11. Dennis Mahon, 'It's Now War!', *Oklahoma Excalibur* 1 (March/May 1992), p.1.

12. See, e.g., the remarkably sympathetic portrait of Robb by Michael Riley, 'White & Wrong: New Klan, Old Hatred', *Time*, 6 June 1992, pp.25–7. For another view of Robb, see 'Robb's Knights of the KKK Stage Small Comeback', *Monitor* 25 (May 1992), p.11. Cf. the media success of Robb acolyte and former skinhead Shawn Slater; 'Colorado Klansman Refines Message for the '90s', *New York Times*, 22 Feb. 1992, p.10.

13. ADL, *Hate Groups in America: A Record of Bigotry and Violence* (NY: ADL, 1988), pp.3–4; 'The Hate Movement Today: A Chronicle of Violence and Disarray', *ADL Special Report* (1987), p. 4; and 'The Ku Klux Klan: A History of Racism and Violence', *Klanwatch Special Report*, p.47.

14. ADL, 'The KKK Today: A 1991 Status Report', *ADL Special Report* (NY: ADL, 1991), p.21.

15. The reconstruction of Identity history which follows is based primarily on Michael Barkun, *Religion and the Racist Right: The Origins of the Christian Identity Movement* (Chapel Hill, NC: UNC Press, 1994). Cf. my review article, 'The Far Side of the Far Right', *The Christian Century*, 2 Nov. 1994, pp.1019–22.

16. Dan Gayman, 'The Fable of Eve and the Apple', *Zions Watchman* 8 (July 1977), pp.11–12.

17. Dan Gayman, 'Jesus Christ Was Not A Jew', *Zions Watchman* 4 (April 1977), pp.6–8.

18. Barkun, *Religion* (note 15), Ch.4.

19. The most sophisticated version of this conspiratorial scenario may be found in Pastor Earl Jones' newsletter, *Christian Crusade for Truth*, in an ongoing series titled 'Lesson In History'. For a good, book length version of a similarly complex Jewish conspiracy, see Eustace Mullins, *The Curse of Canaan: A Demonology of History* (Staunton, VA: Revelation Books, 1987).

20. See Anti-Defamation League of the B'nai B'rith, '"Identity Churches": A Theology of Hate', *ADL Facts* 28 (Spring 1983); Leonard Zeskind, *The 'Christian Identity' Movement: Analyzing Its Theological Rationalization for Racist and Anti-Semitic Violence* (Atlanta, GA: Center for Democratic Renewal, 1986).

21. ADL, 'Extremism Targets the Prisons', *ADL Special Report* (June 1986), pp.5–8.

22. For details on these Order related activities, see Thomas Martinez with John Gunther, *Brotherhood of Murder* (NY: Pocket Books, 1990); and Kevin Flynn and Gary Gerhardt, *The Silent Brotherhood* (NY: Signet, 1990).

23. Martinez and Gunther (note 22), pp.270–1.

24. 'The White Supremacist Movement: 1992 At A Glance', *Klanwatch Intelligence Report* (Feb. 1993), p.11; 'White Supremacist Movement Reels from Severe Setbacks in 1993', *Klanwatch Intelligence Report* (Feb. 1994), pp.12–13; 'From Aryan Nations to Anti-Hate: Floyd Cochrane Talks About the White Supremacist Movement and the Reasons He Left It',

Klanwatch Intelligence Report (Oct. 1993), pp.4–6.

25. Pete Peters, *Death Penalty for Homosexuals* (Laporte, CO: Scriptures for America, 1993). The timing of the tract's appearance indicates that it was intended as a riposte to Bo Gritz's reluctance to endorse capital punishment for homosexuality before a gathering of Identity ministers during the 1992 American presidential campaign.

26. 'Special Message and Alert from Pastor Peters', Scriptures for America cassette No. 552 (n.d.). The similarity of the tactics employed at Waco with those utilized against the far right wing did not go unnoticed. See Michael Barkun, 'Reflections After Waco: Millennialists and the State', and Jeffrey Kaplan, 'The Millennial Dream', both in James R. Lewis (ed.), *From the Ashes: Making Sense of Waco* (Lanham, MD: Rowman & Littlefield, 1994), pp.41–53.

27. These plans were published under the ungainly title: *Special Report on the Meeting of Christian Men Held in Estes Park, Colorado October 23, 24, 25, 1992 Concerning the Killing of Vickie and Samuel Weaver by the United States Government* (Laporte, CO: Scriptures for America, n.d.). The booklet contains as a bonus a little known but important essay by Louis Beam arguing for the efficacy under the present circumstances of those willing to engage in revolutionary violence to utilize small cell or even 'lone wolf' tactics without recourse to a central organization. See Louis Beam, 'Leaderless Resistance', Ibid., pp.20–23.

28. On Peters' legal dilemma, see 'Identity Minister's Church and Property Seized', *Klanwatch Intelligence Report* (April 1993), p. 4. On the authoritarian personality, see Seymour Martin Lipset and Earl Raab, *The Politics of Unreason: Right Wing Extremism in America, 1790–1977* (Chicago, IL: Univ. of Chicago Press, 1978), pp.477–82. Cf. the criticism of Lipset's findings in James Aho, *The Politics of Righteousness: Idaho Christian Patriotism* (Seattle, WA: Univ. of Washington Press, 1990), Ch. 7.

29. On Gayman's career, see Jeffrey Kaplan, 'The Context of American Millenarian Revolutionary Theology', especially n. 190, pp.81–82 for his denial of any knowledge of Order activities or of conversations he was alleged to have had with Order member Richard Scutari. For the allegations themselves, see Flynn and Gerhardt (note 22), p. 305, n. 6.

30. Church of Israel, 'Articles of Faith and Doctrine' (Schell City, MO: Church of Israel, 10 Jan. 1982), p.31.

31. On submission to state authority, see Dan Gayman, 'Romans 13: A Primer in Government for Patriotic Christians', pamphlet from the Church of Israel, 1989; Idem., 'Rebellion or Repentance: Which Way Modern Israel?', pamphlet from the Church of Israel, 1987; and Idem., 'Christian Conscience Towards Government', pamphlet from the Church of Israel, 1988. Cf. the 4 hour cassette series, 'The Bible and Civil Disobedience', 1 Jan. 1989. On the Phineas Priesthood, see Idem., 'Can There Be Vigilantes in Christendom?', pamphlet from the Church of Israel, 1991.

32. Harold Covington, 'What Have We Learned?', undated pamphlet pub. by the National Socialist Party of America. The quotes are taken from pp.17–18 and 11–13 resp. These sentiments are ubiquitous in the writings of American National Socialists. In George Lincoln Rockwell's view: 'I learned from bitter experience that the human material of the right wing consists 90 percent of cowards, dopes, nuts, one-track minds, blabbermouths, boobs, incurable tight-wads and – worst of all – hobbyists...'. George Lincoln Rockwell, *This Time the World* (Arlington, VA: Parliament House, 1963), p.193.

33. See for an early example James Warner's letter to 'Fellow National Socialists' dated Jan. 1968 which denounces Forbes and explains that his decision to lead a breakaway faction from the NSWPP to form a new American Nazi Party was taken after Matt Koehl failed to resolve a dispute among Los Angeles-based Nazis satisfactorily. A much stronger denunciation of Koehl and the NSWPP is offered in a report marked 'confidential' (on every page!) from the self-styled National Socialist Defense Force Stormtroops Central Command Organization of the National Socialist Party of America. In actuality the work of Harold Covington in the early 1980s, the report, titled 'NSPA Security Division Report on the Current Status of the National Socialist White People's Party (NSWPP)', systematically holds up to ridicule virtually every facet of Koehl's leadership. On the internecine rivalry that pervaded ANP ranks during the Commander's lifetime, see the acerbic record of life in

Rockwell's barracks by A.M. Rosenthall and Arthur Gelb, *One More Victim: The Life and Death of a Jewish American Nazi* (NY: Signet Books, 1967).

34. Conversation with Ron Hand, 12 Sept. 1992.
35. The National Socialist group most involved in this form of revolutionary violence is, unsurprisingly, moribund if not defunct. The National Socialist Liberation Front (NSLF) was founded in the early 1970s by Joseph Tomassi, who was purged from the NSWPP by Koehl on the grounds that he allowed young women and copious amounts of marijuana in party headquarters. Tomassi responded by forming the NSLF on the model of left-wing terrorist groups of the day. Tomassi was assassinated by a NSWPP adherent in 1975, leaving behind a cadre which included David Rust, Karl Hand and James Mason. Both Rust and Hand are currently incarcerated. For Mason's account of the mass action vs. revolutionary violence split in National Socialist ranks, and for some 400+ pp. of that group's newsletter, see James Mason, *Siege* (Denver, CO: Storm Books, 1992).
36. According to Matt Koehl, 'Like a true disciple, he [Rockwell] would be propagating the Millennial Idea as the rallying banner of an embattled race'. ADL, *Extremism on the Right: A Handbook* (NY: ADL, 1988), p.111. Rick Cooper of the National Socialist Vanguard is equally explicit:
    We know 'Armageddon', which many (we included) believe is the biblical word for race war, will climax a tribulation period at which time the bankers will close their doors. What we have been attempting to determine now is a possible trigger incident that will cause the bankers to close their doors.
    [Rick Cooper, 'No Man Knows the Date', *NSV Report* 11/3 (July/Sept. 1993), p.1.] Cf. James M. Rhodes, *The Hitler Movement: A Modern Millenarian Revolution* (Stanford, CA.: Hoover Instn. Press, 1980).
37. Martinez with Gunther (note 22), pp.35–47, 93–100; ADL, *Extremism on the Right: A Handbook*, pp.39–40; 144–5; Laird Wilcox and John George, *Nazis, Communists, Klansmen and Others on the Fringe* (Buffalo, NY: Prometheus, 1992), pp. 364-365.
38. Dr Pierce remains, in fact, perhaps the last man that Church of the Creator creator Ben Klassen could call a friend before Klassen's 1993 suicide. This too was no mean feat, and Pierce's reward was the opportunity to buy Klassen's North Carolina property at the bargain price of $100,000. ['Church of the Creator Founder Ben Klassen Commits Suicide', *Klanwatch Intelligence Report* (Aug. 1993), p. 7.] The article states that Pierce immediately put the property back on the market with an asking price of $300,000. For a remarkable record of the blossoming of the Pierce-Klassen relationship, see the exchange of correspondence in Ben Klassen, *The Klassen Letters Volume One 1969–1976* (Otto, NC: Church of the Creator, 1988), pp.212, 220–2, and 286–8; and Ben Klassen, *The Klassen Letters Volume Two 1976–1981* (Otto, NC: Church of the Creator, 1988), pp. 8–9, 29–33.
39. Andrew Macdonald, *The Turner Diaries* (Arlington, VA: National Vanguard Books, 1978), and Idem., *Hunter* (Arlington, VA: National Vanguard Books, 1989). For a discussion of the impact of the two volumes, see Kaplan (note 2), pp.59–60, 65 n.28.
40. Lauck's current loner status in the world of National Socialism may have been the result of an ill-starred alliance with Frank Collin, the head of the National Socialist Party of America in Chicago in the late 1970s. Collin's reign ended ingloriously, although in the milieu of North American National Socialism, hardly atypically. First, it was revealed that Collin was half-Jewish – his father had been a prisoner in the Nazi concentration camp at Dachau. As if this were not enough, Harold Covington, his rival for NSPA 'power', made the fortuitous discovery (while rifling through Collin's desk) that the half-Jewish führer also had a weakness for pedophelia and did not hesitate to photograph his dalliances with young boys. As a result, Collin was sent to prison, Covington inherited the NSPA and moved its operations to North Carolina, and the luckless Lauck found a new calling: translating American neo-Nazi propaganda and smuggling it into Germany [Wilcox and George (note 37), pp. 366–7]. On the Covington/Collin imbroglio, ibid., pp.360–1. Cf. ADL, *Extremism on the Right:* (note 36), pp.118–19. For a first person account of Lauck's meetings with German comrades in third countries, see 'Gerhardt Lauck in Europe', *New Order* 96 (Jan./Feb. 1992), p.3. On Lauck's success in importing National Socialist materials into Germany, see Tamara Jones, "'Farm-

Belt Fuehrer" 'Feeds German Market for Hatred', *Anchorage Daily News*, 9 Sept. 1993, p.1. Lauck was arrested for these activities in Denmark in April 1995 as this volume was going to press.

41. The saga of the NSV is best found in its breezy newsletter, the *NSV Report*. See in particular the *NSV Report* 1/1 (Jan./March 1983) and the *NSV Report* 2/3 (July/Sept. 1984) for the Wolf Stadt dream and biographies of the leaders.

42. These themes are drawn from an 11-year collection of *NSV Reports*. For other views, see Wilcox and George, *Nazis* (note 37), p. 366; and ADL, *Extremism on the Right* (note 36), p.46.

43. Snorri Sturluson, *The Prose Edda*, Jean I. Young, trans. (Berkeley, CA: Univ. of California Press, 1966), p. 86. The marked similarity of this description of Ragnarök, the Twilight of the Gods, to Jewish and Christian apocalyptic texts demonstrates the compatibility of the reconstruction of the Norse tradition with the monotheistic apocalypticists who people the radical right wing. With Ragnarök, most of the gods and a great deal of the potential for human happiness disappeared from the earth, leaving the Odinist/Ásatrú literature to refer to the contemporary world – our world – as the Wolf-Age, based on this and similar texts.

44. To date, there is only one published account of the history of the Ásatrú community which may be thought of in simplified terms as a form of Norse neo-paganism which seeks a fuller, less explicitly racialist reconstruction of the Norse-Germanic pre-Christian tradition than does Odinism. Stephen E. Flowers, 'Revival of Germanic Religion in Contemporary Anglo-American Culture', *Mankind Quarterly* 21/3 (Spring 1981). Stephen Flowers is the birth name of Edred Thorsson, currently a primary Ásatrú theorist and a leader of a wing of the Satanist Temple of Set. A complete documentary history of the Ásatrú/Odinist community will appear as: Jeffrey Kaplan, 'The Reconstruction of the Ásatrú and Odinist Traditions', in James Lewis (ed.), *Magical Religions and Modern Witchcraft* (Albany, NY: SUNY, forthcoming).

45. C.G. Jung, 'Wotan', in Jung, *The Collected Works*, Vol.10, Bollingen Series XX (NY: Pantheon, 1964); A. Rud Mills, *The Odinist Religion: Overcoming Jewish Christianity* (Melbourne, Australia: self-published, c.1930). For a classic example of the primary influence of occult beliefs on neo-Nazi adherents, one need look no farther than the Depression era leader of the fascist Silver Shirts, William D. Pelley. For a perceptive encapsulation of Pelley's syncretic ideology, see Martin E. Marty, *Modern American Religion Volume 2: The Noise and the Conflict 1919–1941* (Chicago, IL: Univ. of Chicago Press, 1991), pp.262–5.

46. Interview with Else Christensen 27 Nov. 1992. Mills is presented to the readers of *The Odinist* in 'The Wisdom of A. Rud Mills', *The Odinist* 65 (1982), p.1. Yockey would deservedly be accorded greater attention than Mills, however. See 'Our View of History', *Odinist* 10 (Dec. 1973), p.1; 'The Structure of History', *Odinist* 11 (March 1974), p.1; and 'More Yockey', *Odinist* 12 (June 1974), p.1.

47. The quote is taken from a typescript of McNallen's summer 1978 statement. The statement is accompanied by an internal NSWPP letter dated 24 June 1978 advising members to eschew their Nazi uniforms and paraphernalia for the 'Odinist' event. The letter is signed by Victor Fox for Commander Vincent, suggesting how this stratagem was hatched. Fox is an Odinist attached to the Ásatrú Alliance where he enjoys according to this research a particularly vile reputation for his overt Nazism and for the reputed dishonesty of his personal dealings. A career officer in the US Army, Fox at this writing is fighting the Army's efforts to discharge him for racist activity. McNallen, after a period of inactivity, emerged in 1994 with a new explicitly National Socialist/Odinist vehicle, the National Socialist Kindred. See the first issue of the NS Kindred's newsletter, 'Why Adolf Hitler Had to be Overcome', *Aryan Destiny!* (n.d.).

48. The seeds of Mrs Christensen's downfall should not have been difficult to foresee. Consider a letter from an Odinist prisoner reprinted on the front page of *Odinist* which decried the rejection faced by prisoners in the Odinist/Ásatrú community upon their release. After all, 'Am I so different just because the genes I inherited from my Aryan ancestors impelled me to seek some adventure? Wasn't our very heritage built on Viking raiders?' 'Brotherhood', *Odinist 67* (1982), p.1.

49. The premier issue of The Odinist appeared in Aug. 1971 and would appear faithfully for 21 years, ending only with Mrs Christensen's incarceration. Reportedly, Steve McNallen, long inactive on the Ásatrú scene, has been given The Odinist mailing list for his own recently revived periodical, The Runestone. The Toronto Sunwheel, which began publication in 1972, should not be confused with the current British Sunwheel, a quasi-Odinist vehicle billed as 'The Voice of National Socialism in Britain'. See Grimnir, 'Editorial', Sunwheel 1 [Britain] (1990), p. 2.

50. Lane was later to resign from the Order on the grounds of the incompatibility of his Odinism and the Christian Identity faith of the majority of Order adherents. David Lane, 'Divided Loyalties', NSV Report 8/3 (July/Sept. 1990), pp.1–2. Lane's philosophy of life is detailed in David Lane, '88 Precepts', WAR 11/1 (n.d.), pp.22–3.

51. Flowers (note 44), p.282. Beinteinsson died in 1993, but during his life he was something of an icon for North American Odinists. The Odinist carries the remarkable story of one young American Odinist who made the journey to see Beinteinsson, only to find the language barrier impassable. The reader is reminded of religious seekers of an earlier day who would make pilgrimages to distant holy men only to discover that they were equipped linguistically and culturally to do little more than stare at the radiant countenance of the learned one, and to write moving accounts of the effect of that worthy's beatific smile which changed the seeker's life. For just such a touching account, see The Odinist 49 (1989), p. 9.

52. The primary texts for the COC are Ben Klassen's Nature's Eternal Religion; The White Man's Bible; Expanding Creativity; Salubrious Living; Building a Whiter and Brighter World, and Rahowa! The Planet is Ours. The last volume, published in 1989, is an acronym of RAcial HOly WAr, and spells out Klassen's dreams for bringing about, in COC parlance, 'A whiter, brighter world'. This output is impressive, but also somewhat less than meets the eye. After The White Man's Bible, most of these volumes merely reprint material from Racial Loyalty. Most recently, several volumes of Klassen's letters have appeared as well. All of the volumes above are published by the Church of the Creator, Otto, NC.

53. Ben Klassen, The White Man's Bible (Otto, NC: Church of the Creator, 1981), pp. 313, 325. All emphasis in original. Klassen is more succinct in Nature's Eternal Religion: 'Christianity was invented by the jews (sic) as a tool with which to destroy the White Race'. Ben Klassen, Nature's Eternal Religion (Otto, NC: Church of the Creator, 1973), p.258.

54. Ibid., pp. 408–9.

55. 'Church of the Creator in Turmoil Over Leadership Change', Klanwatch Intelligence Report 66 (April 1993), p. 1; 'Church of the Creator Founder Ben Klassen Commits Suicide', Klanwatch Intelligence Report 68 (Aug. 1993), p.7.

56. 'Rebuking the US, Jury Acquits 2 in Marshal's Killing in Idaho Siege', New York Times, 9 July 1993, p. 1. Cf. the press accounts of various stages of the Weaver odyssey; 'US Hits Snag in Idaho Siege Trial', New York Times, 23 June 1993, p. 7; and 'Fugitive in Idaho Cabin Plays Role of Folk Hero', New York Times, 26 August 1992, p. 10. For various movement views, see the Christian Identity sources; 'Lesson in Federal Tyranny: The Weaver Family Saga', Jubilee 5/2 (Sept./Oct. 1992), p.1; 'Weaver, Harris Face the Death Penalty', Jubilee 5/3 (Nov./Dec. 1992), p.1; and 'Weaver Trial Update', Jubilee 5/6 (May/June 1993), p.1. The latter issue runs Waco and Weaver news side by side. The view of a movement lawyer, Kirk Lyons, is offered in 'White Separatists Acquitted', The Balance 4/2 (Aug. 1993), p. 1.

57. NSV Report (Jan.–March 1985), p.6.

58. Archibald Roberts, Emerging Struggle for State Sovereignty (Ft. Collins, CO: Betsy Ross, 1979). Cheri Seymour, Committee of the States: Inside the Radical Right (Mariposa, CA: Camden Place Communications, 1991). ADL, 'The Committee of the States', ADL Special Report (Oct. 1987). One could add to this list another Gale creation, the California Rangers, as well.

59. Leon Jaroff, 'Debating the Holocaust', Time Magazine Electronic Edition, 19 Dec. 1993. Perhaps the star exhibit available to anyone with a modem and the address of an IHR FTP site is the Leuchter Report. This document, the work of one Fred Leuchter whose claim to be an engineer was debunked in 1991 when he was forced to admit that his academic background was limited to a BA degree in history, purports to prove on the basis of blueprint

specifications that the gas chambers at Auschwitz, Birkenau and other Nazi concentration camps could not have been responsible for the murder of human beings. A printed version of the work is available from Bradley Smith for $20. Cf. ADL, 'Holocaust "Revisionism"': Reinventing the Big Lie', *ADL Research Report* (Summer 1989).

60. Stanley R. Barrett, *Is God A Racist?: The Right Wing in Canada* (Toronto: Univ. of Toronto Press, 1987), pp.156–65.

61. *Klanwatch Intelligence Report* 68 (Aug. 1993), p.1. Klanwatch prefaces the article with a quote from William Pierce's *Turner Diaries* to the effect that the war against the 'system' has at last begun. James Mason, the National Socialist theorist considered above, is perhaps most notable for his early recognition of the lessons that Charles Manson and his 'Helter Skelter' race war fantasy could teach the movement would Nazis but give him an ear. Mason initiated a correspondence with Manson and his followers and may now be classed as something of a Manson adherent himself. Mason, *Siege* (note 35).

62. *Klanwatch Intelligence Report* 54 (Feb. 1991), p. 2. Bill Moyers, *Hate on Trial*, PBS Documentary, broadcast 5 Feb. 1992.

63. ADL, 'Young Nazi Killers: The Skinhead Danger', *ADL Special Report* (1993), p.5. Previous ADL publications about the skinhead movement were 'Shaved for Battle', *ADL Special Report* (1987); and 'Neo Nazi Skinheads: A 1990 Status Report', *ADL Special Report* (1990).

64. Mark Hamm, *American Skinheads* (Westport, CT: Praeger, 1993), is the sole available academic study.

65. Kaplan (note 2), pp.40–1.

66. Letters dated May–July 1990. Name withheld by request.

67. Ehud Sprinzak, 'The Process of Delegitimization: Towards a Linkage Theory of Political Terrorism', *TPV* 3/1 (Spring 1991), pp.50–68; Idem., 'Right-Wing Terrorism in a Comparative Perspective: The Case of Split Deligitimition', in this volume.

68. Kenneth T. Jackson, *The Ku Klux Klan in the City, 1915–1930* (Chicago, IL: Ivan R. Dee, 1967, 1992).

69. For a view of the trial as seen by one of the defendants, see Lawrence Dennis and Maximillian St. George, *A Trial on Trial: The Great Sedition Trial of 1944* (Torrance, CA: Inst. for Historical Review, 1945, 1984). Before the IHR reprinting, the original edition was published under the aegis of the National Civil Rights Committee. On Smith, Coughlin, *et al.*, see David H. Bennett, *Demagogues in the Depression* (New Brunswick, NJ: Rutgers UP, 1969).

70. Naomi W. Cohen, *Not Free to Desist* (Philadelphia, PA: Jewish Publication Soc. of America, 1972), p. 346.

71. Ibid. The fate of Jews in the Soviet Union was a critical factor in this decision as well.

72. Glen Jeansonne, 'Combating Anti-Semitism: The Case of Gerald L. K. Smith', in David A Gerber (ed.), *Anti-Semitism in American History* (Urbana, IL: Univ. of Illinois Press, 1986), pp.158–60.

73. Smith died on 15 April 1976, but the *Cross and the Flag* went on briefly, as did the dream of a biblical theme park and passion play at Eureka Springs. See *The Cross and the Flag* 36 (Sept. 1977), p.13, for an advertisement for the park and p. 23 for a discussion of the project. For a scholarly view, see Glen Jeansonne, *Gerald L. K. Smith: Minister of Hate* (New Haven, CT: Yale UP, 1988), Ch.11; and Arnold Forster and Benjamin R. Epstein, *The New Anti-Semitism* (NY: McGraw-Hill, 1974), p. 29. On the concept of the 'high priesthood' of watch-dog groups, Jeffrey Kaplan, 'The Anti-Cult Movement in America: An History of Culture Perspective', *SYZYGY* 2:3-4 (Summer/Fall 1993), pp.267–96.

74. Forster and Epstein (note 73), pp.44–5. The Humble Oil Company, e.g., which publicized the passion play in a list of outdoor dramas printed in its *Happy Motoring News*, found its correspondence with the ADL leaked to the press and some credit card holders returned their cards.

75. E.g., Gerald L. K. Smith and the Christian Nationalist Crusade, 'Sex "Education" (?) Phony Name For Academic Pornography Resulting in Corruption of Youth, Free Love, Popularization of Pre-Marital Sex, Libertinism, Repudiation of Moral Standards, Juvenile

Perversion, Community Degeneration, Ridicule of the Church, Evaporation of Religious Standards', unpub. report distr. to *Cross and the Flag* mailing list, n.d. Cf. Idem, ''75 Prostitutes, United States Senators in a Brothel Run by Jews', unpub. pamphlet distr. to *Cross and the Flag* mailing list, n.d.

76. Among them the Order's Tom Martinez. Martinez with Gunther (note 22), p. 22.
77. 'The Jerry Springer Show', *NSV Report* 11/3 (July/Sept. 1993), pp.2–3. This account was privately confirmed in considerably greater detail by a participant in the fiasco.
78. Seymour (note 58), pp.17–18.
79. Sprinzak 1991 (note 67), pp.63–6.
80. For an unparalleled view into the world of the Covenant, Sword and Arm of the Lord, see *CSA. Survival Manual* (no publication data). Cf. the CSA of the Lord newsletter. Richard Snell's musings can best be found in Richard Snell, 'The Shadow of Death! (Is There Life After Death?)' (unpub., c.1986); or his death row newsletter, the *Last Call*.
81. Martinez with Gunther (note 22), p.42; Flynn and Gerhardt (note 22), p.193; and Stanton (note 7), p.185. Cf. Stephen Singular, *Talked to Death: The Life and Murder of Alan Berg* (NY: William Morrow, 1987).
82. Militia of Montana, 'Executive Orders for a New World Order: What You Should Know', (n.d.). One of the first movement newsletters to begin the serious sport of 'bluehat spotting' (i.e., to detect covert movements of UN troops in the USA) was the Christian Identity White Angel Isaac Sons of Lincolnton, North Carolina. This pastime has since become a ubiquitous in movement literature.
83. Martinez with Gunther (note 22), pp.96–100. Martinez appears to suggest that a more important source of tactical advice was drawn from Order member David Lane's 'Bruders Schweigen Manual'. See pp.62–3 for excerpts.
84. Sprinzak 1991 (note 67), p. 66.
85. Anon., *The John Franklin Letters* (NY: The Book Mailer, 1959).

Radical Right Parties in Europe and Anti-Foreign Violence: A Comparative Essay

PETER H. MERKL

This is a comparative survey of contemporary patterns of anti-foreign violence in Europe and some historical antecedents, such as pogroms and individual and small group attacks on visible foreigners. It considers the perpetrators and the long list of different categories of victims, many of them not foreigners at all. Against the background of general youth violence in schools and neighborhoods and waves of asylum-seekers, the motives of anti-foreign violence are examined and attributed to the undereducated, 'no-future' youth or underclass 'losers' of the 'communications revolution' of the 1980s. The skinhead and soccer hooligan anti-foreign violence is, on the whole, not remotely as political as the fascist blackshirts and Nazi stormtroopers of the interwar period were. A look at the evidence from different European countries reveals on the one hand recruitment attempts by extreme right-wing organizations among the skinhead and hooligan groups – but rather limited success. On the other hand, most of the violent actions appear to be uncoordinated and responsive to community panic and media hype regarding the 'floods' of asylum-seekers and illegal immigrants in the offing. By making themselves the executors of the community panic, the otherwise despised skinheads are grasping at personal acceptance and legitimacy.

In the last several years, scholars have made valiant efforts to catalogue and taxonomize the ever-changing scene of radical right parties in various European countries. There is little more to be added except, perhaps, to update and fill in a few gaps created by fast-moving developments. In the meantime, however, the involvement, or alleged involvement, of right-wing parties in waves of anti-foreign violence demands further analysis beyond the sensationalist and superficial attention of the media. We need to investigate what is known so far about the waves of anti-foreign and other right-wing violence in a systematic fashion and carefully consider the significance of different kinds of violence and their possible linkage to these parties. The appearance of large numbers of skinhead gangs, soccer hooligans, and other violent youth who are politicized to only a very limited degree poses major conceptual obstacles to explaining political action. Fortunately, by now there is more comparative evidence available that permits scholarly analysis and detachment, so that we may move beyond the facile interpretations of the 'return of the Nazis' in Germany towards an assessment of similar phenomena with minor variations

all over Europe. We hope to place the anti-foreign violence of recent years
into the broader context of understanding how right-wing extremism and
political violence may interact generally under different circumstances.
When we began our survey of contemporary radical right parties half a
dozen years ago, which resulted in the volume *Encounters with the
Contemporary Radical Right*,[1] the literature was still relatively thin.[2]
However, a new wave of party activities and voter response appeared to be
building up in some countries, including France and West Germany. There
had of course been many fine comparative studies on interwar Fascism in the
late 1960s and the 1970s,[3] culminating in the somewhat politicized 'theories
of fascism', which suggested, in some cases, that contemporary conditions
and governmental policies were very likely to bring about a relapse into a fascism comparable to that between the world wars.[4] We concentrated our survey of the contemporary radical right on empirical investigations rather than
becoming entangled in premature theoretical perspectives or questions of continuity with the interwar period. But even then, the new salience of 'individual crazies' such as racist skinheads and violent soccer hooligans, especially
in post-1989 East Germany, came to the forefront. Was this a new 'social
movement' in *statu nascendi*?[5]

Since the 1980s right-wing agitation in response to the surging immigration and refugee figures has exploded all over Europe and become an object
of concern to the European Union. More or less systematically collected
police statistics have accumulated on anti-foreign violence, and social scientists have begun to analyze them with care.[6] There is much more known now
about neo-fascist agitation and skinheads even in Eastern Europe and the former Soviet Union.[7] In the latter, there has evolved a scenario similar to
Weimar's wounded ultra nationalism and obsessive concern for the *irredenta*
in the successor states following the breakup of the empire; this has evolved
and weighs heavily on Boris Yeltsin's government: Many Russians connected with the old communist party and regime (including the Army, KGB and
state enterprises) feel injured by the fall of communism and its empire. They
are understandably concerned about the fate of Russians now stranded in the
Baltic states, Moldova, the Crimea, and other successor states, not to mention
the Serbs of former Yugoslavia. Dimitrii Vasil'ev's *Pamiat* (the Russian tra-
ditionalist extremist movement discussed in *Encounters*) is stronger than ever
and despises Vladimir Zhirinovsky's Liberal Democratic Party, both because
of Zhirinovsky's alleged half-Jewish parentage and because the Liberal
Democrats 'shamelessly' participated in a democratic election, and did sen-
sationally well.

Elsewhere in Europe, the Italian Social Movement (MSI) surprisingly
metamorphosed into a new party, the National Alliance (AN),[8] doubled its

vote in 1994 and entered the government of Silvio Berlusconi. The French
Front National is still going strong at a level between 10 and 15 per cent and
British nationalist fringe groups have been making a comeback.[9] German rad-
ical right parties hoped for substantial electoral gains in the many local, state,
national, and European elections in 1994. The *Republikaner* (REP) and the
German People's Union (DVU) are rivals for the extreme rightist vote which
capitalized in 1991–93 on the German panic over the arrival of asylum-seekers in several states, achieving 10.9 per cent of REP votes in Baden-
Württemberg, 6 per cent DVU voters in Bremen, and 6.3 per cent in
Schleswig-Holstein, 8.1 per cent REP in Berlin and 8.3 per cent in Hesse in
the local elections in March 1993.[10] Their electoral support declined, however, in the European parliamentary elections and national elections in 1994. A
similar surge of the right-wing vote benefited the Dutch *Centrumdemocraten*,
the Belgian *Vlaams Blok*, the Austrian Freedom Party, and the Italian neo-fascists, all reflecting popular reactions to the influx of refugees and asylum
seekers from Eastern Europe, Africa, and the rest of the world.[11]

    The spectacular increase of the extreme right vote, along with (as we shall
see) an even bigger rise in anti-foreign, seemingly right-wing-inspired violence, has also revived interest in research on possible international connections among those new extremist forces (although so far such connections
have been demonstrated mostly among small racist groups such as the
American Ku Klux Klan, the White Aryan Resistance, the Church of the
Creator, The Order, and their European offspring). On the other hand, we need
to separate all these neo-fascist groups analytically from the new wave of libertarian populist movements such as the Italian Leagues (*Lega Nord*), tax-
payer protest parties in Scandinavia, and similar movements in Canada and
the United States (Ross Perot). The latter may be, at times, demagogic and
irresponsible but they are not by any stretch of the imagination the neo-fascists that their political antagonists have claimed them to be.[12]

Scenarios of Anti-Foreign Violence

While we may be preoccupied with the recent waves of anti-foreign violence
in Europe, we need to remind ourselves that we are dealing with a much
broader phenomenon of violence than the latest skinhead attacks on asylum
seekers from Eastern Europe and Third World countries, which are merely the
tip of a recurrent iceberg. As in North America, the youth scene in schools has
become rather violent. Of course, we are aware of the unsynchronized waves
of anti-foreign violence that seem to characterize the phenomenon in different European countries: Germany in 1991–93, France in 1961, 1973, and
1982, and again in the late 1980s, Sweden in 1989, the Netherlands in the
1970s and early 1980s and in 1992, Great Britain in the early 1970s and early

1980s – the timing often is still something of a mystery. Even the term 'foreigners', if we go back but a few steps into European history, becomes a function of citizenship in the modern integrated nation-state: Segmented, less modern states often denied full citizenship to minorities such as the long-present gypsies and treated them as foreigners to be expelled at will.[13] The Nazi state routinely took away German (and other) citizenship from minorities it wished to expel as undesirable aliens, or worse. 'Foreigners' are created by a deliberate process of exclusion and labeling.

There are certain basic rationales to each wave and culminating event of anti-foreign violence. Each scenario, whether it is a pogrom, a race or anti-foreign riot, or other form of minority discrimination or persecution, begins with the symbolic construction of a macropolitical (sometimes even cosmic[14]) reality: Right-wing governments or parties spread a nationalist ideology, or an interpretion of a major historical event such as a lost war, to set the stage. The ideological interpretation often may have been around for a long time and may be part of the national mythology that gives meaning to events. In any case, it also singles out the target, the scapegoated minority or the foreigners within the walls, and may set them up for the attack by isolating them in ghettos, marking them for discrimination and persecution and, perhaps, also disarming them. The rest of the scenario is less clear and preordained: The attackers may be organized and designated groups, such as a popular militia, or they may just be local drunks or skinhead gangs. The attacks may be triggered by rumors or unexpected events, or they may be so deliberate that church bells are rung or the mayor gives a speech to signal the onslaught. But no matter how anarchic the process, the final outcome is often clear from the beginning.

The nineteenth century riots against immigrant workers during hard times were an early prototype. Belgian workers and their families in France became the targets in 1819, in the 'hungry' 1840s and again in the depressed year of 1892. English and German workers were driven out of France in the 1830s, Savoisards in 1848, and Italians between 1881 and 1897. But the xenophobia of those years simply focused on the scarcity of jobs in the less mobile labor markets of that day. Today, economic arguments are often bandied about but they are rarely true. Even at an unemployment rate around 10 per cent in Germany, few Germans are willing to do the rough and menial work that is done by Turks and other immigrants, at least not at foreigners' wages and under the conditions typical of such employment.

The process leading to racial or xenophobic violence may not be anarchic at all but the firmly steered violence of the state, its troops or police, or at least of regional and local state agencies that direct the action, encourage it, or pointedly fail to curb it. The most extreme form of such state-directed persecution, of course, was the genocide of Jews and gypsies by the Nazis in World War II when they proceeded to exterminate millions in the death camps of the Holocaust, a goal far beyond the usual aim of expelling 'foreigners' from the nation's [conquered] territory.[15] The Serb policies since 1991 of 'ethnic cleansing' by massacres, mass rape, and shelling of civilians are a combination of direct genocide and expulsion by terror. There is also the example of other nationals (for example Poles), military troops or irregulars shortly after the Russian Revolution, when many Tsarist troops thought that their Bolshevik opponents were German sympathizers; and later, during the Russian Civil War, when the Whites regarded their victims as 'Jew-Bolsheviks' while the Reds may have considered them bourgeois traitors. These scenarios of state persecution also began with official beliefs and ideologies, partly old and partly invented, long before the commandos, troops, or police carried out the actual policies. In the case of the Third Reich and its satellite regimes, for example in Vichy France and Antonescu's Romania, there were also first the legal definitions of the Nuremberg Laws, the labeling of Jews with yellow stars,[16] and the apartheid regulations isolating the target populations and confining them step by step to ghettos and camps before the lethal attacks began.

Most other scenarios of anti-foreign persecution by state agencies are more subtle than mass murder, even though they may produce deaths for the purpose of intimidation. A postwar link to the Vichy persecution of French Jews was the massed police attack of 17 October 1961, ordered by the Paris Prefect of Police, Maurice Papon,[17] on a demonstration of 30,000 Algerians (mostly French citizens) of whom over 200 were killed and 10,000 arrested.[18] Even the regime-directed Kristallnacht, the anti-Jewish pogrom of 9 November 1938, was more subtle than Papon: The Third Reich organized civilians and stormtroopers to attack Jewish businesses and residences, as well as their owners, in a pretense of spontaneous public German outrage against the Jews.[19]

More often than engage in direct action, a prejudiced military or police – or the judiciary – may fail to protect foreigners or resident minorities against assaults and discrimination, a common complaint in Britain and France in the 1980s. They may even arrest and punish the victims of anti-foreign persecution by private assailants or deport them for being trouble-makers. Like other police establishments, for example, the starchy British law enforcement community was most reluctant to recognize racial attacks per se as an offense until the Home Office report *Racial Attacks* (1981) and various related public documents made the problems unignorable. Throughout the Nottingham riots of 1958 and the race casualties of the 1960s and 1970s, not to mention the seaport riots against black and Arab seamen of earlier decades, the British police tended to blame the colored victims for the violence.[20] Or they sometimes simply prosecuted each violent act but deported the victimized families afterwards.

The most common role of the police (and at times the military) has been to stand aside and let the *pogromshchiki* do the dirty work. In some 25 anti-gypsy pogroms in the two years following the fall of Ceausescu (1990–91), it was evidently not a matter of persecution by the Romanian state, but the police generally failed to protect the victims or came too late to stop the burning of their houses. Local mayors in some cases headed the mob and priests rang the church bells to start the pogrom by Romanians or other ethnics. To begin with, of course, there was the common belief in the marginality and criminality of the victims as a group, as well as memories of their persecution by the Nazis and Romanian Fascists in World War II. The communist regime already had set out to destroy their cultural identity, and their successors refused to recognize them as citizens.[21] Most tellingly, the aftermath of the pogroms typically was characterized by reluctant official investigations and slow trials promoted mostly by Roma associations in Bucharest. The local authorities, however, simply expelled the gypsies from the neighborhood – which had of course been the point of the pogroms, quite similar to American race riots before the 1960s which also usually ended with the forced exodus of the victimized black population. In the anti-Jewish pogroms of 1881–82, following the assassination of Tsar Alexander II, and in the sanguinary pogroms of 1903–6, likewise, the Russian police and military mostly failed to protect the Jews from the rampaging mobs rather than actively persecuting them.[22] Individuals among the officials, however, may have been among the monarchist counter demonstrators (Black Hundreds) whose demonstrations fed the riots.[23]

How does this compare to the contemporary scenarios of the attacks on the hostels of foreign workers and asylum-seekers, from southeastern France to Rostock-Lichtenhagen and the various Scandinavian sites of such attacks?[24] In France, the *ratonnades* ('rat hunts') against foreign workers really began as long ago as the Algerian War, when off-duty police and the Secret Army Organization (OAS) raided against the shanty towns (*bidonvilles*) of Algerian immigrants.[25] The ideology, of course, derived from the war and the actions were anything but spontaneous. Even long after the war was settled, a wave of violence was unleashed upon North Africans in 1973, including arson and machine-gun assaults on *Sonacotra* (the immigrant workers' hostel association) hostels, bidonvilles, and places inhabited by 'them'. As the justifying ideology evolved into right-wing racism, perpetrators were often led by the neo-fascist *Ordre Nouveau* and its Marseilles Defense Committee, which alleged that the influx of *mahgrebiens* had become a 'flood' against which the natives had to defend themselves by all means necessary. Housing discrimi-

nation and the high price of housing helped to concentrate the target population, though cafés and restaurants catering to 'them' also received their share
of violent attacks. In 1982 another lethal wave of such assaults began. It was
at this time frequently a response to the rise of Islamic fundamentalism and
conflict in the Middle East and of Middle Eastern terrorism in France and the
rest of Europe (especially in 1986). The assailants were often skinheads and
members of the neo-fascist PNFE or Le Pen's *Front National*. The Gulf War
of 1991, too, marked an upward tick in the curve of violence.[26]

In the Netherlands where racial or anti-foreign violence had been rare and
isolated before the 1970s, the arrival of the Moluccans marked a turning point.
In 1971 and 1972 there were anti-Turkish riots in Rotterdam; and the late 1970s
and the 1980s witnessed the first racial fatalities in Dutch cities as well as
attacks on mosques, coffee-houses, and living quarters, mostly traced to skinheads and small neo-Nazi groups. In 1992 a new wave of Dutch anti-Islamic
and anti-Turk violence erupted, including a series of bomb and arson attacks on
mosques. However, none of these quite resembled the pogrom type described
above. Instead, they were often more like massive brawls among youths of different ethnicity or terrorist incidents in the sense of one or a few persons trying
to intimidate the minority with the use of outrageous, lethal force.[27]

This was rather different from the racist violence in Sweden, where over
a hundred attacks on refugee camps occurred in the three years 1989–91. The
ideology behind them evidently represented native opposition to the official
refugee policy, but there was no central direction or campaign by extreme
right-wing organizations, according to the Swedish security police, only
drunk neighborhood youths and long-standing local patterns of hostility to the
refugee presence.[28] Such hostility was expressed by local officials and opinion leaders and by shop and restaurant owners who refused to admit alien
refugees to their premises: a ready demonstration of prejudice and posses-
siveness of turf, and of the principle that collective prejudicial violence usually occurs as the result of *a drawn-out process of escalating actions*, not as a
sudden, unexpected explosion. The 1988 mob of perhaps 70 youths that
attacked the refugee camps in Karlstad with rocks and Molotov cocktails, the
1990–92 incidents in Karlstad/Säffle, and the earlier racist incidents in Växjö
and Landskrona all related more to small-town and rural areas of long-stand-
ing extreme right traditions and neo-Nazi activities than did most of the
Swedish attacks on refugee camps. On the other hand, they also highlighted
significant differences between patterns of urban anti-foreigner violence and
manifestations in rural and small-town areas.[29] Even Spain and Italy are wit-
nessing a rising tide of anti-foreign violence, especially by the Italian
Naziskins whose activities easily outdo the old Blackshirts in anti-Semitism
and racism.

German Pogroms and Small Group Violence

How do the German anti-foreign incidents of 1991–92 compare? While racial incidents and neo-Nazi violence had a long history in West Germany – and had some antecedents in East Germany[30] – they had never before taken on the pogrom-like character of the 5-day siege in Hoyerswerda to some 230 foreigners in September 1991 or the even bigger battle of Rostock-Lichtenhagen in August 1992. In both of these cases, and in about 1,000 cases of arson attempts (mostly against asylum-seekers' hostels) from mid-1991 to the end of 1992, there was obviously an ideology at work that was based on old xenophobic and turf-conscious prejudices and combined with a sense of panic at the sudden 'flood' of refugees and asylum seekers that the locals had been told would descend upon them. Partisan interpretations, in some cases, have spun an elaborate tale of conspiracy from this in which the Kohl administration and other sinister forces in Germany were said to have begun a grand debate on changing the constitutional article (art.16) governing political asylum. This allegedly touched off the great panic that was manipulated by its instigators in order to compel the opposition SPD to give in to the amendment of article 16.[31] Notwithstanding the local xenophobia, the truth is that the upsurge of refugees and asylum-seekers in mid-1991 would have been difficult to hide and that, of course, the article in question – one of the most liberal in the world, but meanwhile amended – had attracted immigrants all along. German administration of asylum police, moreover, had been so cumbersome that a mere claim of asylum often led to a year of free sojourn, or more, which aroused further popular ire.

Whatever the rationale, there was no doubt about the failure of the police efforts to contain the *pogromshchiki* in Hoyerswerda – some say they never tried – and in Rostock where there resulted substantial injuries to scores of policemen. In Rostock-Lichtenhagen, furthermore, decisions at the very top (the state minister of the interior and the police commanders in charge) suddenly suspended the effort at crowd control. In both places, locals and neighbors stood by and cheered and skinheads had traveled for many miles to participate. The role of law enforcement, again, was reminiscent of the deliberate failures of elected sheriffs and police in the Klan lynchings and riots of a by-gone era in America. The goal of the Hoyerswerda and Rostock pogroms, and of the many clandestine attacks on German asylum-seekers' hostels and camps, was the same as with the Romanian pogroms against the gypsies and the Russian pogroms against the Jews: while there may have been injuries and even deaths, the real point was not to kill but to drive 'them' away.[32] And the police of Hoyerswerda and Rostock, and of many another hostel or camp site, did exactly that: They transported 'them' somewhere else.

As in Sweden, the participation of neo-Nazi action groups in such local anti-foreign violence varied greatly with the territory. In some areas with old Nazi traditions and a certain density of neo-Nazis, it was high while, on the average, the locals seem to have had no need for such assistance. In too many cases, still, the perpetrators have not been discovered and tried which makes generalization difficult. The per capita frequency of Swedish attacks on refugee camps – over 100 in three years in a population of 8.6 million with 2.3 per cent foreign immigrants, and 115,000 new refugees in 1991 and 1992[33] – is quite comparable to the 1,000 in Germany in half that period (with a population of nearly 80 million, more than three times the percentage of foreign residents, and six times the number of new asylum-seekers in 1991–92). However, because of the Nazi past, German xenophobic outrages make better news copy than one can get out of those of the duller Swedes. Speaking of the media, we should also mention the very considerable role played by German newspapers and television, not only in talking up the panic at the impending 'flood' of refugees and in spreading unfavorable stereotypes of uncleanliness and criminality of certain kinds of foreigners, but even in calling for action.[34] The role of the media of course can work in either direction. In Germany, elements of the media – regrettably few – helped to mobilize the massive German counter-demonstrations and candle-light processions against the racist outrages of 1992. More characteristically during this period, however, the German media tended to create what Tore Bjørgo and Helmut Willems have called a 'contagion effect', leading to 'copy cat' assaults, lavishing attention upon some of the perpetrators, perhaps helping them recruit more activists, and increasing public panic.[35]

The attention focused on German anti-foreign violence in 1991 and 1992 also highlights two other aspects that deserve mention. While the pogroms and nocturnal attacks upon the hostels and camps of refugees and immigrant workers have attracted public scrutiny, we must not forget that (1) there have been other kinds of assaults on foreigners too, and often in broad daylight and with serious risk to life and limb; and (2) the same perpetrators frequently assault other targets too, including German gays, the homeless, the handicapped, and a variety of random victims.

As for the first point, I have elsewhere coined the concept of 'personal attacks by individuals or small groups' of German skinheads, soccer hooligans, or neo-Nazi youths upon visible foreigners or groups of them.[36] Unlike the attempts to terrorize the refugees in their hostels and cause them to leave, these personal attacks are usually meant to insult, seriously injure and, quite often, to kill the victims. According to the German official federal crime (BKA) statistics, such assaults on foreigners jumped sharply in mid-1991 from modest levels of fewer than ten a month to as many as 30 to over 100 per month.[37]

My second point is implicit in a casual look at the 17 reported fatalities of such skinhead and neo-Nazi attacks on persons in 1992: Of the 17 dead, the largest group turn out to be six German homeless men, mostly over 50 years old and evidently the victims of skinheads on 'homeless manhunts' (*Pennerfang*). Another two were Germans who got involved in political arguments with skinheads or soccer hooligans; two more Germans died without obvious political motives. These ten German victims hardly fit the stereotype of racist violence. Of the seven foreign casualties, only one was a young Romanian asylum-seeker, who was slain when about 40 right-wing radicals invaded his hostel in Rostock in March 1992. Two more, an Albanian and a young Pole, had working permits but the latter was killed by skinheads at a discotheque which may have been over a girl as much as over his foreignness.[38] Finally, there was a Vietnamese who was knifed in the streets of Marzahn, a Berlin suburb notorious for its violent skinheads, and the three Turkish women killed in the arson attack at Mölln. My point is simply that the violent youth element in Germany has not particularly selected only foreigners or asylum-seekers to brutalize. Indeed, the attacks by East German skinheads and other violent youths in 1992 also included ethnic German refugees (from Russia or Romania), Russian soldiers, nationals, and war monuments, Ukrainian children from Chernobyl, Polish travelers and street vendors, Jewish cemeteries, German gays and lesbians, handicapped German children, young Turks (who grew up in West Berlin or Germany), elderly Germans, German homeless persons, and young German anti-fascists and anarchists (*Autonome*). While their choice of targets may not earn them a prize for ethical or humanitarian concerns, this obviously makes it difficult to describe them exclusively as the nemesis of foreigners and refugees.[39] In addition to employing this scattershot violence, they are also known to invade and trash restaurants in resorts, or on the way to a soccer game (if they are hooligans), attacking German patrons, passersby, or motorists; trash stores; extort beer or cash from the German proprietors; and, of course, try to beat up the 'hooligans' who came with the opposing team, and an occasional policeman as well.[40]

Racist Offenses and Hate Crimes

The German attacks by individuals and small groups have their equivalents in other European countries and in the United States. Systematic comparison, however, is hampered by the widely differing definitions of offenses among national police forces and also among researchers,[41] not to mention by the number of unreported cases, The British Home Office, for example, estimated in 1981 that there were about 7,000 'racial incidents' involving different racial groups. Ten years later, the Interdepartmental Racial Attacks group of the same ministry accounted for racially-motivated incidents as increasing from about 4,400 to 7,800 between 1988 and 1992. These probably include some cases of arson which we have tried to separate from the small group pattern in the German case: According to the German Security Service (BVS), there were about 1,100 non-arson attacks in 1991 and 1,800 in 1992. Swedish local police departments reported 2,039 cases of 'racist or xenophobic crimes' for 1984–87, with some notable gaps in the reporting. In the Netherlands, cases of racist and extreme right violence rose from a level of well under 50 incidents a year (except for a brief rise in 1983–84) to 270 in 1992 and 352 in 1993.[42]

One of the curiosities in the definitional debate has been the frequent drunkenness of the perpetrators which in Germany and some North European countries tends to depoliticize their acts and perhaps even remove them from crime statistics, when committed in a condition of *Volltrunkenheit*. Racist offenses and skinhead violence, however, are almost always committed while drunk. Another problem lies in the varying sets of victims in different countries: North Africans in France, Moroccans in Belgium, Asians and Afro-Caribbeans in Britain, and East European (among others) asylum-seekers in Italy, Spain, Germany, and Scandinavia. The dubious term 'race' here does not gain in significance when there are no differences in visible skin pigmentation, nor should religious and cultural differences ever be subsumed under the biological concept of 'race'. In the post-communist successor states, ethnic hatreds of a 'non-racial' sort have supplied most of the unrest and violence. Even in very sanguinary civil wars, such as in ex-Yugoslavia, Georgia, or Armenia and Azerbaijan,[43] we hesitate to speak of race or racism.

The definitional question is posed most broadly with the American term of 'hate crimes'. In addition to racial offenses, the concept of hate crime includes attacks on gays and lesbians and, in fact, breaks down its statistics in terms of the different groups of victims. Unfortunately, the invitation of the FBI for nation-wide reporting in the US has not been followed uniformly, although certain states (New Jersey) and counties (Los Angeles) regularly report their hate crimes and there are also national organizations of victimized groups that publish an annual tally. The American-Arab Anti-Discrimination Committee, for example, noted a quintupling of acts of violence, harassment, and intimidation against Arab-Americans throughout the United States with the outbreak of the Gulf War of 1991. The Jewish Anti-Defamation League reported a record level of 1,685 anti-Semitic incidents for 1990, including 927 acts of destruction and vandalism (arson, bombings, cemetery desecrations, swastikas daubed on buildings and other objects) and 758 incidents of harassment, assaults (one assassination: Meir Kahane), and threats. In 1992, they reported similar figures (1,730) while a National Gay and Lesbian Task Force reported 1,001 anti-gay incidents in five major cities that year. The 1992 report of the Los Angeles County Human Relations Commission documented 736 incidents involving African-American (168), gay (147), Jewish (119), and Latino (89) victims, an 11 per cent increase from the previous year. A majority (434) were considered racially motivated,[44] but it was not clear[45] what the authors of the report did with the local Asians – an estimated 3,500 Asian-owned businesses were reported damaged or destroyed in the Los Angeles riots of 1992, especially of Koreans in black neighborhoods. In any event, the time may not be far when social scientists might be able to draw their conclusions from similarly inclusive hate crimes statistics in all the major industrial nations.[46]

Different Kinds of Violence

Violence against humans has been with us ever since Cain slew Abel. It is obviously one of the most common forms of interaction among members of our species even though its purpose and severity may vary widely. Some basic distinctions with regard to the functions of violence in human intercourse appear essential to establishing its relationship to political groups and to prejudicial actions towards foreigners or minority groups. The first of these distinguishes public, or political, from private violence, as for instance in a homicide committed for reasons of jealousy, revenge, or robbery. When the police find a body of a member of one group and establishes that the killer(s) was of another group, such a finding obviously falls short of 'proving' a racist or prejudicial intent, because the motive could have been private in character. Proving present intent requires eyewitness testimony, preferably from impartial witnesses and, if possible, from acquaintances of both the victim and the assailant, as well as some background knowledge about both. It would be a rare case in which an assailant simply admitted that he had killed the other fellow because the latter belonged to 'that group'. More likely several motives will be offered, some of them private, and our analysis will be greatly complicated thereby.

Once we are in the realm of public or political violence, we face a second crucial distinction, namely between violence ordered by constituted state authority and the political violence of such organizations in the public realm as trade unions, corporations, political parties and social movements. The state, of course, claims a monopoly on the use of violence and may use it without question against its enemies, external and internal, or even just against whoever it regards as a law-breaker or disturber of the domestic peace. Hence we cannot simply regard as 'racist' a police action that carries out a prejudicial law or orders of the legitimate authority – the policemen involved may not be prejudiced at all – even though we may be very critical of the law itself and may wish to protest against it by legitimate means. Organizational 'voluntary political violence' on the other hand, is always proscribed in principle but frequently condoned if it appears to serve widely recognized purposes, as in a strike, and remains within reasonable, voluntarily accepted limits: Strikers are not supposed to inflict serious bodily injury, burn down the factory, or block the passage of traffic through the town. Some of these ground rules are codified in advanced industrial societies, many are merely understood and accepted, and all of them get broken at times.

The fine distinctions and ground rules literally enter a state of limbo when violent militias like the Nazi stormtroopers or communist Red Guards or revolutionary armies confront other groups or the state itself. Their violence is, of course, illegitimate and this is particularly true of what they may inflict upon their enemies or other groups. Bloody street fighting, for example between the Weimar stormtroopers and the communist Red Front organization – with hundreds of casualties in 1931 and 1932[47] – was clearly an illegitimate use of violent force and yet the state proved quite unable to stop it despite prosecuting many of the perpetrators. From the moment the Nazis won power, moreover, their previously illegal violence suddenly became clothed in the mantle of the legitimate state authority[48] so that they could thenceforth brutalize their enemies legally – and the latter might have done the same to them, had the communists won.

This is as good a place as any to state a major point that has consistently been missed by mindless journalists and others ignorant of Weimar history, as compared to the anti-foreign violence in Germany today: It is completely in error to believe that the Weimar movement consisted of neighborhood youth gangs venting their prejudices on foreigners or Jews. The Nazi instrument of political violence, the *Sturm-Abteilung* (SA) stormtroopers, were a militarily organized and commanded army which wore uniforms and which was tightly disciplined to forestall individual or spontaneous actions. Its chief enemy in countless bloody street fights were young communists (Red Front) and republican guards (*Reichsbanner*) who were nearly as much under military discipline as the SA was. The SA spent most of its time marching in formation in order to propagandize and recruit people for the cause, to protect the party's rallies and speakers, and to marshal its major electioneering efforts. Such tight military control from the top, by the way, also marked the Baader-Meinhof (Red Army Faction) terrorists, the Italian Red Brigades, and other terrorist organizations that never intended to leave the action to the spontaneity of prejudiced individuals or small groups.[49]

But let us come back to the question of the legitimacy of political violence. Revolutionary armies in a civil war operate similarly to the brown or red paramilitaries of Weimar, but often at the expense of legitimate state authority within the territories they control. As long as a civil war is still raging back and forth, however, woe to unpopular, distrusted minorities like the Jews in the Russian Civil War of 1919–21 who got victimized by both sides, and without recourse to any authority. It seems actually better to have been in a state-sponsored pogrom like the others mentioned above in which the authorities, while not exactly protecting the minority, at least took on the responsibility of guiding most of them to a safer place.[50]

The question now arises: in what sense of the word can the violence of neo-fascist parties, so-called action groups like VAM (the Swedish White Aryan Resistance) or the Dutch or German Action Groups of the National Socialists (ANS), or European skinhead gangs and hooligans of uncertain degrees of politicization be compared to these violent party militias and revolutionary armies of an earlier day? None of these kinds of political violence is legitimate either, although it may seem so to the camp followers or, in the case of a pogrom like the ones in Hoyerswerda and Rostock, to a significant part of the community. In a democratic society, numbers confer a semblance of authority, and cooperation with at least some of the rules of the democratic game adds some authority. If the mighty electorally successful *Front National* (FN), for example, says that the French people have 'a right to defend themselves' against the alleged onslaught of alien Muslim culture, it carries a lot more weight than if a small action group like *Ordre Nouveau* or if individual 'crazies' justify their actions with such a claim. A prejudicial media campaign or news of large numbers endorsing the neo-Nazi slogan 'Out with the foreigners' or 'Germans in their own country' likewise carries far more authority than the mutterings of a beer-sodden juvenile skinhead gang or hooligan mob.[51]

The democratic calculus of authority, in other words, leaves individual crazies, activist groups, and low-class neighborhood gangs in about the same limbo of authority that characterizes terrorists: They may pretend to be the representatives or even the saviors of all Germans, or all Europeans, or even of the entire white race[52] but it seems to take a lot of beer, or hard liquor, to make themselves believe it. The constituencies they claim have never really endorsed their actions – this is why they are so eager for any sign of even partial community support, a sympathetic newspaper report, or an encouraging public opinion poll – and the constituencies often express their massive condemnation, as in the case of the German candlelight parades against racism after the terrible year of 1992. Of course, the gangs still have their prejudiced opinions and can practice the 'propaganda of the deed', just as the left-wing terrorists do, saying to themselves: Once we attack the asylum-seekers' hostel in the middle of the night, the locals will applaud our deed. And they have the painful, daily despair of the socially marginalized, the 'no-future' kids,

whose great yearning is to find someone they regard as even lower than themselves, and against whom they can discharge all their self-hatred and
contempt.

Thus two powerful motives, I think, explain what the skinhead gangs do:
(1) They try to spearhead community support by terrorizing refugee camps
and hostels, to make 'them' go away, and (2) they vent their self-hatred in
vicious individual and small group attacks on a wide variety of targets they
perceive as even weaker and more contemptible than themselves: asylum-
seekers, especially gypsies and visible people of color, the homeless and inebriated, the handicapped, gays or lesbians. Their attacks (and their own
humor) eloquently speak of these displacements with the crudest of insults.
Their mistreatment of their victims is designed to humiliate and brutalize – in
the sense of turning the victim into a brute beast – and quite often to maim or
kill. These dual motives together represent a more persuasive explanation of
skinhead activity that the allegedly direct chain of command from the neo-fascist parties, which has never been demonstrated.

This account would not be complete if we did not also mention the
increasingly violent youth scene in schools and neighborhoods of most industrial countries today. It is not only in the big cities of the United States that we
find violence among school children and a growing need to protect them from
each other. Britain and Germany are not far behind, except that the control of
gun ownership has limited the weaponry of young Britons and Germans to
bicycle chains, nunchakus, baseball bats, knives, and other weapons, but not
guns. There are no drive-by shootings as yet, the likes of which killed 800
young Los Angelenos in that fateful year of 1992 – the same year in which
Europe was racked by anti-foreign and other youth violence.

The mention of youth should also remind us once more that most of the
perpetrators and many of their victims (at least in small group attacks) tend to
be very young. Young immigrants, Turks, Afro-Caribbeans, Asians, North
Africans – or Latinos in the United States – long ago began to form their own
youth gangs which give them both sense of belonging and physical protection
against the hostile skinhead groups of the majority (or the adult world of both,
their own minority and the hostile majority). Their recreational lives
inevitably bring them into contact and conflict with the rival gangs, for example at discos, ball games, rock concerts, and other festivals, and especially at
night and on weekends. The intergroup contacts – and conflicts over girl
friends, possessions, dress and musical fashions, hair styles and a hundred
other obsessions of volatile youth – are far more pervasive than any political
concern which moves only a few people. In France, for example, where educational failure, rundown ghettos, and youth unemployment have long threatened the integrating power of the French melting pot, immigrant youth has

exploded repeatedly in rage against police prejudice and racial violence, and against the smugness of the *beati possidentes*.

One of the wilder pastimes of French youth has been their nocturnal 'rodeos', as in the 1980s in Lyon, which involve stealing, racing, and finally crashing cars so they erupt in flames. This is a surefire way for thrill seekers to get the attention of the police and of the adult world, and this is true not only of France. In other countries too, outrageous youthful actions – for example of German skinhead attacks against foreigners, or of a youngster screaming the Nazi salute *'Heil Hitler'* in school – are a reliable method for *epâter le bourgeois*. What the adult world clearly needs to cope with the unrest of youth (right-wing or otherwise) in advanced industrial societies is a lot more patience than it has exhibited, and a major attempt at urban amelioration, cleaning up the ghettos, improving the schools, helping youth to find its way before it goes astray in self-destructive ways, such as in a violent, beer-swilling, skinhead gang or in fighting during half-time at a soccer match. Politics has little to do with it, except perhaps for the 1980s politics of urban neglect by the adult world. Some day in the future, perhaps, social historians will see the 1980s as a truly horrible period – but not because of the misconduct of youth, but because of the greed and self-centeredness of a generation of neglectful parents and adults, who voted for the social cutbacks of a Margaret Thatcher, Helmut Kohl, or Ronald Reagan without regard for the consequences. One of these consequences is the rising dragon seed of neglected youth.

Radical Right Movements and Anti-Foreign Violence

One of the more intriguing perspectives of studying assaults on foreigners concerns the dichotomous interpretations placed on racist or anti-foreign violence by (a) some conservative politicians and 'see-no-evil' policemen who interpret the violent incidents as isolated 'boyish tricks and drunken pranks'; and (b) anti-fascist groups that see them solely as the machinations of racist or neo-Nazi organizations. The anti-fascist or anti-racist organizations deserve a lot of credit for fighting[53] and exposing neo-fascist groups and for collecting a cumulative record of racist incidents. But they do tend to paint all the perpetrators with the same brown brush as if the questions of whether or not these are politically organized incidents did not exist. They also tend to ignore the very considerable role played by the violent 'contagion from the left' in raising the general and right-wing levels of violent conflict by mutual escalation in some settings, for example in large cities and some university towns of Germany.

What levels of organization between racist incidents and groups or parties of the extreme right have been observed by various researchers during the recent waves of anti-foreign violence? Tore Bjørgo remarks that

> my examination of groups which have carried out terrorist attacks
> against immigrants and asylum-seekers in Scandinavia revealed a wide
> variety of organisational levels. At the highest level we find formal
> political organisations and parties or their armed wings. At the lowest
> level of organisation are youth gangs or groups of friends with no for-
> mal structure, no ideology and no political orientation above a general
> hostility towards 'foreigners'. Between these extremes we find youth
> gangs and informal youth movements with more defined group identi-
> ties, shared symbols and slogans, some racist ideology, and sometimes
> with ties to right-wing political organisations.'

Significantly, the waves of anti-foreign violence involve 'the more apolitical
youth gangs', Bjørgo adds. He emphasizes the need to examine the role of the
media and other stimuli in triggering such violence, as well as the complex
motivations at play which may remain obscure if we decide prematurely that
that the violence was caused by racism alone. The complicated dynamic of
events in Scandinavia serve as an example of the cryptic roots of violence.
There, Bjørgo concludes, the use of 'terrorist violence' against foreigners was
evidently pioneered by organized right-wing activists but subsequently picked
up by unaffiliated members of youth gangs with strong anti-immigrant racist
views, often with criminal records, and evidently exposed not only to the
activists' racist propaganda, but also to their use of bombs and Molotov cocktails. In Norway, the use of explosives has persisted in recent anti-foreign incidents. Unemployment has little to do with the current wave of violence, at
least in Sweden[54] where violent outrages began a year prior to the rise in
unemployment, but the government's restriction of the country's liberal immigration policy may well have legitimized the violence. In Denmark, the place
of neo-Nazi involvement in anti-foreign violence was supplanted by street
attacks by small gangs of 'Green Jackets' inspired by international White
Power propaganda, carrying out hit-and-run raids in the 1980s.

In how many of the 168 'terrorist' actions[55] against foreigners and asylum-
seekers in Scandinavia during 1982–92 could a political organization be
implicated? Since only about one-third of the perpetrators were known and
caught, and some trials had not yet been concluded, Bjørgo estimated that
only between one-fifth and one-third of the resolved cases revealed the
involvement of 'organized political activists' – a difficult judgment call to
begin with; moreover, some of those activists had kept their membership hidden while others had clearly acted on their own rather than on behalf of the
organization involved. 'The majority of the solved actions were perpetrated
by unorganised, generally apolitical youth gangs who were often feared and

despised in their local communities for their arbitrary violence and criminal-ity.' The unsolved cases, too, seemed to suggest some 'organization' but a majority appeared to be 'unorganized', local affairs.[56] Quite typically, Scandinavian right-wing activist groups try to recruit the violent gang mem-bers only *after* the latter have attacked immigrants or asylum-seekers. Sometimes also, there may be a small core of group members with strong racist views or connections while the larger circle just goes along, or tries to impress each other with occasional expressions or acts of prejudice, often under the influence of alcohol.[57]

Jaap van Donselaar, writing about the same question in the Netherlands, also concluded at first that there had been 'no concrete evidence... conform-ing' to a 'Weberian "ideal type" of violent offence of a racist nature attribut-able to any extreme right organisation'. There have been a few cases of direct involvement by such groups in racist violence,[58] such as a raid by the *Nationale Centrum Partij* on illegal immigrants camping in a church. Van Donselaar's description of right-wing politics shows why such action is rare and atypical: there are strong pressures within such parties to refrain from vio-lence so that the party does not get in trouble with the police and courts, and so that its candidates for public office can maintain a respectable image. Even when racist violence increases substantially at the same time as a rise in the right-wing vote, 'nothing in police investigations indicates a country-wide campaign', according to the Dutch Home Office. This still leaves the possi-bility that the police have not yet discovered the linkage. Even the activist youth organizations of some extreme right parties, which were meant to be a kind of buffer between the adult party and the excesses of the young, have not been found to have been involved in the violence, it would appear. They may engage more in propaganda and 'expressive' posturing such as has also been reported for Scandinavia.[59]

The recent wave of racist violence in Germany in many ways seems to conform to these models, in particular that of the Netherlands. The right-wing parties, despite their temporary increase in voting support, are wary of being blamed for the violent activities of the skinhead and hooligan 'scene', and even shy away from obvious expressions of racism because of the long-stand-ing laws arrayed against any revival of Nazism, including the advocacy of anti-Semitism, race hatred, and hostility towards other nations. The violent youth scene, on the other hand, seems to range from unorganized and hardly politicized neighborhood gangs and soccer rowdies – probably the vast major-ity – to the so called neo-Nazi action groups which, however, engage mostly in propagandistic posturing and recruitment efforts among the skinheads and not so much in violence itself. Helmut Willems' study of the suspects in vio-lent anti-foreign incidents found links to skinhead and other xenophobic groups – but less often to right-wing extremist groups – and particularly to 'everyday leisure time groups and cliques of friends which are neither politically oriented (right-wing) nor to be regarded as formal groups or organizations'. The majority were 'ordinary, youthful first-time offenders,' often acting out the small group dynamics of their clique. 'So far they hardly exhibit common organization and supralocal structures and right-wing efforts at steering and organizing them have been of rather limited success.'[60] Again, there are also regional differences which show up certain 'traditional' Nazi or neo-Nazi strongholds as more organized among a vast sea of unorganized, local outbreaks that may enjoy some community support if they promise to chase away the immigrants or asylum-seekers.[61]

In analyzing the patterns of street attacks on individuals, small groups, and symbolic targets such as Soviet war or concentration camp memorials, moreover, we found noticeable differences between the less political, garden variety human targets, including the homeless, homosexuals, and even the handicapped – and certain, more political, motifs: The latter kind tends towards anti-Semitism (for example, Jewish cemeteries) and highly symbolic targets, regardless of whether there are any Jews visible or whether a memorial is controversial in a particular neighborhood.[62] These latter cases are selective enough to appear political and it seems likely – though perpetrators are rarely caught – that they are committed by sympathizers or members of right extremist organizations. Quite often, the perpetrators also leave a message behind to make sure everybody gets the point. The small number of these cases does not detract from their significance. But it would be difficult to overlook the vast preponderance of the unorganized, unpolitical, and less political outrages against asylum-seekers and other visible foreigners.

NOTES

1. Peter H. Merkl and Leonard Weinberg (eds.), *Encounters with the Contemporary Radical Right* (Boulder, CO: Westview Press, 1993).
2. There were, of course, earlier books and articles on particular countries such as West Germany, Britain and Italy. We were not aware of several comparative projects that were being assembled, such as the collection edited by Lucia Choles *et al.*, *Neofascism in Europe* (London and NY: Longman, 1991) or of Paul Hainsworth (ed.), *The Extreme Right in Europe and America Since 1945* (London: Pinter, 1990) or of his 1992 update.
3. See, e.g., Stein Larsen *et al.* (eds.), *Who Were the Fascists? Social Roots of European Fascism* (Oslo: Norwegian UP, 1980).
4. The argument skillfully combined capitalistic policies and business-oriented politicians with the unemployment and economic troubles of the energy crisis to predict a return to the Nazi years of war and racist dictatorship.
5. See 'A New Lease on Life for the Radical Right?', in Merkl and Weinberg, *Encounters* (note 1), pp.204–26.
6. E.g., Helmut Willems, *Fremendenfeindliche Gewalt: Einstellungen, Täter, Konflikt-eskala-tion* (Opladen: Leske + Budrich, 1993).

7. See, e.g., the work of Thomas Szayna on Hungary, Poland, and the Czech and Slovak republics, 'Ultranationalism in Central Europe', *Orbis* 37/4 (Fall 1993), pp.527–50.

8. The American press, for unknown reasons, at first insisted on referring to the AN as a 'conservative party' which perhaps mirrors public confusion about this term since the Reagan years. It is difficult to imagine the American media using such a label for Germany's neofascist *Republikaner* party, which was actually named after Reagan's Republican Party in the mid 1980s.

9. Since the British National Party (BNP) won a seat on the council of the Isle of Dogs in London's East End in Sept. 1993, racial attacks there have tripled. This was the fifth such win in Britain. The BNP hoped for two more seats, for control of the council, and for a total of 30 council seats throughout Britain in the next local elections.

10. According to an INFAS poll in the midst of the panic of 1992, 19 per cent of West Germans and 12 per cent of East Germany, especially young people under 25, were ready to vote for a 'party to the right of the CDU/CSU', and by 1993, various sources predicted a veritable tidal wave of the radical right.

11. See the accounts by Jaap van Donselaar and Helene Lööw in Tore Bjørgo and Rob Witte (eds.), *Racist Violence in Europe* (London: Macmillan, 1993), and the table in Merkl and Weinberg (note 1), p.3.

12. The Italian *Lega Nord* is perhaps the most egregious example of a concerted campaign by the media and their competitors to smear them as fascistic. Rising from several regional antecedents such as the *Lega Lombarda*, they reached substantial strength in Northern Italy amid the crisis of the Christian Democrats. The new Berlusconi party, *Forza Italia*, however, may already have outdone them in becoming the leading national libertarian party and successor to the once mighty Christian Democrats. The media and supermarket tycoon Berlusconi suggests parallels ranging from Ross Perot to Alfred Hugenberg of the Weimar Republic, who helped Hitler into the saddle. For Italy, a lot will depend on which one of these he resembles more. See also Adrian Lytteton, 'Italy: The Triumph of TV', *New York Review of Books*, 11 Aug. 1994, pp.25–9.

13. In a manner of speaking, this is still the custom in former Yugoslavia, especially in Bosnia where Serb 'ethnic cleansers' have expelled long-resident Muslim and Croat populations as if they were not fellow citizens, but hostile foreigners.

14. Some full-fledged racial or nationalistic ideologies indeed interpret the role of the unique and superior race or nation in terms of a divine mission or cosmic destiny.

15. Earlier Nazi goals still aimed at expulsion, e.g., to Madagascar, and there was still a curious make-believe of 'resettlement' policies and institutional labels being employed in the midst of the genocidal 'ethnic cleansings', massacres, and mobile and stationary mass murder in vans and death camps.

16. Similar labels were invented for gypsies, homosexuals, and other target populations. The Third Reich also attempted to kill its incurably ill population, after having taken away their rights of protection as citizens, also from the control of their families.

17. Papon had been a Vichy official in Bordeaux who had been involved in the deportation of Jews to Nazi death camps.

18. See M. Slitinsky, *L' Affaire Papon* (Paris: Moreau, 1983). The peaceful demonstration was protesting a curfew imposed on 'Algerian' workers of French citizenship by Papon against their appearing in groups.

19. This was supposed to be in retaliation for foreign Jewish criticism and for the assassination attempt against a German diplomat in Paris by a young Jew.

20. See Paul Gordon, 'The Police and Racist Violence in Britain', in Bjørgo and Witte (note 11), pp.167–78, and idem., *Racial Violence and Harassment*, (London: Runnymeade Trust, 1990). The establishment of much-resisted self-defense organizations of Asian and Caribbean immigrants and the race casualties of 1981 turned the tide.

21. See Katrin Reemtsma, 'Between Freedom and Persecution: Roma in Romania', in Bjørgo and Witte (note 11), pp.194–206, and, by the same author, *Roma in Rumänien. Menschenrechtsreport der Gesellschaft für bedrohte Völker* (Göttingen, 1992).

22. The casualties of 1903–6 were in the hundreds. In Odessa alone, some 500 are believed to

have died.
23. See also John D. Klier, 'The Pogrom Tradition in Eastern Europe', in Bjørgo and Witte (note 11), pp.128-138 and the sources cited there. The Tsarist government, however, had established a restricted settlement area for the Jews long before the 1881 pogroms.
24. See Bjørgo, 'Terrorist Violence Against Immigrants and Refugees in Scandinavia: Patterns and Motives', in Bjørgo and Witte (note 11), pp.29–45.
25. See M. Levine, Les Ratonnades d'Octobre, un mentre collectif à Paris en 1961 (Paris: Ramsay, 1985), p.13.
26. In 1991 there were also the riots of immigrant youth (harkis), the second generation in the banlieus of Paris, which began with protests against unemployment, discrimination, and police conduct. C. Lloyd, 'Racist Violence and Anti-Racist Reactions: A View of France', in Bjørgo and Witte (note 11).
27. See Jaap van Donselaar, 'The Extreme Right and Racist Violence in the Netherlands', in Bjørgo and Witte (note 11), pp.46-61 and the sources cited there.
28. This element may also have been present in the Netherlands. The Swedish police also claimed that earlier media attention to racist activist groups may have served as a trigger to action. See Helene Lööw, 'The Cult of Violence: The Swedish Racist Counterculture', in Bjørgo and Witte (note 11), pp.62–79, esp. pp.77–8.
29. This difference appears to be striking in all the countries and is probably due to the high mobility and larger numbers of people living in urban settings, in contrast to the countryside where people tend to know each other more; in rural areas, the experience of the 'strangeness' of foreigners is more pronounced and they are also very likely to be under-policed and governed by informal rather than institutionalized power structures.
30. See this writer's 'Rollerball or Neo-Nazi Violence', in Merkl (ed.), Political Violence and Terror: Motifs and Motivations (Berkeley and Los Angeles: Univ. of California Press, 1986); and for the East German background, see my conclusion to Encounters (note 1), pp.208–14. Contrary to many foreign newspaper accounts there had also been Turkish and other foreign fatalities in West Germany prior to reunification, including fatal arson attacks resembling the one in Mölln, e.g., in Schwandorf in 1988.
31. Willems speaks of 2½ decades of the German partisan blame game between left and right. See Willems, Fremendenfeindliche (note 6), pp.17-18. For a well-argued version of this conspiratorial interpretation, see Graeme Atkinson, the editor of Searchlight, 'Germany: Nationalism, Nazism and Violence', in Bjørgo and Witte (note 11), pp.154–66. Atkinson also adds German unification to the dastardly plots to facilitate the return of Nazism.
32. Injuries and deaths are not only a result of the terrorist component of extremist intimidation, but they are impossible to avoid, given the character of the 'barefoot brigades' of pogromshchiki in Tsarist Russia or post-Ceausescu Romania, or of inebriated skinheads and local riff-raff in Germany, Sweden, and the Netherlands.
33. These are figures cited by Lööw (note 28), p. 77, while Bjørgo lists 94 arson or explosives attacks in Sweden during 1982–92 (mostly in 1990–92). pp.31–32. According to Lööw, there are about 500–600 right-wing radical ('racist') activists in Sweden whereas the German BVS (security service) names about 65,000 organized members of which the neo-Nazis constitute only about 2,500, and the skinheads 5,000.
34. In Rostock, according to a report in Der Spiegel, the Springer Press and a local paper actually demanded that 'something be done' if by a certain date the authorities did not stop the influx of refugees. The Rostock skinhead gangs, who are usually preoccupied with turf fights against each other, evidently took up the hint and 'did something' on that date.
35. See Bjørgo and Witte (note 11), pp.96–112, and esp. Willems' comments on the role of the media (note 6), pp.99–103.
36. See 'Are the Old Nazis Coming Back?' in Merkl (ed.), The Federal Republic at Forty-five, London: Macmillan, forthcoming).
37. There were interesting variations in the distribution of both of these offenses between West and East Germany. While the arson attempts and 'other offenses' were spread fairly evenly through the nation, the attacks on persons ran at over four times the per capita rate in East Germany, a telling sign of the alienation and disorientation of East German youth in the wake

of the fall of the communist regime.
38. The crime statistics of the BKA and Security Service (BVS) are none too clear about defining political or racist motives. There has also been a lot of criticism of their judgments in some cases, and even of their differing figures, by anti-fascist or anti-racist organizations or media such as *Searchlight* or *Antifa Information*. See also Atkinson (note 31), pp.154–5 and Willems (note 6), pp.97–8.
39. Some innovative neo-Nazi spokesmen (there are no women in this capacity) and some very imaginative journalists have attempted to construct from this a neo-Nazi enemy list or demonology, pointing to the long list of kinds of victims of the Third Reich, but this confuses system and movement.
40. See my description of Munich hooligan Chelsea Andy, and his friends, in 'Rollerball' (note 30),. There is by now a large sociological literature on soccer hooligans in English, French, Italian, and other languages.
41. See, e.g., the recurrent discussions about what constitutes 'racist violence' in Bjørgo and Witte (note 11), pp.4–6.
42. See esp. Frank J. Buijs and Jaap van Donselaar, *Extreme-rechts* (Den Haag: Leids Instituutvoor Sociaal Wetenschappelijk Onderzoek (LISWO, 1994), pp.64–73, for statistical details and breakdowns.
43. The real tragedy of the slaughter among Serbs, Croats, and Muslims in fact lies precisely in the absence of differences other than religion and culture. Completely unscrupulous people have set brothers and sisters upon one another in order to profit from the immense cruelty and slaughter.
44. *Los Angeles Times*, 23 March 1993. It is also not clear whether any of the 800 gang fatalities in 1992 found their place in these statistics. See also Mark S. Hamm (ed.), *Hate Crime: International Perspectives on Causes and Control* (Cincinnati, OH: Anderson Publishers, 1994).
45. The National Asian-Pacific American Legal Consortium which claims to represent 7.3 million Asian Americans, has meanwhile reported its own findings that 335 Asians were beaten, vandalized, or threatened in the US in 1993. As many as 30 Asians are said to have died because of hate crimes. The Consortium admitted that its statistics may be incomplete.
46. Considering the very young age of most perpetrators and the juvenile justice regulations of many of the countries concerned, it would also be very helpful if juvenile offenders and their acts were not excluded from the reports. These days a good deal of prejudicial violence, certainly in the US and in Germany, already occurs in the schools which in many cases have become a very unwholesome environment in which to bring up the next generation.
47. See esp. the accounts of political violence among the paramilitary armies of the Weimar Republic that I described in the *Making of a Stormtrooper* (Princeton, NJ: Princeton UP, 1980), Ch.2.
48. Stormtroopers (SA) and SS men were actually sworn in as auxiliary police and could hence forth claim legitimate authority in carrying out arrests, killings, and torture in the jails and first concentration camps of the Third Reich.
49. On the street fighting of the stormtroopers, see Merkl, *Stormtrooper* (note 47), Chs.3 and 4 and Merkl, *Political Violence Under the Swastika: 581 Early Nazis* (Princeton, NJ: Princeton UP, 1975), last part.
50. In the case of the gypsy pogroms, there always were warnings so that people could flee their dwellings before the arsonous mobs arrived and put them to the torch.
51. Twenty-six per cent of Germans agreed with the first and 37 per cent with the second, according to an INFAS poll broadcast on television in Sept. 1992.
52. Their claims are analogous to the Baader-Meinhof terrorists' insistence that they were defending the German and international working-classes against exploitative capitalists, or the developing nations of the Third World against Western neocolonialism and American imperialism; but they had no confirmation, only counter indications, to the effect that any of these constituencies wanted to be represented by them, or saved by their terrorist deeds.
53. Some of their critics, however, claim that their suppression of nativist pride actually encourages racist violence, or that extreme leftist and extreme right-wing activities mutually esca-

late the common level of violence. See, e.g., Iver Frigaard, 'Terrorism in Nordic Perspective', in E. Ellingsen (ed.), *International Terrorism as a Political Weapon* (Oslo: The Norwegian Atlantic Committee, 1988); or the writings by Klaus Farin and E. Seidel-Pielen on skinheads in German cities, e.g., *Krieg in den Städten* (Berlin: Rotbuchverlag, 1991), and *Skinheads* (Munich: Beck, 1993).

54. In Denmark, moreover, where unemployment has been at the highest level of the three main Scandinavian countries, the level of anti-foreign violence has remained low [Bjørgo (note 24), pp.30–3]. The Swedish neo-Nazi Nordic National [*Reich*] Party and its activist RAG squads seem to have pioneered the use of fire bombs in 1985.

55. Bjørgo's numbers did not include acts of street violence, vandalism, or unsubstantiated threats nor were attacks on anti fascists and homosexuals included. [Bjørgo (note 24), p.44n].

56. Ibid., pp.34–35. The Scandinavian police seem to agree with this assessment, which is not to say that the unpolitical groups have not 'borrowed' far right slogans, or that theirs may not be 'copy cat' crimes.

57. The question of what makes these acts political is answered by (a) their selective victimization of foreigners, (b) the existing right-wing propaganda, and (c) instances of community support experienced after such violent incidents. See Bjørgo (note 24), pp.37–42.

58. See Donselaar (note 27), pp.46–7. Dutch skinhead groups and their violence tend to 'drift around' among several extreme right organizations and not really to belong to any of them. Ibid., p. 50. A series of 1992 racist bombings in the Hague also turned out to have no link to any extreme right organization. Ibid., p.54. More recently, however, he has revised his views somewhat, finding a higher amount of organizational involvement. Buijs and Donselaar (note 42), pp.64–7.

59. Ibid., pp.55–60. On Scandinavia, see Lööw (note 28) and Bjørgo (note 24) in this volume.

60. Willems (note 6), pp.246–7, also pp.178ff.

61. This is particularly true of the attacks on refugee camps and asylum-seeker hostels. Attacks on small groups or individuals also are typical of unorganized youth, but rarely enjoy community support. An example to the contrary were the Magdeburg street riots of May 1994, where skinheads attacked and chased away black Africans who were suspected of selling crack to juveniles. There were not only signs of community support but also of police tolerance of the violence.

62. See Merkl, 'Are the Old Nazis Coming Back?' in Merkl, *The Federal Republic* (note 36). Such incidents, by the way, are only a small percentage (2–3 per cent) of the 1992 total but, interestingly, they are more heavily concentrated in West Germany – unlike other small group attacks – where extreme right parties are strong and well-established.

Racist Violence and Criminal Behaviour in Sweden: Myths and Reality

HELÉNE LÖÖW

Since World War II, Swedish national socialists and right wing extremists have been divided into two main factions: *nationalists*, who are parliamentarian, non-racist but ethnocentric, non-revolutionary; and *race ideologists*, who are revolutionary, racist and internationally oriented. During the 1980s a new generation took over, and activities increased. The militant racist subculture, consisting of small independent networks, exists within a long tradition of organised racism or extreme nationalism in Sweden. The organised activists of small militant race-ideologist sects can be described as the most extreme form of the organised hostility towards refugees and migrants, while the unorganised perpetrators of attacks against refugee hostels can be regarded as the extreme expression of an established mentality in the local community. The organised and unorganised exist in a symbiosis. The perpetrators of violence are in most cases to be found at the intersection between the subculture of 'white power' and the general hostility towards refugees in the community.

Much of the public debate in Sweden during the early 1990s has been focused on the issues of racism and xenophobia. Racist violence and the question of whether racist organisations should be banned or not have been important issues in this debate. In the media debate, the racist/xenophobic violence has been said to be either the work of organised racists or drunken pranks committed by unemployed, frustrated youngsters. But who are the perpetrators? What are their motives? To what extent is the violence emanating from racist/extreme nationalistic organisations and to what degree is it unorganised? Is there a connection between the attacks on refugee hostels, asylum seekers and immigrants, local non-violent protests and organised racism/extreme nationalism? It is not possible to answer these questions fully in a short contribution. The aim here is to try to shed some light on these questions through a case study of the criminality among racist/xenophobic gangs in the cities of Göteborg/Borås, Karlstad/Säffle, Växjö and Malmö from the mid 1980s until 1992–93. The issue of attacks against refugee hostels and asylum seekers, the perpetrators and their motives will also be addressed. Initially, however, it is necessary to describe briefly the organised racist activities and to explore the new radical and revolutionary racism which has emerged in Sweden during the 1980s and early 1990s, including the various organisations, their ideology, and political strategies.[1]

The history of postwar national socialism in Sweden starts immediately after the war when – in addition to *Svensk Socialistisk Samling,* the largest of the national socialist parties of the 1930s – several small national socialist groups were active.

In 1956 *Nordiska Rikspartiet* (the Nordic National [*Reich*] Party, NRP) was founded by Göran Oredsson.[2] In the late 1960s NRP experienced some minor success when local branches were established around the country. In the south of Sweden there were several very active local branches, which had close contacts with the Danish national socialists and others. In Göteborg (Gothenburg), there was a strong local branch, with its own party headquarters and a bookstore. A conflict between the Göteborg branch and the NRP leadership, however, led to a split in the movement. After the split, a period of decline in the activities followed, the number of members decreased and the local branches disappeared one by one.[3] The NRP is ideologically a classical national socialist party, and suffers from lack of financial support from older and younger generations of national socialists, internal struggles, splits, and acts of violence carried out by its members and sympathisers. Since the early years of the NRP, members and sympathisers have been convicted for inciting racial hatred, for bombings, assault and battery, and harassment.[4] In 1974 members of *Riksaktionsgruppen* (the National Action Group, RAG)[5] threw a smoke grenade into the Stockholm office of the right-wing extremist organisation *Demokratisk Allians* (Democratic Alliance) which resulted in the injury of one person. During the same year members of the NRP carried out a similar attack on a Stockholm cinema that was showing the movie 'Springtime for Hitler'. These perpetrators were subsequently sent to prison.[6] The first half of the 1980s saw increasing activity from a younger generation of NRP activists, especially on the west coast of Sweden.

Despite NRP's lack of political support, the party has played an important role as a bridge between the pre-war national socialists and the revolutionary, internationally oriented, 'racial socialists' of the 1990s.[7] Some key activists in the contemporary racist underground are former NRP members.[8] Concerning the role of the NRP, one activist stated: 'I admire the people behind it, who have continued despite the hatred they have been subject to ... But I don't know if they themselves ever really have believed that they would once gain power .... I don't know and maybe someone will say the same about me in 30 years time.'[9] Today NRP's political activity is limited to various publications.

One of the right-wing extremist parties of the 1930s which survived the war was *Sveriges Nationella Förbund* (Sweden's National Association, SNF). SNF's activities have, however, been limited since the war. During the 1960s and 1970s the activities were mainly run from cover or sub-organisations. The 1980s were characterised by internal splits and the organisation was divided into three factions, two in Malmö and one in Stockholm. One of the Malmö factions – headed by Lars Göran Hedengård – is part of the US-based organisation NSDAP-AO.[10] The group's activities are, however, very limited. The group is rarely heard of, apart from occasional issues of their magazine.

In the late 1970s the anti-immigration group *Bevara Sverige Svenskt* (Keep Sweden Swedish, BSS) was established. BSS became the embryo of the parliamentarian anti-immigration parties, of which several emerged and grew during the 1980s.[11] The most 'successful' party before the parliamentary election in 1991 was *Sverigedemokraterna* (Swedish Democratic Party, SD). There are several reasons why the SD grew in 1989–90. First, the public debate reinforced SD's argumentation. In this debate, refugees were no longer seen as a resource but as a problem. The more restricted asylum legislation and the change in the public opinion to one more against refugees and immigrants contributed to legitimatizing SD's aims as well.[12] In addition, the victory of the 'No' side on the question of refugee reception in the local referendum in the small rural community of Sjöbo in the south of Sweden in 1988 also had the effect of giving legitimacy to the anti-immigrant stance.

In the 1991 election, SD had competition from *Sjöbopartiet* (The Sjöbo Party) and *Framstegspartiet* (The Progressive Party), whose anti-immigration programme strongly resembled SD's. *Framstegspartiet/Sjöbopartiet*, which ran in the election as a coalition, received 27,637 votes at the local level. *Framstegspartiet* gained 12 seats in local councils, all in the south of Sweden. SD received 4,889 votes on the national level and two seats in local councils.

During 1992, the activities from the parliamentarian anti-immigration parties declined. The reasons for this were twofold: First, part of the base of recruitment for the parliamentarians was undermined by the rise of the populist and to a certain extent anti-immigrant *Ny Demokrati* (New Democracy) and the established political parties' more restrictive attitudes in questions concerning refugees and immigration; second, younger members left in favour of revolutionary racial-ideologist groups, who were considered more active and militant. The above-mentioned factors have contributed to internal conflicts within the parliamentarian groups, paralysing party activities. However, when *Ny Demokrati* – also plagued by internal splits and scandals – began to lose more and more of its political support during 1993, SD again increased its activities and is to some extent gaining support among the generation born in the 1960s and 1970s. In the 1994 election SD took five seats in local assemblies and received approximately 13,000 votes in the general election.

Ideologically, the parliamentarian parties are neither national socialist nor racist – which does not mean that no individuals or factions inside the parties harbour such ideas. The parliamentarians are not opposed to immigration in the general sense of the word; the rejection is directed towards immigrants/refugees from southern Europe and outside Europe, and is based on notions of ethnicity and culture.[13] The parliamentarian groups – officially – strongly condemn violence against refugees and attacks against refugee hostels. However, functionaries occasionally express understanding for the acts. Or to quote an SD functionary:

> We have no need for it [violence]. We have other ways of expressing our thoughts ... however, I would not feel sorry if anyone planted a bomb at the Bureau of Immigration .... just hope that none of our members were responsible for it .... I wouldn't cry, that's for sure, it is the right place to plant a bomb if you should attack any one at all.[14]

The Radical Racists

Within the network of readers and publishers of various racist underground magazines, and among the young NRP activists of the 1980s, a new militant-racist underground emerged. Originally, this network consisted of a small group of young men in their early to mid-20s. In spite of their youth, they all had long experience of political activity in a variety of national socialist and racist groups, including some with as much as ten years of activism.[15] The network is based on local cells, led by a local leader/organiser, thus rejecting the notion of organisational hierarchy. The network does not have a single figurehead, but prefers to organise under several key activists. The strategy behind this organisational set-up, or rather non-organisational set-up, is that the network should distribute propaganda material in order to attract people with racist ideas. Those who are attracted, however, cannot join existing groups directly. They have to start their own racist activity and/or gradually qualify themselves, in order one day to be acknowledged as part of the racist underground. The status of an individual or of a group depends on its previous 'record', its personality, and the 'mythology' surrounding the group or individual. The struggle is collective as well as individual, and every individual or group is free to choose their own means of struggle. The exclusiveness of the network does not repel potential racist activists. On the contrary, it heightens the attraction of the movement and sometimes encourages individuals/groups to increase their activity, or in some cases even to commit acts of violence or other criminal acts in order to qualify as members.[16] One activist stated that his group received numbers of letters from teenagers who wanted them to suggest targets for attacks. The activist added: 'There are lots of letters from young blokes, they are so desperate in a way, and I can very well imagine them doing drastic things, things that might not be so bloody wise, they must have some patience.'[17] Gary Yarbrough, convicted member of The Order and a role model for some Swedish racists, explained the need for a change in strategy in the following way:

> During the past decades the ... tactics used by our various organisations have been open and public, i.e. producing publications, gaining subscribers and supporters and recruiting members, which unfortunately [has meant] that our cause attracts and gets its fair share of mentally unstable people, psychopaths, neurotics and ... whose hearts do not belong to our good cause ... [We should instead] limit the number of members to a small and dedicated number of loyal fighters. Recruit quality not quantity. Publication and distribution of literature and propaganda should be the main function for every official organisation. This strategy should prevent or at least limit the number of unwanted elements who voluntarily join our activities.[18]

To have participated in demonstrations, internal meetings, concerts and ritual celebrations has became a status symbol among a growing number of young men, who have gradually tried to copy the lifestyle of the network.

Kreativistens Kyrka is a Swedish offshoot of the US Organisation *Church of the Creator* (COTC). It was founded in Sweden in 1988 by Tommy Rydén, a long time activist in racist and nationalist organisations.[19] In October 1990 Rydén was sentenced to pay a fine for incitement to racial hatred.[20] Rydén appealed the verdict to a higher court, which upheld the verdict *and* increased his sentence to four months of imprisonment.[21]

In the late autumn of 1992 a faction headed by Rydén broke all relations with the US parent church and established an independent organisation called *Ben Klassen Academy,* named after the founder of COTC. The split was the result of organisational conflicts.[22] In April 1993 Rydén returned to the parent church since the faction he belonged to had won the battle for control over the organisation. He was also appointed leader of the Swedish COTC.[23] A few months after the suicide of COCT founder Ben Klassen in August 1993, Rydén once again left the parent church and transformed his movement into *DeVries Institutet (DeVries Institute)*. The institute is said to be a non-profit information centre, which focuses on questions like eugenics, salubrious living and legalisation of euthanasia.[24] During the summer of 1994 Rydén, however, started *Den Reorganiserade Kreativistens Kyrka* (The Reorganised COTC), which is said to function as an order. In the group's introductory leaflet it is pointed out that a potential member should be at least 18 years old, bound to silence about the group's activities and willing to give loyalty towards his 'comrades' priority over anything else. In the leaflet it is also stated: 'Our organisational model is the catholic Opus Dei and Jesuit order – we are a priestly order, not a traditional organisation. But our teaching is social Darwinism and free from all kinds of gods and myths. Our race is our religion.' The group maintains contact with like-minded splinter-groups of COTC around the world.[25] The organisational set-up of the COTC is a Swedish invention; the US COTC is, according to Jeffrey Kaplan, more of a mail order ministry.[26] COTC is not national socialist, but considers national socialism as the only ideology which has 'seriously challenged the Jews'.[27]

In addition to the COTC, the racist counterculture also includes *Riksfronten* (the National [*Reich*] Front). As the fastest growing race ideological group, it has established several local branches around the country during 1992–1993.[28] In 1993 *Riksfronten* established itself as the open political front of the network. In the autumn of 1993 the organisation published a political programme in which it stated: 'Riksfronten will run in the elections in order to give the people an alternative to the misgovernment .... Riksfronten is neither populist nor democratic but a militant liberation organisation for Sweden's survival.'[29] *Riksfronten* is organised according to the same principles as the Fascist and National Socialist organisations of the 1930s.[30]

In May 1993 it seemed as if the previous differences between the various organisations within the network had been put aside in favour of a united front.[31] In 1993 the network's main publication, the magazine *Storm,* ceased to appear – the bank account and official post box address were closed – after a final issue which, among other things, contained lists of 'enemies of the white race', complete with adresses, telephone numbers, etc.[32] The paper was, however, soon to reappear under a new name with new post box addresses and bank accounts, and in 1994 *Storm* was replaced by *Blod & Ära* (Blood & Honour).[33] During 1993 the network formed a prison organisation, which first existed under the name of *NS Ledung*, and later changed its name to *Thuleringen* (The ring of Thule). *Thuleringen* is, however, not an organisation in the proper sense. It is said to function as an educational group and runs a racist book club for imprisoned activists and publishes a magazine called *Gryning* (Dawn)[34] which contains ideological as well as historical articles.[35] During 1994 the production and distribution network *Motstånd* (Resistance) – which is part of the larger racist network – came into being. The aim of *Motstånd* is to create an alternative infrastructure and an alternative lifestyle. *Motstånd* provides activists with propaganda material such as CDs and T-shirts, and encourages activists and sympathisers to organise rock concerts, sell T-shirts, CDs, books, etc. The money the network earns should be used to start import companies, record companies, printing factories, pubs and cafés.[36] The purpose of the alternative infrastructure is both to serve as a recruitment base for the movement's more militant groups, and to provide the movement with the necessary financial resources.

It should, however, be stated that the Swedish racist counterculture is relatively small. Although the movement has grown slowly during the past two years, the estimated number of activists, members and sympathisers of the network remained, by the end of 1993, at no more than 200.[37] The total number of 'White Power activists' and more or less active sympathisers of different age groups was 500–700.[38]

Ideology

All the organisations discussed above are parts of a radical racist counterculture with its own vocabulary and mythology. The network's rhetoric is a mixture of national socialist terminology of the 1930s and the contemporary code used by the American Ku Klux Klan and White Supremacist groups.[39] A study of the magazines, leaflets, and propaganda material issued by the network reveals that some of the articles and symbols are taken from the Swedish and international national socialist literature of the 1930s or are glorified descriptions of the old movements.[40]

The links between the old and the new movements can also be found in the music of the 'White Power' movement – 'White Power' groups like *Odins Änglar* (Odin's Angels) put music to lyrics written by the ideologists of the old movements.[41] They can also be found in the rituals that take place during party rallies – when the battle songs of the national socialist movements of the 1930s are sung.[42] Some local branches of the network have taken the names and numbers of the local branches of the national socialist movements of the 1930s.[43] Some of the old national socialists and members of the generation of activists who were active during the 1950s to 1980s are also part of the racist subculture of the 1990s. There are no age barriers – everyone who believes in the concept of racism and who is accepted by the network is considered a 'brother or sister' – in spite of age, social position and education. Everyone who is defined as being outside the movement is regarded as either an 'enemy of the race' or an 'unenlightened white'.[44] One of the members of the old generation of national socialists, a former Waffen SS volunteer, explained why he had chosen to associate himself with the new generation of race ideologists:

> We are not ordinary people, when you have done what I have done and seen what I have seen, you never become ordinary again, and that is why I'm here, because the boys they are like we were. They are us and we are them, we are the same kind of people.[45]

Some of the activists are even the children and grandchildren of the old generation of activists in the biological meaning of the word. To belong to a fam-

ily with a long history of activism in national socialist, fascist or racist organisations gives an individual a high status within the group, but at the same
time expectations are high.

Members of the old national socialist movements have played an important
role for some of the modern activists in the process of becoming politically
active. A member of a militant racist group recounts how his racist activism
started:

> At first I thought the Nazis were just shit, I hated Germans, everything
> German, but I was interested in the Second World War. I read everything
> I could find about it. And it became sort of an awakening. I suddenly
> woke up. I and my friends went to a meeting where an old national
> socialist spoke. He spoke about democracy, the hypocrisy, the double
> standard, the lies, it was like something fell from my eyes. I woke up.
> We walked away as different human beings...But it is hard to be like us
> ... I have asked myself hundreds of times why I'm doing this. Why I'm
> not doing something else with my life, but I cannot do that, this is my
> life, there is nothing to do about it.[46]

Anti-Semitism is as important to the racist activists of the 1990s as it was to
the national socialists of the 1930s. One leading Swedish Creator, explained
why:

> Anti-Semitism to us is based on history ... We can trace the Jews as the
> root of all evil ... destroyers of the Roman Empire ... the American Civil
> War, the First World War, the Second World War ... in addition to which
> they own most of the world's financial assets ... they have got the white
> man down on his knees with taxes and so forth ... taken our cultural
> inheritance away from us ... and bring hordes of non-whites to mix with
> us ... in order to exterminate the white race.[47]

Anti-Semitism is extreme in some factions of the racist counterculture. One
activist within the network gave the following answer as to what his opinion
was about the Holocaust;

> You mean Auschwitz and that kind of crap, it was necessary, complete-
> ly necessary. It might sound awful to say like that, but it was necessary.
> I don't belong to those who say that it never happened, bloody hell it
> happened ... and do you know what the real horror is? ... They were so
> close to succeeding, so close to the dream, the new society. We whites
> are being exterminated, don't you understand that, and they [the nation-
> al socialists] were so close to succeeding in cleansing the world of the
> vermin ... of course I get upset, reading about the exterminations, bloody

hell it was brutal, but it had to be done and must be done again ... I want you to understand that, it is important to me.[48]

Others among the hardcore anti-Semites are obsessed by the idea that the Holocaust did *not* happen, and explain their anti-Semitism almost in terms of a religious awakening. Or to quote one long-time anti-Semite:

First I belonged to a leftist group, I have always been committed to some cause. Then one day someone gave me a leaflet. That leaflet changed my life, even if it was only three pages long. When I had read it I understood that it all was a lie, the Holocaust had never happened, it was a dizzy feeling ... At first I was ashamed, I did not dare to tell anyone that I had these thoughts, these doubts. I didn't even dare to tell my girlfriends that I had become an anti-Semite, did not dare to tell anyone about what I had discovered, it was awful. At my work as a teacher in a public school I had to pretend that nothing had happened, but now ... when I have met others who feel like I do, I dare to come out more and more as an open anti-Semite.[49]

To some of the Holocaust-deniers, their obsession has become a substitute religion, in which the revisionist literature has received almost the status of 'holy books' and the leading revisionists have been turned into prophets. Other revisionists, however, strongly resemble other kinds of 'conspiracy theorists'.

A key word in the counter culture of the 'White Power' movements is 'race consciousness'. The activists believe that inside every human being there is a slumbering racial instinct – an instinct they want to awaken through propaganda. 'Purity' is another important theme in the rhetoric of the movement. The idea of purity is naturally a central part of racial ideology. Immigration of non-whites is for instance seen as a 'disease'. Members of other races, homosexuals, etc. are looked upon as 'sub-humans' or 'vermin'.

This corresponds closely to Ehud Sprinzak's observation that racist ideology is based on the belief that certain people do not belong to the relevant community, that they are by definition outsiders and should be treated accordingly. Therefore terrorism against groups considered to be inferior is a control mechanism, a means of assuring that they do not multiply and prevail. 'This attitude is perhaps the reason why most particularistic terrorists never attempt to apologise for their brutal actions and why so few explanatory ideologies of terrorism exist in this cultural milieu. Acts that are reasonable and natural do not require justification', Sprinzak states.[50]

The idea of purity and the importance of a healthy lifestyle is also found in the recommendations to the activists of how they should live.[51] Many of the activists in the racist counter culture are also genuinely concerned about issues such as environmental protection, animal rights, anti-drug activities and anti-pornography.[52] Some activists for instance support Greenpeace and various organisations for animal protection.[53] The democratic state is regarded as 'impure', 'perverted' and full of 'decadence', 'disloyal' and 'hypocritical'.[54]

It is quite common for activists to share a flat. This perpetuates the tendency of activists to refer to their fellow members as 'family' or 'brothers and sisters'.[55] For young activists with no family of their own or having bad relationships with their relatives, the group step by step becomes the only 'real' family they have ever known. The older activists become their big brothers or substitute fathers and the pre-war generation becomes their grandfathers. Activists, with or without families of their own, often tend progressively to break the remaining connections with the outside world, in favour of a life among likeminded. The surrounding society gradually becomes an 'alien world' full of enemies against which the activists have to defend themselves.

Loyalty towards the group, its ideas, and its cause is extremely important to the activists. Loyalty is not only meant to bind the members of a particular network or activist cell, but includes all 'White Warriors'. Names and addresses of jailed activists from a variety of nations frequently appear in 'White-Power' magazines around the world to arise sentiments of loyalty and support for all brothers-in-arms.[56] The 'international-racist underground's' loyalty also extends to Swedish 'white prisoners of war' and their families.[57] In 1993 *Ariska Frihetsfonden* (Aryan Liberation Foundation) was founded. The organisation gives imprisoned activists financial and moral support.[58] *Ariska Frihetsfonden* also sells 'supporter T-shirts', with profits going to imprisoned activists.[59] Activists on the outside 'adopt' imprisoned activists and support them morally and financially.[60] The network defines two kinds of imprisoned members. The first is *prisoners of war*. To be qualified as such, the activist must have taken part in a war against a power hostile towards the white race, and have acted as a soldier. However, the activist must not necessarily have taken part in an armed action personally; accomplices are also qualified. The second category is *political prisoners*. To qualify as such, the activist must be serving a sentence because of racist beliefs or actions triggered by that belief. The beliefs or actions may or may not be legal, and the activist takes action as an individual, not as a member of an organisation. Prisoners who have received a higher sentence because of their racist ideas are also qualified.[61] *Ariska Frihetsfonden* does not, however, support activists serving prison sentences for drunk driving, etc.[62] A group of imprisoned activists have lately started campaigns in order to force society to acknowledge them as 'political prisoners'.[63]

The formation of the contemporary ideology and strategy of this revitalised radical racist enclave is based on a combination of historical traditions of pre-war Swedish National Socialism, ideas from the NRP of the late 1970s and early 1980s, influences from American White supremacy groups such as The Order, and the skinhead press described above. During the late 1980s and early 1990s the racist counterculture gradually developed a political agenda which operates on three different levels. The first is official public propaganda activities. Distribution of various types of propaganda material has increased rapidly during the early 1990s. The second level consists of public demonstrations and rallies. The third level of activity centres on the militant cells of individuals who in the recent past have carried out bank robberies to amass a 'war chest' to support the cause and to give financial support to activists who are often unemployed.

The notion of a threatening social conspiracy managed by 'lying media', Jews and homosexuals, has deepened during the past year, and the hardcore activists have, step by step, broken their remaining contacts with the surrounding society – in favour of a more or less outlaw existence.[64] In the early to mid-1980s the main enemies of the racist counterculture were individuals considered either to be 'racially inferior' or 'traitors'. During the late 1980s the rhetoric of the movement began to change. The main enemies were no longer specific minorities or individuals, but the state itself. But on a day-to-day basis, the primary enemy remained anti-racist and watch-dog groups.[65] In this respect the Swedish racist counter culture fits well into the model of racist terrorism presented by Sprinzak.[66]

The idea of the history of mankind as a never-ending struggle between different races is central to the ideology of the revolutionary racists. To modern race ideologists, the notion of struggle is vital. The activists regard themselves as 'White Warriors' in an 'International Aryan Resistance movement'. The modern militant racism is not primarily nationalistic, it is internationally oriented. The network continuously reminds its members to prepare themselves, physically and mentally, for the inevitable and imminent 'holy racial war'. The race war is not only an armed war, it is a 'birthrate' war as well. Women are by some parts of the network regarded as objects in this racial war. One creator explained it as follows: 'Yes, of course, they [non-white men] are a threat. It is a threat to our race if they take our women.'[67] 'The struggle over the women' is considered a part of the notion of the 'holy racial war'. In some circles, cases of rape by non-white perpetrators are regarded as 'extreme anti-white activities', that is, a deliberate act from the enemy's side in the ongoing race war.[68]

Modern race ideologists are also primarily revolutionary and look back on the German national socialism of the early 1920s as a source of inspiration.

Many of the leading activists of the movement also claim that their goal is not only a racial hegemony, but a total transformation of the society and the individual.[69] In this respect they resemble the classic national socialist and fascist movements.[70]

The network does not openly encourage acts of violence, but states that every activist has to be prepared to use violence 'if the situation calls for it', i.e. if the network considers itself attacked or is banned.[71] On the other hand, the network does not condemn violent or criminal acts committed by individual members of the underground – on the contrary it 'understands' them.[72] The movement also wants to attract individuals with a potential for action. Tommy Rydén explained the recruitment strategy:

> I hope that we will attract many, many militant individuals, who are ready to do anything when the situation calls for it, but who are stable and do not commit attacks at the present time, because we don't gain anything from such actions, not as a group. But who can defend us in case the group is threatened. We do not want cowards .... Well, no Swedish Democrats, who do not dare to clearly take a stand for the cause.[73]

Racist Violence

> *Hell if it had blown up ... What the devil, then they would bloody hell have had to move the whole fucking refugee hostel ... but there were lots of attacks around Sweden by that time. Everyone was doing it, so I guess someone wanted to join in.*[74]

Before addressing the issue of racist/xenophobic violence, it is necessary to briefly examine Swedish refugee policy. The Swedish system for refugee reception underwent major changes during the 1980s. First, the number of refugees and asylum seekers placed in local communities increased. The table below shows the number of refugees, relatives and other immigrants between 1987 and 1993.[75]

TABLE 1
NUMBERS OF REFUGEES, RELATIVES AND OTHER MIGRANTS, 1987–1993

Year	Refugees	Relatives	Others	Total
1987	16,545	9,884	2,237	28,666
1988	19,490	11,401	2,115	33,006
1989	29,968	12,599	1,775	44,342
1990	18,028	17,032	2,323	37,383
1991	25,532	14,361	2,355	42,248
1992	19,903	12,550	2,364	34,817
1993	44,079	12,199	2,650	58,928

Second, the organisation for refugee reception underwent several changes. In 1985 a new reform to make the system more efficient was introduced. The refugees should now be placed in local communities that have previous experience of refugees or immigrants and that have an already existing community service for minority groups. The labour market in the region should further allow the refugees who were granted a permit to stay the possibility to gain employment in the area. The system for community reception was voluntary, namely, a community could refuse to participate if it considered itself unable to live up to the standard. The main reasons behind this reform were, on the one hand, to take the pressure off the big cities, which until then had taken the majority of the refugees and, on the other hand, to shorten the period of time from the refugee's arrival until a decision had been taken whether the refugee would be allowed to stay or not. The idea behind the reform was also to speed up the integration process. The reform was based on the premises that Sweden should receive approximately 5,000 refugees a year. However, the number of refugees increased rapidly from the mid-1980s (see Table 1 above) and the need for housing facilities, etc., became more and more pressing. The number of communities that SIV (the State Bureau of Immigration) signed contracts with increased, and the original plan to place refugees only in communities with an existing competence and with reasonable possibilities for the refugees to support themselves was gradually abandoned. In the end not even the argument that the community lacked sufficient housing facilities for the refugees was accepted by SIV as a reason for a community to refuse. The so-called whole Sweden strategy was born, that is, that all Swedish communities should take refugees – not only those communities with realistic possibilities to integrate them.[76] In the early stage of the reform the refugees and asylum seekers were housed in the local communities, but due to lack of housing facilities etc, a system of refugee hostels was created. The hostels themselves often consisted of hotels, holiday centres, closed schools etc in the various local communities. The refugees were not allowed to work. 'The whole Sweden' strategy also meant that refugees were placed in small rural communities lacking previous experience with refugees or migrants, and in many cases with a high unemployment rate.

During the same period attitudes towards immigrants and refugees became more negative. Lange and Westin claim in a study that this change in public opinion was caused by the high number (by Swedish standards) of asylum seekers, the social problems surrounding certain refugee hostels, the economic costs of refugee reception, the exploitation of the immigrant issue by *Ny Demokrati* and locally-based populist parties, and the decision to send refugees with a permit to stay to small rural communities with high unemployment rates. The fact that the government on several occasions made the asylum legislation more restrictive in order to reduce the number of refugees, and ultimately to decrease the number of people granted permission to stay, has been taken as a confirmation that the refugees are a 'burden on society'. It was no longer considered morally wrong to criticise migration.[77]

Between 1990 and 1993 there were 567 attacks against asylum-seekers and refugee hostels or local representatives for immigration issues.[78] But who are the perpetrators? And what are their motives? There is, unfortunately, very little official data available regarding the total number of attacks, the perpetrators and their underlying motives. However, three reports made by the Swedish security police concerning crimes with racist or xenophobic motives, covering the years 1990–91, 1992 and 1993 respectively, give us some clues as to who the perpetrators are.

FIGURE 1
AGE AT THE TIME THE CRIME WAS COMMITTED AMONG 165 SENTENCED/
SUSPECTED PERPETRATORS 1990–1993[79]

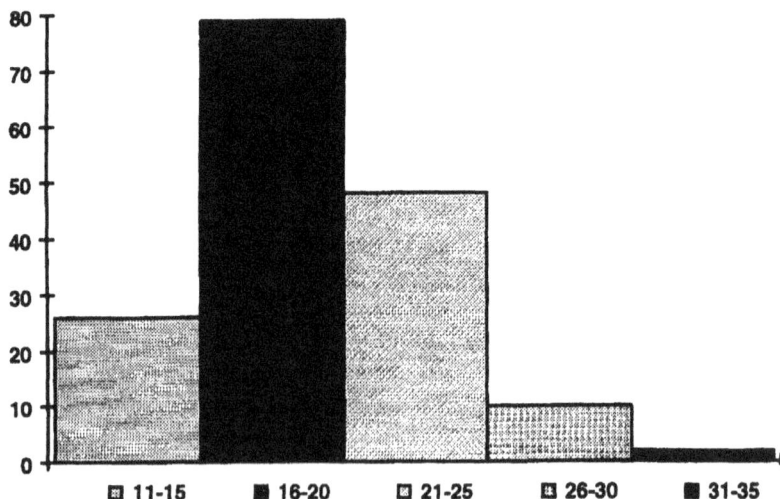

The majority of the suspected/convicted perpetrators were between 16 and 20 years of age at the time of the crime. The reports from the security police also show that 86 of the 165 suspected/convicted perpetrators had been convicted previously (47 had a long criminal record, the remaining 39 were convicted for minor offences, whereas 69 had no previous criminal record). Almost all (162) came from the town/village where the crime was committed or from the area nearby. The reports also show that very few of the suspected/convicted perpetrators can be tied to racist/extreme nationalistic organisations.[80] It is interesting to note that only half of the suspected/convicted perpetrators in 1990–92[81] were reported to have been drunk at the time of the offence – a fact that does not correspond with the stereotypical image of perpetrators as being young, drunk losers with nothing else to do. This raises the interesting question of why sober men from the local community, many with no or only a minor criminal record, suddenly decide to attack the local refugee hostel. This is, in my opinion, a far more interesting question than why drunks belonging to the local group of social losers commit similar attacks.

In addition to the above-mentioned offences, there are 124 cases of incitement of racial hatred and 81 cases of discrimination listed for 1992. The last category also includes cases of discrimination against homosexuals and religious minorities. Unfortunately, it is not possible at this stage of the research to present more detailed information about these types of crimes and the perpetrators. It can, however, be stated that typical offences within this category are restaurants refusing migrants access to their establishments, housing companies discriminating against immigrants and members of the gypsy minority, shopkeepers refusing to allow refugees to enter to the shop or letting them enter only five at a time or only in the company of staff from the refugee hostel or after they have paid an 'entrance fee' of maybe 100 Swedish crowns. The reason for this is often that the shopkeepers suspect refugees of stealing.[82] One example of the latter was the effort by an association for shopowners in the district of Norrbotten to limit the refugees' access to the shops to restricted hours, because they believed that the refugees were responsible for the increasing rate of shoplifting in the area. In some shop windows signs like 'immigrants not allowed to enter' could be found.[83] The 1993 report lists 32 cases of incitement of racial hatred, but 18 of these cases are reports of a Holocaust revisionist flyer from *Radio Islam*.[84] Six reports concern material issued by SD, one case concerning *Riksfronten*, whereas the remaining are anonymous. The 1993 report also includes 140 cases of illegal discrimination. Of these, 102 cases are based on information from the victim, that is, the victim claimed that he/she has been subject to discrimination. In 35 of these cases, racist/xenophobic motives could be ruled out (another 3 cases were discharged as miscoded). About half (72 cases) concerned restaurants.[85]

The 1992 police report includes 359 reported crimes, but 18 of the cases have been written off as not racist/xenophobic or not a criminal offence. Of the remaining 341 cases, 161 were found to have been directed against asylum-seekers/refugee hostels and 180 against members of immigrant groups by

Swedes engaged in anti-racist activities, by public officials at the immigrant offices, and by local and state politicians. Apart from the above-mentioned cases, the report also includes crimes with race-ideologist or right-wing extremist origin without racist/xenophobic motives – four cases of armed robbery, one theft and two cases of illegal possession of weapons.[86] The report also shows the following figures regarding violence and attacks of a more serious kind in 1990–92:

TABLE 2
SERIOUS ATTACKS AGAINST ASYLUM-SEEKERS AND REFUGEE HOSTELS 1990–1992[87]

Crime	1990	1991	1992
Fire/explosion	20	18	25
Assault & battery	4	1	7
Total	24	29	32

The figures above indicate a minor increase in serious attacks, that is, incidents that have or could have meant serious risk to the lives of the victim(s). It should, however, be noted that seven of the cases listed for 1992 are attempted murders committed by the so-called revolver/laser man, who killed one migrant and tried to kill 10 others. He was sentenced in January 1994 to life imprisonment for one homicide, ten cases of attempted murder and ten cases of armed robbery.[88] The 1993 report lists 1,033 criminal cases. Due to changes in the system for reporting these crimes, it is not meaningful to compare these figures with those for previous years. Even if the routines for registering racist/xenophobic crimes have improved during the year, there are still difficulties when it comes to the big cities. The difficulties in 'capturing' all the crimes in the above-mentioned categories are mainly related to reorganisations within the police department. The 1993 report lists 787 cases where circumstances indicated that the motive behind the crime was political, xenophobic or racist in nature; 289 crimes where alleged political/xenophobic/racist motives can be excluded; 143 crimes where the motive could not be determined; 53 anti-Semitic crimes; 6 anti-homosexual crimes; and 67 crimes with other forms of right-wing extremist connection. Of the total, over half (396) of these crimes were directed against refugee hostels or against representatives involved in immigrant issues.[89]

These results indicate that perpetrators tend to be men from the local community. Slightly more than half of them were drunk at the time of the offence. But even if it is hard to trace deeper ideological motives behind the attacks and the violence, a survey of court material, police investigations and verdicts shows that the predominant motive behind the crimes *is* hostility towards refugees and minority groups. A survey of the motives behind attacks committed in 1988–92, based on verdicts and police interrogations with convicted perpetrators, points to three main categories. The first category could be labelled *'private motives'*, that is, the offender claims, for instance, that he or persons close to him have been robbed or, more commonly, believe that they have been robbed by refugees from the local refugee hostel. Other common motives which can be brought to this category are statements like 'the refugees behave badly, insult us Swedes, laugh at us', etc. The second main group of motives can be labelled as *'frustration and protest motives'*, namely, the perpetrator claims that he wants to put 'the refugee question on the political agenda', 'awaken people', etc. In some cases perpetrators claim that attacking the refugee hostel is the only remaining way to protest, beacause 'the politicians do not listen'. Perpetrators falling within this category tend to state that the attack was not directed against the refugees, but against the politicians and the society. In some cases the perpetrators see themselves as some kind of 'local heroes', and claim that 'everyone in the village thinks like us, but no one except us dares to do anything about the refugees' or 'the refugees are what people talk about around here, everyone is against them'. In some cases the perpetrators have indeed received some kind of passive support and understanding from part of the local population. The third main category can be labelled as *'hate and dislike'*. The perpetrators belonging to this category claim that they 'hate the bastards', 'can't stand Arabs', etc.

A few examples are illustrative. A 23-year-old man who together with a friend threw a Molotov cocktail at a refugee hostel in Fagersta in 1992 claimed that his motive was to scare the refugees, which – according to him – 'made too many demands on Swedish society'.[90] One of the two men, who also set fire to a refugee centre in Tyringe in October 1990, claimed at his trial that he 'could not stand Arabs'. The second perpetrator added that he had 'nothing against foreigners, not more than people in general'. He had, however, agreed to help his friend to 'burn out refugees' on the condition that there were no people in the house they set fire to. Inside the building that the two men eventually set fire to, there were actually eleven people, including six children.[91]

In June 1990 two young men in Mellösa, after provoking a fight with a gypsy family, set fire to their house. The fire caused severe material damage. In its verdict the court stated: 'Under no circumstances can this violence [from members of the victim family while trying to get rid of the two men] in any way excuse or even be regarded as an explanation to the acts of the accused. Behind this is instead, without any doubt, an unpleasant element of xenophobia.'[92]

The police reports indicate that few of the actual perpetrators are organised racists, xenophobics or right-wing extremists. But is there a correlation between the number of racist/xenophobic crimes and the level of activism, that is, number of local branches, distribution of propaganda material, etc., in the various regions? The figures below show a comparison between the number of racist/xenophobic crimes 1993 and the level of racist/anti-immigration activity 1990–94.

TABLE 3

COMPARISON OF THE NUMBER OF RACIST/XENOPHOBIC CRIMES IN 1993, AND THE LEVEL OF RACIST/ANTI-IMMIGRATION ACTIVITY, 1990-1994.[93]

County (by official letter symbols)	Number of racist/xenophobic crimes 1993	Level of activity 1990–94
AB	223	High
C	26	Low
D	19	Low
E	25	High
F	25	High
G	18	High
H	15	High
I	7	Negligible
K	38	High
L	19	Low
M	58	High
N	34	Negligible
O	72	High
P	60	High
R	18	Low
S	60	High
T	19	Low
U	59	High
X	15	Low
W	72	High
Y	92	Negligible
Z	10	Negligible
AC	20	Negligible
BD	29	Negligible

The figures show that in several counties with a fairly high rate of racist/xeno-phobic crimes, there is also a high level of activity among various racist/extreme nationalistic groups. That is, however, not the case in certain regions in the north of Sweden, which have a fairly high level of crimes, but no noticeable activity at all. There seems nonetheless to be some correlation in the western and southern parts of Sweden, while the case is the opposite in the north of Sweden, where racist groups show virtually no activity at all. The existence of xenophobic and racist activities is, as the figure shows, of course not the only explanation as to why violence occurs more in certain regions. Other dimensions, such as unemployment levels, structural changes within the local labour market, the religious make-up of the area, the number of immigrants and refugees (and from which part of the world they came), and local protest groups must be added too in order to get a more complete picture of this complex problem.

The 1992 report made by the Swedish security police also includes a survey of 92 suspected/sentenced perpetrators of other crimes with racist/xenophobic overtones, that is, attacks on targets other than asylum seekers and refugee hostels.

> A number of the suspected/sentenced perpetrators have contacts in right wing circles. In most cases they belong to gangs surrounding an individual who is active in extreme right-wing organisations and harbour racist and right-wing extremist ideas. The perpetrators are, however, seldom politically active. They often have a criminal record before they 'find' VAM or other extreme right-wing organisations.[94]

The survey indicates that crimes with racist/xenophobic motives against members of minority groups, to a higher extent than attacks against refugee hostels and asylum seekers, are committed by gangs surrounding organised racists. It should also be pointed out that some of the criminal activities that can be traced to organised individuals, or can be said to be the result of organised activities, are threats and harassment against public persons, local politicians, officials at the immigration bureau, homosexuals, journalists, intellectuals, anti-racists etc. However, the majority of offences involving threats and harassment of a racist/xenophobic nature directed at these categories of targets are committed by individuals with no connection whatsoever to any extremist organisation.

A conclusion of these surveys is that attacks against refugee hostels and asylum seekers are only rarely the work of organised racists/xenophobics. The increase in serious violence is not part of a directed campaign from race ideologists or extreme nationalist organisations, but the work of local unorganised individuals with racist or xenophobic ideas. In some cases the attacks on the local refugee hostels and asylum seekers are the end result of a long history of escalating hostility in the local community: hostility from local politicians who oppose the establishment of a refugee centre in the community, from local protest groups against the refugee hostel, and from shop owners or restaurants who refuse to let the refugees have access to their establishments. Setting fire to the refugee hostels could to a certain extent be seen as the most extreme expression of an existing mentality within the local community.[95]

In the following three examples, this process will be described. During

Spring 1990 the small community of Kimstad, on the outskirts of the city of Norrköping, became nationally known because of local protests against the establishment of a refugee hostel in the community. Kimstad figured daily in the television news and in the newspapers. In February 1990 an information meeting about the planned refugee hostel turned into chaos with some participants screaming racist slogans. According to some sources, members of the extreme nationalistic and anti-immigration organisations SD and *Framstegspartiet* took part in the meeting. They were, however, not from the local community, but had travelled to the meeting in order to try to exploit politically the local hostility. During Spring 1990 a local politician from *Moderata Samlingspartiet* (The Conservatives) joined the protesters.[96] The protests in Kimstad culminated when someone set fire to the refugee hostel, which was partly burnt down. The perpetrator or perpetrators were never found. After the fire and the refugees' subsequent arrival, there has been no sign of protest in the community. According to Leif Stenberg, the fright from the incident remains: 'Some still don't say hallo to each other ... Many ties of friendship have broken among grown ups as well as among youngsters. People don't want to talk about what they think about the refugee question any more.'[97]

The incidents in Kimstad do not only serve as an example of the underlying processes, partly stirred up by of the media, which culminated in an attack on the local refugee centre. The Kimstad example also shows how anti-immigration organisations, which previously had not existed in the local community, try to exploit politically the existing local hostility towards the refugee hostel. Similar cases occurred in other places during 1989–91. Attacks have frequently been carried out where there have been strong local protests against the establishment of a refugee hostel. The example of Kimstad, however, differs from the pattern in many other small communities in one important respect: in Kimstad the anti-immigration groups never managed to establish themselves politically. They disappeared from the local political scene after the attack on the refugee hostel.

The following example – the town of Mariestad – shows the opposite: how an anti-immigration/racist organisation – active for decades in the area – was 'reactivated' when the issue of establishing a refugee centre became part of the political agenda.[98] In May 1990 a refugee centre opened in Mariestad. During the autumn it was turned into a refugee hostel. The hostel issue was a recurring topic in the letters-to-the-editor columns in the local newspapers. The animated debate heated up when a local politician from the conservative party raised the question of whether the town should take any more refugees. During the debate in the local papers, SD, a group which had been active in the area for a long time, started a propaganda campaign, which led to a new round in the letters-to-the-editor columns. This time the debate was carried on mainly between the youth organisation of the Social Democratic Party and SD. In late May 1990 a series of attacks was launched. The day before the opening of the refugee hostel someone set fire to a tractor tyre at the steps to the refugee hostel. The night after, a shop owned by migrants was petrol-bombed.

As a response to the attacks, local anti-racists held demonstrations. They received bomb threats and a bombing took place at the facilities of a local Free Church,[99] whose members were involved in solidarity work for the refugees. During the summer of 1990 several attacks occurred, directed against local companies and schools. Then finally, a couple of men with ties to extremist organisations (NRP and SD) were arrested for the bombing of a local school.[100] At first the accused confessed to the attack.[101] Two of the accused later withdrew their confessions – while the third suspect was con-victed for the bombing of the school.[102]

After the wave of attacks during the summer of 1990, things returned to normal. The summer of 1991 set off a new series of attacks – this time against large election posters and one school.[103] The perpetrators were never caught. SD and smaller more militant groups still maintain a relatively high level of activity in the town.

In the small village of Överum – a local community with a population of approximately 2,000 inhabitants – hostility toward the 250 refugees at the nearby refugee hostel increased during the spring of 1990. In the summer of 1990 the tense situation exploded into riots between refugees and the local population. Several people were injured during the riots. The police set up day and night surveillance of the area in order to stop the violence. The local police force also started to investigate the underlying reasons for the riots and could establish that the hostility from the locals in Överum had its roots in 'anger concerning the behaviour of certain refugees', who were said to have stolen goods in shops and gardens, borrowed a lifeboat for a fishing trip, etc. This information was new to the police, since nobody had reported the inci-dents to the police. The locals nevertheless claimed that the police were unin-terested in their problems and ignorant. The police, the Bureau of Immigration and the local council set up a contact group in which they also chose to include 'some of the more loudmouthed critics from the local popu-lation'. The result of the group's work was that all crimes were reported and prosecuted. Education in the Swedish legal system was provided at the refugee hostel. The distrust of some of the refugees turned out to be so deep that they were moved to other refugee hostels. The riots were over in a cou-ple of days and the police considered the situation as stable after one to two months. The contact group, however, continued its work despite the fact that the immediate crisis was overcome.[104]

The examples above point to the existence of a potential for violence in the local communities – a potential due either to existing extremist groups or to an accelerating local hostility with its roots in a breakdown of communication between the locals and the authorities, combined with a growing distrust of the refugees or a combination of both factors.

Four Case Studies

The following survey is focused on racist/xenophobic criminality between 1985 and 1992 in four areas of Sweden.[105] The survey is based on verdicts and in some cases preliminary investigations made by the local police. The survey does not cover all crimes of the above-mentioned categories in the areas, because it is not possible to get information about the total number of crimes with racist/xenophobic motives. Relevant cases cannot be extracted from official crime statistics, because no separate code exists for these crimes, apart from the category 'incitement of racial hatred'. The survey has therefore been limited to cases where it has been possible to obtain court material from the incidents in question.[106] The survey is also restricted to convictions until the turn of the year 1992–93. The cities of Karlstad/Säffle, Växjö, Göteborg/Borås and Malmö have been chosen because in these areas organised as well as unorganised racist activities can be found. The aim of the study has been to explore the possible interplay between the two and to determine whether the crimes committed by organised racists differ from the crimes committed by unorganised racists.[107] It should be noted, however, that not all activists in these cities are included in the survey. There are two reasons for this. First, not all activists have criminal records, secondly, not all activists are known to the author. This survey is part of a larger research project which covers the whole country and the years 1980–94.[108] The perpetrators have been divided into three categories: *Activists* are individuals with a long documented history of activism in various racist/national socialist or extreme nationalist groups. *Sympathisers* are individuals belonging to groups surrounding activists. These individuals are distinguished according to two premises. Either they commit racist/xenophobic crimes together with activists; and/or racist or extreme nationalistic material, such as magazines, stickers, books, correspondence etc., are listed among the items found during the police search of the perpetrator's home. *Unorganised perpetrators* are individuals where no connection to racist/nationalistic groups can be established.

SWEDEN   141

The Karlstad/Säffle Group

This area is characterised by a long history of organised national socialism and hostility towards migrants and refugees. In some communities there is an unbroken chain of organised national socialism and racism which goes back to the mid-1920s. Between the 1950s and the 1970s most of the activities were restricted to the hidden subculture of 'White Power'. It was in the 1980s and early 1990s that the organisations took their activities out into the open. At the same time, as the propaganda activities became visible, racist-motivated criminality increased. During the first half of the 1980s the anti-immigration organisation BSS had an active local branch in Karlstad. NRP also had some activities going on in the city.[109] During the era of the *Vit Rebell* magazine at the end of the 1980s, the local racist scene, whose members had grown tired of NRP as well as SD, went under the name of *Karlstad SA*.[110] In 1985 anti-Semitic propaganda was spread in the area by a group called *Frispråkig Nationell Förening* (The Outspoken National Association).[111] In June 1990 a faction of the local racist scene formed a branch of *Kreativistens Kyrka*.[112] In 1989 members and sympathisers of SD could be found in Karlstad.[113] The same year Säffle was the target for SD's propaganda campaigns, and a local branch of the party was established the following year.[114]

In the following, some examples of criminal offences with racist/xenophobic motives found in the area will be presented. In October 1987 two Karlstad activists attacked a young Swede who had infuriated them the previous year by pulling down a sticker from the anti-immigration organisation BSS.[115] In November 1990 the Jewish cemetery was vandalised.[116] The perpetrators were never found. In December the same year two drunken young men from Säffle threatened some refugees with a knife. Later the same night the young men tried to set fire to the refugee centre. At the trial they claimed that there were 'too many immigrants' in the city and that their aim had been to 'scare them away'.[117] During the night of 11 April 1992 four drunk skinheads harassed and injured one migrant and one Swede, smashed the windows of a café belonging to the Swedish church and a shop for immigrants. Two of the skinheads later returned and set fire to the place. Later the same night they set fire to several entrance halls in a housing complex where many immigrant families lived.[118]

The survey of the Karlstad/Säffle group includes 19 convicted perpetrators, all men, among whom five can be considered as hardcore racist activists.[119] The total number of convictions for the whole group is 57; ten of the 19 individuals in the survey were convicted more than once, one individual a total of 12 times; only two in the group were convicted only of so-called 'ordinary criminality', that is, crimes without racist/xenophobic/ideological motives,[120] nine were convicted only of crimes related to either their ideolog-

ical beliefs or their racist/xenophobic values; the remaining nine were convicted for both 'ideological' or value-related crimes and ordinary criminal
offences.

The more or less ideologically motivated criminality mainly involves
theft, grand theft, stealing of weapons and military equipment, Xerox
machines, etc., which can be used for political activities. This category also
includes assault and battery, where the victims were migrants, refugees and
local anti-racists; damage, threats, and arson. These kinds of offences were
found also among the unorganised perpetrators. The so-called ordinary criminality in the group includes car thefts, assaults, forgery, illegal driving,
receiving stolen goods, reckless driving, assault of public servants, offences
against the law of public military service, harassment, damage, etc.[121] The
results of the study of the Karlstad/Säffle group follow the same pattern as the
previously presented surveys made by the Swedish security police, that the
groups or individuals around the organised racists commit a large proportion
of the racist crimes. It, must, however, be pointed out that there are several
serious cases of assault and battery that can be directly linked to the perpetrators' racist ideas. Three of the five activists were convicted for 'ordinary'
criminal offences. Organised racists/extreme nationalists have also on at least
two occasions participated in direct attacks against the local refugee hostel
and against asylum seekers. Part of the ideologically motivated criminality is
directed against Swedish anti-racists. Another share of it consists of stealing
weapons and military equipment which can be used for political activities.

The Göteborg/Borås Group

The seaport city of Göteborg on the west coast became a centre for anti-
Semitic activities early on. Between 1919 and 1931 Barthold Lundén, a leading Swedish anti-Semite, published the highly anti-Semitic paper *Vidi*. In
1923 Lundén founded *Svenska Antisemitiska Föreningen* (Sweden's Anti-
Semitic Organisation).[122] During the 1920s and 1930s Göteborg also became
a centre for national socialist activities. After the war the national socialist
organisations continued their existence as a hidden subculture. Alongside the
national socialists, *Nysvenska Rörelsen* (the New Swedish Movement, NSR)
had a local branch in Göteborg from the 1940s onwards.[123] The organisation
held meetings in their own neighborhoods in the city until the late 1980s.[124]
During the first years of the 1990s the activities declined. The NSR, howeve-
er, still has some activities in the city. But since the death of their leader Per
Engdahl in May 1994, the group has started to orient itself toward the racist
counterculture.[125] During the 1950s a group called *NS-Information* (National
Swedish Information) distributed anti-Semitic propaganda to schoolchild-
ren.[126] And during the 1960s Göteborg became the centre of the activities of

NRP.[127] NRP, however, lost its appeal to the younger generations after the trials against members and former members of the NRP branch in Göteborg 1985–87, when the NRP leadership distanced itself from the defendants. One group of former NRP members carried on with limited activities under the name of *Nationalsocialistiska Arbetarepartiet*.[128] During the *Vit Rebell* era the group existed under the name *Göteborgs SA*.[129] The Göteborg group also calls themselves *Göteborgs and Borås SA* or *Västfront SA*. *Västfront SA* also includes a group of activists from the nearby inland city of Borås. In Göteborg, there is also a group called *Unga Nationalsocialister i Sverige* (Young National Socialists in Sweden). Alongside the revolutionary groups, Göteborg has also seen increasing activity from parliamentarian anti-immigration parties during the 1980s, and a local branch of *BSS* was formed early in the decade.[130] *Sverigepartiet* – the forerunner of *Sverigedemokraterna* was established in 1986 and an active SD branch has existed ever since.[131] During the early 1990s there has been an animated debate about the location of a mosque in the city. The anti-mosque side includes both the local SD branch, some clergy of the Swedish state church and a local populist party, *Hisingens kommunalförening*. The organisation ran in the church council elections in 1991 with the anti-mosque stance as the main issue, and was very successful (it obtained 50 per cent of the seats on the parish council).[132]

Crimes motivated either by xenophobic or racist ideas have continued in Göteborg since the so-called NRP trials in the mid-1980s. In the following, a few examples of this type of criminal offences will be described. On 30 May 1990 two young men threw Molotov cocktails at the refugee hostel in Partille, a suburb of Göteborg. In November 1991 the same men attacked with explosives another refugee hostel in the Göteborg area. The bomb caused substantial material damage. During the trial the accused claimed that they themselves and persons close to them on several occasions had been assaulted and robbed by foreigners. One of the perpetrators stated at the trial that 'He wanted to scare people and get attention and from some kind of demonstration show that something was wrong'.[133] On the night of 12 August 1990 two members of the local racist scene arrived at the entrance of Touch, a local club for homosexuals, harassing visitors of the club. One of the activists shouted that he wanted to see 'blood float' and 'my grandfather had people like you gassed in the concentration camps 40 years ago'. Guests and members of the staff tried to chase the two activists away. The activists, however, surrounded one of their pursuers and stabbed him to death.[134] Activists from local racist movements still – sometimes almost daily – hang outside Touch, threatening, beating and harassing staff and guests.[135] In November 1992 a gang of skinheads – among them several leading activists – started to sing racist songs at a trolley bus, harassing black passengers, attacking and beating a immigrant.

The accused activists denied the charges, and stated that they were merely 'singing battle songs on the tram and none of the passengers minded'. Two activists were convicted, however.[136] In July 1992 a gang of Borås skinheads attacked four refugees from Somalia, who were severely beaten and badly injured.[137] In 1990 letter bombs were sent to two well known anti-racists in Göteborg.[138] The following year, a powerful letter bomb was sent to a married couple well known for their anti-racist activities.[139] Those responsible for the letter bombs have not yet been found.

A survey of 42 convicted activist/sympathisers and unorganised perpetrators from Göteborg and Borås between the years 1985 and 1992, all men, shows that 15 individuals were sentenced during the so-called NRP trials of 1985–87. Six of them are still active in various racist organisations and one in SD. There is no evidence of any political activity for the years following the convictions for the other eight former NRP activists. The total number of convictions for the entire group is 89. Half (21) of the perpetrators have more than one sentence and the largest number of individual convictions is seven. Nineteen offenders were convicted of both 'ordinary' criminal offences and crimes motivated either by ideological or xenophobic ideas. Eight individuals were convicted only of 'ordinary' criminal offences.[140] Only 15 offenders had convictions for crimes related to xenophobic or racist values; among this group, seven were convicted during the NRP trials and have since then not been convicted of any criminal offences. The so-called ordinary criminality basically involves assault and battery, narcotic crimes,[141] grand theft, grand forgery, stealing, damage, car theft, arson, attempted theft, illegal entrance, dealing in stolen goods, illegal driving, drunk driving, assault on public officials, violation of the military laws, illegal threats, etc. The ideologically motivated or xenophobic crimes were homicide, preparations for assault and battery, threats, misconduct, preparation for damage, arson, forgery of documents, assault and battery, grievous assault and battery, incitement to danger, armed robbery,[142] damage, theft, illegal possession of arms, illegal entry constituting public danger and attempted murder.[143]

The Göteborg group is described by other activists as special.[144] The group is the largest and best organised in the country. The activists also have their own premises –what they call an 'SA hostel'. The group is also the faction – apart from *Kreativistens Kyrka*, which has taken the hardest stand on the question of sobriety.[145] The number of drunken participants in public demonstrations has been reduced to a minimum during the last couple of years. In this matter the West coast activists differ from those from Stockholm.[146] The West Coast group also seems to differ regarding the nature of criminality. This group has the largest number of serious crimes with ideological motives, being responsible for two homicides of homosexuals, serious cases of assault and battery, one attempted murder and arson attacks. The Göteborgs/Borås group also have, with a few individual exceptions, a lower degree of so-called ordinary crimes. Of the 42 perpetrators in the survey, 19 can be regarded as organised activists; 13 of these have a long history of documented activities in various organisations, while 6 have been added during the last couple of years. Within this group of activists, the age differences are also larger than in activist groups from other areas – varying from individuals born in the 1940s to individuals born in the mid-1970s.[147] No activist has been convicted for attacks against refugee hostels, which is in accordance with the police reports.[148]

Regarding the question of terror as a political weapon, members of the hardcore activist group responded: 'We are totally against terrorism, terror affects the innocent, the national socialists have always been against that, but the Jews are not innocent.' However, referring to attacks on refugee hostels, one member ironically added: 'They [the refugees] are not my people, they have no business being here in the first place, so if someone burns down a refugee hostel or two, what the hell .... They should be used to it anyway.' Another activist obviously despised the perpetrators of these crimes and stated: 'Most of the people [who have] done it, have been stupid, ignorant bloody peasants, who cry during the police interrogations that they were just so drunk and if they had been sober they would never done it; they are nothing to take seriously'.[149]

The survey indicates that part of the old NRP branch is still politically active. There has been, however, substantial recruitment of new members to the group during the early 1990s. The Göteborgs/Borås group have managed to create a relatively disciplined activist group with a profile of their own. Surrounding these hardcore groups, sympathisers with racist/xenophobic ideas can be found. Among the individuals in the survey there are also unorganised perpetrators with no known connection either to the activist group or to sympathisers. Among the crimes the activists have committed, there are, as in the case of Karlstad/Säffle, thefts of weapons, explosives, etc., which could be used in the political activities. Members of the local homosexual community are often found among the victims. The victim group also includes individuals working in sex shops, the homeless, drug addicts, political opponents (mainly communists and liberals), alcoholics, adopted children, anti-racists, immigrants and – in one case – members of the Church of Scientology.

The Växjö Group

The first branch of a national socialist party was founded in Växjö 1934. It was a local branch of *Nationalsocialistiska Arbetarepartiet*, which existed until 1944. During the late 1940s *Nysvenska Rörelsen* had certain activities in the inland city.[150] In August 1963 the former corporal 'Svensson' was charged with grand forgery, threats, abusing a public servant and incitement of racial hatred. He was also the leader and founder of a by now long forgotten organisation called *Nationella Nyhedniska Fascistpartiet* (The National Neo-Pagan Fascist Party), founded in January 1963.[151] 'Svensson' then started to distribute a rather odd collection of flyers in the area. The party leader also started to send hate mail to public servants. In the letters he threatened people with acts of reprisals the day the party had gained power.[152]

'Svensson' was not the only one conducting racist/national socialist activities in the area. He had competition from other extremist parties. The NRP was by that time established in the area. The local NRP branch was headed by Nils Erik Rydström – another eccentric character in the history of Swedish national socialism.[153] But according to the police, neither the NRP nor *Nationella Nyhedniska Fascistpartiet* had any major success in the area.[154] According to the police interrogation, 'Svensson' refused to accept any other label for himself than 'resistance fighter'. He considered himself a 'political prisoner', harassed and imprisoned by the 'corrupt society', which acted on orders from the 'Jewish world conspiracy'. He refused to volunteer any kind of information regarding the party, its activities and members. The number of members was most likely limited to himself and a handful of others. 'Svensson' was suspected of a weapon burglary in Växjö in November 1962 because of the summons he had given members/sympathisers to collect weapons to use in the political activities. The police could, however, not tie him to the crime. The party leader explained that he had not intended that members should collect firearms, 'only' truncheons, knives and explosives. The members were encouraged to carry knives and truncheons to meetings in case they were attacked.[155] The leader of *Nationella Nyhedniska Fascistpartiet* was eventually sentenced to psychiatric treatment. It did not, however, restrict his political activities. From the psychiatric ward at the prison of Malmö on the south-west coast he managed in 1964 to distribute large amounts of anti-Semitic propaganda around the country.[156]

It is interesting to note that despite the criminal offences 'Svensson' was charged with and his perception of the society and his ideological beliefs – and apart from his bizarre ideas about his own role within the party[157] – 'Svensson' was regarded by the court and the media as a raving maniac. Almost 30 years later individuals stating that they are 'political prisoners' imprisoned by the 'Zionist Occupational Government' and who publicly express their ideas about a 'Jewish world conspiracy' in court are looked upon not as individuals in need of psychiatric treatment, but as ordinary everyday criminals or political activists. Until the late 1980s psychiatric evaluations in many cases were ordered on individuals charged with incitement of racial hatred, especially in cases where the defendant had expressed ideas of the existence of a 'Jewish world conspiracy', etc., in order to determine whether they were suffering from any mental disorders or not. This does not seem to be the case today, which indicates that a change in attitudes towards these kind of activists has taken place.

Nationella Nyhedniska Fascistpartiet disappeared from the local extremist scene but the NRP continued its activities. In the beginning of the 1980s its level of activity was relatively high. In 1986 some Växjö activists were sentenced in connection with the so-called NRP trials in Göteborg. Among other things, they were convicted of threats to local journalists, immigrants and anti-racists, harassment and damage.[158] Some of the activists continued their political activities after the trials and became members of the race ideological network in due time. In addition to the militant race ideologists, SD has established a branch in the city – in fact one of the most active SD branches in the country.[159]

In the following paragraphs, a few examples of the nature of the racist/xenophobic criminality in the area will be presented. In 1989 one active sympathiser – who also belongs to the racist underground in Karlstad – together with two other skinheads attacked an 89 year old hunter with the purpose of stealing his hunting rifles.[160] In January 1992 four individuals attacked the premises of an organisation for homosexuals. Two of the attackers wore masks and one was armed with a machete. The gang vandalised the club and physically attacked club members. At the trial all four claimed that they were innocent. They were convicted, however.[161] The previous year one activist – member of various racist organisations since the mid 1980s – was sentenced for assault and battery, having beaten his victim at a private party. The reason for the attack was that the victim did not share his national socialist opinion about homosexuals and migrants.[162]

A survey of the nine convicted perpetrators in Växjö, all men, gives the following result:[163] The total number of convictions was 28; six perpetrators were convicted more then once, one having been sentenced nine times and one seven times. Five of the perpetrators included in the survey belonged to the group of NRP members convicted during 1985–87. Two of them have not been involved in any ideologically motivated criminality since these earlier convictions.[164] Two of the convicted NRP activists have continued their criminal as well as their political activities. Since the NRP trials they have, among other things, been convicted of assault and battery of homosexuals. Six perpetrators were convicted of so-called ordinary crimes as well as ideologically motivated crimes, of these one was sentenced in the NRP trials.

In a broader sense, the offences could be said to be motivated by ideological or xenophobic ideas. They involved threats, harassment, theft, damage, forgery, false alarm, assault and battery, illegal entrance and arson. The so-called ordinary criminality of the group mainly involved theft, car theft, attempted theft, damage, illegal possession of arms, illegal driving, drunk driving, threats, assault and battery, burglary, careless driving, narcotic crimes, etc.[165]

In contrast to the Karlstad/Säffle group, the survey of the Växjö group shows that no attacks on refugee hostels or asylum seekers have taken place – at least not that anyone has been convicted of. The arson attack was directed at the office of a communist organisation in Göteborg, and took place in connection with the so-called NRP trials. The violence which has occurred has mainly been directed against members of the local homosexual community and local anti-racists. It should also be stated that the two individuals known to be hard core activists have a substantial ordinary criminal record as well. The activist and sympathiser group is also rather eccentric. Members have for instance legally changed their first names to Himmler, Göring, Goebbels etc. They are also in the habit of driving around in the area in replicas of SS uniforms. Among the criminal offences tied to the activist group, there is – as in the case of the Karlstad/Säffle group – theft of weapons which could be used in the political struggle. It should, however, be stressed that weapons can be used in ordinary criminal activities as well. It is not, especially since the group is heavily criminal, necessarily so that the weapons should be used for political means.

The Malmö Group

The first anti-Semitic organisation in the southern seaport city of Malmö was founded as early as 1924 – *Organisationen Svenske* (The Swede Organisation), headed by Gottfrid Mortens. During the 1930s the city was the centre for activities of national socialists from the south of Sweden, and in the early 1950s Malmö became the centre for *Nysvenska Rörelsen*. The NRP has been established in Malmö for decades.[166] Malmö is also the centre of the faction of *Sveriges Nationella Förbund* which is a part of NSDAP-AO.[167] In the early 1990s *Malmö VAM* was founded. Since the late 1960s Malmö has also been the centre of *Svenska Folkets Väl* (The Swedish League), which at the present mainly distributes leaflets and stickers. *Svenska Folkets Väl* first came to public attention in 1968 when the organisation tried to register as a political party. However, it never managed to collect the necessary 1000 names required of an organisation to be allowed to register as a political party.[168] Originally, the organisation was a party of discontent, and the main issue was environmental protection. During later years the main issues have become anti-immigration and anti-abortion.[169] In the early 1980s BSS was established in Malmö.[170] They were followed by *Sverigepartiet* and later *Sverige-*

demokraterna.[171] Malmö is also the centre for *Skånepartiet,* under the leadership of Carl P. Herslow. The party was founded in 1978 and ran in the 1979 election, with little success. In the 1985 election *Skånepartiet* had the question of immigration as its main platform, and took five seats on the local council. Ideologically *Skånepartiet* is a local populist party of discontent.[172] In the 1988 election, the party lost two of its seats in the local council.[173]

In the following, some cases with racist or xenophobic motives will be presented. On midsummer's eve 1988 a 14-year-old immigrant boy was severely beaten by a gang of youngsters. Among the perpetrators there was a leading local functionary from the SD.[174] In June 1990 five youths, four boys and one girl, set fire to the Serbian Orthodox church in Malmö. They had originally planned a cross burning, something they had done the previous year. In the verdict the following statement by the court is to be found: 'The cross burning was to X and his friends a way of demonstrating against the official immigrant policy.' When the group did not manage to collect enough material for making a cross, they got the idea to set fire to the church instead. According to some of the perpetrators, the aim was not to burn it down but to 'mark it'.[175] In January 1991 a gang of skinheads attacked and assaulted a young Swedish couple outside a grocery. The incident took place after what one of the convicted skinheads characterised as a 'political discussion'.[176] In 1991 a 23-year-old skinhead from the city of Kalmar was shot to death by a police officer during a fight outside a hot-dog stand.[177] The incident, which occurred in the early hours of 30 November 1991, the same day as the yearly nationalist anniversary of the death of King Charles XII, aroused strong feelings among the skinheads and extreme nationalists. Some time after the incident a local activist printed and distributed a flyer in which the police officer was said to be a 'murderer in the service of the state'. The flyer also included a photograph, the address and other personal information about the police officer. A 19-year-old skinhead activist was charged with instigation of rebellion, but charges were dismissed. The court stated:

> The background for the flyer is the incident on 30 November of the previous year, when a skinhead was shot to death in Malmö by police officer, XX. YY felt very badly about the case. According to him the police investigation was unnecessarily prolonged. He had the impression that the authorities were trying to cover up the incident ... The purpose of the flyer was not to encourage anyone to commit a crime against XX. Firstly YY wishes that XX should be charged with the serious crime he has committed. If you have shot a human being to death you are a murderer. It is not only important that a trial be held. It is equally important to get people to commit themselves in the case, which has the character of a miscarriage of justice. They can do this by writing in the papers,

exercising their right to vote, call on politicians, etc. ... The flyer ... can according to the court be interpreted as an exhortation to people to act up against lacking rule of law etc. ... If, however, the receivers of a text like this one have a spirit of violence, it can be interpreted as an exhortation to crime. It can, however, according to the court, not be proved that the individuals that YY has distributed the flyer to are violent to any appreciable degree.[178]

The racist and extreme nationalist groups, as well as the militant anti-racist groups have for decades distributed prints and flyers with personal information about disliked individuals or published photographs, names, addresses, telephone numbers, etc., of political opponents, public servants and others in various magazines, as well as, in the case of extreme nationalist groups, personal information about members of immigrant or refugee communities who have committed crimes against Swedes.[179] The dismissal of the charges against the Malmö skinhead implies that this is a perfectly legal way of conducting political activity, unless it is directly said in the text that person X or Y should be subject to harassment, assault and battery, etc. The tendency to print personal information about disliked individuals has increased during the early 1990s. Information of this kind is also often to be found in racist as well as in anti-racist electronic bulletin board systems (BBS).

A survey of the 16 convicted Malmö activists/sympathisers and unorganised perpetrators with xenophobic/racist values – 15 men and one women – gives the following result: the total number of convictions – 31, six perpetrators convicted more than once, and the largest number of convictions for one single individual – six. Eight perpetrators were convicted for so-called ordinary criminality, as well as criminality related either to their political conviction or to a generally hostile attitude towards migrants/refugees. Only six had convictions for racist/xenophobic crimes only, and two were convicted only for so-called ordinary criminality. Two of the individuals in this survey can be regarded as organised hardcore activists. The so-called ordinary criminality found within the group consists of attempted theft, assault and battery, dealing in stolen goods, car theft, damage, assault and battery of a public servant, and illegal entrance. In a broader sense of the word, criminal offences can be related either to the perpetrators' ideological conviction or general hostility towards migrant/refugees. These offences consist of arson, assault and battery and harassment.[180] A closer look at the verdicts reveals that the victim group consists of members of minority groups and Swedes who have expressed opinions regarding the official immigration policy different from that of the perpetrator. The Serbian Orthodox church has twice been attacked, but by different perpetrators. The two activists included in this survey were convicted of so-called ordinary as well as ideologically motivated criminality. As in the Karlstad/Säffle case, some of the street violence offences have been committed by gangs close to organised racists. No Malmö activist has, however, been convicted of any attacks on refugee hostels. Offenders already convicted of such attacks, moreover, have after their convictions started to orient themselves towards the activist group and its sympathisers.[181] The Malmö group also differs from other groups in another aspect: Among activists or sympathisers there are no known cases of thefts of weapons or explosives that might be used in the political struggle.

Similarities, Differences and General Tendencies

FIGURE 2
AGE DISTRIBUTION BASED ON THE YEAR OF BIRTH AMONG 86 CONVICTED
ACTIVISTS/SYMPATHISERS AND UNORGANISED PERPETRATORS IN
KARLSTAD/SÄFFLE, VÄXJÖ, GÖTEBORG/BORÅS AND MALMÖ

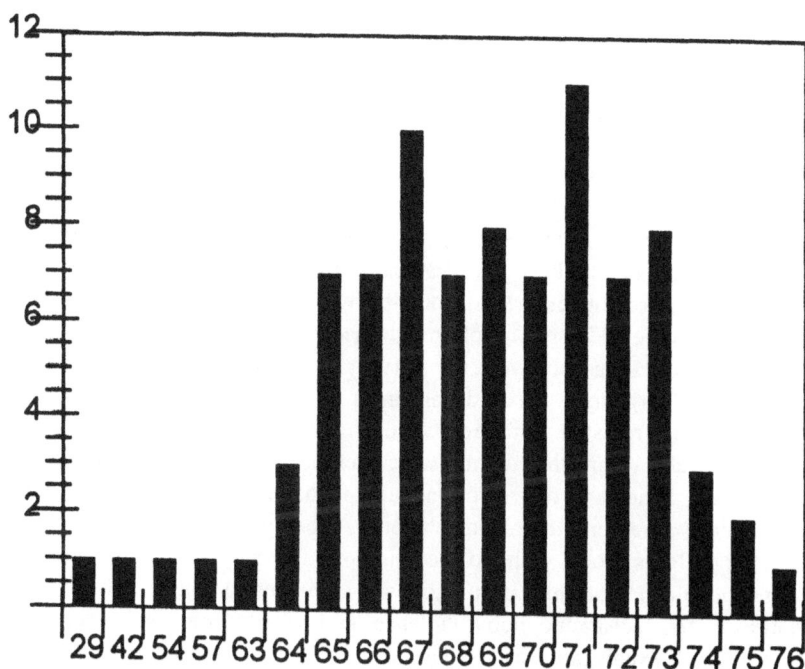

The diagram indicates that the majority of the perpetrators were born between 1965 and 1973 – all those born before 1960 are to be found in the Göteborgs/Borås group. The total number of convictions adds up to 205 verdicts, which gives an average of two convictions per individual. The figures below show the distribution of different categories of perpetrators.

TABLE 4
DISTRIBUTION OF DIFFERENT CATEGORIES OF PERPETRATORS.

Individuals with one conviction	Individuals with more than one conviction	Convicted of ordinary and xenophobic crimes	Convicted only of xenophobic crimes
42	44	43	33

The number of activists included in this survey, individuals with a documented history of involvement in racist/extreme nationalistic groups, is 28, approximately one third of the investigated population. No activists, apart from the Karlstad/Säffle group, have been convicted of attacks against refugee hostels. The result of this survey indicates the same pattern as the previously presented reports made by the security police, i.e., the attacks against refugees centres and refugees have only in exceptional cases been committed by organised racists or ethnocentrics. The survey also points to differences among the various groups. The Växjö group consists of very few organised racists who have a substantial criminal record. The main target for the group is the local homosexual population. There is no evidence of attacks on either immigrants or refugees found in the survey of the Växjö group. Surrounding the activists there is a group of sympathisers with more or less formulated racist or xenophobic values. The Karlstad/Säffle and Malmö group also consists of a hard-core of activists, surrounded by groups of sympathisers. To this pattern should be added groups of unorganised perpetrators. However, there is no evidence of contacts between the activists and the unorganised offenders.

The Göteborg/Borås group differs from the pattern of the other groups. This group has registered the most serious crimes with ideological motives: two homicides where the victims were members of the local homosexual community, some cases of grievous assault and battery, one attempted murder and a series of arson attacks. In relation to other groups in the survey, the Göteborgs/Borås group, with the exception of a few perpetrators, has a lower degree of so-called ordinary criminality and a broader distribution of age. The victims of the racist/xenophobic violence tend to be asylum seekers, immigrants, homosexuals, anti-racists. The result of the police reports from 1990 to 1993 and the survey of perpetrators presented above corresponds well with surveys made in other countries. Christopher T. Husbands' study of convicted activists in the former West Germany in 1981–85 shows for instance that the typical perpetrator is a man of approximately 21 years of age and that 95 per cent of the convicted activists were men.[182] Husbands, however, points out that even if direct physical attacks against immigrants/refugees causing bodily harm or material damage often is carried out by younger men, there are other types of incidents which could be classified as racist/xenophobic. Husbands points to the following:

> For example, there are some older and more middle class racists who do not attack black people on the streets or in their homes, even if they might have done so had they been younger and not middle class ... However, they may not be above making malicious and anonymous reports to child-protection agencies or environmental health services about purported child abuse or infraction of health regulations either by individual black households or perhaps by ethnically owned restaurants.[183]

This type of harassment described by Husbands is harder to investigate than actual physical attacks, but it points to the possibility that different age groups or social groups choose different methods to express a similar dislike. The younger perpetrator of an attack on a refugee hostel is not necessarily more hostile than the older man or woman who sends anonymous notes to various authorities concerning their immigrant neighbour.

Long traditions of organised racist or extreme nationalism, as well as populist groups trying to exploit local dissatisfaction with the current immigration and refugee policy are apparent in the Göteborg/Borås and Malmö cases. The organised activities have in all the cities in the survey been subject to a revitalisation during the 1980s, when a new generation – born between the late 1950s and the early 1970s took over. In Malmö and Göteborg there are unbroken traditions of organised national socialist, racist and nationalistic parliamentarian activism from the early 1920s until the present day. In both cities the activities of various organisations increased in the 1980s when the younger generation of activists took over. This generational shift took place at the same time as public opinion regarding immigration and refugee questions became more negative – which contributed to the increasing activism of organised racists and nationalists.

The organised activists of small extreme race ideologist sects can be described as the most extreme form – the horror version – of the organised hostility towards refugees and immigrants, while the unorganised perpetrators of attacks against refugee hostels can be regarded as the extremist expression of an established mentality in the area. The organised and unorganised exist in a symbioses. The perpetrators of violence – often young local men – are in most cases to be found at the intersection between the subculture of 'white power' and the general hostility towards refugees in the community.

NOTES

1. This essay is part of a project titled '*Xenophobia and Counter reactions 1930–90*', sponsored by The Swedish Council for Social Research.
2. Hans Lindquist, *Fascism idag; Förtrupper eller eftersläntare?* (Stockholm: Federativ, 1979), p.24.
3. Lindquist *Fascism*, pp.24–5.
4. Heléne Lööw, 'Återkommande mönster', *Invandrare och Minoriteter*, no. 5–6 (1990), p.29–30 ('Lööw 1990 I').
5. RAG was an SA–type of sub–organisation to the NRP.
6. Lindquist 1979 (note 2), p.26f.
7. The radical racist groups are anti–immigration only to a degree. They can accept, and sometimes even welcome, immigrants as long as the immigrants are white.
8. Tape recorded interviews with TM, 15 Aug. 1991 ('TM 15/8 1991'); members of the Göteborg branch of the revolutionary racists, 1 Sept. 1991 ('GBG 1/9 1991'); DT, 20 Sept. 1991, ('DT 20/9 1991'); LL, Dec. 1991 ('LL 12/12 1991'; 'Gregor', 12 Jan. 1992. See also Heléne Lööw, '*The Cult of Violence: The Swedish Racist Counterculture*', in Tore Bjørgo and Rob Witte (eds.), *Racist Violence in Europe* (Basingstoke: Macmillan, 1993) ('Lööw 1993 I').
9. TM, 15 Aug. 1991 (note 8).
10. See, for instance, *Sveriges Nationella Förbund, Riksorganisationen* (Winter 1992/93), p.2.
11. The term 'parliamentarian' is used here to denote organizations working within the system of electoral politics, without necessarily being represented in the parliament (*Riksdagen*). BSS was never a political party but a campaign organisation whose aim was to bring about a national referendum regarding immigration from outside of Europe. BSS was never a large organisation. In 1984 the group is said to have had around 300 active members (Source who wishes to be anonymous).
12. For the change in the public opinion, see Anders Lange and Charles Westin, *Ungdom om invandringen II: Förhållningsätt till invandring och invandrare 1993*, preliminary version (CEIFO, Stockholms universitet, Nov. 1993); idem, *Den mångtydiga toleransen; Förhållningssätt till invandring och invandrare 1993*, preliminary version (CEIFO, Stockholms universitet, Nov. 1993); Charles Westin, *Den toleranta opinionen; Inställningen till invandrare 1987* (Rapport nr 8 från DEIFO); Marie Demker, 'Stäng gränserna!?'; Svenskarnas åsikter om flyktingmottagning', in Sören Holmberg and Lennart Weibull (eds.), *Perspektiv på krisen*, (SOM No 9, 1992).
13. Nationalism among the parliamentarian groups is tightly linked to ideas such as the banning of abortion, banning of pornography, etc., and to national romantic notions about Sweden's historical traditions (cf. Heléne Lööw, 'Dom har ockuperat mitt land', *Anno 1992*).
14. Tape-recorded interview with SD functionary TR, 19 March 1991.
15. Lööw 1990 I (note 4), p.48f.
16. Cf. Judgment DB nr. 222 B 196/92, Klippans Tingsrätt; Judgment DB nr. 39 B 1286/93, Hovrätten för västra Sverige.
17. Tape–recorded interview with MS, 4 July 1994 ('MS 4 July 1994').
18. Gary Lee Yarbrough, 'Aktuellt Stormalarm', *Gryning* nr. 3 (June 1993), p 4. This imprisoned member of the Order is (honorary) editor of the ideological journal of the Swedish network.
19. Anna–Lena Lodenius and Stieg Larsson, *Extremhögern*, 1991, p.173f.
20. Judgment DB nr. 584, Jönköpings tingsrött 1990.
21. Judgment DB nr. 3027, Göta Hovrätt, 3 avd, rotel 9, 1991.
22. Cirkulär Jan. 1993, Ben Klassen Akademin.
23. *Ben Klassen Akademin*, Internal letter April 1993.
24. On Ben Klassen's death see COTC; 12 Aug. 1993, Dr Rick McCarty, PM; *Bäste vän av religionen Kreativitet*, Tommy R. Rydén, Aug. 1993. The DeVries Institute is named after the author of the book *Salubrious Living*, a book which serves as a kind of 'health guide'

SWEDEN   155

for COTC. For information about the institute, cf. *Lite Information* (Winter 1993); *Till er föräldrar, är vi nazister?* leaflets (Feb. 1994).

25. *Ansökan om medlemskap i den reorganiserade Kreativistens Kyrka*, leaflet (July 1994).
26. See Kaplan in this volume.
27. Ben Klassen, 'We must learn to distinguish clearly between our friends, our enemies, and the mugwumps', *Racial Loyalty* (May 1991), pp.1–2.
28. *Rikslarm* (Autumn issue, 1992), p.2. In Feb. 1994 RF had established itself in five districts, Stockholm, Linköping, Göteborgs and Bohus län, Bergslagen and Skåne. RF has also decided to form a *Frontorganisation* and a women's league (Letter to the author, Linköping , 4 Feb. 1994, TM).
29. *Riksfronten: Program för 2000–talet*, p.10.
30. *Detta är Riksfronten* (Introductory leaflet, Dec. 1993), p.1.
31. The local branch in Skåne, has, however, kept the name VAM.
32. 'Med lögnen som vapen' and 'Från personregistret', *Storm* nr. 9–10 (1993), p.6–7. A new issue of *Storm* has, however, during Aug.1994 been issued by a group that calls itself *Unga Nationalsocialister i Stockholm* (Young National Socialists in Stockholm).
33. The change of name, bank accounts and box addresses follows a pattern since the era of the first white power youth magazine *Streetfight*. When the authorities show interest in the paper, it disappears and the activists responsible for the paper try to wipe out all evidence, i.e., post box addresses, bank accounts, etc. in order to avoid being prosecuted for inciting racial hatred or instigating rebellion or inciting harassment and assault of people singled out as enemies of the network.
34. Jonas Ledin, 'Ledare', *Gryning*, No.3 (June 1994), p.2. On the editorial board of *Gryning*, there are three imprisoned Swedish activists and one American – Gary Yarbrough, cf. *Gryning* nr.1 (1994), p.2.
35. *Gryning* nr.2 (1993); *Wärendsbladet*, nr.11 (1993); *Blod & Åra*, nr.1 (1993), p.2. There have, however, been cases reported of leading activists who have assaulted immigrant prisoners (Judgment DB 689 B 729/91), and activists have been moved to other prisons for racists activities (anonymous sources).
36. *Motstånd, Sanningen är vårt vapen!*, leaflet (Summer 1994).
37. Kenneth Johansson, *Political violence in Sweden; A study of three cases of systematic use of political violence by Swedish organizatons and the international influences on their use of violence* (Statsvetenskapliga institutionen, Lunds Universitet, mastersutbildning, VT 1993), p.20.
38. There are no exact figures of the number of activists or sympathisers. The figure 500–700 is based on an estimation of the number of activists and more or less active sympathisers with *Riksfronten*, Ben Klassen *Akademin/Kreativistens Kyrka/DeVries institutet*, the former VAM network, NRP, members of parliamentarian groups who hold 'double memberships' and sympathisers who are older national socialists, and once were active in the pre–war and wartime organisations.
39. This becomes apparent when you compare the vocabulary used in the organisational press and by the informants with national socialist texts from the 1930s and literature from American White Power groups.
40. See, for instance, Léon Degrelle, 'Adolf Hitlers politiska testamente', *Storm* nr.9–10 (1993), p.18–19, Håkan Bengtsson, *Det hemliga världskriget: sanningen om frimureriet* (leaflet); Sven Olov Lindholm (once the leader of SSS) *Rädda den vita rasen* (a poem), p.2; 'Operation Werwolf', *Storm* nr. 3 (1991), p.3; 'Vår ära heter trohet', *Storm* nr. 4 (1991) p.4; 'Idelogisk skolning en del av kampen', ibid., nr. 4 (1991), p.5; 'Död åt ZOG', ibid., nr. 7–8 (1992), p.18; '20 April 1993', *Arisk Revolution*, nr. 1 (1993), p.5; 'Det röda packets dubbelmoral', *Arisk Revolution* nr. 1 (1993), p.9; Sven Olov Lindholm, 'Sången om Goliat', *Gryning*, nr. 1 (1994), p.1; 'Rättning och disciplin i leden', ibid., p.9; Örnulf Tigerstedt, 'Den nya puritanismen', *Rikslarm* nr. 1 (1994), p.9–11.
41. *Blå Gult Blod*, Odins Änglar CD 1994, Song, 'Karl XII', text Per Engdahl. It should also be stated that the record company – *Ragnarock records* – is run by Lars Magnus Westrup, once an activist in *Nordisk Ungdom*.

42. Föreningen Sveriges Framtid/ Riksfronten rally at Medborgarhuset in Stockholm, 30 Nov. 1991, observations by the author.
43. The Linköping branch of *Riksfronten*, for instance, calls itself *Linköping SA Storm 38*, which is the same name and number as the Linköping SA unit of *Nationalsocialistiska Arbetarepartiet* (The National Socialist Workers Party) during the 1930s and 1940s, *Blod & Åra* nr. 2, p.3 and list of SSS local branches (in the author's possession).
44. 'We show our own people, young as well as old, women as well as men, solidarity and love. But those who are white and betray our people by race mixing we consider as aliens.' *'Jag är vit jag bryr mig om!'*, leaflet, Kreativistens Kyrka, Karlstad 1991.
45. Interview with person who wants to remain anonymous, 29 Aug. 1991.
46. Interview with person who wants to remain anonymous, 17 May 1991.
47. DT, 20 Sept. 1991 (note 8).
48. As note 46.
49. Interview with anonymous activist, 3 April 1991.
50. Sprinzak in this volume.
51. See for instance, *'Vad tror kreativister på?'*, leaflet (1991); 'Kvinnans livsuppgift', *RAHOWA*, nr. 3, (1991), p.3–4.
52. Heléne Lööw, 'Från nassar till seriösa patrioter', *Tvärsnitt* No.3 (1991).
53. 'Gregor', 12 Jan. 1992 (note 8), and note 46.
54. See for instance, 'Tack demokrater', *Sveriges Framtid* nr. 3/4 (1990), p.6; 'En introduktion till Riksfronten', *Rikslarm* (Summer 1992), p.5; 'Bygg på sanningen', *Sveriges Framtid* (Spring/Summer 1990), p.4.
55. See, for instance, 'Klas Lund visar vägen', *Storm* nr. 4 (1992), p.6.
56. As an example see *Storm* nr. 5–6 1991, p.4; *NS Kampfrut* Nov.–Dec. (1988), p.10, *Racial Loyalty* (May 1991), p.4; *The New Order* (Nov.–Dec. 1991); p.8; *Today's Aryan Woman* (April–June 1991), pp.11–14; *Race and Reality*, nr. 6 (1994), p.26, *Storm* nr. 5–6 (1991), p.4.
57. In the American magazine WAR the following ad was run, for example: 'Private letters ... Klas Lund, the young man who was labelled "the country's most dangerous Nazi" after his attempt to start an armed resistance group were published in a newspaper ... in an effort to hurt him. Lund reads English and can be reached at the following address ...' (*WAR*, 'International News', Aug. 1992). WAR's International News is a regular feature by Tommy Rydén. The strong emphasis on international solidarity has helped to generate a loose international network that acts as an 'Amnesty international for white prisoners of war'.
58. *Den Ariska Frihetsfonden*, leaflet (Dec. 1993).
59. *Blod & Ära*, nr. 2 (1994), p.10.
60. MS, 4 July 1994 (note 17).
61. Lindholm (note 40), p.21.
62. MS 4 July 1994 (note 17).
63. See for instance 'Vänersborgs fängelset JO-anmält'; *Trollhättans tidning* (15 April 1994); 'Allt fler fAngar', *Kumla tidning* (20 April 1994).
64. Lööw 1993 I (note 8), p.74–75.
65. Cf. 'Anarkister på våldsoffensiv, nationalister på defensiv', *Rikslarm*, No. 1 (Jan. 1994), p.5.
66. Sprinzak in this volume.
67. DT, 20 Sept. 1991 (note 8).
68. Vad försiggå i vårt fosterland?, *VAM Samhällsdebatt* nr. 1 (1992), p.2.
69. Cf. TM, 15 Aug. 1991 (note 8); tape–recorded interview with Tommy Rydén, 17 July 1991 ('TR 17 July 1991'); MS 4 July 1994 (note 17); tape–recorded interview with Karl Jonas Ledin and Christopher Ragne, 26 Oct. 1994.
70. Sprinzak in this volume.
71. See for instance *Så du vill starta ett raskrig eh?*, *Vår ras är vår framtid, Res svärdet mot SOR!* och *Vitt Ariskt Motstånd*, VAM leaflets, 1991. Calls for violence do, however, appear in *Werwolf*, a paper which is not for public distribution, only for the activists.

72. See for instance 'Ledare', *Rikslarm* (Autumn 1992, p.3; 'Jibbie Jahoo', *Storm, nr.* 3 (1991), p.2; 'Hell Orden', *Storm* nr. 4 (1991), p.2; 'Våra Ariska Hjältar', ibid., nr. 4 (1991), p.12f.; 'Den svenska orden', ibid., nr. 5–6 (1991), p.6; *Res svärdet mot SOR*, VAM leaflet (1991).

73. TR, 17 July 1991 (note 69).

74. Tape-recorded interview with Marcus Koch, SD–functionary, and at present member of the local council in Dals Ed, 20 March 1991. The incident referred to in the quotation is an attack against the refugee camp Vildmarksporten in Dals-Ed.

75. Source for table: *Statens invandrarverk*, 1993. Note: Family members have been counted together with refugees. The label 'relatives' includes persons married to Swedes etc. Others include labour, adoptive children etc. Persons from the Nordic countries are not counted.

76. Maritta Soininen, '1985 års flyktingomhändertagande: Från reformbeslut till genomförande under öndrade vilkor', in *Invandring, forskning, politik: En vänbok till Tomas Hammar* (Stockholm: CEIFO 1993).

77. Lange and Westin (2nd citation, note 12), p.77.

78. The crimes in question were harassment and battery, arson, damage, giving rise to danger, threats, instigation to rebellion, cross burning, stealing, burglary, attempted murder, attempted manslaughter, incitement of racial hatred, insult, theft, forgery, harassment, and illegal threats.

79. Sources for figure: 'Analys och bearbetning av utredning rörande attentat mot flyktingförläggningar och brott riktade mot invandrare och flyktingar' (covering 1990–91), dated 11 Feb. 1992, SÄK Stockholm (cited as SÄK 1990–91); 'Kartläggning av främlingsfientliga angrepp' (covering 1992), Säkerhetspolisen, dated 9 March 1993 (cited as SÄK 1992); 'Sammanställning 1993 avseende förekomsten av rasism och främlingsfientlighet inom riket', SÄK, författningsskyddet, Stockholm, dated 27 Sept. 1994 (cited as SÄK 1993). Note: 159 of the suspected/convicted perpetrators were men and six women. For 1993 there is one perpetrator aged 43 at the time of the crime, who has not been included in the figure.

80. During 1990–91, one person claiming he was a former member of NRP and SD. For 1992 the report lists two VAM activists, 3 VAM symphatisers, 1 SD member and 3 SD symphatisers. The 1993 report lists 2 local VAM–leaders, 7 VAM sympathisers, 1 local leader of *Riksfronten*, 2 sympathisers of *Riksfronten*, and 4 sympathisers with 'right-wing extremism' (It is not clear if sympathiser with right-wing extremism means SD or another extreme nationalist group or general sympathiser with right wing extremist values). Sources: SÄK 1990–91; SÄK 1992; SÄK 1993 (note 79).

81. Information regarding the perpetrators' drunkenness is available only for the years 1990–92.

82. See, for instance, 'Vägrade en invandrare att flytta in – åtalades inte', *Folket*, 15 Aug. 1992; 'Inget krogbesök utan legitimation', *Nya Norrland*, 9 Feb. 1992; 'Badförbud för flyktingar', *Expressen*, 28 March 1992.

83. 'Flyktingar skall tvingas handla under bevakning', *Expressen*, 8 Aug. 1992; 'Det strider mot lagen', *Norrländska Socialdemokraten*, 8 Aug. 1992; 'Butiker stoppar flyktingar', *Dagbladet*, 29 Sept. 1992; 'Anmäld för diskriminering', *Norrbottens Kuriren*, 10 Dec. 1992.

84. Even if the flyer was anti-Semitic, it did not fall under the definition of incitement of racial hatred, so no charges were pressed.

85. SÄK 1993 (note 79), pp.17–19.

86. SÄK 1990–91 (note 79), pp.3–4.

87. Source for table: SÄK 1990–91 (note 79), p.5.

88. See for instance 'Lasermannen i lång intervju', *Arbetet*, 12 Jan. 1994; 'Livstid', *Expressen*, 15 Jan. 1994.

89. SÄK 1993 (note 79), p.14–15.

90. Helené Lööw, 'Vit makt – en mörk historia', in *Uppväxtvillkor* nr. 3 (1993), p.18.

91. Judgment DB nr. 363 B 307/90 Hässleholms Tingsrätt.

92. Judgment DB nr. 241 B 227/90 Katrineholms Tingsrätt.
93. The figures are based on the following sources: publications from various organisations, racist activity reported in the local press, police sources; SÄK 1993 (note 79).
94. SÄK 1990–91 (note 79), pp.14–15.
95. Lööw 1993 I (note 8), p.19.
96. The politician in question, however, left the party after the incidents in Kimstad and started to publish a magazine *Fri Information* (Free information) 1991, which focuses on the question of immigration.
97. Leif Stenberg, 'När Kimstad blev riksbekant', *Pockettidningen R*, No.2–3 (1991), p.10–18.
98. In Mariestad there is an almost unbroken tradition of organised racist and extreme nationalist activity going back to the 1930s. During 1934–38 a national socialist party was represented in the local council.
99. A 'free church' is a church which is not aligned with the official Lutheran 'state church' of Sweden.
100. Torbjörn Jonsson, *Flyktingdebatten i TSL*, B–uppsats Historiska Institutionen ,Göteborgs Universitet, VT 1993.
101. TT telegram, 23 Aug. 1990.
102. Judgment DB nr. 191 B 117/90, B 152/90 Mariestads Tingsrätt.
103. 'Ny våg av bombdåd i Mariestad', *Svenska Dagbladet*, 22 Aug. 1991.
104. *Oroligheter i Överum*, report presented by police officer Lennart Nyberg, 7 Nov. 1990, at Löckeby.
105. The survey also includes ideologically motivated crimes directed against homosexuals, anti-racists and local politicians.
106. Data about incidents have been collected from news clippings about different incidents. I have thereafter examined verdicts and in some cases the police investigations concerning the cases mentioned in the media, information from the local police about racist crimes, and from a survey of the total number of convictions on every individual. This has proved to be a useful method since the perpetrators often tend to repeat this category of crimes.
107. I decided to count the cities of Karlstad/Säffle and the cities of Göteborg/Borås together because the racist counter–culture in these cities operated together.
108. The project is titled 'Organiserad rasism eller fyllegrejor – en studie av rasistiskt våld i Sverige 1980–1994', sponsored by The Swedish Council for Social Research.
109. D T 20/9 1991 (note 8).
110. *Vit Rebell*, nr. 3 (1989); D.T. 20 Sept. 1991 (note 8).
111. Judgment DB nr. 77 B 1267/85, Hovrätten för Västra Sverige. There is, however, no indication that the convicted individual nor his group, had any connections to other racist/anti–Semites in the area.
112. D T 20/9 1991 (note 8).
113. *Medlemsbulletinen* (SD) (Dec. 1989).
114. ibid., (Oct.1989), *Sverige–Kuriren*, nr. 11 (1990).
115. Judgment DB nr. 291 B 130/88 Karlstads Tingsrätt.
116. *Nya Wermlands tidningen*, 12 Nov. 1990.
117. Judgment DB nr. 234 B 200/91 Arvika Tingsrätt.
118. Judgment DB nr. 205 B 131/92 Arvika Tingsrätt.
119. Four of the hardcore activists have a long documented history of membership in various extreme nationalistic and race ideologist groups.
120. These two have been suspected of racist/xenophobic crimes but the charges have been dropped due to lack of evidence. They have, however, been included in this survey due to the fact that they belong to the group of sympathisers surrounding organised racists.
121. A complete list of verdicts on which the survey of the Karlstad/Säffle group is based, is available from the author.
122. Mattias Tydén, *Svensk antisemitism 1880–1930*, Uppsala Multiethnic Papers 8 (Uppsala: Centre for Multiethnic Research, 1986).
123. Cf. *Vägen Framåt*, 2 June 1946; 21 Jan. 1947; 26 Dec. 1948; 21 Feb. 1949; 9 April 1950;

9 Dec. 1951; and 31 Aug. 1952.

124. Cf., e.g., *Nysvenska rörelsen, ortsförbund Göteborg* (invitation to meeting, Jan. 1988).

Leading activists from the militant racist underground participated in the meetings during the late 1980s, cf. Göteborgs Tingsrätt Judgment DB nr. 779 B 3422/90.

125. Anonymous sources.

126. 'Anti–Semit–propaganda spreds bland skolbarn', *Svenska Morgonbladet*, 25 Jan. 1955; 'Torefalk ämnar gå ur föreningen Ej för officer', *Göteborgs Handels och Sjöfartstidning*, 17 Dec. 1954.

127. Lindquist (note 2), p.24–5.

128. GBG 1/9 1991 (note 79). The group was named after a national socialist party active 1933–50.

129. *Vit Rebell*, No. 3 (1989).

130. Lodenius and Larsson (note 19), p.30.

131. Cf., e.g., *Medlemsbulletinen* (Oct. 1989); *Information från SD* (Nov./Dec. 1990); *SD–bulletinen* (March 1990); ibid., (April 1990).

132. Petter Johansson and Lars Winkler, 'Moskén skall byggas men striden är inte över', *Ny i Sverige*, nr. 6 (1991), p.26–30.

133. Judgment DB nr. 715 B 619/91 Mölndals Tingsrätt.

134. Judgment DB nr. 779 B 3422/90 Göteborgs Tingsrätt.

135. In July 1992, for instance, a gang of skinheads stood outside the club singing hate songs about homosexuals. When a guard tried to persuade them to leave, a prominent activist threatened to kill him. Judgment DB nr. 882 B 4907/92 Göteborgs Tingsrätt.

136. Judgment DB nr. 882 B 4907/92 Göteborgs Tingsrätt.

137. Judgment DB nr. 755 B 665792 Borås Tingsrätt.

138. 'Brevbomb mot Hagge', *Expressen*, 19 June 1990; 'Segerstedt Wiberg fick ny brevbomb', *Arbetet*, 31 June 1990.

139. 'Brevbomb mot Unni och Lasse Brandeby', *Aftonbladet*, 31 Dec. 1991.

140. The reason for including these eight perpetrators in the survey is that they have either been suspected of xenophobic crimes, although the charges have been dropped due to lack of evidence, or they have publicly appeared as spokesmen for various racist groups.

141. The charges for violations against narcotic laws is found among individuals who have left the political scene. Drug dealers or drug users are not tolerated within the organisations.

142. The motives underlying bank/post office robberies are probably a mixture of private and ideological.

143. A complete list of verdicts on which the survey of the Göteborg/Borås group is based is available from the author.

144. Interview where source wish to remain anonymous, 21 Sept. 1992.

145. In the flyers and circulars handed out before public demonstrations, it is for instance pointed out that the participants must be sober. *Manifestation 6 November 1992*, flyer; *Anhängarbulletinen* (April 1992).

146. In Stockholm drunk distributors of flyers is a far more common scene.

147. Whole families can be found in the activist group, although not all family members have been convicted of criminal offences.

148. One Göteborg activist, however, claimed that they knew those who were convicted for these two attacks but added, '*we don't mix with them socially or cooperate with them*'. GBG, 18 May 1993.

149. GBG 1 Sept. 1991 (note 8).

150. See *Vägen framåt*, 20 Nov. 1949.

151. KD, nr 121/1963, 'Förundersökningsprotokoll' (Police report), 16 Aug. 1963.

152. State Police, Stockholm, avd II, rotel B, *Kortfattad redogörelse angående Nationella Nyhedniska Fascistpartiet*.

153. Rydström is still politically active and issues a magazine called *Wårendsbladet*. He also supports the new movements, the parliamentarian one as well as the racist revolutionary racists.

154. As note 152.

160 TERROR FROM THE EXTREME RIGHT

155. Interrogation protocol, Criminal Police, Växjö, 5–7 Aug. 1963.
156. *Skånska Dagbladet*, 3 March 1964. The party symbol was a skull with a pipe in its mouth. *Nationella Nyhedniska Fascistpartiet* was strongly anti–Semitic. Anti–Semitism and the notion of an ongoing Jewish world conspiracy was the main ideological theme. In one of the circulars issued by Svensson he stated: 'The discovery of the poisonous substance JEWS is one of the largest revolutions in the history of mankind...How many diseases have not animated from the poisonous substance JEWS! (for example Christianity).' Circular div. *3 Kristendomens sista kullerbyttor.* 'Svensson' did also believe that Jesus was not a Jew but an Aryan, and one of the first 'true anti-Semites'. See *Nationalism och nationalsocialism: De oförsonliga fienderna till allt judiskt* (flyer); and *Människokräk knorrar och skränar när övermänniskan – ulven upptäckes* (circular div. 12).
157. 'Svensson' referred to himself as the 'victor' or Ek Eerier, and claimed in the party programme that the 'Leader must after the takeover (of power) live with his nearest in a guarded area, away from others. The leader must live an abnormal life and be abnormal', cf. *program för Nationella Nyhedniska Fascist partiet.*
158. Judgment DB nr. 276 B 133/86 Växjö Tingsrätt.
159. *SD–bulletinen* (Dec. 1990).
160. Judgment DB nr. 453 B 218/89 Eksjö Tingsrätt.
161. Judgment DB nr. 219 B 50/92, Växjö Tingsräått.
162. Judgment DB nr. 304 B 252/91 B 277/91 Växjö Tingsrätt.
163. In some cases other perpetrators are found in the verdicts. These have, however, not been included in the survey, since there is no proof of them harbouring xenophobic or racist ideas.
164. There is no information available as to whether these three individuals are active in *VAM, Riksfronten* or *Kreativistens Kyrka.*
165. A complete list of verdicts on which the survey of the Växjö group is based, is available from the author.
166. Cf. *Nordisk Kamp,* No.1–2 (1985); *Informationsblad till activa medlemmar* (1985); *Nordisk Kamp,* No.3–4 (1984); ibid., (No.3–4 (1987); ibid., No. 6 (1990).
167. Cf., 'Sveriges Nationella Förbund, riksorganisationen', (Winter 1992/93), p.2.
168. 'Nytt politiskt parti står höger om högern', *SDS,* 2 Aug. 1968. The leader of *Svenska Folkets Väl* was once an activist in the SSS youth movement, NU.
169. *Svenska Folkets Väl,* leaflet; *Svenska Folkets Vål,* Political program; 'Partiprogram av den 5 juli 1970, reviderat den 5. mars 1972' (1983 edition); Géza Nagyn, 'Främlingsrädsla och invandrarfientliga opinionsyttringar i Sverige; Från anonyma brev till organiserad rasism', in *Kulturmöte konflikt eller samarbete, Papers in Anthropological linguistics* II (Göteborg, 1982), pp.171–2.
170. Lodenius and Larsson (note 19), p.30.
171. See, for instance, *Medlemsbulletinen* (Oct. 1989); ibid.,(Dec. 1989); *SD–bulletinen* (April 1990).
172. Thomas Peterson, Mikael Stigendal, Björn Fryklund, *Skånepartiet; Om folkligt missnöje i Malmö* (Lund, 1988).
173. Lodenius and Larsson (note 19), pp.67–8.
174. Lodenius and Larsson (note 19), p.48.
175. Judgment DB nr. 163 B 2938/90, Malmö Tingsrätt.
176. Judgment DB nr. 45 B 4049/90, Malmö Tingsrätt.
177. Judgment DB nr. 181 B 95/92, Malmö Tingsrätt.
178. Judgment DB nr. 102 B 1841/92, Malmö Tingsrätt.
179. Cf. 'Med lögnen som vapen' and 'Från personregistret', *Storm,* No. 9–10 (1993), pp.6–7; *Storm: Organ för det syndikalistiska ungdomsförbundet,* No. 1 (1994), p.3; *BSS Medlembulletin,* No.1 (1981), p.8; *Oliktänkande förföljs,* BSS flyer; *17 årig svensk mördad av invandrare,* SD flyer (Nov. 1992).
180. A complete list of the verdicts on which the survey of the Malmö group is based is available from the author.
181. Police sources.

182. Christopher T. Husbands, 'Militant Neo-nazism in the Federal Republic of Germany in the 1980s', in Luciano Cheles et al.(eds.), Neo Fascism in Europe (Essex: Longman, 1991), p.103.
183. Christopher T. Husbands, 'Racism and Racist Violence: Some Theories and Political Perspectives', in Tore Bjørgo and Rob Witte (eds.), Racist Violence in Europe (Basingstoke: Macmillan, 1993), p.118.

Development, Patterns and Causes of Violence against Foreigners in Germany: Social and Biographical Characteristics of Perpetrators and the Process of Escalation

HELMUT WILLEMS

Acts of violence against foreigners have increased dramatically since 1991 in Germany. The author underlines the wave-like process of escalation and tries to identify triggering and amplifying factors (police reaction, political deficits, public opinion). He analyses police data concerning biographical and socio-demographic characteristics of the perpetrators and discusses some of the prominent scientific interpretations (disintegration, individualisation, right-wing activities) concerning the recent waves of right-wing and xenophobic violence in Germany.

The following presents results from research projects on the development and characteristics of violence against foreigners in Germany between 1991 and 1994. The projects were carried out at the University of Trier under the direction of Professor Dr Roland Eckert and Dr Helmut Willems with the sponsorship of the Ministry for Women and Youth (BMJF), the German Research Community (DFG), and the Ministry of the Interior. The project was motivated by the realisation that still relatively little is known about three central aspects of the escalation of xenophobic violence in the early 1990s:

(a) the *general political* and *specific local* conditions that cause sections of society (particularly youths) to develop a greater degree of xenophobic attitudes and a greater propensity to xenophobic violence;

(b) the specific social and biographical *traits* which characterise these groups of *violent* criminals and those disposed to violence. To date we have been able to derive only relatively inaccurately from general questionnaires how xenophobia, propensity to violence, and intention to act against foreigners are embedded in social structures. Moreover, very little is known about the actual crimes and their perpetrators. An analysis of the perpetrators of xenophobic violence, their economic and social status, their political convictions, as well as their biographical background is indispensable, therefore, both for the furtherance of scientific knowledge as well as for social, political, police, and educational dealings with these groups.

(c) *The diffusion and escalation patterns* of xenophobic violence are also completely unresearched. We know little about situational conditions and crystallisation points, triggering factors and opportunity structures, diffusion mechanisms and escalative processes of the recent waves of violence against foreigners.[1] In past decades, right-wing groups usually preferred acts of force by the state to protect law and order against anarchists rather than themselves using violence against the state or opponents. Presumably, however, political conflicts – such as the current conflicts in Germany concerning the integration of foreigners and political asylum – present new opportunities for those right-wing parties and violent groups which do not feel themselves to be represented in established parties and their politics. Therefore it is essential to undertake an analysis of concrete historical incidents of violence in terms of the underlying dynamics of escalation, interaction structures, as well as the general political, but also locally specific requirements and conditions for outbreaks of xenophobic violence.

Accordingly, the research aims and methods for this both theoretically and practically relevant topic can be specified as follows:
1. For the quantitative investigation of the *characteristics of perpetrators* (socio-demographic structures, etc.), data from police records were used. These records cover xenophobic and right-wing motivated criminal and violent acts from 1 January 1991 to 4 April 1992 in a total of ten German states.[2]
2. For the qualitative determination of individual criminal types as well as *biographical and family backgrounds*, we evaluated the court sentence records of about 140 criminals and, in addition, carried out expert interviews with judges, social workers, police officers, etc.
3. For the *reconstruction of the events* and *escalation processes*, documents, news reports, etc., were evaluated and expert interviews likewise carried out.[3]

I. The Development of Xenophobic Violence in the 1990s

To date, the phenomenon of xenophobic violence has been dealt with almost exclusively on the basis of single case studies or representative public opinion polls. But these polls elicit responses concerning not actual violent crimes but the respondent's attitude toward violence, that is, his propensity to and acceptance of violence.

For both a theory of xenophobic violence as well as for political and practical conclusions, precise *figures on the extent of violence* and the change in the level of violence over time are of special importance. The short term fluctuations in the level of violence indicate that the extent of violence in a society not only correlates with overall social conditions and problems, but also varies with political, legal, or social actions and reactions.

Data concerning the development of xenophobic crimes, however, are collected exclusively in reports by the police (and by the *Verfassungsschutz*, the Federal Agency for the Protection of the Constitution). Using data established by police raises questions concerning its quality and validity for the following reasons: (1) Only the criminal and violent xenophobic acts registered with the police (i.e., reported), are included. The number of crimes that are not reported for various reasons remains an open question. It must be presumed that the actual number of xenophobic crimes and acts of violence is higher than the figure obtainable from police statistics. (2) The criteria according to which criminal and violent acts are categorized by the police as xenophobic are by no means unequivocal; the definition and categorization are different for each individual precinct. In some cases all crimes in which foreigners, refugees, or even other victims (gays, handicapped) are harmed are included in the statistics even if it is not clear whether rightist, racist, or other xenophobic motives were actually the underlying cause.

Uncertainties in the evaluation of the data arise, then, without the possibility of estimating the presumed distortions in terms of their quantitative values. Since the various selection mechanisms responsible for possible distortions in police statistics probably tend to compensate one another partially, we can assume that the available figures adequately reproduce the changes in relative values at least. I, therefore, would like to take a look at the development of xenophobic crimes and acts of violence registered by police since these figures offer an important indication as to degree, structure, and dynamic of xenophobic violence. It must, of course, be taken into account that we view violence as a physical infringement and damage or the threat of corresponding infringements – our basis is a narrow concept of violence which is also the foundation of the state's monopoly on the use of force. In Germany, however, many groups and individuals use a different, much broader concept of violence: they consider the insulting and disgracing of foreigners as well as civil rights discrimination to be violence as well. As such they arrive at a much more dramatic image of the xenophobia and the threatening and harrassment of foreigners and political refugees in Germany. Our use of a narrower concept of violence is not because we consider molestation, insults, and discrimination less important and unproblematic in the context of physical violence; it is because our data were obtained on the basis of a narrow definition of violence, and because the limited concept of violence presents a kind of lowest common denominator for the intersubjective analysis of violence. Psychic and structural violence phenomena, though, are strongly dependent on subjective perception and definitions.

First let us observe the temporal development of xenophobic crimes registered by police. Besides the typical violent offences (murder, assault, arson, vandalism with violence), these crimes also include the spreading of propaganda, the use of signs and symbols of unconstitutional organisations, as well as disturbing the peace.

As Figure 1 shows, a *dramatic rise* in the overall number of reported xenophobic crimes first occurs in 1991. From an average of about 250 reported xenophobic crimes per year from 1987 to 1990, the number skyrockets to 2,426 in 1991 – a tenfold increase in the average of the preceding year. This first clear break in the development of xenophobic crimes is in its magnitude a clear expression of actual change and not the result of strengthened and enhanced police perception. The majority of the 2,426 crimes can be attributed to the distribution of propaganda, disturbance of the peace, vandalism without violence, etc. Yet in typical violent offences, such as attacks against individuals and arson, a dramatic increase compared to the previous year is also discernable.

For 1992 a clear rise in xenophobic crimes to 6,336 is once more detectable and in 1993 figures are again higher than in the year before; although with 6,721 xenophobic crimes it is but only a small increase. I do not intend to list the details of the development of events individually. Summarizing, I would ask only what can be deduced from the data on the development of xenophobic crimes and violence concerning the factors which produce, strengthen, escalate and de-escalate this development.

FIGURE 1
MOST DISTRIBUTION OF CRIMINAL OFFENCES AGAINST FOREIGNERS
JANUARY 1991 TO FEBRUARY 1994

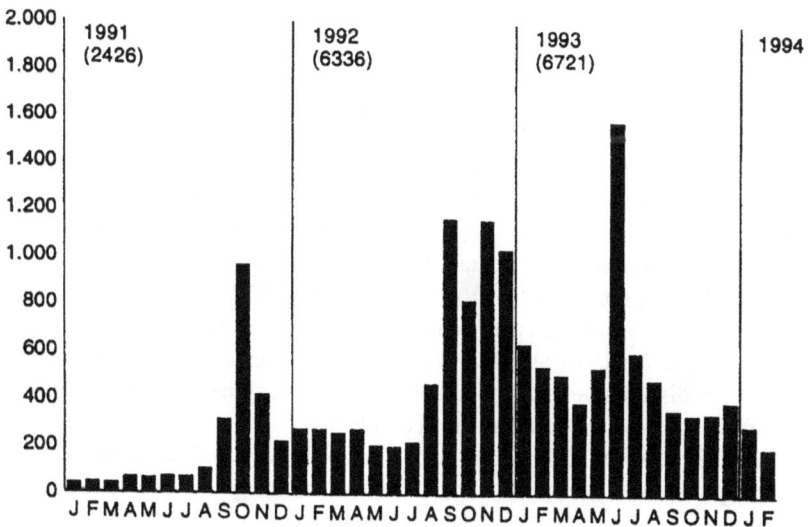

The data support the following points.

1. The increase in xenophobic crimes in 1991, 1992 and the first half of 1993 compared to previous years involves right-wing propaganda offences, violence against individuals, and arson against housing for refugees and foreigners to virtually the same extent. The changes in the three categories of perpetrators are nearly synchronous. From this we may infer that the activities of right-wing parties, violent xenophobic skinhead groups and frustrated youths from refugee neighborhoods have all found a common conflict and *crystallization point* in resisting housing for foreigners and political refugees.

2. The quantitative escalation and dramatic increase in xenophobic events are not continuous but erratic. Dramatic individual occurrences trigger *waves of escalation* and mobilization. The wave of violence reaches its first peak directly after the attacks on homes for foreigners and refugees at the end of September 1991 in Hoyerswerda, which ended in the evacuation of all refugees from the affected lodgings. This 'success' of the perpetrators in Hoyerswerda represents a central mobilization factor in the further development of the violence: directly thereafter, imitation throughout the entire Federal Republic caused the number of xenophobic crimes and violent offences to peak and, at the same time, bring about a diffusion of the violence, in particular through the activation of violently disposed groups elsewhere. The same *mobilization and recruitment effect* can also be observed *after* the *'successful' riots* in Rostock at the end of August 1992 and even after the Solingen murder (June 1993) where five Turkish women died after their house had been set afire.

3. Large-scale waves of escalation and mobilisation do not simply ebb back to pre-escalation levels; they lead to a *stabilization of xenophobic crimes* at a higher level for some time at least. In the weeks following the events in Rostock we could determine that the escalation had become constant and everyday over a long period. The reasons for this development remain largely uninvestigated. *Changed expectations for the success* of violent acts due to successful predecessors as well as *reduced expectations of sanctions* due to scant state reactions offer a partial explanation. Also possible, however, is that other, better organized right-wing groups and parties deliberately attempt to escalate the riots and instrumentalize them for their own political aims.

4. Following the events in Mölln in November 1992 and particularly after the protest demonstrations and candlelight marches against racism and violence, *a reduction in violent crimes* and in the tolerance of and propensity to violence is discernable in the population, even if not at the relatively low level that existed before 1991. What has occurred?

(a) The events in Mölln (arson with two people killed) shocked sections of violently disposed youth groups and cliques: for many, the events in Mölln went too far. Some realized only afterwards what they had gotten themselves involved in.

(b) With the protest demonstrations the till then silent majority made its voice heard. This made it clear to the right-wing, racist, and xenophobic groups that they are a minority as before, are by no means supported by a large section of the population, and in future can no longer count on the same tolerance in the population as was partially the case in 1991–92.

(c) These changes in the mood of the population as well as determined proceedings by the state against right-wing groups and criminals have changed the perpetrator's expectations of success and the risks involved.

5. For the period between July 1993 and September 1994, a clear reduction of criminal offences against foreigners is discernible. This decline in xenophobic violence should obviously not be understood as an all clear signal. On the contrary: the cycles of mobilization, with their ups and downs in terms of the support and participation of larger sections of the population, seem rather to be typical for the genesis of a *xenophobic social movement* which has developed in the last few years and whose end is not yet foreseeable. And more than this: the consequence of the *polarization* of the xenophobic and right-wing scene may be a *radicalization* and hardening of the propensity to violence among some groups to the point of *right-wing terrorism*.

II. Suspect Characteristics, Biographical Backgrounds, Types of Perpetrators

The evaluation of police files to gain information about the protagonists of xenophobic violence is not unproblematic. First of all, the data deal not with actual convicted criminals but suspects. Second, the selection processes influencing the inclusion of police investigations are not controllable. As such, we do not know which distortions adversely affect the results obtained. Third, we have no influence over what data are obtained nor over how they are obtained. A complete and detailed collection of information on suspects is hindered since suspects are not obliged to provide more than a few particulars in police investigations. Voluntary information for sociologically interesting questions about family structures, social status, biographical data, or motives is provided by only a few.

Due to these problems, the evaluation of police reports is meaningful and valid only for specific hypotheses. The following data from the project mentioned above, based on the evaluation of 1,398 police reports on perpetrators of xenophobic violence between January 1991 and April 1992, must, therefore, be considered with reservations and can be adequately interpreted only in context with other information won from questionnaires or qualitative studies. What do we know about the perpetrators?

(a) According to the analysis of police records, over 95 per cent of xenophobic crimes and violence are committed by men, by very *young men* in particular. More than 75 per cent of the suspects investigated are 20 years old or younger; over 35 per cent under 18. Only about 5 per cent of the suspects are over 30 years old. Furthermore the propensity to xenophobic violence and violence itself seems to correlate more strongly with *lower levels of education* (grades 9/10) and with *apprentices* and *skilled manual workers*. Indications of a dominance of deficient family structures, special social problems (like high unemployment, lack of school certificates), and a predominantly lower class social origin could be found for subsections of the suspects.

(b) Typically, xenophobic crimes and violence are *group offences*. This is true for over 90 per cent of the investigated cases. Fifteen to twenty per cent of the suspects classify themselves or could be classified according to prior police information as members of a xenophobic right-wing group. Corresponding figures are also mentioned by the *Verfassungsschutz*, the Federal Agency for the Protection of the Constitution.[4] Particularly evident is an involvement and membership in the skinhead subculture (in about 30 per cent of all cases) and in other xenophobic youth groups.

(c) For the first waves of xenophobic violence from mid-1991 to mid-1993, at least, there are only few indications of planned, organized, or even directed actions. The actions are usually preceeded by *spontaneous* decisions under a strong influence of alcohol. The increase registered by police in repeat and multiple crimes by the same person does, however, indicate that xenophobic activities have become routine in particular groups.

(d) The indication that up to 10 per cent of the suspects already had *prior records* for politically motivated crimes and that almost 35 per cent have prior records for other crimes may be particularly important. Even if distortions due to police investigations play a decided role, it must be remembered that violently disposed groups and skinhead subcultures, fascists, hooligans, etc., are of particular importance not only in terms of xenophobic violence but also quite obviously as a problem group from the perspective of youth criminality.

On the basis of police data as well as an analysis of court records of about 140 criminals, four different types of perpetrators could be identified, which differ both in their political-ideological orientation and propensity to violence and xenophobia as well as in their biographical experiences and family backgrounds. This analytical differentiation of types of perpetrators is one indicator for the heterogeneity of the xenophobic movement which attracts activists and supporters far beyond the extremist right margin.

FIGURE 2
FOUR TYPES OF PERPETRATORS: ATTITUDES AND MOTIVES

TYPES OF PERPETRATORS — IDEOLOGY, ATTITUDES, MOTIVES	Type 1. Right-wing activist	Type 2. Ethnocentristic youth	Type 3. Criminal youth	Type 4. Fellow traveller
Right-wing Ideology	strongly right-wing ideology and identity	partly right-wing ideology and slogans	partly right-wing ideology and slogans	no right-wing ideology
Ethnic prejudices & hostility against foreigners	strongly racist ideology and hostility against foreigners	strongly ethnocentristic attitudes and hostility towards foreigners	partly racist and ethnocentristic attitudes and feelings	no firm racist or ethnocentristic attitudes
Propensity to violence	politically motivated and legitimized willingness to resort to violence (instrumental violence)	propensity to violence as expression of subcultural values and as means of provocation (expressive or hedonistic violence)	violence as normal everyday means of dealing with conflicts (no legitimization needed)	violent behavior as result of group dynamics & peer expectations (no general propensity to violence)
Prior police records	some prior police records for multiple political crimes	some prior police records for juvenile crimes	multiple prior police records & criminal career patterns	no prior police records

FIGURE 3
SOCIAL AND BIOGRAPHICAL CHARACTERISTICS OF PERPETRATORS

TYPES OF PERPETRATORS / SOCIO-BIOGRAPHICAL CHARACTERISTICS	Type 1. Right-wing activist	Type 2. Ethnocentristic youth	Type 3. Criminal youth	Type 4. Fellow traveller
Family of origin	• lower- and middle-class • no problem families	• lower middle-class • problem families	• lower-class • multiple problem families • socialization deficits	• lower- and middle-class • no-problem families
Private or job problems	• no private or job problems	• some private and job problems	• multiple private and job problems	• no private and job problems
Educational level & success	• low and middle educational level • successful	• low educational level • partly unsuccessful	• unsuccessful in school • often no exams • drop outs	• low and middle educational level • successful
Job training	• successful job training	• some unsuccessful job training	• often no job training	• successful job training
Occupation/ unemployment	• low unemployment	• higher unemployment	• high and recurring unemployment	• low unemployment

Type 1: Politically motivated, right-wing extremists: The role of extremist parties

This type generally either has contacts with right-wing extremist parties and groups or is a member of such a group. Often he has already been politically active in this field, whether in the preparation of meetings or in the distribution of right-wing magazines, films, etc. In other contexts and cliques this type also makes his appearance with the corresponding arguments and slogans. In court he often demonstratively expresses right-wing and neo-Nazi thoughts.

The right-wing extremist frequently tries to act as an agitator in concrete situations as well as in the preliminary stages of violent events and crimes to influence the groups and persons involved. Since the willingness to submit to party ideologies and the corresponding discipline is generally low among the politically unbound youth groups and subcultures, the influence of right-wing parties is more on an ideological than on an organizational (and operational) level.

Fundamentally we can assume that an ideologically legitimized, strategically directed and disciplined propensity to violence against concrete victim groups is present in this case. The propensity is often racially motivated but not concentrated only against foreigners. Rather it is directed depending on the situation against everything "non-German", "unmanly", "weak" or against any opponent to the new right parties.

More so than the other types, the right-wing extremist appears to have successful school degrees (often even a higher educational level), successful job training, as well as a steady job.

Type 2: The xenophobe or ethnocentrist youth: The role of skinhead and fascist subcultures

The second type identified is the xenophobic youth who – unlike type 1 – represents no firm right-wing political ideas or ideologies and who neither is a member of right-wing parties or groups nor has been active in this field. Many of these youths, whose attitudes range from hostility to hatred against foreigners, are to be found in the skinhead, hooligan, and fascist subcultures but also in various youth leisure cliques. Even if xenophobic prejudices and nationalist mottos are represented here, these youths did mark themselves off from the right-wing parties and their goals in the past.

In this case, violence against foreigners is legitimized less by means of racist and right-wing ideologies than by diffuse feelings of threat, disadvantage, and unequal treatment of 'Germans' versus 'Foreigners', political refugees in particular. Racist prejudices and sterotypes, however, can easily follow. The current or expected future competition for jobs, housing, and material and financial aid appears to be the dominant theme here and the central reason for the legitimation of the use of violence. The propensity to violence in these groups is diffuse in the sense that it is neither politically disciplined nor strategically integrated. All the same, via the existence of xenophobic attitudes and stereotypes, the propensity to violence in concrete situations is, of course, deliberately directed against certain victim groups, foreigners and refugees in particular. The attitudes towards violence represent a mixture between instrumental and expressive orientations. On the one hand, an attempt is made to draw attention to personal fears, problems and conflicts and, if need be, to solve them by spreading fear and fright amongst the victims; on the other hand, however, it is in no way discernable amongst these groups that violence might be organized as a political protest and used for attaining general political goals. In addition, the desire for action as well as a propensity to and acceptance of violence as an aspect of manly self-portrayal and self-definition all play a central role.

In terms of social-structural and biographical traits, these youths differ from the first type: the lower school degree (grade 9/10) is more frequent, with unemployment somewhat higher on the whole. In addition, school and family problems and deficits are more often reported.

Type 3: Criminal and marginalized youths: losers and drop-outs

This type is generally composed mostly of somewhat older youths with markedly negative (private as well as professional) careers and usually more or less pronounced criminal careers. Many of these youths have, in part, a long list of prior offences (ranging from theft to assault), have frequently confessed in court, and some have also been sentenced to jail terms.

As a rule there is a high proportion of school dropouts as well as of youths with incomplete or interrupted job training who then also change jobs frequently and are affected to a much greater extent by unemployment than the other types. In terms of family background there is an especially high ratio of problem families: On the one hand, the number of incomplete or single parent families is particularly high here. At the same time, however, the family communication structures and upbringing are described as especially problematic. Parental alcohol abuse as well as the use of violence as a means of discipline and communication in the family are reported. Neglect by the parents, with children being left alone at a very early age, as well as being shuffled back and forth between different counseling centers, is quite frequent.

Even if we are not dealing with a type having a marked right-wing ideological background and political interests (like type 1), xenophobic slogans and nationalist mottos are nevertheless widespread among this group. These

mottoes and slogans seem to have an important psychic significance, particularly in dealing with personal experiences of failure and poor prospects for the
future.

In terms of the propensity to violence, this is a markedly action-oriented,
aggressive, and violently disposed type. Here violence is seen not as means of
political conflict, but as a normal element of daily life and conflict resolution
which needs no specific legitimation. In this respect there is a relatively constant and high but quite diffuse – concerning the choice of victim – potential
for violence that is also closely linked to the self-portrayal and experience of
these youths. The propensity to violence does not direct itself, therefore,
exclusively against foreigners, but is used in a variety of daily situations, partly within the group itself. Due to the increased propensity to violence and personal experience with the use of violence, and also due to a higher risk potential, these youths often appear in the primary stages of xenophobic actions as
initiators, and in concrete situations appear particularly aggressive.

Type 4: Fellow-travellers
In this type we find neither an identification with right-wing extremist views
nor a corresponding, deeply seated xenophobia.

The youths are mostly from intact, often middle-class families and do not
have serious private or professional problems. As a rule, they have both a
completed school education (grade 10 or 12) as well as adequate job training,
and a stable job. Prior offences are extremely rare. Fellow-travellers are found
in both youth skinhead and fascist groups but more frequently in young music
or leisure cliques where community orientation and group solidarity play
important roles.

In terms of the development of the propensity to violence as well as participation in xenophobic crimes, aspects of group dynamic (pressure to conform, loyality, solidarity, etc.) are usually foremost. A fundamentally deep-
seated propensity to violence is just as uncommon as general xenophobia. On
the contrary, an important motive for the crimes seems to be the desire to
prove oneself in front of friends or not to leave them in the lurch. These
youths, therefore, appear more frequently not as the main protagonists or initiators but as fellow-travellers and supporters. To be sure, they do not withdraw from the scene of the crime, or stop their friends from committing
crimes, but they are very seldom violent themselves.

On the basis of the currently available results as well as insights from
other areas, a quantitative determination of the various criminal types can be
estimated only approximately. The right-wing, politically motivated type 1
criminal is noticeably less frequent than the other types. We estimate the percentage of type 1 at around 15 per cent of the total, with the percentage of the

other types hovering at around 25–30 per cent each (with distortions due to police methods undoubtedly present). What conclusions do these results allow then in terms of the public and scientific interpretation of xenophobic violence?

III. Individualization, Disintegration, or Anomie? General Causes of Xenophobic Violence

1. Is the current xenophobic violence motivated most by right-wing, racial or social concerns?

The xenophobic violence of 1991 and 1992 can by no means be seen as being organized, directed or even motivated exclusively by right-wing extremists and ideas. On the contrary, the analysis of the various criminal profiles shows that besides right-wing motivated political extremists, sections of the normal – initially unpolitical – youth groups and gangs have found a field of political action and confirmation. On the whole the group of perpetrators is too heterogeneous both in their motives and in their group orientation and world views to allow them to be sweepingly labeled as racist or right-wing. Rather there is a broad mixture of differing motives for violence: playing important roles are (a) political, right-wing motives and racist ideologies and legitimization, (b) unpolitical (expressive) motives for violence and a desire for action, and (c) social protest motives. Referring to Sprinzak's typology of right-wing terrorism elements, at least four of his five general types can be identified here: revolutionary, reactive, racist and youth counterculture terrorism.[5] It is important to note, however, that until today reactive motives and violently-disposed youth groups have been foremost. Ideological or political convictions are not the common bond among these heterogeneous groups and protagonists, but rather diffuse ideas of a general threat and disadvantage of Germans versus foreigners (political refugees in particular) and the resulting xenophobic and hostile feelings. This idea attaches itself predominantly to the government's transfer payments and aid to refugees, but can also generally settle in the fear of competition in a period of economic recession, increased unemployment, etc. This is particularly true for the new East German states, where the experience of competition and feelings of threat are widespread and xenophobic beliefs and propensity to violence are likewise more strongly pronounced. Such xenophobic attitudes can easily expand beyond political refugees to all foreigners whose rights to government assistance can be denied.

2. Is the violence a result of experiences of disintegration and loss of social status?

Theories of deviant behavior and violence have always tried to use general social structures and changes as an explanation for increasing propensities to violence and acts of violence; such factors include, for example, social tensions, a high degree of social inequality, or injustice and discrimination against social groups. Today as well such causal explanations are also offered. Xenophobic violence is described by many – based on the research by Wilhelm Heitmeyer[6] – as a consequence of experiences of social disintegration: the breakdown of family structures, professional integration, political and institutional loyalties and identification. From Robert K. Merton,[7] however, we know that social-structural explanatory models have decisive weaknesses. People do not react uniformly but variably to conflictive, contradictory, or lawless structures and situations depending on their concrete needs and desires, their competence, and on opportunity structures. Furthermore, a look at the past and at other current societies shows that xenophobic violence and ethnic conflicts often occur precisely in highly integrated societies – namely, where particularistic orientations toward personal relations, kin, and ethnic group present central mechanisms of integration. As a result, the use of the disintegration concept for the explanation of xenophobic violence has well-known limits.

The results of our research underline this as well. Just as the attribution to aggressive and xenophobic youth subcultures cannot generally be described as an effect of disintegration, individual experiences of disintegration (dropping out of school, unemployment, deficient family structures, lack of relationships) could be found only for a sub-section of the perpetrators. Dominating personal experiences of disintegration or loss of social status as a central explanatory factor for xenophobic violence can at best be assumed for the criminal youths described in type 3: youths with an accumulation of problems at home and at school.

Nevertheless, economic pressures and high unemployment in connection with the immigration of new ethnic groups matter in explaining xenophobic violence. Economic problems and high unemployment stir up fears in individuals (even if they are not yet affected) because they fear the future consequences for themselves or for groups they are in solidarity with. Disappointment with the welfare state and social market economy are particularly noticeable in the former East German states following reunification. In such a situation, the considerable influx of immigrants and refugees and their support by the state are perceived by many as direct competition and as a threat to their desired social status and, apart from individual and direct fear of competition, as unjustifiable and exaggerated. Not personal experiences of disintegration and loss of status but rather conceptions of unjust distribution and a perceived preferential treatment of foreigners (relative deprivation) as well as real or perceived threats play a decisive role, therefore, in explaining the underlying causes of violence against foreigners. To emphasize the relevance of real or perceived threats as prerequisite for political violence and particularistic terrorism, Sprinzak uses the term 'reactive terrorism'.[8]

3. The role of individualization as an explanatory model

The concept of individualization is relevant here in terms of social structural changes that are characteristic for developed modern societies and, above all, for the relationship between individuals and society.[9] The concept describes the loss of importance of traditional environments, social classes, and neighborhoods in providing individual support, direction, and careers. Social classes and traditional lifestyles previously offered orientation patterns for the following generation. Today, individuals are increasingly freed from traditional bonds and support relationships, like family and relatives, and are thrown back on themselves and their individual fate with all the liberties and chances but also all the risks and contradictions involved. The consequences of this development are visible only in broad outline. I would like to mention some of these aspects here since they may have some connection to the violence:

*   With the individualization of personal decisions and ways of life, the number of choices an individual faces has risen considerably. A greater need for orientation develops, especially amongst youths; while at the same time, however, traditional orientations, identities, and life styles are devalued. It is possible that this development produces amongst some youths a need for and susceptibility to simple radical ideologies, feelings of belonging, and opportunities for identification. Especially, ideologies based on natural criteria like race, sex, or nation mediate more stable experiences of identity because they cannot be threatened by the possibility of being different. Such ideologies can be the point of departure for the legitimization of violent acts against outsiders.
*   Individualization produces a situation in which the social sanctions of milieus and neighborhood have only a limited reach. Neighbors and relatives have lost their power to control and socialize in so far as they have become largely irrelevant for planning one's own life and can be escaped through mobility. To use violence as a means to an end or simply to follow one's aggressive impulses is made easily possible then because long term disadvantages are not necessarily associated therewith. The strategic importance of a civilized compulsion to self-discipline is partially lost through individualization.
*   The expansion of competitive relationships not only in the job market but also in leisure and private relationships develops a compulsion to create a self-image and a pressure to self-assertion which young people feel in par-

ticular. This strengthens the expansion of an individualistic orientation of competition and success as the dominating value, against which solidarity and empathetic competences often cannot assert themselves.

From these individualization tendencies, orientation problems, experiences of anomie, and a onesidedness of personal values can definitely be deduced.[10] They are difficult for many a youth to deal with. Nevertheless this does not immediately lead to a violent disposition or violence itself. A variety of other forms of coping with problems and strains exists – plainly recognizable in the fact that violent youths represent only a minority of youths overall, whereas individualization affects almost all.

Individualization and disintegration theses therefore are too general and abstract to explain very specific violent forms of assimilation and reaction to the structural changes described. Decisive, rather, is that in light of individualization, increasingly specific youth subcultures can form in modern societies. Many of these subcultures crystallize around violent affects, traditional masculine ideals of fighters or warriors, or radical political ideas. For the explanation of the propensity to violence especially of youths, individualization is not so much the decisive factor as is the existence of a differentiated system of youth groups and subcultures in which violent motives arise and strengthen themselves and which also become active in current social conflicts and problems.

IV. The Importance of State Reactions and Perceived Changes in Public Opinion for the Legitimization and Escalation of Violence

So far I have predominantly followed an individualistic – perpetrator oriented – perspective and have attempted to identify various types and motives as well as to hint at the general causes of the recent violence. Admittedly, such a perspective does not altogether suffice to explain the escalation and development of violence over the past few years.[11] In addition, it inhibits the view of the involvement of other social protagonists and groups. Therefore, I would like to supplement this perspective with another that embeds the violent activities of individuals and groups in a net of social relationships in which other protagonists and institutions and their actions or inactions also play an important role. This type of perspective attempts to understand violence not as a characteristic of individuals or groups, but as a product of interaction and communication processes. The perspective itself proceeds from the thesis that propensity to, legitimization of, and concepts of the costs and risks of violence are first generated and modified in these interaction processes. I would like to conclude with four theses that support these assumptions.

Thesis 1: The German asylum procedure has promoted interaction processes and experiences between refugees and the native population that are perceived by many as conflicts and burdens and that became the crystallization points for the development of corresponding attitudes and a disposition to violence.

The current asylum procedure has dumped the main financial, housing and social burdens of political refugees largely on the local authorities. Due to the great influx of refugees in recent years the local authorities are frequently overburdened with fulfilling the allocations and their freedom of activity is correspondingly limited. The consequence: Neighbors and residents of refugee housing are confronted with decisions in which they were not a part and which for this reason alone are difficult to accept. Thus the interaction between refugees and local residents are often characterized from the outset by rejection, distrust, and suspicion without having to assume xenophobic motives for the rejection. In addition, residents often feel – particularly after a certain concentration of refugees – deeply disturbed in their accustomed order and lifestyle. Racist prejudices, ethnic sterotypes, and xenophobic-nationalist slogans become more evident and plausible for many citizens in the face of these experiences and represent a first phase in the development of new ethnic conflicts. An analysis of the events in the primary stages of xenophobic riots in the last two years has shown that considerable tensions often preceded the riots and that protest against and resistance to refugee housing had already been manifested in most cases. The existing tensions and indignation were usually not taken seriously or were underestimated. Attempts by politicians to mediate, discuss, and find acceptable solutions were rare and usually, as in Rostock-Lichtenhagen, too late. The development of xenophobic attitudes up to the tolerance and willingness toward the use of violence was therefore influenced considerably by political and bureaucratic action/inaction in the primary stages and the learning experiences conditioned thereby.

Thesis 2: The conflict over asylum and the inability of political leaders to present quick decisions and better concepts have changed the political opportunity structures for right-wing and violently disposed groups.

In view of the aforementioned new social conflicts and burdens to the local communities, and the worry of native inhabitant groups due to an increased immigration of refugees in particular, there was a build-up of expectations of political solutions in the population. At the same time, the political parties proved themselves largely incapable of reaching a consensus on the matter, developing common concepts or even making clear that local concerns and problems were being taken seriously. In this situation right-wing groups with their xenophobic demands and even with violent acts gained an audience and influence for themselves. They could bring their radical slogans into the public discussion and clearly influence public opinion regarding the asylum problem. This in turn got the established democratic parties moving, which then had to adapt their platforms for election reasons. The result was that previously marginalized and taboo political themes and demands were taken up by the large parties and could now take their place on the formal political agenda. A problematic definition of radical minorities was thus made politically viable, and xenophobic attitudes and violence legitimized. This can be interpreted as one important phase in the process of delegitimization that leads to political violence and terrorism.[12]

Thesis 3: *The weakness of state authority, particularly in the new Eastern states, made possible successes for the violent perpetrators, and contributed to the change in the cost-risk structures of violence.*

An inadequate police presence at the beginning of the riots in Hoyerswerda and Rostock, along with operational mistakes by the police, opened the opportunity for violent groups to use violence against refugees and also against the police almost without risk. Here, for a time at least, the state monopoly on the use of force was lifted. For the psychological dynamic of the riots these preliminary successes were of great importance. The sight of police retreating in the face of violence leads to a euphoric sense of power and a contagious and stimulating experience of lawlessness in violent groups, which is of great significance for the subsequent course of riot events. Violence seems to be employable without risk and thus becomes attractive for those who normally avoid high risk action.

Furthermore, violent groups experience that the massive use of force is successful: not only in that it can be carried out without risk, but also in that it does obtain political objectives. Through the use of violence in Hoyerswerda and Rostock, it was possible to force the evacuation of refugees and 'clean the city of foreigners', as it is expressed in the xenophobic jargon. These experiences of the successful use of violence are of decisive importance for the diffusion and escalation of the violence. Learning by direct success or by the models of others is of great significance for the explanation of a wave-like escalation and expansion of violence after spectacular individual successes.

Thesis 4: *The change in public opinion, particularly the increase of xeno-phobic attitudes in sections of the population in recent years, opens new pos-sibilities of self-definition and the feeling of collective importance for stigma-tized and violent groups of youth.*

Xenophobic violence as well as fascist and skinhead groups have not emerged just since 1991. Important, however, is that these groups which had already demonstrated xenophobic and nationalist tendencies in the 1980s were mar-ginalized, stigmatized, and discredited then precisely because of these traits. With the conflict over asylum rights in the 1990s and the associated legitima-tion of xenophobic attitudes, public opinion has changed considerably (not least because of local problems, conflicts, and experiences). In a relatively short period, xenophobic attitudes and a corresponding tolerance of violence have grown considerably in sections of the population. This is of great impor-tance both for the self-definition of right-wing and violent groups as well as for the further escalation of the violence. Right-wing and aggressive youths experience that their propensity to violence against foreigners now does not lead to social bans, stigmatization, and sanctions as before, but, on the con-trary, finds understanding, sympathy, and support within sections of the pop-ulation. For the first time these groups can experience a new self-definition and collective meaning as representatives of general interests through the unspoken or open support of parts of the population. Many perceive them-selves, thus, as the national avant garde, warriors for German interests, and have ascribed to themselves an historic significance in this role: either as the front-fighters of a larger xenophobic-nationalistic social movement whose first formation in waves of mobilization we recently observed,[13] or as radical right-wing extremists and terrorists who will continue to operate even with-out the support of larger parts of the population.

V. Conclusion

The development and expansion of xenophobic attitudes and violence cannot be traced back solely to personality deficits and socialization problems of individual perpetrators or to social, economic and cultural crises of the soci-ety as a whole. What we have to take into account in order to understand and explain what has happened, is the manner in which the immigration and inte-gration of foreigners are currently organized in Germany.

What we have observed in Germany, as well as in other European coun-tries is the emergence of new ethnic conflicts and the origin of xenophobic nationalist movements which reach far beyond the right-wing political mar-gin into the centre of society as a whole. The conflict about asylum is only the prelude to a new fundamental conflict: the conflict over immigration and by extension over the future definition of our society as a multicultural and multi-ethnic society. Youth violence gains political importance in these conflicts and is, under certain conditions, an efficient means of promoting change, as can be judged from the political processes brought about by the violence. Where right-wing or racist movements develop from here depends on (a) whether we are in a position *to allow and control immigration*, namely, to set quotas; (b) whether we are ready and willing to guarantee integration not only economically and socially but also legally; (c) whether we are capable of furthering and facilitating the necessary *learning processes* which are a prerequisite both to overcoming ethnocentric perspectives as well as to developing tolerance and solidarity beyond cultural borders; and d) whether *confidence in the social market economy* can be restored to all those who see themselves (or others close to them) as threatened by unemployment, rent increases and erosion of social aid.

NOTES

1. This is true for the discourse in Germany, whereas escalation has been a central issue for Scandinavian researchers in the field. See Tore Bjørgo, 'Terrorist Violence against Immigrants and Refugees in Scandinavia: Patterns and Motives', in idem. and Rob Witte (eds.), *Racist Violence in Europe* (Basingstoke: Macmillan, 1993).
2. A follow-up study for the period between May 1992 and Dec, 1993 has just been finished. See Helmut Willems, 'Analyse fremdenfeindlicher Straftäter' (Bonn: Bundesministerium des Innern, 1994).
3. For more detailed analysis, see Helmut Willems (together with R. Eckert, S. Würtz et al.), *Fremdenfeindliche Gewalt. Einstellungen, Täter, Konflikteskalation* (Opladen: Leske + Budrich, 1993).
4. Bundesministerium des Innern (Hg.), *Verfassungsschutzbericht 1991* (Bonn 1992).
5. See Sprinzak in this volume.
6. Wilhelm Heitmeyer, 'Hostility and Violence towards Foreigners in Germany', in Bjørgo and Witte (note 1), pp.17–28.
7. Robert K. Merton, 'Sozialstruktur und Anomie', in F. Sack und R. König, *Kriminalsoziologie* (Frankfurt: Suhrkamp, 1979).
8. See Sprinzak in this volume.
9. P. L. Berger, B. Berger and H. Kellner, *Das Unbehagen in der Modernität* (Frankfurt: Suhrkamp, 1973); U. Beck., *Risikogesellschaft. Auf dem Weg in eine andere Moderne* (Frankfurt: Suhrkamp, 1986).
10. Wilhelm Heitmeyer, *Die Bielefelder Rechtsextremismus-Studie* (Weinheim, Müchen: Juventa-Verlag, 1992).
11. Helmut Willems, 'Gewalt und Fremdenfeindlichkeit: Anmerkungen zum gegenwärtigen Gewaltdiskurs', in Hans-Uwe Otto und Roland Merten (eds.), *Rechtsradikale Gewalt im vereinigten Deutschland* (Bonn: Leske + Budrich, 1993), pp. 88–108.
12. See Ehud Sprinzak, 'The Process of Delegitimization', *Terrorism and Political Violence* 3/1 (Spring 1991), pp.50–68.
13. Helmut Willems, 'Kollektive Gewalt gegen Fremde: Historische Episode oder Genese einersozialen Bewegung von Rechts?', in Rainer Erb und Werner Bergmann (eds.), *Neonazismus und rechte Subkultur* (Berlin: Metropol Verlag, 1994).

Extreme Nationalism and Violent Discourses in Scandinavia: 'The Resistance', 'Traitors', and 'Foreign Invaders'

TORE BJØRGO[1]

This is a comparative analysis of neo-Nazis and anti-immigration activists in Norway, Denmark and Sweden with regard to their rhetoric and justifications for violence against 'foreigners' and political opponents, and actual patterns of violence and harassment. Different traditions of nationalism in the three Scandinavian countries, and highly dissimilar historical experiences – especially during World War II – influence the rhetorical strategies of the two types of extreme nationalists, and their respective abilities to appropriate national symbols. However, based on divergent historical analogies, most extreme nationalist groups present themselves as a 'resistance movement' fighting 'foreign invaders' and 'traitors'.

> We are the resistance movement, fighting the Muslim invasion of our country and the national traitors assisting them. Unless the treacherous immigration policy is reversed, a civil war will break out! [Arne Myrdal, leader of the organization 'Norway Against Immigration', NMI c.1989].[2]

> In our resistance struggle for ... the survival of the white race ... we must turn the battle axe against our common enemy – the Zionist Occupation Government (ZOG) [and] the liberal racial traitors, the keen servants of the crook-noses who are demolishing our country piece by piece. [In the racial war,] the ends justify the means [from Storm, the magazine of the 'White Aryan Resistance' in Sweden, 1992].[3]

In Scandinavia, two different types of extreme nationalists – on the one hand, neo-Nazis[4] and others with a clear racist ideology, and on the other, anti-immigration activists – seek support for their views from their interpretations of historic events. History comes to serve as mythological justification of their political messages and as legitimation for the use of violence against immigrants and political opponents. The highly dissimilar experiences of Norway, Denmark and Sweden during World War II, and the different traditions of nationalism, can be shown to have strongly influenced the discourses and rhetorical strategies developed by organised anti-immigrant and neo-Nazi activists in the three countries.[5] Although these discourses are shaped by specific historical circumstances, they are varieties of similar discourses developed by right-wing extremist groups in many other countries. The idomatic form may differ greatly but the structure of the discourse is often the same.

One discourse used by Norwegian and Danish anti-immigrant activists seeks to establish an analogy between present-day opposition to immigration, on the one hand, and the resistance against the Nazi forces of occupation during World War II, on the other. The implicit claim is that it is just as necessary and justified to fight – with violence if required – against today's 'national traitors' and 'foreign invaders' as it was when Norway and Denmark came under German occupation. A Swedish variant – due to lack of more recent historical models of popular armed resistance – draws an analogy back to the so-called Engelbrekt rebellion against German tax collectors during the fifteenth century.

Another discourse of a very different origin, used mainly by Swedish neo-Nazis and racial ideologists, speaks of the 'White Resistance Movement' and its fight against the 'Zionist Occupation Government' (ZOG) and the 'racial traitors'. This revolutionary version of 'Jewish World Conspiracy' theory was taken over from American racists and neo-Nazis. The notion of ZOG refers to the entire political, economic and cultural establishment, regarded as subservient tools and lackeys of the Jews. It is this Jewish-controlled elite that has to be overthrown and exterminated before the new and racially pure Aryan society can rise from the ruins.

Although the ideological points of departure for these two discourses are fundamentally different, the argumentation and conclusions are strikingly similar: A civil war will inevitably break out if immigration is not halted. When this situation arises, the 'resistance movement' will wage a just war against the 'traitors' and 'foreign invaders'. The radical racist ZOG discourse goes considerably further in terms of justifying extreme violence than the more 'moderate' nationalist anti-immigrant activists normally do in their rhetoric – but it is a matter of degree, not a difference of principle. Moreover, those activists who claim to be the heirs of the wartime resistance movement also demonstrably cooperate closely with today's political heirs of the quislings in collecting a 'traitor register' on political opponents.

It is mainly through their *discourses* that we are able to study the ideologies, political cultures and central aspects of the behaviour of extremist groups or movements. Discourses are empirical objects open to direct observation in ways which 'cultures' and 'ideologies' are not. By analysing statements, verbal exchanges, texts, and other forms of communicative interaction, we see how these groups, to use Berger and Luckman's formulation, 'construct their social realities'[6] – and further, how they try to influence social realities through these discursive practices.

The concept of discourse is used differently by various authors.[7] It is used here to refer to the process of communicative interaction whereby people through speech, texts, and other social practices codify and reflect on their experiences. While developing specific ways of speaking about certain topics, these discursive practices 'systematically form the objects of which they speak', as Michel Foucault puts it. Discourses are products of our experiences but are also constitutive of the social realities in which we live and the truths with which we work.[8] When ideas and arguments are exchanged within a group or a moral community, these notions may gradually become 'common property'. During this communicative interaction, sets of conventionally linked concepts are established, determining premises for interpreting situations and making decisions. Such conclusions and choices may appear logical and justified within the context of the relevant discourse and the moral community sharing it. To outsiders who do not reason in terms of this discourse, however, the act may seem irrational or even reprehensible. To bring out their reasoning and give glimpses into their particular constructions of reality, statements and texts by these groups and activists will be cited at some length in the present study.

The concept of *rhetoric* is used here to refer to a special form of discursive practice with the specific purpose of persuading audiences.[9] Successful rhetoric organizes the experiences of the audiences by creating a context which gives meaning to these experiences. This requires that the rhetorician be able to capture and 'tune in' to the concerns and experiences of his audiences. Political rhetoric normally seeks to promote certain interpretations of current events by presenting them in the light of specific constructions of reality, and to influence the audiences to act in accordance with these conceptions and values.[10]

Nationalisms in Scandinavia

Most Norwegians and Danes relate to national symbols and feelings in ways which differ significantly from the way Swedes do. This has important consequences for the ways in which extreme nationalists can exploit or appropriate national symbols.

The different paths that Sweden and Norway have taken through history have given rise to very different types of nationalism. Danish nationalism may be seen as representing an intermediate form. Sweden's past as an expansive great power in Northern Europe, particularly during the seventeenth and eighteenth centuries, and the way it was influenced by the political culture of Prussia/Germany, shaped Swedish nationalism. The notion of a 'Greater

Sweden' was alive in influential circles way into the twentieth century – at least until the middle of World War II.[11]

At times in its history, Denmark competed with Sweden in being the dominant regional power. Although it had (and to some extent still has) considerable possessions overseas, these were generally not results of military conquests, as was the case with the Swedish empire. With the exception of the wish in some circles to recover parts of southern Schleswig from Germany after the two World Wars, there is virtually nothing left of any notion of a 'Greater Denmark'. After having received a blow as a great power during the seventeenth century, Denmark lost practically all wars in which it was involved. Pacifism has thus become a far more prominent characteristic than militarism in present Danish political culture during the last century.

For Norway, the 'golden age' ended with the collapse of the kingdom and the incorporation of Norway under Danish rule during the fourteenth century. Thenceforth Norway was the underdog in Scandinavia – first during more than 450 years as an underdeveloped part of the union with Denmark, subsequently in a forced but somewhat more equal union with Sweden (1814–1905). The emerging Norwegian nationalism in the early nineteenth century (and even before) was predominantly a national liberation movement, closely linked to the development of democratic values and institutions, and occurring in an age of flourishing national culture.[12] The 1814 Constitution became a powerful national symbol of democracy and liberation. After Norway finally got its full independence in 1905, there was, however, in some circles a wish to re-acquire former Norwegian territories from Sweden and Denmark, but these tendencies towards revanchism were limited and not very aggressive.

During the twentieth century, World War II was the single event which most significantly affected the development of nationalism in Scandinavia (a summary of Scandinavian war history is given in endnote.[13] The wartime experiences of occupation and resistance in Norway and Denmark made national feelings a legitimate and uniting force in ways which have no parallels in recent Swedish history. The Swedish people has never undergone a national crisis where patriotism and national feelings have played a similar positive and uniting role in the struggle for freedom and democracy. To many Swedes today, national feelings and symbols seem problematic, even dubious. This was reflected when pupils at a school outside the town of Kalmar during Spring 1992 were preparing the programme for the end-of-term celebration, and proposed the national anthem '*Du gamla du fria*' as one of the items. However, this was rejected by the headmaster, who feared that the anthem could be exploited to stir up nationalist and racist sentiments. In this context, the strong wishes of the pupils to sing the national anthem was judged as suspect. The headmaster of the school stated that

We can never know for sure whether there are racist motives involved. We are so unaccustomed to singing *'Du gamla du fria'* in Sweden that we do not know what to think when the pupils want to.[14]

This decision was revoked after heavy criticism from leading politicians and the media; nevertheless, similar 'bans' of singing the national anthem have taken place at other schools, indicating widespread uneasiness about national feelings in Swedish society.[15] As nationalist symbols and sentiments are not much used and embraced by most Swedes (except in connection with sports), these symbols have to a large extent been appropriated and monopolized by right-wing, racist and neo-Nazi groups – who all wave the flag and sing *'Du gamla du fria'* with great enthusiasm.[16] Thus, the headmaster's worries were not entirely unfounded.

In Norway and Denmark, by contrast, it would be almost unthinkable to question the appropriateness of singing the respective national anthems on such occasions.[17] Broad-based support for national symbols and feelings is legitimated by the struggle against Nazi occupation (and for Norway's part, also the previous struggle to gain independence from Danish and Swedish dominance and the concurrent development of democracy). Norwegian anti-immigrant and neo-Nazi groups have made vigorous attempts to appropriate national symbols, but face great difficulties in doing so as long as most of the population celebrates Constitution Day (17 May) with such great festivities, in which flag-waving children play a prominent role. The celebration of the Swedish National Day is, by comparison, a very low-key event with limited participation by the general public.[18]

The main national celebrations of the extreme right in Sweden are the annual marches to commemorate the warrior kings of Sweden's glorious imperial past during the seventeenth and eighteenth centuries, in particular Karl XII and Gustav II Adolf. It is a paradox, however, that self-declared 'Norwegian patriots' go to Stockholm and Lund each 30 November to commemorate the death-day of Karl XII, who was killed by a bullet during his attempt to invade Norway in 1718. The Norwegian activists explain this by saying that they go to Sweden to celebrate the kind of nationalism and warrior heroism which Karl XII represents. At the same time, they also use the opportunity to strengthen their ties with their present political models and allies – the relatively extensive movement of neo-Nazis and declared racists in Sweden.[19]

By contrast, due to their outspokenness against racism and xenophobia and their support of refugees and immigrants, the Norwegian and Danish monarchs are unpopular in extreme-right circles.[20] Although the present

Swedish king and his family have spoken out against racism as well, they carry less weight than the Norwegian and Danish Royals due to their respective historical legacies. During the war, King Haakon VII of Norway and King Christian X of Denmark were symbols of opposition to Nazism. King Haakon insisted during the invasion that he would abdicate if the Parliament yielded to German demands. The Swedish King Gustav V, known for his pro-German views during the 1930s and early 1940s, threatened to abdicate *unless* Nazi troops were given free transit in the officially neutral Sweden in 1941.[21]

Swedish history, strongly characterized by great power traditions and ambitions, lends itself to a more aggressive and chauvinistic version of nationalism than does the history of Denmark and – in particular – Norway. Present-day extreme nationalists in Sweden attach themselves to this established 'Greater Sweden' tradition. Notions of brotherhoods of arms, war heroes and 'martyr' worship are central values among groups like *Vitt Ariskt Motstånd* and the nationalist *Sverigedemokraterna*. By contrast, while Swedish national heroes are predominantly warrior kings and soldiers, national heroes in Norway tend to be poets (of pronounced liberal and democratic inclinations), polar explorers and even skiers. Norwegian chauvinists have to go back one thousand years to find suitable historic models of expansionist warriors – the Vikings.

The Vikings, the sagas of ancient kings, and Norse mythology *were* important national symbols in Norway – in particular during the period of national romanticism of the late 1800s. However, this uniting symbolic function was lost after World War II because Vidkun Quisling and his Fascist party *Nasjonal Samling* had linked this symbolism to their discredited form of nationalism. To the political mainstream, this made Vikings and old Norse gods unsuitable as collective national symbols in the postwar era.[22] It is probably due to a sensitivity to this shift in symbolic meaning that today's non-Nazi anti-immigration activists – who want to portray themselves as the successors of the Resistance movement – generally seem to avoid using Norse gods and vikings as national symbols. Groups within the Nazi tradition, on the other hand, focus extensively on Vikings, runes and Norse mythology in their rhetoric. In Sweden, this Viking symbolism was not discredited during the war, and is now much used both by Nazi-inspired racists like *Vitt Ariskt Motstånd* and by non-Nazi nationalists such as *Sverigedemokraterna*. Danish nationalist groups relate to this set of symbols in the same way as the corresponding Norwegian organizations: The more Nazi-oriented, the more Vikings, runes and Norse gods. The petit bourgeois *Danske Forening* (Danish Association) is virtually free of Vikings.

Among modern national symbols, it is noteworthy that the two main representations of modern Sweden, the social democratic welfare state and high-tech industry (such as the car-manufacturers Volvo and Saab-Scania), are both crumbling during the first half of the 1990s. As carriers of national identity these two symbolic complexes have little to offer young Swedes seeking an expression of their Swedishness. To some, old warrior kings and Vikings appear more attractive and meaningful as objects of identification. The present situation in Sweden in this respect does have some parallels with Germany after unification. The German *Wirtschaftswunder* has also lost its lustre as a source of identity, whereas traditional national symbols are linked to historic legacies incompatible with democratic values.

Thus divergent historical experiences in the three Scandinavian countries largely determine which types of nationalism and national symbols extreme nationalist groups may play on – and which symbols they may have prospects of appropriating. Since the political mainstream in Sweden has not embraced the main national symbols such as the flag and the national anthem with much enthusiasm, extreme nationalists have seen their chance to appropriate these symbols. Furthermore, National Socialist and anti-Semitic symbols and notions have not in principle been incompatible with Swedish patriotism. In Norway and Denmark, this has been an almost impossible combination due to the historic legacy of Nazi occupation and the local Nazi traitors during the war – especially among the older generation which still has vivid memories of the occupation. In these two countries, extreme nationalists have also faced many more obstacles in their attempts to take over central national symbols such as the flag, the national anthem, the national day and royal traditions. These symbols are embraced by almost the entire population and by the political establishment, and are firmly linked to anti-Nazi and democratic traditions. However, Norwegian and Danish anti-immigrant nationalists have launched a strong offensive to capture a very central set of national symbols: that of the wartime Resistance Movement against the Nazi occupants and local traitors. Although these symbols are exploited to justify violence against immigrants, political opponents and democratic institutions, the extreme nationalists have met surprisingly little ideological resistance in their attempts to usurp these symbols.

'Resistance' Against 'National Traitors'

By their rhetoric, organized anti-immigrant activists in Norway and Denmark have attempted to establish themselves as the new 'resistance movement', fighting 'foreign invaders' and present-day 'national traitors'. Their rhetorical strategy consists in relating themselves to a set of symbols and values which, in their original version, are held in high esteem by the great majority of the population – symbols which represent true patriotism.

The discourse concerning 'the new resistance movement' and 'the national traitors' draws its symbolic material from a movement which was anti-Nazi (and therefore presumably anti-racist), and which – at least in Norway – saw itself as defending the legally elected institutions of democracy.[23] Today's anti-immigration activists have transformed this symbolic material into a discourse where 'the resistance movement' embodies nationalism and patriotism directed against foreigners (particularly Muslims), and with a threat of violence or other forms of reprisal against the elected institutions and civil servants who determine and administer current immigration policy. By linking their rhetoric to a symbolic material which enjoys general support and evokes powerful emotions among much of the population – particularly the older generation – they hope to mobilise extensive support. However, to accomplish this, they must get people to accept the assumption of a fundamental analogy between resistance against German occupants and resistance against immigrants and asylum-seekers. For most people, this analogy seems too far-fetched – even highly offensive to many of those who personally experienced Nazism during the war. Even so, a tiny minority of the population[24] can be said to have accepted the analogy and support the notion of 'the new resistance movement' against immigrants and 'traitors'.

Arne Myrdal, the former head of *Folkebevegelsen Mot Innvandring* (FMI, the People's Movement Against Immigration)[25] who split off to establish the more militant *Norge Mot Innvandring* (NMI, Norway Against Immigration), has been the leading proponent of violent rhetoric concerning civil war and violent reprisals against political opponents considered 'traitors' due to the immigration issue. He himself has a considerable record of violent behaviour.[26] Yet Myrdal is certainly not the only one among the leaders of anti-immigrant organizations in Scandinavia to harbour such views. Other central leaders of FMI and other nationalist organizations have expressed similar notions publicly – although rarely as bluntly as in Arne Myrdal's civil war romanticism. The common denominator is a discourse based on a metaphor or analogy where the alleged mass immigration of Third World refugees to Norway is portrayed as an 'invasion' comparable to Nazi-Germany's invasion of Norway (and Denmark) in 1940. In this analogy, anti-immigration activists are depicted as 'the resistance movement', while anti-racist activists (often branded as 'red Nazis') as well as politicians and civil servants are 'national traitors'. These people will have to answer for their treason – just like Vidkun Quisling and his party, *Nasjonal Samling*, it is asserted.

FMI spokesman Jan Høeg, who uses every opportunity to stress his active participation in the Resistance during World War II, has played an important role in developing a common discourse among Norwegian and Danish anti-immigrant activists.[27] He writes in the periodical of the sister organisation *Den Danske Forening* (DDF, The Danish Association) about the Norwegian immigration policy:

> Twenty to thirty years from now, Quisling's treason will probably appear relatively insignificant compared with what [prime minister] Gro Harlem Brundtland has commenced in Norway .... Gro Harlem Brundtland's name [will also] be remembered as the name of the traitor who removed Norway's boundary barriers and opened the gates for a free invasion of asylum parasites, deserters, and drug mafias by the thousands. ... Unless the course is altered very soon, we must unfortunately conclude that Norway has got its second traitor government within the span of a few years (*Danskeren*, No. 5, Dec. 1989).

This national traitor analogy is a recurrent theme in pamphlets and other propaganda material published by nationalist and anti-immigrant organizations in Norway as well as in Denmark. In the journal of the crypto-Nazi *Partiet De Nasjonale*, headed by Albert Larsen – himself a former honorary member of *Danmarks Nationalsocialistiske Bevægelse* – we can read:

> If a foreign invasion army had attacked Denmark, defeated the army, conquered the country and installed a Quisling government, we would have had a situation like the one Denmark is in today. We are occupied. The Quislings in government and the *Folketing* (the Parliament) take care of the interests of the immigrant forces, not those of the Danish people. [...] The foreign colonists are given such good conditions that they rapidly can establish themselves, multiply and by a new mass invasion in the longer term take over political power in the country. Many would claim that this take-over has already taken place, as all the state institutions today are programmed to consolidate the immigration forces' grip on the country (*Bavnen – Nationalt tidsskrift*, No. 5, 1993, p.13).

The analogy of the resistance movement serves two important rhetorical purposes. First, it is an attempt to give the nationalism of anti-immigrant activists an aura of legitimacy as good patriotism. If this is accepted, it may counter the claim that anti-immigrant activists are racists colluding with neo-Nazis. The second point made by the analogy – sometimes expressed explicitly, at other times more implicitly – is to legitimate the use of violence and other forms of reprisal against 'the foreign invaders' and the 'national traitors' (*landssvikerne*) – just as the Resistance did against collaborators during the war. Arne Myrdal, the FMI/NMI leader, has declared this in very unambiguous terms in an interview:

The Norwegian population will no longer accept this national treason. When the politicians provoke the people, then youth will take recourse to violence. First against the immigrants, then against those who promote immigration, and finally against the politicians and the System. Then the civil war will break out. It's too bad that the immigrants will be targeted – it is not their fault. They [i.e., the young militants] should rather go for the politicians.

[Interviewer] How?

By beating or killing them. The people will rise against them with violence. The government and the *Storting* are out of touch with the people. When they do not govern the way we want, things will escalate to a civil war. There are many resistance groups, and the boys are armed. I know everything about this, I direct the resistance all over the country. There have been many weapons thefts [from military depots] during the last few years. These weapons end up with the resistance groups. It is not our intention to use the weapons against the immigrants. It is our own national traitors we have to fight against.[28]

In apparent contradiction to this argument, Myrdal also describes immigrants and asylum seekers as 'pioneers' in a Muslim army of conquest. According to this theory, the so-called refugees have come to establish 'bridgeheads' for Islam in Norway. This is part of an evil Muslim conspiracy to establish global Islamic rule.

...all those foreign intruders who came here ... have not come to save their lives, as they have tried to make us believe. They have come for nothing less than taking over our country, to become as numerous as to make the Norwegians a minority in their own country. The Pakistanis in particular are highly determined in this respect. The FMI is a very unpleasant obstacle to their attempt to achieve this goal. It is therefore no wonder that they try to fight us with all possible means.[29]

Thus, the argument goes, the resistance struggle must also involve 'resistance' against the Muslim intruders:

The Muslims have come to conquer Europe. I believe there will be civil war in three years' time. We can either surrender and let them take over our country – rape our country! Or we may prepare ourselves for resistance, and that is what we are doing right now.[30]

Myrdal's successor to the FMI leadership, Bjørn Voldnes, subscribes to the main features of this 'theory'. He speaks of FMI as

> ... the struggle of a few Norwegians against both an anti-national
> political system of government and against a migration of peoples who
> have the overarching goal of exterminating all the European nation-
> states as we know them today. ... The Norwegian people can rest assured
> that the FMI will never give up the struggle to stop these pioneers and
> to send them out of our beloved fatherland.[31]

Several of the central personalities in the anti-immigrant organizations did
in fact take active part in the wartime Resistance. In Norway, these include
Jan Høeg and Gunnar Øi, executive members of the FMI; Vivi Krogh, who
established *Organisasjonen mot skadelig innvandring* (Organization against
Harmful Imigration); and the highly decorated war hero Erik Gjems-Onstad,
a top parliamentary candidate for *Partiet Stopp Innvandringen* (The Stop
Immigration Party), and later, *Fedrelandspartiet* (the Fatherland Party), and
known as a staunch supporter of the South African Apartheid regime. In
Denmark, the anti-immigrant association *Den Danske Forening* was
etablished by a group of persons who had belonged to a militant, nationalist
and conservative faction of the resistance movement on Jutland in western
Denmark who for several decades after the war met annually for political
discussions.[32]

This historical link to the Resistance constitutes an important rhetorical
resource to both Danish and Norwegian anti-immigration activists, and it is
exploited for all it is worth – and even more – to give legitimacy to their
nationalism, anti-immigrant views and militant initiatives. The secretary of
FMI, Gunnar Øi, mailed a series of harassing letters to the female secretary of
a local antiracist organization in Norway, *Brumunddal på nye veier*
(Brumunddal on New Paths). In one of these letters, he wrote:

> Hello, Judas! ... The writer of this letter took an active part in the
> resistance struggle through the war and consequently has had a long
> experience in dealing with small national traitors of your calibre.

Arne Myrdal also has tried – albeit with some credibility problems – to exploit
the legitimacy of the resistance movement:

> In my family, a cousin of my mother was a member of Milorg [the
> Military Resistance Organization] – and they still dare to call me a Nazi!
> Such libel makes me worry that we will have to take recourse to
> weapons in the future.[33]

In 1992 Arne Myrdal and the so-called *Landsforeningen mot landssvikere* (the National Association against Traitors), with links to neo-Nazi activists, intensified their work on building up what they called a 'Traitor Register' (*Landssvikerregister*). Myrdal even applied to the Data Protection Registrar (*Datatilsynet*) for a licence but was – not surprisingly – turned down. All the same, he and his partners continued to register enemies. During the autumn of 1992 his organization Norway Against Immigration (NMI) sent a form to a large number of individuals whom they wanted to have registered in their 'Traitor Register'. Recipients were asked to fill in the form themselves (!) 'to save us the work', as it was stated in the accompanying note. This *could* be interpreted as a joke, but many of the recipients undoubtedly felt it threatening to be registered by extremists. This was probably also the intention of informing them that they were under surveillance. The note also explained who the 'traitors' are:

> When foreign troops invaded and occupied our country in 1940–45, Norwegian traitors who assisted and cooperated with the foreigners were registered in a traitor register by good Norwegians and patriots. This register came to use later during the treason trials.
> Today it is again necessary to register new traitors who take service for the enemy. ... It is useful to assign and register such traitors in three categories:
> *(1) Governmental officials:* Major state/regional/municipal officials who by their acts or statements aid the foreigners and make possible further occupation – also by aggravating the situation of Norwegian patriots (ministers of state, government employees, civil servants, etc.).
> *(2) Political traitors:* Politicians and extremists in parties/groups/ organizations who actively work against Norwegian patriots and assist the foreigners in their occupation of Norway (left-wing extremists, *Blitz* activists [an 'autonomous' group], organized 'antiracists', etc.).
> *(3) Other traitors:* Individuals who by *clear* acts and statements serve the enemy (e.g., 'pro forma' wives of foreign immigrants,[34] dishonest journalists, frequent contributors to newspaper letter-columns, etc.).[35]

Myrdal has also claimed that his group has been registering illegal and criminal immigrants as well as their Norwegian helpers.

> The information [in these registers] will be of great help to us the day the situation really blows up. Because it will – some time in the future. Then there will be a real fight, and it is paramount to be prepared for that, Myrdal asserts to *Aftenposten* [27 March 1992].

At the NMI meeting in Myrdal's house in June 1992, where members of the skinhead band Boot Boys and the neo-Nazi group *Hvit Arisk Motstand*

(HAM, White Aryan Resistance, linked to the Swedish VAM network) were also invited, it was emphasized that the future struggle was to be directed not against immigrants but against 'white traitors'. 'Unfortunately, we will have to fight against our own countrymen, against the immigration commissioners', Myrdal told his followers, according to a report by a local journalist who was present (*Agderposten*, 6 June 1992).

One of those who have felt the effect of this particular type of 'struggle' is the mayor of Ringsaker municipality. He took a strong position against racist tendencies in the municipal centre Brumunddal. During the autumn of 1992 he went public about the protracted and severe harassment he and his family had been exposed to in the form of night-time phone calls, letters with threats to kill him and his family members, a dead rabbit in the mail box, and various mail-order merchandise ordered by others in his name. Even if each individual episode seen in isolation was not particularly serious, the continuous and massive amount of harassment had a severe impact on himself and his family.[36] The police suspected that activists of the local NMI and HAM groups were responsible. The local NMI activist and Myrdal devotee Arild Elvsveen confirmed that they had registered in the 'Traitor Register' the mayors of Ringsaker and the nearby town of Gjøvik (both had strongly opposed local racists).[37]

These registration and harassment activities are clear parallels to the so-called Anti-antifa lists, circulating among German neo-Nazis, with close connections to similar groups in several other countries – including Denmark and Sweden.[38] There are also strong indications that Anti-antifa cells have been established by Norwegian neo-Nazis, although it is still not clear to what extent these groups are attached to the international Anti-antifa network. Most probably, they are linked via Swedish VAM.[39] Arne Myrdal has even stated that 'I support the neo-Nazis' harassment lists in Denmark and Germany. We have for a long time tried to build up something similar in Norway. I support violence, but not murder' (*Dagbladet*, 4 Dec. 1993). Several extreme nationalist groups consider registering and harassing opponents to be their main *raison d'être*. This is for instance the case with the 'patriotic youth organization' called *Djerv* ('Brave'), located in Trondheim, which has stated in a pamphlet that its main tasks were to 'register everyone who agitates for or makes profit from the coloured occupation forces, [... and] carry out active combat training to retaliate against violence and harassment from immigrant groups and left-wing radical mobs'.[40]

Despite Norway's and Denmark's common historical experiences of occupation, there is one important difference which gives today's Danish activists against immigration an extra point. As noted, the Norwegian government actively resisted the German invasion, and was directly involved in organizing the illegal resistance movement after the official capitulation two months later. The collaborator Vidkun Quisling and his fascist party *Nasjonal Samling* became the archetype traitors, while the government-in-exile enjoyed a strong legitimacy among most Norwegians. By contrast, the Danish government capitulated without having been able to offer any serious military resistance. In order to protect Danish interests within the framework of an agreement of cooperation with the German occupants, the government and large parts of the Establishment actively opposed the illegal resistance movement from its very beginning – until popular resistance against the occupying forces became too strong. Thus, many resistance activists held the Danish government to be treacherous. After liberation, a large part of the organized resistance activists still remained partly outside the power elite – quite unlike the situation in Norway. *Den Danske Forening* (DDF) claims that the situation today is analogous to that during the war: The power elite – with the government taking the lead – is serving the 'foreign occupiers'. The anti-immigrant activists of DDF see themselves as representing the same popular and determined resistance which, after five dark years of occupation and official submission, gradually won through and overcame the treacherous course of the authorities during the war.[41]

Compared to the Norwegian FMI/NMI, which under Myrdal's leadership has openly promoted violence and armed 'resistance' and joined forces with violent youth gangs, *Den Danske Forening* presents itself as a more civic organization with professors and Lutheran priests in prominent positions.[42] The DDF has nevertheless been embarrassed by revelations about preparations for future violent action. It was, for instance, documented that the chairman, Ole Hasselbalch, a professor of law, studied bomb-making instructions. He claimed that he just wanted to warn that Danish patriots might take resort to arms because they saw no other options. However, in an internal DDF paper he wrote that 'unless one wants to see the country turned into a ruin, one is left using physical means to prevent the policy of destruction being carried out'. A leading DDF member – a policeman by profession – provoked strong reactions when he stated publicly that 'I do not disagree with those holding that it is necessary to resort to violence and weapons to bring attention to the problems of foreigners in Denmark.'[43]

Since Sweden avoided German occupation during World War II, one would have to go as far back as the 1430s to find Swedish historical models of popular, armed resistance to foreign occupants and their collaborators. The so-called Engelbrekt Rebellion was a popular uprising against extortionist German tax collectors during the rule of King Erik XIII (of Pomerania). The heroic leader of this struggle for liberty, Engelbrekt Engelbrektson (who descended   from a German noble family!), was immortalised in the

Engelbrekt Ballad (*Engelbrekt-visan*). He is celebrated by the nationalist, anti-immigrant party *Sverigedemokraterna* (SD) during the 'Engelbrekt March' every 25 April. The SD's predecessor, *Bevara Sverige Svenskt* (BSS, Keep Sweden Swedish), rewrote the Engelbrekt Ballad, replacing the German tax collectors with today's immigrants in the role of foreign occupants. Anti-immigrant resistance was equated with the Engelbrekt Rebellion.[44] However, this analogy is made primarily in the rhetoric of the anti-immigrant organisations and parties that operate within the parliamentary political system. When militant Swedish racists operating *outside* the political system address the issue of resistance and race war, they speak instead about the struggle against the Zionist Occupation Government (ZOG) and its lackeys.

The ZOG Discourse: the *'White Resistance Movement'* against the *'Zionist Occupation Government'*

While Norwegian and Danish anti-immigrant activists compare their struggle against immigrants and their helpers with the anti-Nazi resistance, the rhetoric of Swedish neo-Nazi groups like the *Vitt Ariskt Motstånd* (VAM, White Aryan Resistance) take rather the opposite point of departure. They see their fight as a direct extension of Nazi Germany's struggle against the 'insidious influence' of the Jews. Swedish neo-Nazis (and their less numerous Norwegian and Danish counterparts) base their ideas of the 'Great Race War' against the 'Zionist Occupation Government' and their lackeys on the old notions of a 'Jewish World Conspiracy' aimed at destroying the white race and subjugating the entire world under Jewish domination. More specifically, it is the way these ideas were further developed into a highly violent revolutionary and terrorist doctrine by North American racist movements during the 1970s and 1980s which was adopted by local Swedish neo-Nazis during the late 1980s.[45]

An important and – in racist circles – highly influential representation of the ZOG ideology is presented in literary form through the novel *The Turner Diaries* (1980), written by the US racist leader William Pierce under the pseudonym Andrew Macdonald. The novel describes – in blood-dripping detail – the revenge taken on the racial traitors after the white resistance movement has seized power in a coup. A subsequent novel by the same author, *Hunter* (1989) describes how an individual white man, the 'lone hunter', can wage his private war against powerful Jews, media people, politicians and others considered ZOG lackeys and racial traitors. The sinister thing about these novels is that they can serve in many capacities: as exciting entertainment, as propaganda for a racist worldview, as ideological instruction, as handbooks of terrorism, and as models of action for young activists in the militant neo-Nazi and racist sub-cultures.[46]

Within the framework of the ZOG ideology, immigration is presented as a strategic weapon in the hands of the Jews in their ongoing race war against the Aryans. Through their 'malicious scheme of racial mixing' – and with the help of their Liberal lackeys – ZOG disseminates perverted humanistic ideas of 'a common human race', tolerance and multi-cultural societies. The pervasive feeling of fear that the social world they know – and the race they belong to – is threatened with annihilation, is apparent in the following excerpt from an editorial in the VAM magazine *Storm* (No. 7–8, 1992):

> Our wonderful race is on the brink of *total* extermination. It is *our* assignment to save the *remnants* out of the decadence and misery of the present situation and restore it [i.e., our race] to its former honour and greatness. This can *only* take place in *one* way, by struggle!
>
> Unless *we* take responsibility to recreate the *natural* world order, *everything* of beauty and value will be lost *forever*. No people has perished by hunger, war or disease, but rather because its blood has been *tarnished* [Italics were upper-case in original].

The idea that it is really the Jews who are behind the immigration problem and the wave of refugees is fundamental to the way most neo-Nazis perceive the issue of immigration. This view is also shared by the less militant Norwegian organisation *Zorn 88*:

> As National Socialists we are more concerned with exposing the worldwide Zionist activities of deceit and banditry, and attacking the actual *cause* of the immigration problem, rather than turning against the individual *immigrant*.[47]

The militant activists of the VAM network will also often claim that in the race war it is more important to fight the Jews and their obedient servants within politics, the bureaucracy and the media than going after the individual immigrant, who is merely a small pawn in a large game. The terrorist-oriented VAM cell *Werwolf* declares in its magazine:

> Let us once and for all state clearly that the primary targets of the national revolution are not refugee camps or individual niggers. Attacks on these are generally a waste of our resources. Attacks must be aimed at newspapers, politicians, journalists and the police/prosecuting authorities. They are the ones who constitute a great but not insurmountable obstacle in our fight for freedom. Far too long have these traitors escaped unpunished, despite their maladministration of Sweden, with mass immigration, increasing homosexuality, assaults on minors, giving Sweden away to the EC, etc.

After every article harassing national movements, heavy attacks must be aimed at the newspapers and journalists who are responsible. Everything from bomb threats to grievous bodily harm and murder. For every national soldier who is sentenced to imprisonment we shall extract bitter revenge. We shall attack judges, jurors, prosecutors, witnesses and policemen.[48]

Swedish neo-Nazi groups have long traditions of publishing in their journals lists containing names, addresses, phone numbers and other information on their enemies, often with a thinly veiled call to harass or physically attack the persons in question. For instance, the VAM journal *Storm* (No. 9–10, 1993) published detailed information about nine named 'racial traitors', including two prominent journalists, two left-wing activists, an academic researcher, a social democratic member of parliament, a youth worker, the head of the Police Union, and the National Police Chief. Harassment by phone and mail appeared to be the recommended form of action – although in the case of a female journalist there was an appeal to 'young aspiring soldiers [to volunteer for] the noble pioneer mission ... of ending her career'.

The virulent racism and anti-semitism of the ZOG discourse have the potential of attracting support from only a very marginal part of the population. For most anti-immigrant activists and 'moderate' nationalists this discourse is far too extreme.[49] Thus, the symbolic 'capital' is unsuitable for creating a rhetoric with any potential of winning support from larger segments of the population. On the other hand, this is hardly the objective of VAM activists. Within Nazi groupings and among young people who are attracted by their kind of rebellion against society, this extreme discourse serves as a test to cull the 'soft' from the 'strong'.[50] Groups like VAM, *Kreativistens Kyrka* (Church of the Creator, a kind of racist religion) and *Föreningen Sveriges Framtid/Riksfronten* (Association for Sweden's Future/National Front) want to be an elite, not a mass movement. As a banner of rebellion and a boundary marker against the rest of the society, this extreme discourse is highly functional. The reactions of disgust and dissociation from the surrounding masses merely serve to strengthen group identity and solidarity. But as a basis for more extensive political mobilisation aimed at winning political influence in the public arena, the ZOG discourse is totally unsuitable, as it is completely without any links to values and symbols shared by the ordinary public. However, their rhetoric is not directed at society at large but at a small segment of the populace who are alienated from society and its predominant values.[51]

Although a marginal phenomenon, the Nazi-affiliated ZOG discourse has won somewhat larger support among racist and nationalist youth groups in Sweden than in Norway and Denmark.[52] This may be explained by the fact that in Sweden there is no contradiction in terms between being both a patriot and a national socialist. Swedish wartime National Socialists were not considered traitors. In Norway and Denmark, where many still remember the Nazi occupation and the local collaborating Nazis during the war, it is far more difficult to 'sell' Nazism and patriotism in the same 'package'. Nazism is still too firmly associated with treason.

In comparison, the rhetorical discourse which attempts to establish an analogy between the present-day resistance to immigration and the Resistance against Nazi occupation has a much larger potential of mass mobilization – even if this discourse is too much to swallow for most people. It should also be noted that whereas the 'resistance movement' analogy was developed locally on the basis of events which many of the activists themselves have experienced, the ZOG discourse was imported from abroad and adopted almost without attempts to transform it to fit a local context – even to the point of keeping the English abbreviation.

Paradoxically, some of the Nazi-inspired organizations have also tried to exploit the analogy to the wartime resistance movement. Even Norwegian Quisling-followers in the partly Nazi *Nasjonalt Folkeparti* (NF, The National People's Party, dissolved in 1991) tried to use this discourse in pamphlets to encourage people to 'join the national Home Front'[53] against an 'invasion of foreign peoples' where 'the uniform of the occupiers is their skin colour'. However, the link between NF and similar parties to wartime collaborators represents a credibility problem when they try to exploit this popular analogy in their rhetoric.

A local neo-Nazi grouping in Norway apparently tried to solve this problem by establishing two formally separate organizations: *Birkebeiner-gruppa* (the 'Birkebeiner group', referring to a twelfth century rebel army in Norway) and *Hvit Arisk Motstand* (HAM, 'White Aryan Resistance'). However, both organizations were headed by the same person, the skinhead Jan Holthe, and there was a considerable overlap in terms of members.[54] HAM was a declared National Socialist organization, and a sub-division of the Swedish *Vitt Ariskt Motstånd* (VAM). As its model, HAM made extensive use of the ZOG discourse. *Birkebeinergruppa*, on the other hand, defined itself as a 'pro-nationalist organization, and certainly not a national socialist one'.[55] This organization aimed at reaching wider circles of 'action-oriented, national-minded young people' – young and militant Norwegian patriots who do not want to associate themselves with Nazism and swastikas. To reach these youngsters, the discourse of the new resistance movement and the national traitors is more functional than the ZOG discourse. However, in such a close organizational collaboration the different discourses tend to get mixed up – especially since HAM and *Birkebeinergruppa* shared not merely the

same the mailbox, leader and core members – but also a common membership magazine, *Vikingen*. The magazine made liberal use of both discourses
without any attempt to make any editorial distinctions between what was
directed at which members. One likely interpretation is that the neo-Nazis
conciously tried to introduce their ideological notions to young nationalists
who do not consider themselves neo-Nazis. If the ZOG discourse is accepted
in wider circles, it will contribute to reinforcing the tendency that Nazism and
patriotism seem less incompatible to the younger generation than it does to
those with personal experience of the Nazi occupation. Nevertheless, the
formal distinction between the two organizations was important because it
enabled anti-immigrant activists like NMI leader Arne Myrdal to cooperate
openly with *Birkebeinergruppa* and Jan Holthe, and still claim not to
collaborate with Nazis.

A set of symbols which to some extent has served as a bridge between the
two types of groups and their respective discourses is taken from the Ku Klux
Klan tradition. The American, anti-black Ku Klux Klan movement has
provided symbols, rituals and slogans used both by neo-Nazis and by some of
the more racist and militant anti-immigrant activists in Scandinavia. Unlike
the other two discourses, these symbols are not elaborated much at the verbal
level. They are mainly expressed through ritual acts such as burning crosses,
the use of white robes, the use of the 'South State' (Confederate) flag, and the
slogan 'White Power'. Racist vandalism against, for example, immigrant
shops is often accompanied by 'KKK' and 'WP' graffiti.

Although unabashedly racist, in Europe the Ku Klux Klan symbols do not
carry the same stigma of treason and Holocaust as the Nazi legacy does. Thus,
particularly in Norway and Denmark, these symbols provide racist activists
with a set of symbols which is compatible – or at least not completely at odds
– with their proclaimed patriotism. Some of these rather unsophisticated
racists seem to be fully aware of this point. One of the leaders of the Danish
Grønjakkerne (the Green Jackets), a violent and criminal youth gang which
became increasingly racist and gained notority for the way they terrorized
immigrant neighbours during the mid-1980s,[56] commented upon their use of
symbols:

> The South State Flag represents the Ku Klux Klan, in other words, the
> struggle against negroes, communists, homosexuals and Jews. Many of
> us sympathized with the Klan because they were undisguised racists –
> people knew what they stood for. However, we could not run around
> burning crosses all the time; using the South State Flag was more
> convenient. We used the flag the same way the Nazis use the Swasika.
> However, if *we* had used the Swasika, it would have offended many old
> Resistance fighters. Although a few of us sympathized with DNSB

(Denmark's National Socialist Movement), most of us felt that to kill six million Jews was to exaggerate a little bit.[57]

Whereas the leaders of the pronounced nationalist anti-immigration organizations as a rule will try to prevent young activists from using swastikas and other Nazi symbols and slogans, the undisguised use of the Confederate Flag and some other KKK symbols appears to be accepted – if not directly approved. This indicates that these racist symbols are not seen as being directly incompatible with their discourse on the resistance movement and the national traitors.

Violence – Rhetoric and Reality

Although right-wing extremists and racists tend to be highly violent in their discourse, their practice rarely approaches the level of violence one could expect from their rhetoric. Still, there have been so many acts of violence, harassment and threats that their violent propaganda cannot be characterized as 'merely rhetorical'. Close to 200 attacks (involving the use of bombs, Molotov cocktails and guns) have been directed at asylum-seekers and immigrant targets in the Scandinavian countries during the past decade, with an alarming increase in Sweden since 1990. However, most of these attacks have been carried out by local youth gangs – often influenced by racist propaganda – rather than by organized activists themselves. Such activists have, on the other hand, been heavily involved in another type of violence – street violence or assaults on 'foreigners' and homosexuals, particularly in Sweden and to some extent in Denmark.[58]

Many of the violent activities of the organized groups are focused on 'traitors'. In all three countries, anti-racist activists and organizations have been targets of bombings and arson attacks. These cases are often unsolved, but racist militants remain prime suspects. In Denmark, an activist of *Internationale Socialister* was killed by a powerful parcel bomb in 1992. In Sweden, several leading anti-racist activists and local politicians have received letter bombs and parcel bombs. A powerful bomb was also found at the scene of an anti-racist demonstration in 1992.[59] Several activists of the neo-Nazi *Nordiska Rikspartiet* were convicted of arson and threats in 1985. In Norway, activists of *Nasjonalt Folkeparti* the same year attempted to carry out bombing attacks against the homes of a communist party leader and a journalist who had written a book on the neo-Nazis. In 1994 a powerful bomb was thrown at the autonomous 'Blitz House' in Oslo – a stronghold of militant anti-racists – causing extensive material damage and endangering several persons. Neo-Nazis or extreme nationalists – possibly linked to *Anti-Antifa* – are prime suspects, but evidence is lacking.

More common than physical violence are the systematic campaigns to threaten and harass anti-racists and other 'traitors'. Although several leading activists from groups such as *Nordiska Rikspartiet, Vitt Ariskt Motstånd, Nationalpartiet Danmark* and *Folkebevegelsen Mot Innvandring* have been linked to or even convicted of making such threats, most cases are never solved because perpetrators are anonymous. The full range of alleged 'ZOG lackeys' and 'national traitors' are among those targeted, including politicians, police officers, journalists, researchers, anti-racist activists and individuals who have publicly expressed opinions in favour of immigrants or in opposition to racism. Sometimes harassment campaigns prove to be highly effective. There are many cases of individuals who have quit their public activities against racism after being intimidated by various forms of harassment and repeated threats against themselves or their families.[60] Actual physical violence may not be necessary if threats can suffice.

However, it must be noted that anti-immigrant and racist activists are themselves targets of violent attacks by anti-racist militants, particularly in connection with counter-demonstrations and blockades of public meetings organized by nationalist and racist groups. It is a stated policy of several of the left-wing radical groups to prevent – by violent means if necessary – racists and fascists from 'taking over the streets' by staging their public meetings and marches. Violence from the left commonly involves beatings and stone throwing, occasionally causing severe injuries. During 1994 Swedish anti-racist militants and immigrant youth gangs have in some cases outdone their Nazi opponents in the use of terrorist violence, brutal assaults and, possibly, even murder.[61] Thus, some of the violence and harassment from racist and anti-immigrant groups against radical anti-racist activists may be seen as motivated primarily by feelings of revenge rather than by lofty ideological considerations. However, anti-racist violence and harrassment against nationalists – and the often conspicuous lack of response from the police and other authorities – also serve to strengthen the notion of a threatening conspiracy of evil forces. Communists, the liberal media and the authorities are seen as collaborating in their persecution of nationalists.

A common explanation of why right-wing extremists and racists resort to violence is that they do not get outlet for their views through ordinary channels of the political system. This situation may lead to an accumulation of pressure and aggression which finds explosive outlets – the so-called pressure cooker effect. This explanation has been presented by extremists themselves as well as by outside observers.[62] This is partly correct: There *is* a certain connection between the use of violence and being hindered – by violence, legal bans or censorship – in presenting their views in public. However, it is a mistaken – or at least an overly simplified – understanding of the mechanisms involved to see the use of violence by the extreme right as the result of such a 'pressure cooker effect'. Many of the violent (as well as many of the non-violent) activists of the extreme right have had numerous opportunities to present their views in the mass media or in other public contexts. Arne Myrdal may serve as an example. His media statements and readers' letters may be counted by the hundreds. He has also staged more than 20 'popular meetings' in various localities – although these meetings have often been disturbed or interrupted by counter-demonstrators. Although he gets less access to the media than he would have liked, he has had the opportunity to propagate his views more than most non-establishment activists can ever dream of. Still, Myrdal has been convicted twice for serious counts of violence. Thus, his violence cannot be explained as a result of being unable to get his message out through more conventional methods. However, it is rather the case that every time he is hindered in his intention to stage a street meeting – whether it is by militant anti-racists throwing stones and eggs, or by police chiefs turning down his request – it is experienced as a provocation, and used as a justification for his own propagation of violence and attacks on 'mock democracy'. What strongly influences extreme nationalists to resort to (or at least to justify) violence is the experience that their right to free expression is obstructed in concrete situations, rather than a sense that they are unable to disseminate their message more generally.

When *Nordiska Rikspartiet* (in 1983–85) and *Norsk Front/Nasjonalt Folkeparti* (in 1979 and 1985) used bombs, Molotov cocktails and other terrorist means against adversaries on the radical left, it was after periods of repeated assaults and humiliations from leftist anti-racist groups. The use of weapons and bombs was seen as a natural and legitimate response in this context – particularly since nationalist and neo-Nazi organizations were normally unable to mobilize sufficient numbers to challenge the leftist counter-demonstrators in street fights. Terrorist tactics were considered legitimate means of self defence and 'a natural extension of the political struggle in a world full of powerful secret enemies'.[63]

When extreme nationalists have started systematically to register their political opponents, it may be seen as a reaction to similar campaigns by leftist anti-racists. For instance, during the late 1970s and early 1980s, a Marxist-Leninist party in Norway, AKP(m-l), ran an extensive intelligence operation in order to keep right-wing extremists under close surveillance.[64] On some occasions, vital information on violent crimes being prepared or committed by right-wing extremists was relayed to the Security Police, helping to solve cases or pre-empting attacks. However, some of this information on right-wing extremists was also used to harrass these political opponents. More recently, the paper of the militant autonomous group *Blitz*

published names and pictures of known and alleged neo-Nazis under the title
'Wanted Dead'. Each picture had a field to check off 'when you have put an
end to that pig' (*Smørsyra*, No.13, 1992). Similar lists and pictures of left-
wing activists published in nationalist magazines such as *Ung Front* and
Norsk Blad may be seen as a direct response to this. The *Blitz* group is
considered by some of the extreme nationalist groups as their main enemy,
and is highly exposed to actions of revenge. Similarly, the German *Antifa* has
for years focused much of its anti-fascist effort on publishing names,
addresses and pictures of right-wing extremists. These opponents have often
been subjected to harassment and violence, including several fatal attacks.
The *Anti-Antifa* phenomenon may also here be seen to some extent as a
counter-reaction and escalation in a spiral of violence – using even stronger
and more terroristic forms of violence, and with vengefulness reinforced by
an extremely violent ideology.[65]

Different Sources – Parallel Content

Although the ideological points of departure are different for nationalist anti-
immigration activists and racial revolutionary neo-Nazi groups, the content of
their rhetoric is strikingly similar.

Today's situation is defined as an *invasion/occupation* where the *foreign
occupants* are supported by local *traitors*. These traitors are identified as the
political Establishment which by its immigration policy has laid the country
open to foreigners who want to take it away from the indigenous population.
The media, anti-racists and anyone who in one way or another takes a stand
against racism or in support of immigrants and refugees, as well as local
women who have intimate relations with foreign men, are all considered
among the traitors who are leading the nation/race towards annihilation. The
only force to stand up against this coalition – which is indeed a *conspiracy* of
evil forces – is a *resistance movement* of true patriots. To save the nation/race
from total disaster this resistance movement will, if necessary, wage a *civil
war/race war* – partly against the 'foreign invaders', but primarily against the
'traitors'.

The content and the structure in this rhetoric are almost identical whether
used by nationalist anti-immigrant activists or by racial revolutionaries like
the neo-Nazis. The main difference relates to the sources and the basis of
legitimacy, and to who is identified as the foreign enemy. Nationalist anti-
immigration activists in Norway and Denmark take the anti-Nazi resistance
during World War II as their model and basis of legitimacy. Racial
revolutionary groups all over Scandinavia, on the other hand, take their
ideological material and symbols from National Socialism and related racist
movements. The first type of activist stresses nation, while the second puts

more emphasis on the notion of race. Although nation and race tend to intermingle in the rhetoric, the new generation of racists tend to be more internationally oriented – they proclaim their solidarity with the white or Aryan race. To nationalist anti-immigration activists, the threat is primarily conceived as cultural mixing, while neo-Nazi and racist ideologists see racial mixing as the great threat.

There is in fact a fundamental dilemma built into all nationalisms with racist ideological elements: the question of whether race or nation should take precedence in cases of conflict.[66] The tension between these two contradictory ideological principles has been a factor of discord and division within the National Socialist movement since its early days. Collaboration and treason have been common solutions to this ideological and political dilemma, illustrated by the behaviour of *Nasjonal Samling* and *Danmarks National-socialistiske Arbejderparti* during the Nazi occupation, and the way many British nationalists praise Britain's arch-enemy, Adolf Hitler. When Norwegian neo-Nazis and racists go to Sweden to celebrate with their Swedish partners the king who tried to conquer Norway, Karl XII, it may be seen as an expression of the same unsolved dilemma of double loyalties.

When it comes to the question of who the main foreign enemy is, national socialists and some other racial ideologists claim that we are facing a *Jewish* conspiracy to annihilate the white race and gain world domination. The other category of anti-immigrant activists claim that there is a *Muslim* conspiracy to conquer Europe and subjugate it under the rule of Islam. The similarities as well as the differences are illustrated by Kaj Wilhelmsen, leader of *Nationalpartiet Danmark*,[67] explaining one of the differences between the national socialists and the nationalist anti-immigration activists which his party represents:

> The national socialists are concerned about the Jews while we are concerned about the Arabs. The Muslims have become many while there are few Jews living here. As an ethnic minority, the Jews are dying out in Denmark, and do not constitute a threat to the Danish people. Therefore we are not that concerned about them. *Danmarks Nationalsocialistiske Bevægelse* (DNSB, Denmark's National Socialist Movement) does have many positive features, like their immigration policy and their 'green' policy. However, much else is outdated. Their economic policy was relevant back in the 1920s. And their views on the Jews are nonsense in relation to the present situation.[68]

Neo-Nazis and other radical racial ideologists share with the nationalist anti-immigration activists the idea that immigrants and refugees are merely instruments in a larger malicious scheme – although they may differ as to when these immigrant groups are seen as independent actors or as relatively passive agents for the actual schemers. Accordingly, there is also some variation as to what degree immigrant groups are seen as a main enemy in the approaching racial/civil war – although there is no doubt that they will be expelled from the country, if necessary, by violence. There is, on the other hand, full agreement that on the day of retribution, true patriots will direct their wrath at the national/racial traitors – those who have laid the country open for the foreign invaders. Descriptions of what is to be done to the traitors are graphic: 'Beat or kill them' (NMI leader Arne Myrdal), 'hang [them] by their neck by a rope' (leader of HAM/*Birkebeinergruppa*), 'two million in this country have to be exterminated because they are racially inferior or traitors' (leading Swedish VAM activist) – or at best, 'send them to imprisonment with hard labour on [the Arctic island] Svalbard' (leader of the Norwegian neo-Nazi organization *Zorn 88*), or 'treat them as was done to traitors after the war' (FMI activist).[69]

In political rhetoric, it is standard procedure to try to present oneself and one's cause as just and legitimate, while simultaneously discrediting the opponent. The 'traitor' rhetoric takes a long step further by seeking to justify the use of extensive violence against political opponents, government officials and immigrants.

To sum up, then, although the two discourses used by nationalist anti-immigrant activists and by neo-Nazis have different sources, the main lines of argumentation and the practical conclusions drawn from them are similar indeed. Unless the flow of immigrants is halted, a civil war is unavoidable. In such a situation, the 'resistance movement' will have to wage a just struggle against the 'traitors'. The revolutionary, racist ZOG discourse goes considerably further in justifying extreme violence than do the 'moderate' nationalist anti-immigrant activists in their rhetoric. However, this is a difference of degree, not of kind. Those adhering to the ZOG ideology claim that the racial war has already started, while the anti-immigration activists claim that a civil war is bound to break out in the (near) future unless their warnings against the present 'suicidal' immigration policy are heeded.[70] This indicates that some militant neo-Nazi groups have reached a further stage in their radicalization towards terrorism compared to most anti-immigrant organizations.

In Ehud Sprinzak's analytical scheme[71] of three stages in the process of delegitimization (crisis of confidence, conflict of legitimacy and crisis of legitimacy), groups like *Norge Mot Innvandring* and *Den Danske Forening* have reached the first or second stage whereas neo-Nazi groups such as VAM and *Werwolf* have reached – or are very close to reaching – the third and final stage of radicalization. Those adhering to the ZOG ideology claim that the

Zionist takeover is already accomplished, and that the racial war has already started. The entire political establishment is in principle identified with ZOG, and its members are therefore legitimate targets of violence from the 'resistance movement'. Ideologically, the process of radicalization is completed, but the urge for violent action is checked by tactical considerations, such as the need to build organizational and military strength and infrastructure, and the realization that premature action would give the police an opportunity to round up the activists, who are in most cases known to the security services.

Most anti-immigration activists consider the foreign (Islamic) invasion as something which *is about* to happen, but that the takeover may be halted if the authorities heed their warnings and bring the flood of foreigners to a full stop. The enemy is identified as treacherous and corrupt individuals and groups within the power establishment, but the political system itself may not necessarily be considered beyond rescue. A civil war is considered as a future consequence of the present suicidal immigration policy.[72] Thus, organizations like *Den Danske Forening* and *Norge Mot Innvandring* call on their supporters to prepare for a future armed resistance struggle when the civil war eventually breaks out. They are rather restrained when it comes to inciting acts of violence here and now – except against groups which physically attack good patriots. They do, however, threaten political opponents that they will be targets of violent reprisals when the Day of Retribution comes. But there are divided views among anti-immigration activists concerning how far they consider developments to have progressed. The more moderate seem to believe that it is still possible to stop the process by normal political means. The more radical activists claim that the occupation is already an established fact. As the action group *Djerv* put it in a pamphlet: 'Until all intruders are swept out of the country and the traitors are made to pay for their treason, [we] consider Norway to be an occupied country – with all the consequences this necessarily must involve.'

Conspiracy Theories and Historic Analogies: Some Comparative Perspectives

Are these types of discourse – and the underlying pattern they share – unique to the Scandinavian scene, or are they just varieties of a more general type of discourse characteristic of right-wing extremism as such?

Obviously, the ZOG discourse and the notion of the Jewish world conspiracy are truly international. However, this specific discourse, or at least idiomatic varieties of it such as the notion of 'ZOG', have been spread through cultural diffusion and various forms of communication. Books and pamphlets like *The Protocols of the Elders of Zion* and *The Turner Diaries* have mattered in disseminating and popularizing these antiSemitic ideas. Certain religious traditions, represented in Christianity as well as in Islam, have also been instrumental in spreading anti-Jewish ideas.

Conspiracy theories are recurring themes in right-wing extremism – although conspiracy theories also appear in other parts of the political spectrum and in different cultural and political contexts.[73] The conspiracy view of political life is based on the notion that events should be seen in terms of an evil conspiracy to take over the world. Powerful and insidious plotters use their agents to subvert independent nations and races by poisoning the minds of ordinary people. To those who accept the premises of conspiracy theory, every event can be integrated into their world view, and no empirical fact can disprove it. Seemingly contradictory principles like capitalism and communism may all be explained as parts of a large-scale Jewish plot to subvert, exploit and delude. A catastrophe is soon about to happen unless the conspiracy is exposed and the warnings – from those few who have seen the horrible truth – are heeded.

The most common form of conspiracy theory in right-wing extremist circles is undoubtedly the anti-Semitic variety. However, some observers, such as Michael Billig,[74] argue that these anti-Semitic conspiracy theories are essential and non-substitutable traits of right-wing extremism. He claims that although fascist groups may have found new targets for their anti-immigrant rhetoric (now directed at Muslim rather than Jewish immigrants), they have not adjusted the targets of their conspiracy theories accordingly. The anti-Islamic theme has not supplanted the themes of a Jewish or Zionist conspiracy, he argues – probably stretching his case too far.[75]

Norwegian and Danish anti-immigrant activists have actually done some inventive ideological work by integrating a theory of an Islamic conspiracy to conquer and dominate the world with their own notion of resistance against foreign invaders and local traitors. It should be noted that the idea of an Islamic conspiracy plays a relatively minor role in the overall discourse, particularly when compared with more grandiose theories of Jewish conspiracies current in many right-wing extremist circles. It is also significant that Jewish conspiracy theories are almost completely absent from the discourse of leading Norwegian and Danish anti-immigration activists. This is so partly because anti-Semitism is too closely associated with Nazism, and partly because these activists feel threatened by Islam and Muslims, not by Jews, Judaism or Zionism. Thus, contrary to Billig's view, an anti-Islamic conspiracy theory *does* indeed serve as a substitute – and not as a supplement – to anti-Semitic conspiracy theories, at least in this particular brand of right-wing extremist discourse. The image of the Islamic threat parallels *some* aspects of the Jewish conspiracy theory, but it is far from a carbon copy.

Whereas anti-Semites hold that communism, capitalism and even liberalism were created as parts of the Great Zionist Conspiracy, the Islamic conspiracy theorists are more modest in their claims. They hold that the 'waves' of Muslim immigrants and asylum seekers are parts of a coordinated plan to conquer Europe for Islam, serving as vanguards to establish bridgeheads in preparation for the final *Jihad*.

This relatively simple conspiracy theory offers few clues to explain why local 'traitors' are assisting the Muslim conquerors – apart from their 'internationalist', 'communist' and 'unpatriotic' orientation. Anti-Semitic conspiracy theorists are able to present elaborated explanations of why liberalism was created by the Jews in order to destroy the white race by poisoning the minds of naive Christian whites with destructive ideas of 'multi-culturalism' and 'racial equality'.[76] No anti-immigrant activist has yet to my knowledge come up with similar theories, or claimed that liberalism was an Islamic invention. Thus, theories of Islamic conspiracies are so far not nearly so elaborated, sophisticated and pervasive as the corresponding Jewish conspiracy theories. However, as fear of Islam is more and more replacing communism as the perceived main threat to Western Civilisation, Islamic conspiracy theories are likely to become more and more elaborated and appealing. Considered in this perspective, one may expect that anti-Jewish conspiracy theories will be less likely to have a mass appeal in this part of the world during the coming years, but rather be the preoccupation of a relatively small fringe. However, as has already been demonstrated, seemingly incompatible discourses and conspiracy theories are fully able to coexist, and even to feed on each other. Many individuals seem to be able to shift between these discourses without being much troubled by logical inconsistencies and ideological contradictions.

Conspiracy theories are in most cases closely linked to notions of agents and traitors: corrupted persons and groups who are betraying their own people to foreign enemies. These alleged traitors – the enemies within – are often the objects of even more intense hatred and violence than is reserved for external enemies.[77]

The same structure in enemy images is found in the German National Socialist tradition, which describes a double set of enemies as *Volksfremden* and *Volksfeinde* – 'aliens to the people' and 'enemies of the people'. The first category refers to those who are enemies because they belong to another race; the second refers to those who are part of the people by birth but betray it. In his rhetoric, Hitler described the future victims of his extermination camps and wars of expansion as the real aggressors. The victims became culprits and *vice versa*, and his military aggression was justified as 'self-defence'.[78] Almost 50 years after the fall of *Das dritte Reich*, the leader of the Republikaner Party, the former SS officer Franz Schönhuber, describes the German Central Council of Jews as 'the fifth occupation power on German soil'.[79]

The way Norwegian and Danish anti-immigration activists make use of history, and their analogy between resistance against immigration and wartime resistance against Nazi occupation, is certainly not unique to the Scandinavian context. The same type of analogy is also made in some other countries which were under German occupation during World War II. In the Netherlands, leading anti-immigration activists also speak about their political struggle as a 'resistance movement'. The youth movement of the nationalist, anti-immigrant *Centrumpartij* (CP, the Center Party, founded 1980) used the name *Jonge Geuzen*. This was a clear reference to the name of the first Dutch resistance group fighting the Nazi occupants. It is notable, however, that even this wartime resistance group took the name *Goezen* from the Dutch 'water guerrillas' fighting the Spanish occupation during the Eighty Years' War (1568–1648). Thus, the militant anti-immigrant activists of the 1980s, *Jonge Geuzen*, tried to present themselves as part of a long tradition of Dutch resistance against foreign occupants.[80] We have already discussed a similar case from Sweden, referring to the way the anti-immigrant organizations *Bevara Sverige Svenskt* and *Sverigedemokraterna* used the Engelbrekt Rebellion of the 1430s as their model of a popular, armed resistance against foreign domination – in that case against extortionist German tax collectors.

The late Rabbi Meir Kahane and his 'quasi-fascist' Kach movement in Israel is representing a totally different political and historical tradition. Kahane, whose ideology may be described as 'catastrophic messianism',[81] advocated the forced expulsion of Arabs from Israel. As a 'demographic timebomb', the Arab minority would eventually outnumber the Jews and take over the state, he claimed. The Arabs were the ultimate Gentiles, who had persecuted the Jews for millenia and sought their destruction, and time was now ripe for revenge. Kahane's other main enemy were those he called the 'Hellenized Jews' who were corrupted by gentile values of liberalism, democracy, secularism and suicidal notions of peace. The term 'Hellenized Jews' is the focus of the root metaphor in Kahane's rhetoric. He made an analogy between the situation of today's Israel and the successful Maccabee revolt against the Greek occupation of Jerusalem, suppression of Jewish values, and the profanation of the Temple (during the 160s BC). The violent struggle was also directed against the Jewish elites who had compromised their Jewish identity, collaborated with the enemy, and been open to Hellenist culture and foreign influences:

> The bitter battle some 2500 years ago was between those Jews who sought to create a truly Jewish culture and society as opposed to those

who sought to be Greeks in form and idea. The latter came to be known as the Hellenists and the real battle of the Maccabees was against them, against the perversion and corruption of the Jewish people into a hideous, Hebrew caricature of foreign, gentilized, culture. That is precisely what the struggle is today in the Jewish state. ... The Jews against the Hellenists. The real struggle.

... And so [the Hellenized Jew] marches for the enemy, and decries the punishment of the enemy, and weeps for the pain of the enemy, until he becomes the enemy ... of all that is sacredly Jewish.[82]

... a huge struggle is going on today, much larger than the Jewish-Arab crises, the struggle between the Jews and the Hellenized. This is the modern phase of an ancient war. ... The first person killed by the Maccabees was a Jew who wanted to eat pork.[83]

The idiomatic content of Kahane's rhetoric is shaped by his peculiar brand of fundamentalist Judaism and the unique historic experiences of the Jewish people. However, the way he exploits historic events for a present political struggle, as well as the structure of his argument, is strikingly similar to the discourse of Scandinavian (and other) anti-immigrant activists. The same themes are prominent: The foreign enemy and the traitors and the resistance movement fighting them both. In several respects, Kahane is also turning anti-Semitic conspiracy theories upside down: Liberalism and democracy are presented as 'gentile' notions which corrupt the Jewish people and lead to treason and national destruction.

Extreme nationalist, right-wing and racist groups seek models for action and justification of violence in historic traditions, and in established national symbols which they re-interpret to fill with their own ideological content. Some themes are of particular importance to almost all these groups: notions of conspiracies and impending threats of national or racial disaster, and the triangular relation between alleged domestic traitors serving foreign forces of invasion/occupation and the resistance movement of true patriots fighting both these categories of enemies. These discourses serve to legitimatize the use of violence and endow present-day militant nationalists and racists with a sense of legitimacy.

212 TERROR FROM THE EXTREME RIGHT

NOTES

1. This study is financed by a grant from the Norwegian Council for Applied Social Research (NORAS). During my work on this study I have received useful comments and suggestions from (among others) Alex P. Schmid, Jaap van Donselaar, Heléne Lööw, Erik Jensen, Daniel Heradstveit, Iver B. Neumann, Ola Tunander, Theo Barth, Øystein Sørensen and Bernt Hagtvedt.
2. The statement was repeated in various forms during this researcher's interviews with Arne Myrdal, 23 June and 12 Aug. 1989, when he was still the leader of *Folkebevegelsen mot Innvandring* (FMI, The People's Movement Against Immigration). He later broke away and established the more militant *Norge Mot Innvandring* (NMI, Norway Against Immigration).
3. From a dialogue between two imprisoned activists in the militant *Vitt Ariskt Motstånd* (VAM, White Aryan Resistance) network in Sweden, published in the VAM magazine *Storm No.* 5–6 (1992), pp.14–16.
4. *Neo-Nazism* is used here as a designation of a racist ideology consisting of elements from several sources and traditions: German national socialism, American racism, and South African apartheid ideology. In addition, the style and music is often inspired by the fascist part of the British skinhead movement. Thus, what is here called 'neo-Nazism' differs significantly from 'classic' national socialism.
5. In English usage, the term 'Scandinavia' is sometimes used interchangeably with the 'Nordic countries'. In local usage, 'Scandinavia' refers to Sweden, Norway and Denmark only, whereas the 'Nordic countries' (*Norden*) in addition to these three also include Finland, Iceland and the semi-independent island communities Åland and the Faroe Islands.
6. P. Berger and T. Luckman, *The Social Construction of Reality* (London: Penguin Books, 1985).
7. See e.g. 'Introduction' in C.A. Lutz and L. Abu-Lughod (eds.), *Language and the Politics of Emotion* (Cambridge: CUP, 1990); Randi Kårhus, 'Diskurs som analytisk begrep', *Norsk antropologisk tidsskrift*, 2/3, (1992).
8. Michel Foucault, *The Archeology of Knowledge and the Discourse on Language* (NY: Pantheon, 1972), p.49; Lutz and Abu-Lughod *Language*, pp.9–10.
9. Whereas the notion of discourse focuses on communicative interaction, the notion of rhetoric is often seen as a one-way communication – speeches rather than conversations. There are various definitions and approaches to the concept of rhetoric and rhetorical analysis. For further discussion, see D. Heradstveit and T. Bjørgo, *Politisk kommunikasjon: Introduksjon til semiotikk og retorikk* (Oslo: TANO, 1992); Robert Paine (ed.), *Politically Speaking: Cross-Cultural Studies of Rhetoric* (Philadelphia, PA: Inst. for the Study of Human Issues, 1981).
10. There is not necessarily a direct causal link from ideology and rhetoric to action. Most rhetoric leads to little or no real action. Neither do ideology and rhetoric always precede action. In many cases, action comes first; subsequently, the actor tries to work out a convenient justification. Most acts of racist violence, at least in Scandinavia, is perpetrated by individuals and small groups – often petty-criminal youth gangs – which initially neither hold an explicit ideology nor have any direct relations to political organisations. Frequently, perpetrators of racist actions are approached by anti-immigrant or racist organisations only *after* they have carried out an arson attack or similar spectacular action. At that stage they may suddenly find themselves hailed as patriots or 'white resistance fighters'. For more detailed analysis of these processes, see T. Bjørgo, 'Terrorist Violence against Immigrants and Refugees in Scandinavia: Patterns and Motives' (Ch.3) and 'Role of the Media in Racist Violence' (Ch.7), in Tore Bjørgo and Rob Witte (eds.), *Racist Violence in Europe* (Basingstoke: Macmillan, 1993). (Also pub. in Norwegian by Tiden Norsk Forlag, 1993.)
11. Notions and ambitions of a 'Greater Sweden' enjoyed considerable support among the Swedish military leadership during the first years of the war. Several generals wanted Sweden to join Germany in going to war against the Soviet Union, and presented detailed plans for an invasion to the Cabinet in 1941 (Cf. Karl Molin, *Hemmakriget* (Stockholm: Tidens förlag, 1982), p.44; Heléne Lööw, 'Hakkorset og Wasakärven: En studie av

nationalsocialismen i Sverige 1924-1950' (PhD dissertation from Historiska Inst., Göteborg, 1990, p.44). Later, when it was clear that Germany would lose the war, anti-Nazi elements got the upper hand in the military leadership. Still, neither the military, the police nor the state bureaucracy purged pro-German or Nazi-sympathizing elements after the war.

12. Norwegian nineteenth century nationalism was largely shaped by liberal, open-minded poets with an international perspective, in particular Bjørnstjerne Bjørnson and Henrik Wergeland. Nikolai Grundtvig played a similar role in relation to Danish nationalism.

13. *Background on World War II in Scandinavia:* In Norway, Vidkun Quisling became the symbol of national treason when he tried to carry out a coup d'etat against the legal Norwegian government on the eve of the German invasion (9 April 1940) and later collaborated closely with the Nazi occupants. Two years later, he and members of his fascist party, *Nasjonal Samling* (NS), were installed as the Norwegian government by the German occupation authorities. The legal Norwegian government had capitulated following two months of military resistance after the invasion. The king and his cabinet escaped to London and established themselves as government in exile. The illegal resistance movement in Norway (subsequently consolidated in *Milorg*) was actively supported by – and under the command of – this government in exile, which continued the struggle from London [H.F.Dahl, B.Hagtvet and G. Hjeltnes, *Den norske nasjonalsosialismen* (Oslo: Pax, 1990); H.F.Dahl, *Vidkun Quisling, I-II* (Oslo: Aschehoug, 1991/1992)].

In Denmark, however, the wartime resistance movement was actively *opposed* by the government which had capitualted without any military resistance and had agreed to govern under German occupation until 1943. Initially, this accommodation policy to secure Danish interests had broad public support. However, during 1942, the resistance movement gradually won increasing popular support for a more active Danish resistance, such as general strikes, sabotage and – towards the end of the war – liquidation of informers. The most impressive part of the Danish Resistance was the unprecedented rescue of the Jews. When the German forces on 1 Oct. 1943 started their *razzia* to deport the Jewish local population and the Jewish refugees from Germany, ordinary Danes hid their Jewish neighbors and shipped them over to safety in Sweden. Only 284 of Denmark's 7,500 Jews were captured in the *razzia* [Politikens forlag, *Besettelsestidens Hvem Hva Hvor* (Copenhagen, 1993); H. Poulsen and M. Djursaa, 'Social Basis of Nazism in Denmark: The DNSAP', in Ugelvik Larsen et al, *Who were the Fascists?* (Oslo: Universitetsforlaget, 1980)].

After the war, to have taken an active part in the resistance was a main source of prestige and influence in Norway, but less so in Denmark where resistance activists remained to some degree outside the Establishment. Following the 1945 parliamentary election in Norway, more than 100 of the 150 delegates elected to the *Storting* had either been actively involved in the resistance movement, suffered captivity in German concentration camps or had a similar background. Collaborators and traitors were totally discredited and excluded from all influence and access to political power for a long time to come. After the war, 46,000 Norwegian citizens were found guilty of national treason (*landssvik*) or membership in *Nasjonal Samling*. Twenty-five Norwegians were executed for war crimes and treason – among them Quisling. At least one hundred had been liquidated by the resistance movement during the war itself (according to the historian Ivar Kraglund at Norway's Resistance Museum; personal communication). In Denmark, 13,500 were convicted of treason and 46 executed, while 300–400 informers had been liquidated by the resistance movement [Ditlev Tamm, *Retsopgøret efter besettelsen* (Copenhagen: Jurist-og økonomforbundets forlag, 1984), pp.270, 661–2)].

Neutral Sweden avoided a wartime invasion by, among other things, accepting the transit of German troop transports and by ensuring continued deliveries of high-grade iron ore to the German arms industry. Both before and during the war Sweden had several significant National Socialist and Fascist parties. These organizations lost much of their support towards the end of the war and afterwards. Still, although most of them were disbanded, Nazi organizations were never banned. Even though more than 500 Swedes had volunteered for the German SS to fight against the Soviet Union, Sweden's National socialists were never branded as traitors after the war – unlike their Danish and Norwegiasn counterparts. However, some Swedish Nazis were convicted of espionage for Germany. Cf. Lööw (note 11).

14. This quote and other information is taken from *Tidningarnas Telegrambyrå* (TT) 2 April 1993, and *TT* and *Aftonbladet*, 3 April 1992. Similar events took place at several other Swedish schools.

15. This uneasiness with nationalist and ethnic feelings has also been reflected in Swedish minority policies. Whereas Norway, Denmark and Finland have to some extent based their minority policies on forms of conflict management where ethno-cultural categories have been made relevant, the 'Swedish model' has tried to transform conflicts between ethno-cultural groups into conflicts between socio-economic groups, which may be solved through redistribution of economic resources as in labour conflicts. This is discussed by Gabriele Winai Ström, 'Etniska konflikter och politiska lösningar', in G. Ström (ed.), *Konfliktlösning i det flerkulturella samhället: En antologi* (Uppsala/Stockholm: Institutionen för freds- og konfliktforskning /Regeringskansliets offsetsentral, 1988, new ed. 1992).

16. The second verse of the national anthem in particular seems to rouse the spirits of Swedish extreme nationalists:
    You are throned on the memories of olden great days
    when the honour of your name spread over the earth.
    I know that you are and will remain [or *become*] *what you were.*
    Oh, may I live, may I die in the Nordic North!

17. However, the Norwegian and Danish national anthems contain little or nothing similar to the imperial connotations of the Swedish anthem. Whereas the Danish national anthem is a poetic description of the Danish landscape, the Norwegian anthem focuses on the longing and struggle for freedom, justice and peace.

18. Recently, there has been a campaign in Sweden to 'take back the national symbols from the racists', using the Norwegians' celebration of their national day as a much admired model (cf. *Aftonbladet*, 18 May 1994). It will, however, be problematic to adopt the *form* of a national celebration without its historical *content*, which is closely linked to events which find no parallels in Swedish history.

19. These are explanations given in 'patriotic' magazines like *Norsk Blad*, *Boot Boys* and *Ung Front*, as well as in my own interviews with activists. To sceptical outsiders, however, two other interpretations are even more obvious: Either the Norwegian right-wing extremists who celebrate Karl XII should be considered national traitors and quislings, or they participate in the commemoration in order to celebrate – in secrecy – the unknown Norwegian soldier who fired the fateful bullet.

20. The former leader of the People's Movement Against Immigration (FMI), Arne Myrdal, spends a full page of his book *Sannheten skal frem* (Lunderød forlag, 1990, pp.7–8) rebuking Crown Princess (at the time, now Queen) Sonja for her work on behalf of refugees. Anti-immigration activists have also reacted angrily when the late King Olav, King Harald of Norway and Queen Margrethe of Denmark in several of their New Year's speeches have condemned racism and xenophobic nationalism (e.g., an acid comment on the Danish queen in *Danskeren*, No. 6, Dec. 1993, p.21). The frontpage title of the newspaper *Ekstrabladet*, 2 Jan. 1994, reads: 'The Xenophobes Rage: Shut Up, Margrethe!'

21. The King's statement was recounted by prime minister Per Albin Hansson as a threat to abdicate when he presented King Gustav's view to a cabinet meeting during the so-called Midsummer crisis of 1941. However, Swedish historians are divided as to the realities behind this alleged threat. See H. de Geer and J. Torbacke (eds.), *Problem i Modern Historia. 'Sverige'* (Lund: Studentlitteratur, 1976).

22. One example was the so-called Eidsvoll Monument, a huge column decorated in Viking style, initiated by the government several decades before the war to commemorate the Constitution worked out by the first national assembly at Eidsvoll in 1814. After the war, the public financing of the work was halted, partly because the artist had joined Quisling's *Nasjonal Samling* during the war, and partly because the Viking style now gave the wrong connotations.

23. In Denmark, however, these institutions were to some extent discredited by their compliance with the German forces of occupation.
24. The nationalist, anti-immigrant parties which make use of this discourse have never been able to muster as much as one per cent of the vote on a national level in elections in Norway. They have, however, won single seats in a few municipal councils and regional assemblies. In Denmark, *Stop Invandringen* ('Stop Immigration') lists attracted up to 2.4 per cent of the votes in some localities in the 1989 local elections. Nationalist and racist parties are too small to qualify for parliamentary elections in Denmark.
25. Arne Myrdal was squeezed out of the FMI leadership in April 1991; he had become an embarrassment to the organization for his not-so-subtle incitements to violence and his record of violence (cf. next note).
26. Myrdal was sentenced to one year in prison for preparing to blow up an asylum centre in 1989 (*Agder Lagmannsrett*, 12 Sept. 1989; *Norges Høyesterett*, 24 May 1990); he later got 7 months in prison (reduced to 4 months on appeal) for inciting and leading a band of followers to attack a group of anti-racist demonstrators with sticks and clubs in 1991 (*Sand Herredsrett*, 24 Nov. 1992; *Høyesterett*, 8 Oct. 1993). Arne Myrdal, born in 1935, has had a varied career, although limited formal education. He has been a low-ranking military officer, an unsuccessful businessman (convicted several times of economic offences), and the author of a highly controversial book on local history. He was also a rebellious local councillor of the Labour Party – from which he split off to establish a competing local party which failed to win any seats in the subsequent election.
27. One example of how Danish and Norwegian anti-immigration activists have developed a common discourse is the notion of 'red Nazis', used to denote leftist and militant anti-racists. Whether this notion was originally coined in Denmark or in Norway is not clear, but it is much used by activists in both countries.
28. Quoted from this researcher's interview with Arne Myrdal, 23 June 1989.
29. Arne Myrdal, *Sannheten skal fram* (The Truth Must be Told) (Oslo: Lunderød Forlag, 1990), pp.3–4. This 'theory' is a recurrent theme in Myrdal's book, mentioned, e.g., on pp. 12, 17, 25 and 31.
30. Quoted from my own interview with Arne Myrdal, 12 Aug. 1989.
31. Cited from 'A greeting from the FMI' on the back cover of Myrdal's book *Sannheten skal fram*, signed by the managing leader of the FMI, Bjørn Voldnes, Feb. 1990.
32. Among the leading persons in this group, which convened annually in the small town of Ranum, was a well-known resistance leader, Jens Tolstrup, who was later seen as linked with the Danish Association, without being a formal member. Another resistance figure was Wilhelm Krarup, the father of the main motivating force of the Danish Association, the clergyman Søren Krarup. Like his son, Wilhelm Krarup was a Lutheran minister.
33. Arne Myrdal, quoted in *Verdens Gang* (VG), 10 Nov. 1991, after his unsuccessful 'popular meeting' in Oslo where 10,000 people literally turned their backs on him in a massive demonstration of disgust.
34. Women having relations with male foreigners have also in many cases been subjects to systematic harassment. This is a main topic in a 'School Edition' of Myrdal's FMI periodical *Norge Er Vårt* ('Norway Is Ours'):

    Women who had affairs with Germans [during the war], we used to refer to as 'German whores' and 'German mattresses'. Today, women who have relations with asylum immigrants should be spoken of as *asylum mattresses*.
    Remember that!

35. Quoted verbatim from the note dispatched with a 'Traitor Register' form mailed to this researcher, with a request that it be filled in 'to save us the work' (!).
36. The mayor related his experiences as a victim of harassment during a speech at a seminar on racism and legislation against racism in Oslo, 1 Dec. 1992. For a theoretical discussion of how harassment works, see Ben Bowling, 'Racial Harassment and the Process of Victimisation: Conceptual and methodological implications for the local crime survey', *British Journal of Criminology* 33/2 (Spring 1993).
37. This is evident from a dialogue between Arne Myrdal and Arild Elvsveen reproduced in the

HAM magazine *Vikingen* 2/2 (1992), where Elvsveen presents himself as one of the founders of *Landsforeningen mot landssvikere* (the National Association against Traitors). Cf. *Hamar Arbeiderblad*, 30 June and 1 July 1992. However, investigation carried out by the police and the Data Protection Registrar has not yet found sufficient evidence to prove that the information collected on political opponents has been systematized to such a degree that it counts as a 'register' in the legal sense.

38. Such a list, in the form of the journal *Der Einblick*, No.1, contained detailed information on some 400 German anti-fascists, journalists, teachers, professors and politicians. It was distributed through a mailbox in the Danish town Randers, belonging to *Danmarks National-socialistiske Bevægelse* (cf. *Politiken*, 4 Dec. 1993). In Dec. 1993, advanced letter bombs were sent to ten prominent Austrians who had engaged in supporting refugees. Several were seriously wounded, including the Mayor of Vienna. The Swedish and Danish neo-Nazis' links to the international Anti-Antifa network are well documented (e.g. *Jyllandsposten*, 19 Dec. 1993; and *Searchlight*, January 1994).

39. The Norwegian right-wing extremist Johnny Olsen, convicted of a double killing in 1981, stated (in *Dagbladet*, 16 Jan. 1994) that there were two Anti-Antifa cells (totalling 8-9 members) in Norway. They maintained surveillance of individuals and planned to murder Norwegian anti-Fascists. Olsen warned against further escalation of the conflict between nationalists and militant anti-racists, and feared that it would end in a bloodbath.

40. Also reported in *Folk & Røvere*, No. 5, (Oct./Nov. 1993), and *Adresseavisen*, 5 Nov. 1993.

41. Ole Hasselbalch, *Viljen til modstand* ('The Determination to Resist') (Tidehvervs forlag, 1990), pp.66–71. Hasselbalch, a professor of Law, is chairman of *Den Danske Forening*. The same themes are reported from a DDF summer meeting by Peter Kramer, 'Venner ser på Danmarks kort', *Fri Aktuelt*, 21 June 1991. Why the DDF use the term 'national treason' on the present immigration policy is also discussed in *Danskeren*, Feb. 1992, sp. issue, p.15.

42. See Steven Sampson, '"The Threat to Danishness": Danish Culture as seen by Den Danske Forening', in Jan Hjarnø (ed.), *Proceedings of the 9th Nordic Seminar on Migration Research* (København: Nordisk Ministerråd, forthcoming). A more direct parallel to DDF in Norway is *Den Norske Forening* (The Norwegian Assoc.). DNF attempts to reach more influential circles in Norwegian society, circles which have kept themselves at a safe distance from the somewhat disreputable FMI. As DNF is not a political party, it has tried to attract politicians from mainstream parties like the conservative *Høyre* ('Right') and the populist *Fremskrittspartiet* ('The Progressive Party'). In spite of some successful initiatives, DNF has remained a relatively marginal group of persons who are also active in other anti-immigrant organizations.

43. *Berlingske Tidende*, 1 Sept. 1991.

44. Refugees and immigrants were mentioned as 'occupiers' for the first time in the local, BSS-affiliated radio station *Öppet Forum* (Open Forum) in 1983, according to the Swedish historian Heléne Lööw (personal communication), who has extensively studied the history of racist organizations in Sweden. The Engelbrekt Ballad could be ordered from a BSS mail-order list in 1983. Cf. Anna-Lena Lodenius and Stieg Larsson, *Extremhögern* (Stockholm: Tiden, 1991), pp.30–1. The Sweden Democrats have presented their own history in the pamphlet *Sverigedemokraterna – 1988-1991 – Et partis framväkst* (Stockholm, 1993), where the Engelbrekt March is also discussed.

45. For the background of the ZOG ideology, see Michael Barkun, 'Millenarian Aspects of "White Supremacist" Movements', *Terrorism and Political Violence* [hereafter *TPV*] 1/4 (Oct. 1989), pp.409–35, and idem., 'Review of J. Aho: The Politics of Righteousness: Idaho Christian Patriotism', *TPV* 3/3 (Autumn 1991), pp.149–57. The ZOG discourse was used publicly for the first time by Swedish neo-Nazis in 1989 in the skinhead magazine *Vit Rebell* (White Rebel, the predecessor to the more influential *Storm* magazine), but the notion of ZOG became more broadly accepted in militant racist circles in 1990. The Norwegian skinhead magazine *Boot Boys* used the ZOG formula for the first time in Oct. 1991, obviously a result of influence from Sweden.

46. Andrew Macdonald, *The Turner Diaries* (Hillsboro, NC: National Vanguard Books, 1980); and *Hunter* (ibid., 1989). For a more detailed account of these books and the role they play

SCANDINAVIA   217

in militant racial sub-cultures, and about the ZOG ideology and VAM network in general, see Bjørgo, 'Militant neo-Nazism in Sweden', *TPV* 5/3 (Autumn 1993), pp.28–57; T. Bjørgo and D. Heradstveit, *Politisk terrorisme* (Oslo: TANO, 1993), pp.175–7; and H. Lööw, 'The Cult of Violence: Swedish Racist Counter-Culture', in Bjørgo and Witte (1993) (note 10), pp.62–79.

47. Erik Rune Hansen, editor of the Zorn 88 periodical *Gjallarhorn*, No. 1/1 (Autumn 1989). The name *Zorn* means 'holy wrath' in German, *88* is a common Nazi code for twice the eighth letter of the alphabet, 'H H', meaning 'Heil Hitler'.

48. Cited from *Werwolf*, No. 9 (undated, 1992). This internal VAM magazine is probably edited by Göran Gullvang, one of the most notorious neo-Nazis in Sweden, convicted of several violent offences, including participation in the killing of a homosexual. Part of his reputation also stems from the alleged fact that both his grandfathers were Norwegian quislings (one of them a guard in a German prison camp, Grini) who fled to Sweden after the war (Swedish police source).

49. Norwegian and Danish anti-immigrant parties and organizations like FMI, DDF, *Fedrelandspartiet* and *Stopp innvandringen* painstakingly avoid using concepts like Jews, Zionism and race in order not to be linked to the discredited Nazi tradition. There is no trace of anti-semitism in the public statements of these organizations.

50. Cf. *Storm*, No.5–6, 1991, p.16.

51. This is evident from the fact that these extremist groups are conducting very active and organized recruiting activities among prison inmates (cf. *Storm* No.7–8, 1992, p.17).

52. Lööw (Ref. 46, p.62) estimated the number of activists, members and sympathisers of the Swedish racist counterculture to be 500–600, growing slowly. However, their message seems to have an appeal to considerably wider sections of the youth population. In Norway, I estimate the number of young racists who would subscribe to the ZOG and Nazi discourse to be fewer than 100, based on available knowledge of the size of the relevant groups (the wartime generation of old Nazis is not included). More general racist notions are much more widespread. The Danish situation is numerically much like the Norwegian one.

53. *Hjemmefronten* (the Home Front) was one of the names of the Norwegian anti-Nazi Resistance Movement during the war.

54. *Hvit Arisk Motstand* had hardly more than 5–10 members, while *Birkebeinergruppa* probably consisted of 20–40 more or less active members. As far as is known, practically all the HAM activists were also members of *Birkebeinergruppa*. However, the groups never took off, and they are likely to disintegrate completely after the leader, Jan Holthe (28), became a father and announced that he had broken with his extremist past (*Dagbladet*, 11 May 1994).

55. Cited from the membership magazine *Vikingen* 2/2 (1992), p.2. This article also states that *Birkebeinergruppa* was 'initiated by HAM and is in theory subordinate to this organization – although for all practical purposes, including ideology and mode of action, BB is free to make its own decisions'.

56. *Grønjakkerne* were an offshoot of the so-called *Rockerne* in Denmark, which were part of a youth sub-culture emerging in many European countries during the late 1960s and 1970s, strongly inspired by American models. Cultivating an image of being outlaws, they used the 'South State' (Confederate) Flag or 'Stars and Bars' as a symbol of rebellion and freedom along with Harley-Davidson motorcycles (for those who could afford them) and heavy rock 'n roll music. Although this sub-culture was predominantly unpolitical, many of its adherents were fully aware of the anti-black/pro-slavery connotations of some of their symbols. The pro-American tendency also often gave it an anti-leftist slant, partly because of the controversy surrounding the US role in the Vietnam War, making this sub-culture an alternative to the more student-dominated youth rebellion of the left. Partly as a reaction to increasing immigration, some of these groups during the 1980s gradually turned more racist and started to use other symbols from the South State tradition, relating more directly to Ku Klux Klan-style racism, and sometimes gravitating towards right-wing politics. Some leaders of anti-immigrant and right-wing extremist organizations (such as Arne Myrdal of FMI/NMI, Poul Heinrich Riis-Knudsen of *Danmarks Nationalsocialistiske Bevægelse* and Albert

Larsen of *Partiet de Nationale*) actively tried to recruit these groups in order to use them as stormtroopers or street activists.

57. Two former 'Green Jacket' members from the Studsgårdsgade group, one of them a leading figure, the other a follower, interviewed by this researcher in Copenhagen, 4 June 1991. Interestingly, the adoption of the Ku Klux Klan symbols influenced not only the form, but also the content of racism, especially in Denmark. Slavery – a rather alien phenomenon in a Danish context – was introduced as a theme in racist harassment and jokes. Immigrants were called 'slaves', and a common racist joke could go like this: 'I have nothing against foreign workers *(fremmedarbejdere)* – everyone should have one.'

58. Cf. Bjørgo, 'Terrorist Violence against Immigrants and Refugees in Scandinavia: Patterns and Motives', in Bjørgo and Witte (note 10); Heléne Lööw, 'Rasistisk och främlingsfientlig brottslighet: Myter och verklighet', in Jan Hjarnø (ed.), *Proceedings of the 9th Nordic Seminar on Migration Research* (København: Nordisk Ministerråd, forthcoming). These findings are supported by a report on attacks on immigrants, refugees and asylum centres, published by the Swedish Security Police (SÄPO), 9 March 1993. Both Lööw and SÄPO are using a wider definition of violent attacks than the one my own statistics is based on, resulting in considerably higher figures. Lööw reports (with support from police statistics) that in 1990–92 there were 213 attacks against asylum seekers and refugee centres in Sweden, a figure which includes assault, maltreatment, arson, vandalism against property, causing danger to persons, causing unrest, and theft. See also her analysis of more recent data in the present volume.

59. See *Searchlight*, Jan. 1993 (p.18) for details. In Jan. 1994 an anti-racist activist received by mail a VCR cassette which turned out to contain high explosives and pieces of metal. The deadly cassette bomb was constructed to explode if it was inserted into a VCR machine. The recipient noted that the cassette was a bit heavier than it should be, and turned it over to the police.

60. For instance, a leading reporter in the Norwegian Broadcasting Company (NRK) had to abstain from further reporting on racist groups after a series of grave threats against herself and her family. The local anti-racist organization *Brumunddal på nye veier* changed its leader four times during its first year of existence, as well as several other members of the board, due to threats and harassment. Cf. Frøydis Eidheim, *Hva har skjedd i Brumunddal* (Oslo: NIBR-rapport 1993:20, 1993), p.64; Henrik Lunde, *Aller ytterst: De rasistiske grupperinger i dagens Norge* (Oslo: Antirasistisk Senter, 1993), p.98.

61. By the end of 1994 there were several extremely brutal attacks on neo-Nazis and skinheads in Stockholm. One 16-year-old boy who was member of a skinhead rock band was murdered and grotesquely mutilated. His attackers apparently cut off his right hand and took it with them, possibly a reference to the skinheads' Hitler salutes. Another skinhead is missing and is feared to have been killed as his chopped-off hand has been found, whereas a third barely survived a vicious knifing from a group of attackers. So far, perpetrators have not been apprehended.

62. This is an important point in the argument of the chairman of *Den Danske Forening*, Ole Hasselbalch, in his book *Viljen til modstand* ['Determination to Resist'] (Tidehvervs forlag, 1990), and used by him to justify the possible use of violence in the future: '[The politicians of the majority] deprive opponents to immigration of their right to speak for their cause ... by claiming that they are 'racists' [... and] create a false democracy where unwanted political currents are made illegal so that they cannot find outlets *within* the institutions of democracy. If this happens, it will of course contribute strongly to justifying physical resistance' (p.68). The notion of a 'pressure cooker effect' was coined by the head of the anti-terror section of the Norwegian Security Police, Iver Frigaard, 'Terrorism in a Nordic Perspective', in E. Ellingsen (ed.), *International Terrorism as a Political Weapon* (Oslo: Den norske Atlanterhavskomité, 1988), p.50. I myself have argued in similar terms [in T. Bjørgo and D.Heradstveit, *Politisk vald og terrorisme i Norge* (NUPI arbeidsnotat No. 5, 1988), pp.157–70], but I later modified this explanation.

63. Cited from Lööw, 'The Cult of Violence: The Swedish Racist Counterculture', in Bjørgo and Witte (note 10), pp.71–2. Cf. Bjørgo, 'Politisk vold og terrorisme: Relevans for

SCANDINAVIA   219

Norge', Part II in Bjørgo and Heradstveit (note 62), pp.157–61, 166. This point is also
confirmed in my own interviews with leading *Nasjonalt Folkeparti* activists at the time, Ole
Kristian Brastad and NF leader Jan Ødegaard.
64. I have interviewed several AKP activists who were actively involved in this operation.
65. Cf. leading expert on right-wing extremism in the German *Verfassungsschutz*, Ernst Uhrlau,
'*Gibt es neue Aufschaukelungs-Phänomene?*', Paper at a conference on right-wing
extremism at the Univ. of Bielefeldt, 6–8 Oct. 1993. An interesting trait about the *Anti-Antifa*
is that they use the left-wing terrorist *Rote Armee Fraktion* as a model. In the magazine
Angriff (cited in *Der Spiegel*, 29 Nov. 1993) they speak of themselves as '*einer Art Brauner
Armee Fraktion*', emphasizing that they have much to learn from the Red Army Faction
about '*Konspiration, die Logistik und Vernetzung*'. Although the ultimate goals and the
world views differ, the State is the common enemy which must be attacked with effective
strikes, it is stated. Another conspicuous parallel is the logo of a terror manual circulating (as
a computer file) in the Anti-antifa network, *Handbuch für improvisierte Sprengtechnik*
('published' by 'Autorenkollektiv Werwolf' at 'Horst-Vessel-Verlag). It is the same logo as
used by Red Army Faction – a machine-gun superimposed on a star – with the exception that
the star is exchanged with a Swastika.
66. The Norwegian historian Øystein Sørensen has discussed this dilemma in his book *Hitler
eller Quisling?* (Oslo: Cappelen, 1989) and his comment (in response to a Norwegian version
of the present article), 'Nasjonalisme og rasisme – et historisk apropos', *Internasjonal
Politikk* 52/1 (1994).
67. *Nasjonalpartiet Danmark* had its origin in *Borgerlisterne Stop Innvandringen* ('the Citizen
Lists Stop Immigration') which was organized by *Den Danske Forening* for local elections
in 1989. After the (unsuccessful) elections, some of the local Citizen Lists decided to
establish a nationwide party – against the wishes of the DDF. This caused a breach between
the DDF and what became *Nasjonalpartiet Danmark*.
68. From this researcher's interview with Kaj Wilhelmsen, 4 May 1992.
69. The VAM activist was interviewed and cited by Lööw (note 10), p.62. The citation by the
HAM/Birkebeiner leader is taken from an editorial in the membership magazine *Vikingen* 2/2
(1992), p.3. The other statements have been made in interviews that I myself conducted.
70. The idea that the racial war already rages is expressed in various forms in the VAM magazine
Storm. The typical position of anti-immigration activists, which foresees civil war, armed
resistance and violent attacks on traitors as a future development, is argued by DDF's
chairman, Prof. Ole Hasselbalch (note 62), pp.66–71.
71. See Ehud Sprinzak, 'The Process of Delegitimization: Towards a Linkage Theory of Political Terrorism', *TPV* 3/1 (Spring 1991), pp.50–68 and his contribution (Ch. 2) in the present
volume.
72. See note 70.
73. The Moscow Processes during Stalin's reign of terror exemplify an extreme case of 'left-
wing' conspiracy theory, whereas my study of agent and conspiracy accusations in
Palestinian politics represents a completely different context [T. Bjørgo, *Conspiracy Rhetoric
in Arab Politics: The Palestinian Case* (NUPI Report No.111, Oslo: Oct. 1987)]. For a more
general approach to conspiracy theories, see C.F. Graumann and S. Moscovici (eds.),
Changing Conceptions of Conspiracy (NY: Springer Verlag, 1987).
74. Michael Billig, 'The Extreme Right: Continuities in Anti-Semitic Conspiracy Theory in
Post-War Europe', in Roger Eatwell and Noël O'Sullivan (eds.), *The Nature of the Right:
American and European Policies and Political Thought Since 1789* (London: Pinter
Publishers, 1989), pp.162–4.
75. Billig (ibid.) is using Jean-Marie Le Pen's *Front National* and the magazine of its anti-
Islamic faction, *Vanguard*, as his main example. In order to distance itself from *FN*'s pro-
Islamic faction, *Vanguard* (Nov./Dec. 1987) attacks Islam as 'the third deadly enemy of the
white race, apart from communism and capitalism'. According to Billig, the ideology of
Front National – as expressed in its publications – conceives of communism and capitalism
as the outward form of a single enemy, Zionism (this view is probably not shared by
everyone within the *FN*). But the anti-Islamic theme was added as a complicating factor

which was not really integrated into this conspiracy theory, either as controlling the other two enemies (communism and capitalism), or as being controlled by them. When Billig asks why an anti-Islamic conspiracy theory has not been slotted conveniently into an ideological space previously occupied by an anti-Semitic conspiracy theory, his answer is that it is easier to adapt old arguments than to invent new ones. However, his argument and example are not quite convincing. One cannot expect an Islamic conspiracy theory to be an exact carbon copy of the Jewish conspiracy theory. Even the most inventive conspiracy theorist would not dream up the idea that capitalism and communism were invented and controlled by Muslims. Conspiracy theories need a grain of truth to work – isolated facts to which grand theories can be attached ('Karl Marx was a Jew'; 'many of the world's wealthiest capitalists are Jewish', etc.).

76. See, e.g., Andrew Macdonald's (pseudonym for William L. Pierce) *The Turner Diaries*, p.42; and *Hunter* (note 46), chs.12–16.
77. This point was clearly demonstrated in my study of conspiracy rhetoric and agent accusations in Palestinian politics during the mid-1980s (Bjørgo, note 73). What has made such accusations particularly pervasive and serious in Palestinian society, is that they are often true – whereas such accusations are also often made for political or other reasons to discredit persons and groups. During six years of Intifada, at least 964 Palestinians were killed by other Palestinians, accused of being collaborators and agents of the Israeli security service, *Shin Bet*. Israeli and Palestinian researchers assess that merely about half of these accused agents were really collaborators (*Aftenposten*, 18 Jan. 1994).
78. Cf. Jaap van Donselaar, 'The Extreme Right and Racist Violence in the Netherlands', in Bjørgo and Witte (note 10), p.59. Ch. 15 of Adolf Hitler's *Mein Kampf* (Vol. 2) was titled *Notwehr als Recht*.
79. Schönhuber implicitly refers to the US, British, French and Soviet forces of occupation after the defeat of Germany. Cited in *Der Spiegel*, No.18 (1994), p.48.
80. This paragraph is based on information from the leading researcher on the Dutch extreme right, Dr Jaap van Donselaar (personal communication). Cf. van Donselaar, 'The Extreme Right and Racist Violence in the Netherlands', in Bjørgo and Witte (note 10).
81. The terms are used by Ehud Sprinzak, *The Ascendance of Israel's Radical Right* (Oxford: OUP, 1991), Ch.7.
82. Rabbi Meir Kahane, *40 years* (Miami Beach, FL: Inst. of the Jewish Idea, 1983), pp.36, 39, 45.
83. Kahane, who as a member of Knesset debated a bill to bar the production and selling of pork. Cited from Sprinzak (note 81), p.230.

Italian Neo-Fascist Terrorism:
A Comparative Perspective

LEONARD WEINBERG

Right-wing violence in Italy has displayed characteristics that set it apart from the violent operations of rightist groups active in the other Western democracies. In the Italian case the violence has been protracted, stretching from the immediate postwar period to our own time. For the most part, it has been aimed at Communists and other leftists rather than racial or ethnic minorities. And it has appeared in a variety of forms, ranging from street-corner brawling to terrorist bombing campaigns to schemes designed to achieve a *coup d'état*. In addition to offering a detailed account of neo-Fascist violence in Italy over the past four decades, this study places the phenomenon in the general context of Italian politics and seeks to explain the violence by reference to the Cold War-based objectives of various anti-communist organizations.

I.

It is hardly uncommon for a political scientist who has devoted any length of time to the study of a particular country or a particular kind of political phenomenon to claim that the subject of her/his inquiries is somehow unique. No other country and no other type of political phenomenon is at all comparable to the one with which the observer has become intrigued. These assertions are all too familiar. Despite the frequency with which these claims are made, it is difficult to place the Italian experience with right-wing violence in the context of a discussion of contemporary far right terrorism in the other Western democracies without stressing some of the unusual features involved.

In most of the other western and industrialized democracies where right-wing violence has achieved some measure of significance the principal targets have been racial, religious or ethnic minority groups whose life styles or claims to equality of status with members of the majority population have often aroused a violent backlash by right-wing groups. Further, although there are probably exceptions here and there, campaigns of rightist violence are typically linked to a conspiratorial world-view in which Jews play a central role. Whether the immediate targets of the violence are Turks resident in Germany, Algerians in France or African-Americans in the United States, those perpetrating the violence oftentimes see mysterious and powerful Jewish forces at work, forces seeking to weaken the power of the dominant population and take control of the national government. Accordingly, for both members of the Order in the United States and followers of the White Aryan Resistance in Sweden, the respective governments of the two countries have fallen under the control of ZOG (the Zionist Occupation Government).

If this is the general pattern, the Italian experience represents a deviation from it. By and large neo-Fascist groups in Italy have not conducted violent operations against minorities of one kind or another. There have been some exceptions. Some violence has been directed against the country's Slovenian minority in Friuli Venezia-Giulia in connection with the extension of regional autonomy to that area.[1] At the time the Israeli government put Adolph Eichmann on trial in Jerusalem in 1961 neo-Fascist youth carried out attacks against Jews in the Trastevere section of Rome.[2] Presently, non-white immigrants to Italy from outside the European Union have become the targets of violent attack by members of the *Movimento Politico* and the Nazi-skinhead gangs in various cities, Rome especially. Despite these and other episodes and despite the fact that leaders of such important neo-Fascist bands as *Avanguardia Nazionale* and *Ordine Nuovo* described themselves and their followers as 'spiritual racists', the major preoccupation of violent radical rightists has been with the communist threat to Italian society.[3] For the neo-Fascists, the 'Reds' have been the ultimate targets for their campaigns of terrorist violence.

The fact that from the end of World War II to the disintegration of the Soviet Bloc itself Italy had the largest communist party of any country in the West represents the most powerful explanation for neo-Fascist violence and that particular kind of violence to which the label terrorism should be attached. Beyond the Italian Communist Party (PCI), with its mass membership, sizable share of the electorate and ties to the Soviet Union, Italy also possessed a complex Marxist subculture containing, from time to time, revolutionary political movements, student groups, labor unions, mass circulation newspapers and magazines, and many of the country's leading artists, scientists and intellectuals.[4] In general, the more closely the PCI approached the keys to national political power and the more threatening the Marxist subculture appeared to anti-communists, the more serious the manifestations of neo-Fascist violence.

The PCI's size and influence plus the vigor of Italy's Marxist subculture did not go unnoticed by the United States and other members of NATO. Aside from domestic considerations, the prospect of a communist Italy aroused fear among those seeking to prevent Soviet domination of Western Europe. As a result, there developed a common interest between those seeking to keep Italy out of the Soviet orbit and various neo-Fascist groups which, though ardently anti-American for social and cultural reasons, were willing to use violence to prevent a communist Italy.[5]

As well as in its anti-communist focus neo-Fascist violence in Italy also seems to differ from far right violence in the other western democracies in lasting longest. In the Italian case we are not dealing with a short-term episode triggered by the appearance of members of a racial minority in a new community or by the establishment of a mosque in a city where none had existed before. Instead, we confront a protracted series of events dating back to the immediate postwar years and continuing over more than four decades. Illustratively, among the first manifestations of neo-Fascist terrorism in postwar Italy were the brief seizure of a Roman radio station (whose employees were forced to broadcast a recording of *Giovinezza*, the Fascist anthem); the detonation of a bomb aboard an Italian ship, at Taranto, intended to be turned over to the Soviet Union as war reparation; and the explosion of a series of bombs in Rome and other cities on 28 October 1950 to commemorate the 28th anniversary of Mussolini's March on Rome.[6] Thus, when neo-Fascists set off an explosive in the waiting room of the Bologna railroad station in August 1980, a terrorist attack in which more than 80 bystanders lost their lives, the event, though the most lethal, was only one of a long list of such occurrences dating back to a time when the country's anti-Fascist republican constitution had barely been written. In fact, we could do worse than consider neo-Fascist violence in postwar Italy in effect as part of a continuing struggle between the forces that rallied to Mussolini's Salo' Republic and the Resistance groups which were formed to liberate the country from Nazi-Fascist control during World War II.

Not only has neo-Fascist violence in Italy been prolonged compared to other western democracies, the events involved have been both more numerous and variegated than the democratic norm. For instance, a report commissioned by the regional government of Lombardy produced a chronology of more than 1,200 acts of violence carried out between 1969 and 1974 by Mussolini Action Squads and other neo-Fascist bands in that region alone.[7] Few of the events involved could be defined as terrorism strictly speaking; most were acts of vandalism such as defacing monuments and other symbols of the Resistance, or assaults on individuals or small groups of individuals, students not uncommonly, suspected of leftist sympathies. And by most accounts Rome and the rest of Lazio was the site of even more neo-Fascist violence than Lombardy during the same period.[8]

In addition to the frequency with which neo-Fascist groups carried out these low level acts of violence and aggression, they were also responsible for the commission of a high proportion of terrorist attacks during the so-called *anni di piombo*, the terrorist dominated 'years of lead', between 1969 and 1982. In these years left-wing revolutionary groups such as the Red Brigades and Front Line received the bulk of the publicity, at least outside Italy. But if we consider the sheer volume of terrorist attacks and the number of people killed as a result of them, then the neo-Fascist groups emerge as the most brutal.[9]

Neo-Fascist violence has also encompassed a wide range of activities, from street corner brawls with leftist *liceo* students in Milan and Rome to widespread urban rioting and massacres of many innocent bank customers, railroad passengers and simple passersby in various bombing operations. Illustratively, leaders of the *Fronte Nazionale, Ordine Nuovo* and *Avanguardia Nazionale* encouraged the mass rioting and protests in the southern city of Reggio Calabria after its rival, Catanzaro, was chosen as the capital of the new regional government in 1970.[10] Other neo-Fascist militants were responsible for the *stragi* or massacres committed at Piazza Fontana in Milan, aboard the express train 'Italicus' between Florence and Bologna, at Piazza della Loggia in Brescia and other venues where time-bombs were exploded to sow mass panic and promote military intervention in Italian politics by killing large numbers of people on an anonymous basis.

II.

If the overall contour of Far Right violence in Italy seems unusual when viewed against the experiences of other Western democracies, how does it look when placed in the context of Ehud Sprinzak's linkage theory of political terrorism? (Our current exploration of this question will perforce be incomplete given the recent vintage of Sprinzak's latest conclusions; this contribution addresses an earlier version of Sprinzak's work.) To what extent does Sprinzak's conceptualization conform to the realities of right-wing violence and terrorism in Italy? The answer, at least a preliminary one, is that it fits in some important respects but is wide of the mark in others.

Sprinzak's formulation certainly applies in the sense that neo-Fascists unleashed campaigns of mass violence, street corner brawling and campus confrontations, and full-fledged terrorism, the *stragi*, in the late 1960s and early 1970s out of fear that the *Partito Communista Italia* (PCI) and the extra-parliamentary movements to its left, for example, *Potere Operaio* (Worker Power), *Lotta Continua* (Continuous Struggle), represented an immediate revolutionary threat to Italian society. In these years we can observe a rapid proliferation of violent neo-Fascist groups organized in various parts of Italy. Important and already existing groups such as the *Fronte Nazionale, Ordine Nuovo* and *Avanguardia Nazionale*, increased in size and stepped up their operations.[11] As we shall see, the 'strategy of tensions' was pursued. There was an intent to replace the existing parliamentary regime with a military-dominated one. Further, by the mid-1970s important neo-Fascist bands reached the conclusion that the Italian state was beyond redemption and began launching terrorist assaults against it, particularly against members of the judiciary committed to uncovering neo-Fascist schemes.[12]

On the other hand, there are at least three ways in which the Italian case does not seem to fit the conceptualization. First, Italy's violent neo-Fascist groups, at least the most visible and influential ones, were not narrowly particularistic in the way Sprinzak conceives them to be. They were guided by a set of universal and 'spiritual' principles articulated by the philosopher Giulio Cesare Evola. A full explication of Evola's philosophy is well beyond the scope of this inquiry. It must suffice to note that Evola (memorialized as 'our Marcuse, only better' by Giorgio Almirante, leader of the Italian Social Movement, after Evola's death in 1974) stressed the decay of Italian society and Western societies in general caused by the influences of materialism, liberalism, democracy, socialism and communism. In the midst of this decadence, there were some signs of spiritual vitality. The latter were reflected in heroic, selfless 'orders' displaying the 'legionnaire spirit'. The Romanian Iron Guard, the Spanish Falange and, above all, the Nazi SS provided modern examples of the kind of elite of heroes that Evola believed could still be achieved despite the decadence of the modern world. Further, the state, according to Evola, was the supreme human achievement which should dominate society the way the male 'spirit' should dominate the female.[13] These ideas and others like them that Evola expressed may not seem especially attractive to social scientists committed to liberal democratic values; nonetheless they were widely discussed among Italy's neo-Fascist ideologues who used them as a rationale for the various violent operations on which their cohorts embarked.

A second way in which the Italian experience does not conform to Sprinzak's view of the dynamics of particularistic terrorist organizations concerns the issue of state delegitimation. In the case of Italy we are dealing with a situation in which the state, as defined by the republican constitution of 1948, never managed to acquire the widespread legitimacy achieved by its counterparts in other parts of Europe; the Italian state seems to suffer from a chronic condition of weak legitimacy. It is true that the country's transparently neo-Fascist political party, the *Movimento Sociale Italiano* (MSI), expressed its lukewarm support for the existing democratic system when it was created in 1946. But this was done for tactical reasons. The MSI's founders wished to avoid legal proscription.[14] But the violent extraparliamentary groups with which this analysis is principally concerned never were willing to make such a tactical concession. Either as admirers of the defunct Fascist dictatorship of

Mussolini or the Nazi regime in Germany or as followers of Evola the important leaders of Italy's violent postwar neo-Fascist groups, for instance, Giuseppe 'Pino' Rauti, Clemente Graziani, Ellio Massagrande, Stefano delle Chiaie, Paolo Signorelli, regarded the whole apparatus of parliamentary democracy with the utmost contempt. At one point during the late 1960s, Rauti and the others, consistent with Evola's views, referred to the 'sane forces' inside the state that could be called to rescue Italy as it went through a time of peril caused by the communist threat. The allusion was to the *carabinieri* and officers in the Italian military establishment whom the neo-Fascist leadership wished to enlist in a scheme to stage a *coup d'état*. The neo-Fascists' crisis of delegitimacy was not especially profound because they never accorded the Italian state much legitimacy in the first place.

Third, Sprinzak sees the violent conduct of particularistic terrorist organizations as the outgrowth of a gestative phase, a period before which the groups embark on terrorist campaigns. There is, he believes, a movement from non-violence to violence to terrorism. The Italian neo-Fascist case is, as has already been claimed and as will be evident in greater detail below, one involving protracted episodes of violence dating back to the immediate postwar years. There have been peaks and valleys to be sure but neo-Fascist activity in the almost half century since the conclusion of World War II has displayed a persistent strain of violence.

III.

The best way to demonstrate the accuracy of this generalization, and of the others that preceded it, is by reviewing the pattern of neo-Fascist conduct in Italy from the immediate *dopoguerra* to the present. This historical experience may be divided into several phases.

First, in the years following the liberation of Italy in April 1945 we can observe the formation of a long list of clandestine neo-Fascist bands committed to the anti-Communist cause.[15] With names like the *Orso Nero*, *Partito Fascista Democratico*, *Fronte Antibolscevico italiano*, *Squadre di Azione Mussolini* and most significantly the *Fasci d'Azione Rivoluzionaria* (FAR) with its *Esercito Clandestino Anticomunista*, these were groups committed to the prevention of a PCI victory and the restoration of a Fascist dictatorship along the radical lines of the Salo' Republic (1943–45). The context for the various operations of these underground groups was an environment in which the avowal of Fascism and the formation of groups committed to its cause were made illegal by the Allied forces, by the provisional government of the National Liberation Committee (CLN) as Italy resumed its independent path, and by the republican Constitution which went into effect at the beginning of 1948. The atmosphere was also one in which

Resistance groups, the PCI-dominated Garibaldi Brigades, carried out a wave of summary executions against Fascists and Fascist collaborators in Bologna, Modena and other areas of Emilia Romagna; indeed all over central and northern Italy some thousands of Fascists were targets of vigilante justice. It was also widely expected at different times in this era that a communist insurrection was imminent, particularly in the days following the attempt to assassinate the PCI leader Palmiro Togliatti in 1948.

The neo-Fascist groups appeared in Rome first, where it was easier to obtain false identity documents. They became more active in 1946 after the government granted an amnesty to many imprisoned Fascists and as the Allied prisoner of war camps were closed.[16] What followed was a series of terrorist events along with some non-violent escapades designed to catch the attention of Italians nostalgic for a return to the old order and skeptical about the ability of the new Christian Democratic-dominated governments to prevent the PCI from coming to rule Italy. Thus over the next few years bombs exploded in front of various public buildings and the local offices of leftist political parties were the targets of nocturnal attack with Molotov cocktails. Most of the clandestine bands involved in these activities proved to be ephemeral. The exception was *Fasci d'Azione Rivoluzionaria* (FAR), with its secret anti-communist Army. Members of the FAR leadership, which included Evola and such Salo' Republic luminaries as Domenico Leccisi, did not believe in political parties, elections and parliaments; they held the view that the Italian public was becoming so alienated by the new democratic order that the time was not far off when it would support another Fascist seizure of power.[17] This was hardly a realistic appraisal of the situation. In the heated anti-Fascist atmosphere of the *dopoguerra* one would have to be gaga to believe the Italian public would tolerate a neo-Fascist regime just as the catastrophic consequences of the original were beginning to subside.

Whatever the manifold failings of Italy's new democratic institutions, those in power were sufficiently attentive to put FAR outside the law in 1951 and prosecute its leaders for the criminal offense of seeking to reconstitute a Fascist party and of promoting Fascist propaganda. A few FAR diehards retitled their organization the *Legione nera* and expressed their displeasure with the government's action by detonating a few bombs in front of public buildings before ceasing operations.

The end of FAR did not bring an end to neo-Fascism or neo-Fascist violence in Italy. It did however usher in a new phase in their evolution.

During the 1950s the *Movimento Sociale Italiano* (MSI) became the dominant focus of neo-Fascist activity. The *missini* had been organized in 1946 by second echelon figures in the Salo' Republic, individuals who expressed a commitment to its ostensibly radical principles, the Charter of

Verona, and who were sufficiently in touch with reality to recognize that a return of Fascism was a long way off (it would take more than 45 years before their hopes would be realized in 1994). The MSI's founders recognized the necessity of electoral campaigns and the pursuit of political alliances with other forces, such as the Monarchists and even the Christian Democrats, if any of their dreams were to be realized. There was also a realization that repeated exhibitions of *neosquadrismo* would likely mean that the MSI would end as FAR had. In fact it was a close call. Thanks to legislation – the Scelba Law, passed before the 1953 parliamentary elections – the MSI barely avoided proscription.[18]

Despite the danger of being placed *fuorilegge* (outside the law) and the MSI's official policy of seeking to 'insert' itself in the Christian Democratic-dominated system of patronage and clientelism, neo-Fascist violence was never far below the surface. While such MSI leaders as Arturo Michelini and Augusto De Marsanich might present themselves to the public wearing double-breasted suits and as advocates of moderation, the Movement's youth organizations were responsible for a long list of violent attacks during the 1950s and early 1960s. By one count members of the *Fronte della Gioventu'*, *Giovane Italia* and *Fronte Universitario di Azione Nazionale* committed 73 acts of political violence between 1953 and 1961.[19] For the most part these were acts of political vandalism and intimidation, such as ransacking a left-wing bookstore, preventing a Communist from speaking at a university gathering, setting fire to a memorial wreath for those killed while fighting in the Resistance, but there were a handful of murders involved as well.[20]

Also during the 1950s the willingness of the MSI leadership under Michelini to pursue an official course of moderation evoked the resentment of those adults in the Movement who paid more than lipservice to Evola's ideas. In the aftermath of the particularly bitter 1956 national congress, dissidents led by Giuseppe 'Pino' Rauti and Clemente Graziani separated themselves from the MSI and created *Ordine Nuovo* (ON) whose motto, 'Duty is our Honor', and symbol, twin lightning bolts, were borrowed from the Nazi SS and whose outlook was anything but democratic.

In 1960 a group of *Ordine Nuovo* (ON) dissidents led by Stefano Delle Chiaie formed a new group, the *Avanguardia Nazionale Giovanile*, which quickly became involved in a series of street corner brawls with left-wing students at the University of Rome. These adventures culminated in the death of one such student in 1966 and the decision of the authorities to dissolve the organization on the basis of its manifestly Fascist character as well as the criminal conduct of many of its militants. Later Delle Chiaie, whom the press nicknamed the 'Roman Bombardier' because of his favorite form of political expression, would reorganize his group as the *Avanguardia Nazionale* (AN), until it too was dissolved by the courts.

As the 1960s proceeded, events occurred which would provide the setting for the next and most virulent phase of neo-Fascist violence in postwar Italy. Space does not permit a complete accounting but some observations are necessary to place the terrorism in the appropriate context. First, so far as the MSI is concerned, the failure of what became known as the 'Tambroni Experiment' in 1960 to bring about the *missini*'s direct participation in the ruling coalition caused the Movement's moderate leadership to lose credibility, particularly among younger members. Accordingly, the extraparliamentary right groups, with their aversion to empty rhetoric and the prevailing patronage system, became attractive to right-wing youth. Second, the early 1960s witnessed the formation of the Center-Left coalition between the Christian Democrats and the Socialist Party (PSI), a party still nominally committed to Marxism. In 1964, after the PSI leader Pietro Nenni reluctantly agreed to continue the alliance on terms he did not regard as favorable to his party's reformist goals, rumors began to surface about anti-democratic schemes involving the Italian military and its intelligence agency, SIFAR.[21] The press reported the existence of Plan 'Solo', a scheme for what amounted to the seizure of power by the Italian military during a period of governmental instability or in the event of a PCI-led insurrection. The parliamentary inquiry on this matter was inconclusive, but it did disclose the fact that SIFAR had kept dossiers on thousands of left-wing politicians and labor union leaders (the press discussed the possibility that these individuals might be the target of a roundup in the event of a *coup d'état*). In any case SIFAR, some of whose personnel were holdovers from the Fascist era OVRA, was transformed into SID (Defense Intelligence Service) in the hope it would in the future conform to democratic norms.

Other events in the mid-to-late 1960s served to radicalize the Italian political environment. The Vietnam War and the student-led protests against it in other countries had anti-American and anti-NATO consequences in Italy as well. Italian students, particularly those from the major northern universities as well as the University of Rome, became involved in mass protest activities. In Greece in April 1967 the military staged a *coup d'état* against the democratic government in a situation that some Italian journalists believed bore a resemblance to the one taking shape in their own country. There were rumors that prominent Italian neo-Fascists visited Greece in order to hold discussions with the colonels.[22]

In 1968 protests reached enormous proportions as hundreds of thousands of university students staged mass marches and sit-ins and engaged in other forms of direct action. The following year there was the 'Hot Autumn'. As labor contracts came up for renewal for the major industrial firms of northern

Italy there were massive strikes in Genoa, Turin, Milan and other cities. Millions of workers became involved in protests against the prevailing terms of employment.[23] As these events unfolded new extraparliamentary left movements, of which *Lotta Continua, Potere Operaio* and *Autonomia Operaio* were the most prominent, emerged to exploit the situation.[24] In general the extraparliamentary left groups, often inspired by the views of Mao, Trotsky and Castro, believed they confronted a potentially revolutionary situation and did what they could to mobilize students and workers for insurrectionary activities. The Christian Democratic government in Rome appeared virtually helpless in responding to these developments.

It was in this context that the next phase of neo-Fascist violence emerged. Known variously as a 'counter mobilization' or as the 'strategy of tensions', there was a substantial and violent neo-Fascist reaction to these manifestations of left-wing radicalism. The extent to which elements in the military establishment and intelligence service participated remains debatable, but by now it is clear that such collaboration existed, at least for a while.

What we can observe is the following. In 1965 the Parco dei Principi hotel in Rome was the site of a conference on revolutionary warfare sponsored by the Alberto Pollio Institute, a previously unknown foundation. At this gathering a series of lectures were delivered by intelligence officers and figures with backgrounds in *Ordine Nuovo* and *Avanguardia Nazionale*. Italy was defined as the target of a world-wide communist offensive. Considerable discussion was devoted to developing a plan of 'total defense' to meet the threat. There was need, for example, to recruit and train 'counter-revolutionary' soldiers to fight communism by all available means.[25] Later the press would report that SID, and indirectly the American CIA, had begun channeling money to 'patriotic' groups including neo-Fascist ones.

Over the next few years we can observe the formation of many neo-Fascist and patriotic organizations all over the Peninsula. With names like *Comitato di Difesa Civica, Gruppo Alfa, Europa Civilita', Fronte Nazionale Rivoluzionario, Movimento di Azione Rivoluzionario* and *Squadre di Azione Mussolini*, one estimate put the number of such new aggregations at over 50.[26] But the most significant of the new groups to be formed was the *Fronte Nazionale* (FN) headed by Prince Valerio Borghese, a former commander of Fascist forces during World War II and a man later prosecuted as a war criminal. In addition to these developments *Ordine Nuovo* (ON) and *Avanguardia Nazionale* (AN) displayed renewed vitality. At this point the press began to report the establishment of paramilitary training camps in different parts of the country. Furthermore, several right-wing figures sought to make new identities for themselves as revolutionary leftists. Franco Freda and Giovanni Ventura, leaders of neo-Fascist initiatives in earlier years including the Aryan Aristocracy, opened left-wing bookstores and loudly proclaimed their conversions to the cause of red revolution. In 1968 the MSI underwent a change in leadership and outlook. Arturo Michelini, the long-serving party secretary, died and his place was taken by Giorgio Almirante, a man far more committed to Fascist principles than his predecessor. Within a short time, Almirante was able to persuade 'Pino' Rauti and a faction of ON to return to the MSI framework. He was also able to recruit some high-ranking military and naval officers, including the former commander of NATO naval forces in the Mediterranean and the general in charge of SIFAR at the time of the Plan 'Solo' scandal, to run for Parliament as the Movement's candidates. By 1970 and certainly by the 1972 parliamentary elections the MSI presented itself to the country as the party of law and order, advocate of the 'silent majority' of Italians tired of the violence and turmoil that had become part of their daily lives.

It is something of an understatement to say that Italy in the late 1960s and early 1970s had become a place where political violence and turmoil had become relatively common. The journalist Alberto Ronchey began referring to the South Americanization of Italian life.[27] In these years the extraparliamentary left movements were an almost constant source of mass protest in the major cities. These movements also provided the milieu from which the revolutionary terrorist groups emerged. The Red Brigades, for example, grew out of the student protest movement at the University of Trent and the atmosphere of mass worker-student actions in Milan.

In response to these developments, the neo-Fascist 'counter mobilization' took various forms. There were literally thousands of violent street confrontations between neo-Fascist bands and the youthful leftist groups. In Milan, Rome and Naples, particular neighborhoods and *piazze* became identified as 'red' or 'black' much in the manner of criminal gangs currently active in Los Angeles. From time to time members of one neo-Fascist band or another would stage a 'punitive expedition' into the area controlled by leftist students etc..

Far more serious in terms of the number of deaths and injuries involved were the so-called *stragi* or massacres. Between 1969 and 1974 there were three major bombings carried out by neo-Fascist groups which resulted in multiple fatalities. The first and most emblematic occurred on 12 December 1969 at the National Agricultural Bank at Piazza Fontana in Milan – an event that left 17 people dead and another 88 injured.[28] At first the police blamed the revolutionary left for the attack. Two anarchists were quickly arrested and accused of the crime; one of them then allegedly committed suicide by jumping from an upper story window of the Milanese police headquarters.

Within a few months this story unraveled. Based on a number of accounts, the bomb had been planted by the neo-Fascists Freda and Ventura acting in conjunction with 'Pino' Rauti and other like-minded individuals.[29] More disturbing still, journalists and investigating magistrates uncovered evidence of police complicity in a complex neo-Fascist scheme to stage a series of provocative bombings: there were other explosions at the same time as the Piazza Fontana killings, in the hope the Italian public could be led to believe that leftist revolutionaries were responsible. Further, individuals, aside from Freda and Ventura, with neo-Fascist backgrounds were reported to have either created or infiltrated leftist groups with the intent of acting as *provocateurs*. These actions, including other attempted bombings in various locales, were allegedly intended to sustain a high level of tension throughout the country. The hope was that, if the pot could be kept boiling, the public could be made to accept a *coup d'état* by elements in the military acting in conjunction with the neo-Fascists.

This possibility was regarded as sufficiently serious for the PCI headquarters in Rome to circulate a warning in 1970 to key leaders around the country instructing them to avoid sleeping in their own homes. The fear was of an anti-communist roundup that would follow a successful coup. This reaction was far from leftist paranoia. In February 1971 Manlio Brosio, a former civilian head of NATO, made a speech in Rome in which he asserted the right of members of the Atlantic Alliance to intervene in the domestic affairs of any NATO country where Communists appeared on the verge of seizing power.[30] And a few years later Arnaldo Forlani, then secretary of the Christian Democratic Party, referred to the existence of serious anti-democratic schemes during a speech he delivered in La Spezia. He also warned of the possibility of a coup.[31]

In fact, there were at least two attempts to stage such an event. The first occurred in December 1970 and involved a central role for Valerio Borghese. During the evening of 7–8 December, members of Borghese's well-financed *Fronte Nazionale* along with followers of ON and AN assembled in front of key public buildings in Rome including the Viminale, site of the Interior Ministry and the broadcast studios of RAI, the state television network. An anticipated cue from key officials was not forthcoming and the assembled neo-Fascists dispersed.[32] The second episode was discovered in its formative stages. In November 1973 authorities in Liguria uncovered the so-called *Rosa dei Venti* (Compass Rose) organization. Groups of right-wing businessmen with their roots in the Salo' Republic, neo-Fascist figures and members of SID were reported to have been in the process of creating a nationwide network of armed neo-Fascist groups, such as *La Fenice*, *Movimento di Azione Rivoluzionario*, *XVIII Legione*, whose ultimate objective was the establishment of a Salo'-like regime. Arrests followed the disclosures.

In fact, by 1974 the government undertook overdue prosecutions against a long list of violent neo-Fascists. Also, in the wake of the Italicus and Piazza della Loggia bombings, the government formed a special anti-terrorism task force of the *carabinieri* in order to fight neo-Fascist violence. Furthermore, the government sought successfully to have ON, AN and Borghese's FN dissolved as manifestly pro-Fascist, anti-constitutional organizations. Borghese, Delle Chiaie and a long list of other leaders of the 'strategy of tensions' fled abroad to avoid prison terms. There was talk in parliament of reforming the intelligence service so as to make it accountable to democratic authorities.[33] It seemed as if violent neo-Fascism might be reaching the end of the road.

But this was not to be. Although the political terrorism in Italy during the second half of the 1970s was dominated by the exploits of the leftist revolutionary organizations, new groups of violent neo-Fascists arose to take the place of the old ones. A new phase in the postwar history of neo-Fascist violence began with a reassessment of the political situation. The earlier bands of neo-Fascists had hoped that the decay of the Italian state could be arrested by a *coup d'état*. 'Sane' elements in the military and police forces, with advice from the neo-Fascist leadership, would be able to restore order and defeat the Communists' designs. After the events of 1974–75, it was realized that the state was beyond redemption.

The ideological tract that dominated neo-Fascist thinking in this period was Giorgio Freda's *La disintegrazione del sistema*.[34] According to Freda, one of the accused Piazza Fontana bombers, the Italian state needed to be destroyed and replaced by a completely new type of regime, one that incorporated elements of the Mussolini dictatorship with some new arrangements of his own design.

In practical terms, those influenced by Freda's ideas began to think about the means available to destroy the republican state. A loose-knit organization centered in Rome, *Costruiamo L'Azione* (there is no easy way to translate this title) was the first manifestation of this new thinking. The publications of *Costruiamo L'Azione* had kind things to say about Argentina's Montoneros, an ostensibly left Peronist group. The latter was defined as part of the world-wide struggle against American imperialism (the USA was characterized as 'Judenland' for those taken with this outlook). There was also discussion about the possibility of forging alliances with the revolutionary groups active in Italy with which they shared a common interest: one enemy, one struggle. For two years, groups tied to *Costruiamo L'Azione* carried out terrorist attacks against state institutions and personnel in and around Rome, including the killing of a policeman, before the authorities managed to dismantle this organization and arrest many of its core members.[35]

There was no cessation of neo-Fascist terrorism during 1979–81. In Rome bombs were exploded in front of the Campidoglio (the city hall), the foreign ministry, the city's major prison and the building that housed the High Council of the Judiciary. Also in Rome neo-Fascist gunmen killed a judge who was conducting an investigation into their organizations, along with two policemen. Other policemen were shot down in Milan and Padua. Then, of course, there was the August 1980 explosion at the railroad station at Bologna in which 85 people were killed and more than 200 injured, at that time the single worst terrorist incident in the history of postwar Europe.

Two short-lived groups, both Roman in origin,were responsible for most of this violence: *Terza Posizione* (TP) and the *Nuclei Armati Rivoluzionari* (NAR). Ideologues for both groups stressed the idea of armed spontaneity and romanticized the idea of struggle on behalf of a lost cause: they sought to capture the 'legionnaire spirit'. Some became taken with the fantasy writings of J. R. R. Tolkien; a 'Camp Hobbit' was held outside Rome in June 1978.[36] TP's ideological perspective was reflected in its name – Third Position. Its leaders stressed their opposition to both socialism and capitalism. It was neither left nor right but represented a third position.

In the months after the Bologna massacre and the public outcry that followed in its wake, there was a massive roundup of known violent neo-Fascists. Some were able to flee abroad before they could be apprehended. Nonetheless, there were a series of prosecutions the result of which was the dissolution of TP and NAR and long prison sentences for most of their leaders. However, as with the prosecutions undertaken for the other *stragi* so too in this instance: the effort to identify those responsible and then try them dragged on for years. A trial was held in 1987 which resulted in the conviction of a long list of neo-Fascists. But this outcome was reversed on appeal two years later.

The collapse of the NAR and TP initiatives ended another phase in the history of neo-Fascist violence in Italy. The 1980s were not kind to the radical left either. The major revolutionary terrorist groups were dismantled by the authorities. The extraparliamentary left movements dribbled away leaving in their wake a minor political party, the Democratic Proletarians. The PCI lost votes as well as members. Its prospects declined over the decade, so much so that after the events of 1989 the party changed its name to the Democratic Party of the Left (PDS) and abandoned its Marxist world-view. In short, the red threat to Italian society had passed and with it the need for a violent neo-Fascist struggle against Communism.

But just as there was a shift in neo-Fascist targeting from the 'reds' to the state during the 1970s, in recent years neo-Fascist youth have turned their attention from the state to other objects. To date the last phase in the evolution of neo-Fascist violence involves attacks on Asians and Africans who have migrated to Italy, illegally in many cases, in search of better lives. The activities of the Nazi-Skins, etc. in Rome and other cities has now made Italy part of the growing European-wide phenomenon of racist violence.

IV.

Italian politics is to conspiracy theories as air is to fire. There is incessant political gossip and rumor circulating about one secret cabal or another. Much of this gossip must be taken with a grain of salt. Nonetheless, there is now sufficient evidence to suggest the existence of one or more ill-conceived and poorly executed schemes to undermine Italian democracy from the late 1960s through the first half of the next decade.

The relationship between the leaders of the violent neo-Fascist bands and elements in the intelligence agency SID has been well established. General Vito Miceli, head of SID at the time, and several of his subordinates were arrested and accused of providing financial and technical assistance to the neo-Fascists. High-ranking army and air force officers were also implicated.[37] There was talk, apparently well founded, of a 'parallel' SID whose covert operatives devoted themselves to coup-making activities.

The real issue concerns the role of 'occult' forces behind the neo-Fascist/SID nexus. In 1980–81 the Italian public became aware of a secret masonic lodge known as *Propaganda Due* (P2) whose leader, Licio Gelli, was identified as a puppetmaster of Italian politics. A parliamentary investigation disclosed that the membership of P2 included a long list of influential businessmen, center and right-wing politicians, as well as officers from the police and military establishments.[38] General Miceli, for example, had been a member. Under Gelli's anti-Communist direction, P2 had sought to manipulate the Italian political situation. Gelli and his subordinates were accused of seeking to end the communist threat by promoting the strategy of tensions and sponsoring the wave of neo-Fascist bombings. By the mid-1970s, however, Gelli and P2 were said to have abandoned coup-making in favor of an effort to reform and streamline rather than topple the democratic order. As these and a long list of other accusations surfaced in the mid 1980s, Gelli fled the country and spent some years in exile in Latin America and Switzerland. In December 1987 a court in Florence convicted Gelli of financing an armed neo-Fascist band that had planted bombs along railroad tracks in Tuscany between 1973 and 1975. And in 1988 Gelli was sentenced to ten years imprisonment by a Bolognese court for his involvement in the August 1980 railroad station massacre.[39] These convictions did not hold. After Gelli was extradited by the Swiss authorities in 1990, appeals courts overturned both his convictions. And so the whole matter remains moot.

Gladio is the other entity widely suspected of sponsoring neo-Fascist activities. In December 1990, after the Berlin Wall had collapsed and the communist regimes of Eastern Europe had disintegrated, the existence of a NATO-backed group known as *Gladio* created still another scandal in Italian public life. As revealed by Christian Democratic leaders Giulio Andreotti and Francesco Cossiga, *Gladio* was part of an overall NATO plan dating from the 1950s, known as Stay Behind, designed to provide an underground response in the event that one or another of the NATO countries were to fall under Soviet control or come to be dominated by domestic communist parties.[40] *Gladio* represented the Italian application of the overall scheme. Among other things, it involved British intelligence and American CIA training of covert forces ready to react to a communist threat and to make use of secret arms caches spread around the country. Although both Andreotti and Cossiga asserted there was nothing sinister about *Gladio*, many believe that it played a role in the Plan 'Solo' operation of the 1960s and the aborted Compass Rose scheme of the 1970s. The end of the Cold War and the PCI's transformation into the PDS lends a certain historical aura to the *Gladio* episode, rather like one of the early John Le Carré novels.

V.

Now, to what extent do the events just described fit Sprinzak's conceptualization of right-wing terrorism? To elaborate upon what was said earlier in the commentary we should stress that the process of radicalization that occurred among the neo-Fascists in reaction to a perceived revolutionary threat in the late 1960s and the subsequent implementation of the strategy of tensions over the following years, followed by attacks on the state itself, does conform to the pattern Sprinzak identified. Sprinzak's view also seems to hold in connection with the outlook of the neo-Fascists' towards the use of violence. The latter's discourse abounds with approving references to the worth of organized violence. Stefano Delle Chiaie, for example, referred to himself and his followers as an 'elite of heroes' shortly after he and a few other 'heroes' planted a bomb in front of an elementary school. Italian psychiatrists who have interviewed both red and 'black' terrorists in prison have found the latter to be more inherently hostile and violent than the former.

On the other hand, applying the Sprinzak conceptualization to the Italian experience extracts that experience from its historical context. Perhaps this result was inevitable, given the nature of the endeavor. Nonetheless, the violent conflict between revolutionary socialism or communism and fascism in Italy did not begin with a meeting at the Parco Dei Principi hotel in 1965. Rather, it has been a consistent factor in Italian politics from the World War I era. Any analysis that does not take the history of the struggle into consideration loses some understanding of the struggle's meaning for those engaged in it. And to repeat a point made earlier, neo-Fascist violence is a continuing process in Italian public life.

Finally, and perhaps at a more general level, the Sprinzak conceptualization does not take account of the role played by foreign sponsors in particularistic terrorism. In the present case we have the still murky role of NATO in the *Gladio* operation, an effort to manipulate Italian politics. But, during the 1930s the Mussolini dictatorship sought to manipulate Yugoslav politics by sponsoring *Ustasha*, the Croat terrorist group. Violent, pro-Fascist groups in France and several Balkan countries were also the beneficiaries of Mussolini's assistance. The Franco insurgency in Spain might also be mentioned. Contemporary studies of particularistic terrorist groups in Latin America and the Middle East provide substantial evidence that external sponsorship is relatively common, so much so that it should be treated as a variable in efforts to explain the performance of right-wing terrorist groups in different national settings.

NOTES

1. Pietro Secchia, *Lotta AntiFascista e giovani generazioni* (Milan: La Pietra, 1973) pp.80–7.
2. Alfonso Di Nola, *Antisemitismo in Italia 1962/1972* (Florence: Vallecchi editore, 1973) pp.25–31.
3. See, e.g., Franco Ferraresi, 'La destra eversiva', in Franco Ferraresi (ed.), *La destra radicale* (Milan: Feltrinelli, 1984), pp. 66-71.
4. For a discussion see Giuseppe Bedeschi, *La Parabola Del Marxismo in Italia 1945–1983* (Bari: Laterza, 1983).
5. See, e.g., Daniele Barbieri, *Agenda Nera* (Rome: Coines edizioni, 1976), pp.69–86; William Scobie, 'Gladio: The War That Never Was', *World Press Review* 38/2 (1991), p.37.
6. See, e.g., Mario Giovana, *Le nuove camicie nere* (Turin: Edizioni Dell'Albero, 1966), pp.28–37; see also Giulio Caradonna, *Diario di battaglie* (Rome: Europa Press Service, n.d.), pp.17–26.
7. Luigi Majocchi (ed.), *Rapporto sulla Violenza Fascista in Lombardia* (Rome: Cooperativa Scrittori, 1975), pp.15–119.
8. Fabrizio Dentice, 'Come nel '22?', *L'Espresso* 16/51 (Dec.1970), pp.4–5.
9. Donatella della Porta and Maurizio Rossi, *Cifre crudelli: bilancio del terrorismi italiani* (Bologna: Istituto Cattaneo, 1983), pp.18–19.
10. See Fabrizio D'Agostini, *Reggio Calabria* (Milan: Feltrinelli, 1972), pp.19–24.
11. See, e.g., Cesare De Simone, *La Pista Nera* (Rome: Editori Riuniti, 1972); Franco Ferrarotti, *Fascismo Di Ritorno* (Rome: Edizioni della Lega per le autonomie, 1973).
12. Piero Luigi Vigna, 'L'Omicidio Del Magistrato Vittorio Occorsio', *Questione Giustizia* 2/4 (1983), pp.913–33.
13. For an account in English see Richard Drake, *The Revolutionary Mystique and Terrorism in Contemporary Italy* (Bloomington, IN: Indiana UP, 1989), pp.114–34; in Italian see, Anna Jellamo, 'J. Evola, il pensatore della tradizione', in *La destra radicale* (note 3), pp.215–52; Franco Ferraresi, 'I riferimenti teeorico-dottrinali della destra radicale', *Questione Giustizia* 2/4 (1983), pp.881–92.

14. Petra Rosenbaum, *Il nuovo fascismo* (Milan: Feltrinelli,1975), pp.55–60; Piero Ignazi, *Il Polo Escluso* (Bologna: Il Mulino, 1989), pp.15–36.
15. For some sense of the atmosphere see Mario Tedeschi, *Fascisti dopo Mussolini* (Rome: L'Arnia,1950), pp.22–53.
16. Angelo Del Boca and Mario Giovana, *I figli del sole* (Milan: Feltrinelli, 1965), pp.173–221.
17. Pier Giuseppe Murgia, *Ritorneremo!* (Milan: Sugar,1976), p.127.
18. See, e.g., Giorgio Almirante and F. Palamenghi-Crispi, *Il movimento sociale italiano* (Milan: Nuova Accademia,1958); and Giorgio Almirante, *Autobiografia di un 'fucilatore'* (Milan: Edizioni del Borghese, 1974), pp.150–85.
19. Secchia (note 1), pp.80–7.
20. Giulio Salierno, *Autobiografia di un picchiatore fascista* (Turin: Einaudi, 1976).
21. Ruggero Zangrandi, *Inchiesta Sul SIFAR* (Rome: Riuniti,1970), pp.18–63.
22. Enzo Santarelli, *Fascismo E Neofascismo* (Rome: Riuniti,1974), pp.249–54.
23. Domenico Bartoli, <u>Gli italiani nella terra di nessuno</u> (Milan: Mondadori, 1976), pp.51–83.
24. Mino Monicelli, *L'Ultrasinistra in Italia, 1968–1978* (Bari: Laterza,1978), pp.23–44.
25. Ferraresi (note 3), pp.58–9.
26. Paolo Guzzanti, *Il neofascismo e le sue organizzazioni paramilitari* (Rome: PSI, 1973), pp.11–31.
27. Alberto Ronchey, *Accadde in Italia 1968–1977* (Milan: Garzanti, 1977), p.17.
28. Mauro Galleni (ed.), *Rapporto sul Terrorismo* (Milan: Rizzoli, 1981), pp.51–3.
29. Marco Sassano, *La Politica della Strage* (Padova: Marsilio, 1972), pp.39–82.
30. De Simone (note 11), p.124.
31. Barbieri (note 5), p.240.
32. For a discussion see Giampaolo Pansa, *Borghese mi ha detto* (Milan: Palazzi,1971), pp.42–73.
33. Rosario Minna, 'Il terrorismo di destra', pp.59–60.
34. Giorgio Freda, *La disintegrazione del sistema* (Padova: Edizioni AR, 1969).
35. Giancarlo Capaldo et. al., 'L'Eversione Di Destra a Roma Dal '77 Ad Oggi', *Questione Giustizia* 2/4 (1983), pp.935–79.
36. Marco Revelli, 'La nuova destra', in Ferraresi (note 3), p.124.
37. See, e.g., Renzo Vanni, *Trent'anni di regime bianco* (Pisa: Giardini, 1976), pp.348–54.
38. Tina Anselmi, 'Il complotto di Licio Gelli: relazioni di Tina Anselmi, residente dellacommissione parlamentare sulla P2', sp. suppl., *L'Espresso, 20 May 1984.*
39. Philip Willan, *Puppetmasters* (London: Constable, 1992), pp.63–5.
40. *The Economist*, 15 Dec. 1990, pp.47–8.

Right-Wing Terrorism in South Africa

DAVID WELSH

This article reviews the background to the rise of the right wing in South Africa and argues that there has always been a strand in Afrikaner politics with a proclivity to violence. The transformation in South Africa began in the 1980s and accelerated in the 1990s, alienating conservatives and those in the security forces who were still in the grip of the militarist doctrines espoused during the P.W. Botha era. Hit squads, dirty tricks and efforts to destabilise neighbouring governments were part of the state's response to the rise of black militance in the 1980s. Terrorism was also practised by paramilitary right-wing groups, the biggest of which was the *Afrikaner Weerstandsbeweging* (AWB). Eventually the right-wing counterrevolution failed, in large measure because potentially the most effective of the paramilitary forces, led by retired General Constand Viljoen, rejected the option of violence and sought instead a negotiated accommodation.

Racially divided societies structured on rigidly hierarchical bases are not readily amenable to gradual, non-violent transformation. As the American Deep South, Algeria and the former Rhodesia, now Zimbabwe, show, dominant groups will fight tenaciously to preserve their privileges. South Africa differs in major respects from each of these examples, having been effectively an independent state since 1910. Its tortuous transformation into a democratic state, a process that began in the 1980s, provoked a severe backlash from conservative sections of the dominant group. By no means all conservatives and reactionaries who opposed the change had recourse to violence. As this analysis will seek to show, it was precisely the serious divisions over strategies and long-term goals that weakened the right wing and reduced the threat that its potential capacity for counter-revolution might have posed.

The Political Context of the Right Wing

From its inception as an autonomous state in 1910 to the installation of a multiparty Government of National Unity in May 1994, South Africa has been a racial oligarchy. For over half of that period, since 1948, the National Party (NP) has ruled, forming a close, even symbiotic, relationship with the state. Afrikaner nationalism has been the most fully mobilised ethnic movement in South Africa's political history, in the sense that at its apex in the 1960s and 1970s it succeeded in drawing to its banner upwards of 90 per cent of all Afrikaner whites, who number in 1994 over three million. (Significant numbers of English-speaking whites also supported the NP.)

The extent of this mobilisation, however, should not be equated with the solidarity of Afrikaner ethnicity. Early on Afrikaner nationalist leaders realised that their numerical superiority within the white group would enable them to wrest control of the political system provided that a substantial majority of Afrikaners could be mobilised to support the NP. Afrikaner unity, in other words, was not a 'given', even if there was a bedrock of cultural commonalities and a similarity of outlook on racial issues. Unity was an ideal that had to be fought for in the face of numerous divisive factors, including provincial, class and ideological differences. Political rivalry among ambitious leaders was another complicating factor that could thwart *volkseenheid* (literally 'unity of the people').

Ethnic unity was tenuous in 1948, but in the 1950s and 1960s as the NP consolidated its grip on power, the cohesiveness of Afrikaner nationalism appeared to strengthen. Superficial observers described the NP and its array of supporting organisations as 'monolithic' and, while this description was congenial to the leadership, it was misleading. As the 1970s and 1980s would show, Afrikaner nationalism, at least as a mobilised and organised force, was anything but monolithic. The Afrikaner community diversified as a result of urbanisation, the rise of an assertive Afrikaner bourgeoisie and the widening of internal class differences. The NP's apparent electoral invincibility and its tight grip over the state machine even caused some measure of complacency among Afrikaners. It was short-lived: black uprisings and the tightening noose of international opprobrium saw to that.

This brief overview of Afrikaner politics has been necessary because it is crucial to an understanding of the right-wing and its terrorist dimension. The proposition advanced here is that as the NP, formerly the unchallenged custodian of Afrikaner nationalist politics, shifted its centre of gravity in a reformist direction, the right wing, which had previously been comfortably located in the NP, became more exposed and isolated, finally breaking away to establish its own organisational base. As the reformist tide strengthened, a segment of the right wing increasingly threatened recourse to violence in defence of the crumbling old order.

The historical process of this political fragmentation was actually more complex than the simplified account offered by the proposition makes it sound. Fragmentation actually began in 1969 with the breakaway of what became the *Herstigte Nasionale Party* (HNP). The breakaway occurred ostensibly as a reaction to the (marginal) changes initiated by B. J. Vorster

(Prime Minister 1966–78). To suppose that these changes were the thin end of a liberalising wedge, as the HNP maintained, was laughable. The HNP breakaway was not significant in the sense that its crude, racist and rough image appealed to very few voters, as its failure in the 1970 election showed.

In spite of this and subsequent electoral setbacks the HNP survived and continued to inject a steady stream of racist propaganda into the discourse of white politics. To what extent it paved the way for the far more significant breakaway of 1982 and the consequent formation of the Conservative Party, much the biggest right-wing formation, is a difficult question to answer. There is little doubt that some NP MPs agreed with the HNP's sentiments, but declined to join it since it soon became clear that its destination was the political wilderness.

What is also clear is that the uninhibited racism of the HNP and the violent tenor of its language contributed in no small measure to building up a milieu in which random violence against blacks and more sophisticated terrorist acts could be rationalised as legitimate defences against engulfment by the forces of communism. Then, as now, the right wing in South Africa received intellectual succour from comparably racist organisations elsewhere in the world.

If the HNP's breakaway was small, the breakaway of the Conservative Party (CP) was far more serious. This occurred in 1982, after several years in which the spiritual leaders of the right-wingers in the NP caucus, Dr A. P. Treurnicht, had played a cat-and-mouse game with the NP leadership. Treurnicht and a coterie of fellow right-wingers had been uneasy about some of the (limited) reforms made by P. W. Botha, who had become Prime Minister in 1978, but usually the unease took the form of questioning whether this or that change was consistent with the policy of separate development (as apartheid was officially termed). In other words, Treurnicht tried to prevent his differences with Botha from coming to a breaking point, and resorted instead to more subtle and insidious tactics. Not unreasonably the irascible Botha construed these activities as an effort to undermine his leadership – which was undoubtedly the case.

By 1982 Botha had lost his patience. He was in the process of introducing a new constitution which would provide for carefully circumscribed 'power-sharing' between whites, Coloureds and Indians in the context of the Tricameral Parliament. It was a disingenuous attempt to co-opt these minorities, while continuing to exclude blacks. Even this, however, was too much for Treurnicht who, in his accustomed manner, had sniped at the constitutional initiative as a breach of the principle that white political sovereignty must remain inviolate. Essentially Botha flushed Treurnicht out.

The hastily-formed Conservative Party, however, proved to be a tougher nut to crack than the HNP. It was badly beaten in the 1983 referendum in which the white electorate was asked to ratify the new Constitution, but in the elections of 1987 and 1989 it demonstrated that it commanded the support of nearly one-third of the white electorate.

The formation of the CP had several repercussions on the political environment that are of significance for the context of right-wing terrorism. First, the departure of the right-wingers removed a millstone from the NP, especially its growing number of reformist members. The CP's return to the racial orthodoxies of the Verwoerd era were a reminder to these *verligtes* ('enlightened' ones) of what the NP had stood for very recently. It was like the shock of seeing a highly unpleasant image in a mirror. This heightened their determination to put as much ideological distance between themselves and the Conservatives as possible.

State-Sponsored Terrorism

Botha had made some significant changes, but he was in no sense a closet liberal, eager to break out of the political constraints and lead a democratic transformation. By the mid-1980s South Africa was aflame as large-scale protests and increasing black militancy established themselves as permanent features of the political landscape. Botha had run out of reformist steam; increasingly he invoked strong-arm methods of executive rule and coercion, and increasingly he relied upon the security establishment for the interpretation of affairs. The military's doctrine of 'Total Onslaught' was congenial to his thinking. The doctrine maintained that South Africa was the target of an orchestrated, international campaign, directed ultimately by the Soviets, to topple its regime, gain control of its mineral resources and seize command of the Cape sea route.

It was a crude, simplistic dogma that had a critical effect on the mindset of many inside the security establishment. First, it reinforced the anti-communist paranoia, including that prevailing among right-wingers; second, it lent credibility to the view that South Africa was involved in a 'low-intensity' civil war (which was not an inaccurate view); and third, arising out of the previous two considerations, it was deemed to legitimate covert operations against 'the enemy'. In short, it gave agents of the state a relatively free hand to deal with alleged opponents, thus bestowing a general seal of approval on 'hit squads', destabilisation of neighbouring states and other violent actions.

Since South Africa's security forces were historically the cutting edge of white control, the exact date at which state-sponsored terrorism began is arbitrary. The routine torture and sometimes killing of opposition activists intensified in the 1960s when increasingly draconian security legislation provided for the detention of suspects incommunicado – and hence entirely at the mercy of the police. In justifying this shift, Vorster, then Minister of Justice, claimed that 'you could not fight communism with the Queensberry rules'.[1] By 1990 over 60 detained persons had died, the most famous of whom was Steve Biko who suffered a cruel death at the hands of his torturers in 1977.

As guerrilla war in Namibia (South-West Africa) and civil wars in Angola and Mozambique intensified in the late 1970s, South Africa's security forces routinely engaged in destabilisation tactics in the region, aiming to weaken incumbent radical regimes and strengthen rivals like UNITA in Angola and RENAMO in Mozambique. No state that offered sanctuary to the exiled African National Congress (ANC) was safe from either pre-emptive strikes or 'hot-pursuit' raids directed at ANC bases. The covert nature of these operations heightened the already intense shroud of secrecy around South Africa's security establishment and gave it virtually complete license.

Within South Africa, as opposition to apartheid mounted steadily after the Soweto uprising in 1976, so did the use of covert action by the security authorities. Apart from harassment, detention and a wide variety of 'dirty tricks', hit squads were established. Between 1977 and 1989 at least 50 people were assassinated, nearly all of them opponents of apartheid.[2] A farm called Vlakplaas (near Pretoria) was acquired by the police in the late 1960s, ostensibly for the purpose of 'turning' captured ANC guerrillas, so-called 'Askaris'. The Askaris were used for the surveillance of alleged ANC members and the detection of infiltrators, but they soon became involved in hit squad activity under the command of white police officers. Between 1980 and 1991 at least 21 activists were assassinated by hit squads operating out of Vlakplaas.[3] The best-known of these victims was Griffiths Mxenge, a prominent human rights lawyer. His wife, Victoria, also a human rights lawyer, was assassinated four years later in 1985.

Another Vlakplaas officer, Eugene de Kock, is currently (October 1994) on trial, charged with over 100 serious crimes, including murder, fraud, and gun-running. In evidence before the Goldstone Commission in 1994 de Kock was alleged to have been involved in violence aimed at the destabilisation of South Africa, including the organisation of violence emanating from the hostels that accommodate migrant workers. The evidence also alleged that he was involved in the manufacture and purchase of arms, most of them destined for the Inkatha Freedom Party. Other senior officers of the South African Police, including Deputy-Commissioner Lieutenant-General Basie Smit, were also allegedly implicated.[4]

The increasing resistance to apartheid in the 1980s brought the military to the fore. Prior to becoming Prime Minister in 1978, P. W. Botha had served for 12 years as Minister of Defence in which capacity he had sponsored the promotion of many of its senior officers and imbibed much of the military's thinking about the 'total onslaught'. In the Botha era the focus of effective decision-making authority shifted to the State Security Council (SSC) which, in the view of many analysts, eclipsed even the Cabinet in importance. Members of this body included the Prime Minister (after 1983 the State President), the Ministers of Foreign Affairs, Defence, Law and Order (with responsibility for the police) and other Ministers who, apparently, attended on an *ad hoc* basis. Other members included the senior civil servants from the ministries named above and other heads of security agencies. Grundy's assessment is valid: 'The SSC is a body composed of political heavyweights supplemented by the highest-ranking political and government experts in security and strategy. When they recommend policy, the cabinet is not likely to deny them.'[5]

Within the South African Defence Force (SADF) the Military Intelligence Division was reputed to be the most important disseminator of the 'total strategy' doctrines that were supposed to counter the 'total onslaught'.[6] Military Intelligence, as will be argued, also became the key institution for the orchestration of covert actions, including hit squads.

In 1986 the oddly-named Civil Cooperation Bureau (CCB) was created as a covert organisation operating under the aegis of the Special Forces of the SADF. According to a judicial commission that tried (unsuccessfully) to investigate the CCB's activities in 1990,

> The plan was to establish a covert organisation divided in such a way that its operations could not be traced back to the SA Defence Force or the State. Approval in principle for such a covert organisation was granted by the Chief of the SA Defence Force and the Minister of Defence during 1986.[7]

The task of the CCB was 'to disrupt maximally the enemies of the State in support of other parts of the Force and as directly ordered by the C[hief] SADF *(sic)*'.[8] Ostensibly the CCB was required to obey the 'supreme political authority' and its operations were supposed to require the authorisation of the Chief of the SADF, but 'if there are political and strategic implications involved, the matter must be submitted to the Minister of Defence for final approval.'[9]

In theory the 'enemies' that the CCB was to disrupt included right-wing organisations but it is clear that nothing of the kind occurred. Indeed, the chances are that many of the shady characters who were CCB operatives came from the same social milieu as the right-wingers who formed terrorist groups to resist the demise of apartheid. The Commission's efforts to investigate alleged CCB ties to Inkatha and the *Afrikaner Weerstands-beweging* (AWB) led nowhere.[10]

The Harms Commission failed to uncover much about the CCB. First, the judge declined to extend his terms of reference to include CCB activities outside South Africa; second, witness after witness (often appearing in bizarre disguises) proved evasive, refused to incriminate themselves or simply lied; third, documents relating to the CCB 'vanished like mist before the morning sun'.[11] Harms, accordingly, was unable to implicate the CCB in the murders during 1989 of Anton Lubowski, a South-West African Peoples' Organisation activist who was assassinated in Windhoek, or David Webster, an anti-apartheid academic who was killed in Johannesburg. Strong circumstantial evidence pointed at CCB involvement, but in neither case could clinching evidence be found. The Commission had to content itself with broad findings such as:

> The actions of the CCB have contaminated the whole security arm of the State. Their conduct before and during the Commission created suspicions that they have been involved in more crimes of violence than the evidence shows. These suspicions are not necessarily unfounded.[12]

In general the Commission concluded that the political authorities, notably the Ministers of Defence and Law and Order, were unaware of the CCB's activities. The CCB, Harms found, operated according to its own political agenda:

> The CCB neither knows nor recognises any higher authority. Orders by the State President (as commander in chief of the Defence Force), the Minister of Defence and the Chief of the Defence Force were simply ignored. Requests by Parliament, the Auditor-General and the Commission were treated with contempt.[13]

Another theatre of operations for state-sponsored hit squads was the Eastern Cape, the historic cradle of the ANC and one of its strongest areas of support. In the tumultuous years 1985–86, the Eastern Cape, like many other regions, exploded in protest, both in the big cities and small towns. With a situation that threatened to get out of control, covert operations were launched against several activists. The most notorious of these was the killing of Matthew Goniwe and three other activists in June 1985. The assassinations were triggered by a signal sent to the SSC Secretariat on 7 June 1985 by General Joffel van der Westhuizen, Officer Commanding Eastern Province Command, calling for the 'permanent removal from society' of Goniwe and two of the associates who were subsequently assassinated. Twenty days later the bodies of the four were found.

After a lengthy inquiry (which had been reopened after the signal had come to light) Judge Neville Zietsman concluded that he was unable to name the particular individuals responsible for the murders since the necessary link between the signal and the actions of the unknown persons who carried out the assassinations had not been established. He was satisfied, however, that the assassinations were the work of members of the security forces. He named five individuals, including van der Westhuizen and two members of the security police of whom he was suspicious. But, he said, suspicion 'does not mean that there is prima facie proof against them'.[14] Van der Westhuizen, whom the Judge branded a liar, went on to become head of Military Intelligence.

KwaZulu-Natal has been an area of considerable violence since the mid-1980s. The conflict has many causes but primarily it stems from rivalry between Inkatha, which controlled the homeland government in KwaZulu, and the United Democratic Front, which in many respects acted as an internal surrogate of the ANC during the 1980s.[15] Inkatha, led by the mercurial Chief Mangosuthu Buthelezi, regarded the entire region as its fiefdom, and bitterly resented what it regarded as the unwarranted intrusion of competitors. It took stern action against young ANC-inclined 'comrades' who boycotted schools, strikers and others who sought to execute the ANC's call to make South Africa 'ungovernable'.

Without minimising Inkatha's role in the violence in KwaZulu-Natal or in those Witwatersrand areas where Inkatha-controlled hostels have clashed with people in nearby settlements, it should be made clear that the ANC and its internal surrogates have by no means been blameless either in causing the violence or in perpetuating it. It is evident that hostilities between Inkatha and the ANC increased in the late 1970s when the ANC broke with Buthelezi, labeled him a 'collaborator' and targeted him and other homeland leaders as fair game in a 'people's war'. Between 1985 and early 1993 Inkatha claimed to have lost 1,275 members and office-bearers through assassination.[16]

Notwithstanding these qualifications, certain facts bearing upon the role of the state as a sponsor of violence stand out and require brief mention. First, the KwaZulu Police, numbering approximately 4,000, has shown a palpable pro-Inkatha bias, substantially justifying the claim that it is little more than Inkatha's 'private army'.[17] Hit squads operating under the aegis of the KwaZulu Police are currently under investigation. Second, the South African Police have frequently been guilty of sins of commission and omission. Mostly it is accused of favouring Inkatha by its failure to take timely steps to prevent impending violence and, indeed, on occasion of fomenting violence, protecting Inkatha-aligned 'warlords', and failing to investigate violence alleged to have been perpetrated by Inkatha.[18]

The *cause celebre* in this region was the Trust Feed massacre that occurred in December 1988, in which 11 people were killed.[19] After a lengthy trial Captain Brian Mitchell of the South African Police and four African special constables were convicted, Mitchell receiving the death sentence and the others lengthy prison sentences. To many observers the Trust Feed case confirmed suspicions of police complicity in the violence, suspicions that were heightened by the efforts of senior police officers to engage in a cover-up. Had it not been for the honesty and diligence of another police officer, Captain Frank Dutton, it is virtually certain that the murders would have been consigned to the 'unsolved' files.

This account of state-sponsored terrorism makes no claim to being exhaustive. Indeed, no-one could make such a claim since even energetic investigative bodies like the Goldstone Commission have been able to achieve little more than revealing the tip of an iceberg. Whether the proposed Truth Commission, a body to be established by statute with a mandate to investigate political crimes, will uncover the full extent of the atrocities committed by all sides over the past 30 years is doubtful. The state's practitioners of violence were ruthless and skilled, and their skills included an ability to cover their traces and to cover for one another. As the author of a book based largely on the confessions of one of the most notorious hit squad operatives observes:

> As members of the Security Branch [of the police], performing illegal operations inside and outside the borders of the Republic of South Africa, Dirk Coetzee and his colleagues enjoyed special protection. This enabled them to operate above the laws of the country and above the rules and regulations of the South African Police. However, this protection is not statutory and is difficult to define. It is vested in a culture belonging to the close-knit family that the Security Branch is. The culture is a syndrome of arrogant exclusiveness, secrecy, loyalty to one another, mutual trust and understanding and a very special relationship between superiors and subordinates.[20]

To provide perspective it must be recalled that total onslaught thinking legitimated the understanding that South Africa was involved in a war. This was true as well of the ANC and other armed formations, who saw themselves as fighting a 'war of liberation', in which all symbols of the state, including police, troops and other functionaries, were legitimate targets.

Many senior officers in the Defence Force articulated the view that South Africa's problems were '80 per cent political and 20 per cent military'. This could, and in some cases did, lend itself to a reformist view. For others, however, the conflict assumed the proportions of a chiliastic fight between white, Christian civilisation and barbarian hordes acting under communist influence. In a revealing parliamentary speech in 1993 Kobus Jordaan, a member of the liberal Democratic Party but formerly a senior civil servant and a member of the 'inner circle' (his description), provided details of how Military Intelligence had planted individuals in organisations like Inkatha, established African-led puppet political parties, and plotted to remove certain homeland leaders and replace them with more pliable plants.

He described also a meeting of Military Intelligence personnel (no date was mentioned) chaired by General Tienie Groenewald, a former security adviser to the SSC and, during 1985–86, chief director of Military Intelligence. Jordaan and like-minded reformist colleagues had outlined South Africa's options and advocated the 'high risk' option of unbanning the ANC, releasing jailed opponents and forming an interim government of national unity as, in fact, the only solution. Groenewald denounced this view, accusing Jordaan of naiveté and of underestimating the 'enemy' (the ANC) which 'had to be destroyed because that was the only solution for this country'.[21] (Groenewald retired from government service in 1990 and thereafter devoted himself to right-wing politics, in which capacity he became one of the right-wing's leading strategists.[22])

Given the magnitude of the change South Africa has undergone since 1990, and given the strength of right-wing vote in the white electorate (approximately 30 per cent), resistance to change was hardly surprising. That diehards in the security establishment who subscribed to the total onslaught doctrine should have been in the forefront of such resistance is equally unsurprising.

Throughout the negotiating process that began in 1990 the ANC persistently blamed much of the violence on a shadowy 'Third Force' who shot people and set rival factions at one another's throats. Since the transition depended crucially on maintaining the partnership between the NP government and the ANC, the threat posed by these activities was serious since, increasingly, the ANC blamed F. W. de Klerk for orchestrating a sinister campaign to weaken the ANC and strengthen opponents like Inkatha. In October 1991 de Klerk and Nelson Mandela had a flaming row over the latter's accusation that the police were 'the country's killing machine'. Mandela added that 'perhaps the ANC had been naive to trust de Klerk.... It is clear that he has either lost control of the security forces, or else they are doing exactly what he wants them to do.'[23]

Repeatedly de Klerk denied complicity in Third Force activities and undertook to investigate all allegations and to charge those guilty of crimes. Exactly how much de Klerk – and, more pertinently, some of his ministerial colleagues in security portfolios – knew remains open to question. Since much of the alleged Third Force activity was directed at derailing de Klerk's initiatives and since he stood to lose most from an aborted transition, the allegation that de Klerk was the spider at the centre of some sinister web of conspiracy appears improbable. It is also clear that those state operatives whose evidence is on record were animated by a deep hatred of de Klerk and all his works – and relished the possibility of damaging or embarrassing him.[24] Internal evidence from the Goldstone Commission also suggests that de Klerk, on being confronted with evidence, did not hesitate to urge the Commission to proceed with its investigation.[25]

In addition, de Klerk's other actions should be noted: for example, on coming to office in 1989 he immediately downgraded the State Security Council; he tried to inculcate a new culture in the police that would remove them from the front-line of enforcing apartheid laws; and he ordered the disbanding of the Civil Cooperation Bureau when evidence of its nefarious activities emerged.

Critics of de Klerk's *bona fides*, however, would not be satisfied with such evidence, and they would insist that he did not live up to his repeated promise to 'cut to the bone' in having dirty tricks investigated. Certain factors appeared to restrain his zeal: perhaps Mandela's suggestion (quoted above) that he had lost control of the security forces is near the mark. Evidence collected by Heribert Adam and Kogila Moodley shows that de Klerk had to tread carefully in relation to the security forces, whose low morale (especially in the police) had been noted since the high peaks of violence in the 1980s. At various times de Klerk had been faced with the danger of a 'soft coup' – a threat by the security establishment not to take over Pretoria, but, on the contrary, to withdraw cooperation. If certain policies were pursued, he was advised, security could no longer be guaranteed (personal interviews, various dates 1990–92). One of his planned overseas visits was almost cancelled because of this looming rebellion. A reputed judge, commissioned to evaluate the attitudes of leading military figures, reported after extensive interviews that most expressed intense resentment of the government's course and displayed varying degrees of cynicism.[26]

Unofficial Terrorism

An interesting question in establishing the context of right-wing terrorism is the extent to which it was a continuation of that strand of Afrikaner nationalism which, historically, has had a romantic, even Fanonesque, view of violence as an instrument of liberation. In other words, are contemporary terrorists the lineal descendants of earlier violent groups? This is treacherous ground for the political scientist and historian alike since the contexts in which periods of violent resistance have occurred differ in fundamental ways.

Nevertheless, an hypothesis may be advanced:

Gewapende protes (armed protest) is a familiar phenomenon in Afrikaner political history. It was relatively common in the nineteenth century South African Republic (the Transvaal), and it has recurred on three occasions in the period after 1910:

(1) the 1914–15 Rebellion in which a segment of Afrikaners, including some senior army officers, refused to participate in what they called 'England's War'.

(2) the 1922 Rand Revolt in which working-class whites, a majority of whom were Afrikaners, rose up in protest against a decision by the mining houses to change the ratio of white to black miners to the disadvantage of whites.

(3) the violence associated with the Nazi *Ossewabrandwag* (OB) and its satellite organisation *Die Stormjaers* during the early 1940s. This was fundamentally an anti-war campaign that took the form of extensive efforts to sabotage the war effort. Terrorism, in the form of attacks on state officials, troops or other putative 'enemies', was not, however, a marked feature of the OB's activities. Like the *Afrikaner-Weerstandsbeweging* (Afrikaner Resistance Movement) of later years (it was founded in 1973), the OB had a public face and a private cadre of trained men, the *Stormjaers*. The latter 'were organised and disciplined, and they were trained to be prepared for what we always called: The Day [*Ter Dag*] – when a German victory would give us the opportunity to carry out a *coup d'état* or to rise up against Smuts [General J. C. Smuts, the then prime minister of South Africa].'[27]

By the early 1940s the OB had become a formidable organisation and a powerful rival to the NP, which constituted the official parliamentary opposition to Smuts's United Party. The NP opposed the war and officially favoured neutrality, but the OB's flirtation with corporatist ideas and the *führer* principle found no favour with the NP Leader D. F. Malan, who remained firmly committed to constitutional politics. The war years 1941 to roughly 1945 saw a murderous struggle between the OB and the NP, essentially concerning the question of which was to be the major political arm of Afrikaner nationalism. After a bruising struggle Malan won and the OB ultimately petered out.

AWB literature contains several admiring references to the OB, and some of its (elderly) members had been members of the OB as well, but this is insufficient to establish the continuity that is implied by the term lineal descendant.

The 'continuity' hypothesis, at least in respect of the putative link between the OB and the AWB (but also possibly some of the other right-wing organisations that have resorted to terrorism), requires more detailed research.

It would be interesting to know, for instance, the extent to which folk memories of the OB in particular communities and within particular families animated those who joined the AWB. Were they, in other words, genuine carriers of that particular strand of Afrikaner nationalism? Or was past history simply invoked as a source of inspiration?

Another question that would be difficult to answer in view of the large-scale urbanisation of Afrikaners is the extent to which particular regions, like the Western Transvaal, have been the storm-centres of militant action of the romantic-violent kind, and the reasons for such activity. Prima facie, it appears that the Western Transvaal was the area from which many participants in the 1914–15 Rebellion hailed; it was the stronghold of the OB; and it is a stronghold of the AWB in contemporary times.

A third set of issues requiring elaboration is the class composition of romantic-violent right-wing movements over time. An important intervening variable here is the dramatic change that has overtaken the Afrikaner community, namely urbanisation and extensive *embourgeoisement*. In the 1930s many Afrikaners were poverty-stricken: 'poor-whiteism' afflicted one-third of the community; by the 1970s 'poor-whiteism' was only a memory and prosperity had been widely diffused among all whites. Fewer than 10 per cent of Afrikaners could be classified as 'rural', and perhaps no more than 20 per cent were working-class.

Categorical statements about the class composition of the OB are hard to make since it appeared to enjoy support from all strata in the community, and since in none of its propaganda were class issues much to the fore (although, to be sure, socio-economic issues were of great importance to Afrikaners at the time). In contrast, class issues have been a significant tap-root for the modern right wing, even if there is no close fit between class and support for a 'respectable' organisation like the Conservative Party. Overwhelmingly, though, the support-base of bodies like the AWB and others that have resorted to violence lies among poorer and less-educated people. Indeed, in the kind of racist populism that pervades the right wing, the *geldmag* (literally 'money-power'), represented by big capital, is singled out for condemnation.

In his detailed survey of the right wing, Johann van Rooyen acknowledges that while many in the higher income and education categories have supported the Conservative Party the relative income decline experienced at the lower end of the income scale has been a major stimulus to right-wing politics:

> The government's policies aimed at the socio-economic upliftment of blacks through increased spending on education, housing and welfare services, eroded the remaining socio-economic privileges associated with being white in South Africa, and led to a decline in the rate of white

incomes in real terms by almost 10 per cent between 1975 and 1979. The whites at the lower end of the economic scale were affected the most severely, and have supported the right-wing parties because of a firm conviction that their policies, if implemented, would ensure a return to the subsidies and privileges guaranteed by an Afrikaner-dominated government.[28]

The decline in real income continued throughout the 1980s and into the 1990s. If urban white workers felt the hardship of declining income so did many in the 60,000-strong white farming community, historically one of the NP's most important support-bases. Declining commodity prices world-wide, devastating droughts (which are endemic in South Africa), and the steady dismantling of the elaborate system of subsidies and 'soft' loans that had previously cushioned farmers against economic vicissitudes steadily weeded out poorer and less efficient farmers and rendered marginal perhaps as many as one-third of those remaining.

Meanwhile, as the ANC's armed struggle intensified in the 1980s, many white farmers in the border areas of the northern and western Transvaal became increasingly vulnerable to attacks. Compounding this insecurity was a rise in the frequency of criminally-motivated attacks on isolated farms, often involving the brutal slaying of elderly whites. Heightened insecurity, both economic and physical, played into the hands of right-wing organisations, who could portray the government as uncaring and incapable of offering effective protection. More than this the AWB attempted to mount the rural equivalent of a neighbourhood watch and offered tangible assistance to farmers, such as helping them to put out bushfires or providing them with fodder in times of drought – provided that the recipients signed declarations that they opposed moves to abolish racial restrictions on the acquisition of land.[29]

The changes that were overtaking South Africa in the 1980s accelerated dramatically in the 1990s. Insecurity, both physical and psychological, gripped many whites as the previous moorings provided by the apartheid state were torn loose. Uncertainty about their political future was compounded by the reality of declining incomes, fears about job security under a future black-dominated government, and doubts about whether their pensions would be paid. Nearly 50 per cent of all economically active Afrikaners are employed in the public sector, which has historically served as a vast system of affirmative action and sponsored upward mobility for them. That, it was perceived, would change.

The political reactions to this pervasive insecurity were immediate. Right-wing organisations demanded a reinstatement of the old order, and when that had become obviously impossible, the creation of a *volkstaat* in which white

Afrikaners could exercise sovereignty. Reformist Afrikaners, along with other whites, had moved beyond the old political nostrums with their emphasis on blood, *volk* and fatherland. Afrikaner conservatives had never abandoned them and now, in the circumstances of the 1980s and 1990s, they received a new fillip. Events in the former Soviet Union and in Eastern Europe, where ethnic nationalism flared up, resonated with the mood of the right wing and prompted its intellectuals to produce elaborate plans for Afrikaner self-determination. All of these failed on one cardinal point: in no single region of South Africa did a white (let alone Afrikaner) majority exist. No democratic government would tolerate a *volkstaat*, excised from the Republic, in which citizens who were not white would be discriminated against or from which they would be expelled.

The Growth of Terrorism

By 1993 it was apparent that the changes initiated by State President F. W. de Klerk on 2 February 1990 were irrevocable. Indeed, de Klerk appeared to enjoy substantial support in the white community, 68 per cent of whom had endorsed the process in a referendum held in March 1992. Although many supporters of the CP had voted 'Yes', the outcome confirmed what was already known: that the strength of the right-wing was approximately one-third of the white community.

The apparently inexorable march towards democratisation spurred right-wingers into more determined action. As this analysis will show, however, the more desperate right-wingers became, the more organisationally fragmented they became, thus substantially neutralising whatever thrust they may have had as a unified force. According to an estimate by a leading authority on right-wing politics, Dr Wim J. Booyse, in August 1991 there were an estimated 144 right-wing groups in existence, including parties, cultural and youth organisations, churches, trade unions, think-tanks and paramilitary organisations.[30] Many, however, were tiny, numbering only a handful of members and often with overlapping memberships. Later estimates put the number of organisations at 186, though by late 1992 the figures had reportedly dwindled to between 20 and 25.[31] These figures, which are presumably based upon police intelligence sources, have to be treated with caution, in view of the evanescent nature of most of these organisations. Among the more significant paramilitary organisations police sources named:

- The AWB's Wenkommandos and Ystergaarde;
- The Boereweerstandsbeweging;
- The Afrikaner Volksleer;
- Die Wit Wolwe;

- The Afrikaner Monargiste;
- The Foundation for the Survival of Freedom;
- The Ku Klux Klan;
- Orde Boerevolk;
- The Boere Republican Army;
- Pretoria Boere Kommando;
- Boere-Krisis Aksie.

Of these the AWB's paramilitary formations were numerically the largest, estimated by police sources to number a total of 15,000 men. The Orde Boerevolk and the Boere Republican Army were said to be highly active, but their respective memberships and the levels of training of the members were not known with any degree of accuracy.[32]

Other groups that have cropped up include several quasi-religious ones: the Church of the Creator, the Israelites, and the World Apartheid Movement (later said to have changed its name to the World Preservatist (sic) Movement), which claimed to have ties to over 100 right-wing organisations world-wide, including the Ku Klux Klan and several German neo-Nazi movements.[33] Their clandestine nature makes it impossible to give an indication of the size of their memberships and the extent to which, if at all, they have engaged in terrorism. All are fanatical believers in racism, maintaining that blacks are subhuman.

Unfortunately published statistics in the Annual Reports of the Commissioner of the South African Police do not break down the statistics on violent acts committed with political motives by the organisations committing them, which, in any case, is not always known. Prior to 1990 violent acts by right-wing groups were few in number and spasmodic. The most horrifying of these episodes was in November 1988 when a young ex-policeman named Barend Strydom opened fire on blacks milling around during a lunch-hour in central Pretoria. Altogether eight were killed, and in addition Strydom was convicted of killing a black woman elsewhere. He was sentenced to death, but was released from prison in 1993 under the terms of a general amnesty. Strydom claimed to be the leader of a group calling themselves the Wit Wolwe.[34]

In 1990, according to Booyse, 52 acts of   right-wing terror were committed and more than 91 right-wingers were arrested.[35] Of these attacks the most serious was an episode near Durban in October 1990 in which three members of the AWB and the Orde Boerevolk opened fire on a bus, killing seven blacks and wounding 18. It was a retaliatory action for an earlier attack by young black militants who stabbed whites in a Durban shop. The three right-wingers were sentenced to death (but, in view of the suspension of the death penalty, none was executed).[36]

In another episode, court proceedings in November 1990 revealed that Cornelius Lottering and Fanie Goosen, members of a small group calling itself *Die Orde van die Dood*, admitted to having drawn up plans to assassinate seven cabinet ministers. Lottering, who had left the AWB in 1986, made a statement to the court, which provided a chilling insight into the outlook of a racial fanatic. In August 1990 Lottering grabbed a black man (apparently in a completely random way) near Johannesburg and stabbed him 'which [according to Lottering's testimony] did not have the desired effect'. Thereupon Lottering put the man in the boot of his car and drove to a village near Johannesburg:

> The man came and knelt in front of me and I went and squatted in front of him. I decided to try again with my knife and I stabbed him below the jawbone to penetrate into the brain. But the point of attack was not 100 per cent and I could not reach his brain.
> Thereafter the unfortunate victim tried to escape and Lottering shot him, and repeated this to make sure he was dead. Lottering showed no remorse: 'Because the black is my natural enemy and because according to the Bible I may eliminate my enemies, the deed has not troubled me.'[37]

Just as with the case of Barend Strydom, mentioned above, the view that blacks were subhuman and, hence, fair game, was common among the more fanatical right-wingers. As tensions rose during the transition process increasing numbers of random killings occurred. Between the beginning of 1991 and the end of 1993, approximately 40 shooting episodes occurred (which may be an underestimate), several of which involved fatalities. Comparable black killings of whites in an apparently random way also increased, many allegedly being the work of the Azanian People's Liberation Army, the military wing of the Pan Africanist Congress.

Right-wing terrorism took other forms as well: frequently non-white residents who moved into previously white neighbourhoods were subject to intimidation and harassment by vigilante groups; blacks using previously exclusively white recreational facilities could be harassed – as occurred in November 1990 when a group of right-wingers, said to belong to an organisation called *Blanke Beveiligingsburo*, harassed a party of black Sunday School children and tried to prevent them entering a public park in Louis Trichardt (a stronghold of the right wing); bombs were planted in some schools that had opened their doors to all races; and a tidal bathing pool on the Natal South Coast was fouled by chemicals to prevent Indian bathers from using it.

What is surprising about the desegregation of facilities and amenities is not so much that episodes like those cited above occurred, but that, relatively speaking, *so few* occurred.

Bomb attacks occurred frequently in the four-year period of transition. Mostly these were aimed at symbolic targets, like the NP and ANC offices, as well as those of the Congress of South African Trade Unions, and, occasionally, the premises of Afrikaans newspapers that were hostile to the right-wing cause.

Of all the terrorist episodes committed by right-wingers none was more serious in its implications than the assassination of Chris Hani, the charismatic and highly popular ANC / South African Communist Party leader. (Hani's popularity was such that had he lived he may well have been chosen as Nelson Mandela's successor.) Hani and his family had moved into a previously all-white suburb of the East Rand town of Boksburg. On the whole, being a friendly and personable man, Hani had enjoyed easy relationships with his neighbours. On 10 April 1993 he was gunned down in front of his house, having made the serious error of going jogging without his bodyguard. A white neighbour spotted the assassin's car and alerted the police. A Polish immigrant, Janus Waluz, was speedily apprehended. A fellow-conspirator, Clive Derby-Lewis, was subsequently also arrested (his wife, Gay, was also accused, but was acquitted). Waluz had been a member of the AWB since 1986, but, so far as is known, he was not a member of any of its armed formations. Derby-Lewis was a senior member of the Conservative Party and one of its few English-speaking members. Both were convicted and sentenced to death, but in neither case has the execution been carried out.

Hani's assassination rocked the country and angry demonstrations occurred in many centres. It seemed to some as if civil war might erupt, but in spite of the seriousness of the situation that was never on the cards. Calls for peaceful behaviour by the police, together with the fact that it had been a young Afrikaner woman who raised the alarm, all served to calm the situation. Critically, the assassination demonstrated that without the calming influence that the ANC exerted the country might indeed be engulfed in violence. In fact the episode so strengthened the ANC's leverage that the de Klerk government had little option but to acquiesce in its demand that the inflamed tempers of its constituency could be cooled only by fixing the date of the first democratic election (namely, 27 April 1994).

In convicting Waluz and Derby-Lewis, the presiding judge found no evidence to prove that the two were part of a wider conspiracy. The ANC has never accepted this finding, believing that such a wider conspiracy definitely existed, perhaps one that was linked to state-sponsored hit squads. Nelson Mandela shares this view, suggesting that those involved included foreigners.[38]

The killing of Hani underlined one of the great perils of the transition, namely the danger of assassination faced by political leaders. All of those deemed vulnerable took care not to venture forth without bodyguards and tight security was maintained at their offices. However great the precautions, however, a degree of vulnerability is always present. Never was this more so than during the election campaign of April 1994 when the leaders perforce were required to move around among large crowds of people, thus exposing themselves to the assassin's bullet.

This analysis has stressed the fragmentation of the right-wing and its ever-present fissiparous tendencies. Extremist groups no doubt have an inherent tendency toward splits, but in the case of South Africa's right wing the tendency was magnified by the inability of right-wing groups to agree upon *any* long-term policy goal, let alone strategy. All were opposed to the process of democratisation, but that was virtually where agreement ended. Some avoided violent methods, like the Conservative Party with its strong parliamentary base, but warned that if the transition process went further, violent resistance would occur.

The best-known of the paramilitary groups, the AWB, has always adopted a bellicose, menacing stance.[39] Its leader, the demagogic Eugene Terre Blanche, uses violent, threatening language, but generally has claimed that the AWB will use violence only as a means of resistance. Thus:

> When the Government capitulates and all the power is handed over, the Black Revolution will start because law and order will go. Then the [white] resistance movement will take the law and order into their own hands. They will restore law and order. They will fight for it and keep their land.[40]

In a more extravagant statement made several years later, Terre Blanche made the same claim that the AWB would fill the vacuum created by the collapse of law and order. He boasted that the AWB's 10,000 commandos were 'totally spread over South Africa', many of them being former policemen or soldiers trained by the South African Defence Force. He claimed also that 90 per cent of the (white) police were friendly to the AWB, as were those in the Army: '... for 30 years the SADF and the police have been taught that the enemy is the terrorist and the terrorist is the ANC.'[41]

Frequently the AWB claimed that it could wreak havoc by industrial sabotage, thanks to its strength with the urban working class. Repeatedly Terre Blanche boasted that the AWB could bring the country to a standstill:

> We could tell shiftbosses [on the mines] not to go underground and have

3,000 blacks stranded there. We could also tell ESKOM [the parastatal electricity supplier] controllers to switch off the lights to leave the night as dark as Africa.[42]

The belief (or hope?) that in the event of some kind of Armageddon-like showdown, substantial sections of the Army and Police would side with the right-wing resistance has been strong in right-wing circles, as Terre Blanche's statement shows. It is true that security forces tend to attract people with right-wing views, but views like those expressed by Terre Blanche (and many other commentators who have predicted a *coup d'état*) overlook the strength in the South African security forces of the tradition of obedience to the civilian government – even if that government does things that are unpalatable to them.

While, as was shown above, it is true that recalcitrant officers in both the Army and the Police have been a concern to the political leadership, and that many retired officers have come out in support of right-wing causes, neither has shown overt signs of disloyalty or mutiny. Indeed, on two occasions in 1991 police actually fired on right-wingers: in May 1991, 2,000 right-wingers tried to remove a squatter community from Goedgevonden, near Ventersdorp in the Western Transvaal. (The squatters were, in fact, attempting to reclaim land from which they had been dispossessed in 1977.) After unsuccessful attempts had been made to persuade the vigilantes to withdraw, the police opened fire, injuring at least two.[43]

Even more dramatic was the episode in Ventersdorp on 9 August 1991 when 2,000 AWB supporters tried to prevent F. W. de Klerk from holding a public meeting in the village. Some 1,500 police were deployed and in the skirmishes that ensued three AWB supporters were killed and 58 (including 7 policemen) were injured. Numerous blacks were beaten up by the vigilantes, and several were rescued from the crossfire by the police.[44] For the right wing, the Ventersdorp fracas was traumatic. It was, said the well-known right-winger Robert van Tonder, the beginning of the Boers' Third War of Liberation.[45] Subsequent events would show that it was nothing of the kind: right-wing terrorism would intensify, but it proved incapable either of staying de Klerk's hand or plunging the country into civil war.

A further significant consideration in explaining the failure of the right-wing counter-revolution is the success the police have had in tracking down right-wing terrorists. The police claim an 85 per cent success rate. Police work was made difficult by the absence of an overall command structure among the terrorist groups. Even the AWB's paramilitary formations appear to operate on a decentralised basis. The very diversity of the terrorist groups made it difficult to establish patterns. To what extent police were able to infiltrate groups is not known, although police sources have confirmed that it was both difficult and dangerous. It appears, however, to have been successful.

Another factor, mentioned by an anonymous security source, was that the police could not anticipate targets, and their past experience had not trained them to be suspicious of whites.[46] Moreover, many whites own firearms legally so that carrying a weapon is not necessarily prima facie evidence of terrorist intentions. In addition to this weapons are easily and cheaply available on the black market in strife-torn Southern Africa. Access to explosives has also not presented a serious problem. Commercial explosives have evidently been readily filched from the mines, or, as in one celebrated case occurring in April 1990, a large-scale heist of arms and ammunition from an official magazine. (It was, incidentally, a weapon acquired in this haul that killed Chris Hani.) Many white South African men have undergone two-year periods of military training (the system was formally abolished only in 1993), which has created a pool of people skilled in the instruments and methods of violence. Obviously not all of these were right-wing sympathisers, but their existence provided a reservoir from which right-wing organisations could draw some support.

Conclusion

Many analysts predicted that the run-up to the April 1994 election would be a time of violence, from both white and black sources. In the week preceding the election huge bomb blasts on the Witwatersrand killed 20 people. Pessimists believed that right-wing terrorists were living up to their promise of resistance. Very shortly after these episodes, 32 AWB members were arrested, and the terror campaign petered out.

It would be tempting fate to pronounce the attempted counter-revolution over, even though no terror or sabotage incidents have occurred since the election. Even the AWB appears muted, and its major post-election demand has been for amnesty to be extended to its jailed or detained members.

If the counter-revolution has, in fact, petered out, why did this happen when the right wing possessed so many apparently formidable resources? Apart from the effectiveness of the police in apprehending right-wing terrorists, the major part of the explanation must be sought in the ability of the more pragmatic right-wing leaders to carry along a substantial percentage of the right-wing constituency with them in search of a negotiated settlement with the ANC, which constitutes the preponderant element in the Government of National Unity that was installed after the April election. The major figure among the right-wing pragmatists has been General Constand Viljoen, who retired in 1985 as chief of the South African Defence Force.

Viljoen enjoyed a formidable reputation as a 'soldier's soldier' in the

Army, as well as impeccable right-wing credentials. But he was no political neanderthal. Viljoen easily became the most important right-wing leader during the course of a meteoric rise in 1993, eclipsing the lacklustre Ferdi Hartzenberg, who succeeded Treurnicht as leader of the CP, and the demagogic Terre Blanche, whose capacity to inflame audiences remained, even if his reputation had been tarnished by well-attested reports of drunkenness and womanising. Viljoen is as committed to the concept of a *volkstaat* as any of the right-wingers, but his impatience with the unrealistic demands and foolish strategies of his fellow right-wingers grew. Unlike the others, he was prepared to negotiate with the ANC, and it is apparent that he, Mandela, Thabo Mbeki and others developed mutual respect.

The denouement of the threatened right-wing counterrevolution occurred in March 1994 as President Lucas Mangope's Bophuthatswana homeland regime began to totter. Mangope, a member of the Freedom Alliance, asked Constand Viljoen to intervene and, according to Viljoen, specifically asked him not to deploy AWB members. Within 12 hours some 3,000 of Viljoen's men arrived in the Bophuthatswana capital, only to find about 500 AWB members assembling. Viljoen asked them to withdraw to the sidelines, which they declined to do. When remnants of the homeland army still loyal to Mangope were deployed against them they began to pull out in an undisciplined, chaotic way. According to eye-witnesses many opened fire on civilians and attacked journalists. Unconfirmed reports estimated that 13 of the 60 killed in the episode were civilians mowed down by the AWB. In turn, three AWB members were shot in cold blood by homeland troops.[47] Horrifying television footage brought home to many whites what the violent option would entail and thus further discredited it.

Undoubtedly the episode strengthened Viljoen's resolve to seek a separate Afrikaner *volkstaat* by negotiated, constitutional means. Previously, at a 'summit' meeting of right-wing organisations in Pretoria, Viljoen had posed the options: if the *volkstaat* were to be achieved before 27 April 1994 (the date on which inclusive elections would be held), 'we would have to seize it violently'; but, he warned, this would have serious economic and security implications and 'would probably lead to total anarchy'. His suggested alternative, that right-wingers participate in the election to demonstrate their strength and geographical location, was shouted down by the boisterous crowd, which enthusiastically applauded the option of violent seizure.[48]

By breaking ranks and opting to participate in the election, Viljoen shattered whatever tenuous hopes there may have been for right-wing unity, but, most importantly, he defused what could have been an ugly and violent confrontation.

The imponderable question is what might have happened if Viljoen and his forces *had* opted for the violent seizure of some territory, thereafter declaring it to be a sovereign *volkstaat*. It is certainly the case that plans were laid in January 1994 for the unilateral declaration of an independent *volkstaat* (UDI), based upon a *versetkaart* (literally a 'map of resistance') that embraced territory delineated by 60 CP-controlled local authorities.[49] This was one of approximately six different proposals for a *volkstaat*: the very diversity of the areas demarcated in the various plans was a fatal weakness because it diminished whatever collective thrust (and it would have been formidable) the right wing could mobilise.

Had there been agreement, had the UDI been executed, and had Constand Viljoen headed an armed formation in defence of such a *volkstaat*, an ugly situation would have arisen. In those circumstances it is not impossible, given Viljoen's prestige in the Army, that neither the Army nor the Police, or major elements within them, would have refused to take up arms to end the rebellion. As Viljoen had shown in the Bophuthatswana fiasco, his organisational talents were formidable; his forces, moreover, were highly mobile, well-trained and, in many cases, battle-hardened.

An even worse scenario could have been predicted had Viljoen's forces joined arms with Inkatha's. Like the Freedom Front, however, Inkatha decided at the last moment to participate in the election, thus defusing the strong likelihood of intense conflict in many parts of KwaZulu-Natal.

There have been persistent rumours (spread by his opponents in the right wing?) that Viljoen was acting as an agent of the de Klerk government with the express brief of channelling right-wing anger into the constitutional negotiating process. Viljoen indignantly denies this. Nevertheless he did exactly what the rumours imputed to him. He opted also to have his hastily-created party, the Freedom Front, participate in the election in return for a last-minute undertaking from the Multiparty Negotiating Process (as the constitution-making body was called) that a *Volkstaat Council* would be established to serve as a 'constitutional mechanism to enable proponents of the idea of a *volkstaat* to constitutionally pursue the establishment of such a *volkstaat....*'

In the election, which was boycotted by all other right-wing organisations, the Freedom Front won approximately 14 per cent of the estimated white vote at the national level, but 22 per cent at the provincial level.[50] It came nowhere near to demonstrating the degree of support among whites for a *volkstaat* that would have given the concept some semblance of plausibility. The election results, apart from demonstrating again the confusion and divided councils in Afrikaner ranks, tend to confirm that for all the right-wing's vociferousness and apparent militancy the actual extent and solidity of the groundswell for a *volkstaat* was limited. A survey conducted

among 800 whites in November 1993 showed that 28 per cent favoured a
volkstaat and 22 per cent thought it was a viable concept. In response to the
question 'Would you personally be prepared to move to such a (white)
volkstaat?', however, only 14 per cent said yes.[51]

The conventional view of why the right-wing counter-revolution petered
out so ignominiously is that when the crunch came the huge majority of right-
wingers decided that they had too much to lose and that, especially after the
Bophuthatswana fiasco, violent insurrection lacked the romance which they
may previously have attributed to it. As a local wit put it, 'the pension proved
mightier than the sword'. The AWB's boasts were shown to have been largely
hot air, and Terre Blanche himself to be little more than a swaggering bully
with minimal organisational ability.

There is much truth in this view and, together with the effectiveness of the
Police in nipping violence in the bud, it explains a great deal. Police sources
were somewhat coy about revealing their capacity to insert informers into the
paramilitary organisations, but, as was argued above, it was generally
successful. What has not been mentioned is the fact that detained right-
wingers have 'sung like canaries', leading the Police to entire networks. Why
this should be so is unclear.

Further factors, however, need to be considered. De Klerk and his
negotiators managed to secure reasonably equitable terms for whites in the
constitutional negotiations, while Mandela and his team came across as
generous and committed to reconciliation. The impact of these intangible
factors is impossible to measure but it is reasonable to suppose that they
contributed to a climate in which, together with the factors mentioned above,
taking one's chances in a democratic state seemed preferable to the misery of
chaos of a counter-revolution which most of the right-wingers knew in their
hearts must fail.

NOTES

1. John D'Oliveira, *Vorster – The Man* (Johannesburg: Ernest Stanton, 1977), p.125.
2. Patrick Laurence, *Death Squads – Apartheid's Secret Weapon* (London: Penguin Books, 1990), p.2.
3. Jacques Pauw, *In the Heart of the Whore – The Story of Apartheid's Death Squads* (Johannesburg: Southern Book Publishers, 1991), pp.270–88.
4. *Report of the Commission of Inquiry regarding the Prevention of Public Violence* (Goldstone Commission) (Pretoria: Government Printer, 18 March 1994), pp.1–4.
5. Kenneth W. Grundy, *The Militarization of South African Politics* (Bloomington, IN: Indiana UP, 1986), p.51.
6. Philip H. Frankel, *Pretoria's Praetorians – Civil-Military Relations in South Africa* (Cambridge: CUP, 1984), p.65.
7. *Commission of Inquiry into Certain Alleged Murders* (Harms Commission) (Pretoria:

Government Printer, 109/1990), p.37.
8. Ibid., p.35.
9. Ibid., p.42.
10. Ibid., p.56.
11. Ibid., p.38.
12. Ibid., p.54.
13. Ibid., p.55.
14. *Sunday Tribune*, 29 May 1994; *Rapport*, 29 May 1994.
15. For fuller accounts see Anthony Minnaar (ed.), *Patterns of Violence – Case Studies of Conflict in Natal* (Pretoria: Human Sciences Res. Council, 1993).
16. John Kane-Berman, *Political Violence in South Africa* (Johannesburg: SA Inst. of Race Relations, 1993), p.73.
17. Jenny Irish and Howard Varney, 'The KwaZulu Police: Obstacle to Peace?' in Minnaar (ed.) (note 15), pp.49–55.
18. Tim Smith, 'The Warlord and the Police', in Minnaar (note 15), pp.57–60.
19. Deneys Coombe, 'The Trust Feed killings', in Anthony Minnaar, Ian Liebenberg and Charl Schutte (eds.), *The Hidden Hand – Covert Operations in South Africa* (Pretoria: Human Sciences Research Council, 1994), pp.191–211.
20. Pauw (note 3), p.62.
21. *Debates of Parliament*, 31 March 1993, col. 4011. Anton Harber and Barbara Ludman (eds.), *Weekly Mail and Guardian A-Z of South African Politics* (London: Penguin Books, 1994), pp.49–50.
22. Harber and Ludman (note 21), pp.49–50.
23. *Business Day*, 20 Oct. 1991.
24. Laurence (note 2), p.60; Goldstone Commission (note 4), p.8.
25. Goldstone Commission (note 4), p.8.
26. Heribert Adam and Kogila Moodley, *Negotiated Revolution – Society and Politics in Post-Apartheid South Africa* (Johannesburg: Jonathan Ball, 1993), p.155.
27. Quoted in P.F. van der Schyff, 'Verset teen "Empire-oorlog"', in idem. (ed.), *Die Ossewabrandwag – Vuurtjie in Droë Gras* (Potchefstroom: Dept. of History, Potchefstroom Univ., 1991), p. 226 (trans. from Afrikaans).
28. Johann van Rooyen, *Hard Right – The New White Power in South Africa* (London: I.B. Taurus, 1994), p.34.
29. *Sunday Tribune* (Durban), 29 Sept. 1991.
30. Ibid., 18 Aug. 1991.
31. Ibid., 29 Nov. 1992.
32. *Cape Times* (Cape Town), 4 Jan. 1992.
33. *Argus*, 15 July 1993.
34. *Race Relations Survey 1988/89* (Johannesburg: SA Inst. of Race Relations, 1989), p.618.
35. *Weekly Mail* (Johannesburg), 1 March 1991.
36. *Race Relations Survey 1991/92*, p.487.
37. *Die Burger* (Cape Town), 13 Nov. 1990.
38. *The Citizen*, 5 May 1993.
39. See Arthur Kemp, *Victory or Violence – The Story of the AWB* (Pretoria: Forma Publishers, 1990).
40. Interview with Terre Blanche, in Michael Abeldas and Alan Fischer (eds.), *A Question of Survival – Conversations with key South Africans* (Johannesburg: Jonathan Ball Publishers, 1987), p.179.
41. *Rapport*, 12 May 1991.
42. *Sunday Times*, 2 Feb. 1992.
43. Ibid., 11 Aug. 1991.
44. *Die Burger*, 12 Aug. 1992.
45. *Cape Times*, 6 Jan. 1992.
46. *Weekly Mail*, 4–10 March 1994.
47. *Rapport*, 13 March 1994; *Sunday Times*, 13 March 1994.

48. *Citizen*, 31 Jan. 1994.
49. *Rapport*, 15 Feb. 1994.
50. Andrew Reynolds, 'The Results', in Andrew Reynolds (ed.), *Election '94 South Africa – The Campaign, Results and Future Prospects* (Cape Town: David Philip, 1994), p.195.
51. *Beeld*, 25 Nov. 1993.

Wrapping Up in Something Long: Intimidation and Violence by Right-Wing Groups in Postwar Japan

KENNETH SZYMKOWIAK
and PATRICIA G. STEINHOFF

Political organizations enjoy considerable legal protection under Japan's postwar constitution, and right-wing organizations acquired additional political protection during four decades of uninterrupted rule by the conservative Liberal Democratic Party. These circumstances facilitated the development or re-emergence of (1) complex links and overlapping memberships between right-wing political groups, organized crime groups (*yakuza*), and professional corporate extortionists (*sōkaiya*); (2) tolerance and encouragement by state authorities of the use of violence by such groups as forms of private policing; and (3) the formation of bogus right-wing groups to facilitate extortion, intimidation, and political corruption under cover of legal protections afforded to political organizations. This situation is reassessed in light of new legislation, current changes in the Japanese political situation and a recent influx of foreign workers.

A frequently quoted Japanese proverb advises people to 'Wrap up in something long', meaning that one can best survive by seeking the protection of the powerful. On the surface, the radical right in contemporary Japan seems to have succeeded in doing just that, since incidents of intimidation and violence by right-wing groups occur with some frequency and appear to receive sufficient political support to be beyond the range of effective police control. But surface appearances can be very deceiving in Japan, as the following examples suggest.

Example I. During the 1980s the *Asahi*, Japan's most respected national newspaper company, was subjected to a series of violent attacks by a shadowy group calling itself the *Sekihōtai* (Red Revenge Squad) that made rambling right-wing demands. One *Asahi* reporter was killed and several were injured in the attacks, but the perpetrators were never arrested and the group itself remained unknown except for the communiques associated with the *Asahi* attacks.[1] In an apparently unrelated incident in 1993, Shūsuke Nomura, a radical right activist who had spent 18 years in prison for two previous political attacks, demanded a meeting with the president of the *Asahi* newspaper company. After making a formal speech he pulled out two pistols, aimed them at his waist, and dramatically shot himself to death.

Example II. In 1983 an unknown young writer won a literary prize for a novel centering on two attempts to assassinate the emperor, one based on historical fact and the other apparently fictional. The prize included publication of the novel in the literary journal *Bungei*, and subsequent publication in book form. After the magazine publication, a story appeared in a rival publisher's weekly magazine sensationalizing the content of the novel as disrespectful toward the emperor, and a radical right organization promptly took up the cause. The local police station called the publisher of *Bungei* to report that right-wing sound trucks were on their way to the publisher's offices, and a member of the security police advised the company to cooperate with the right-wing organization in order to avoid trouble. Faced with this advice from the police, after a week of haranguing from sound trucks and high-pressure demands from the right-wing group, the publisher agreed not to publish the novel in book form.[2]

Example III. In the fall of 1988, when all of Japan was awaiting the imminent death of the Emperor Hirohito, Nagasaki Mayor Hitoshi Motoshima found himself thrust into the center of public controversy after commenting in the city assembly that Emperor Hirohito was at least partially responsible for Japan's involvement in World War II. The mayor was stripped of his affiliation with the local Liberal Democratic Party organization, and 85 right-wing sound trucks converged on city hall to call for his death as divine retribution. The mayor refused to retract his statement, and received 7,300 letters of support from citizens all around the country, which were later published as a book. In January 1990, just after the period of mourning for the emperor's death had ended, Mayor Motoshima was shot in an assassination attempt by Kazumi Tajiri, a 40-year-old member of the radical right-wing group *Seiki Juku* (Right Spirit Academy). Several months earlier, Tajiri and two other *Seiki Juku* members had been arrested for attempting to extort money from a Tokyo corporation.[3]

Example IV. As he was seeking to become Japan's prime minister in mid-1987, Liberal Democratic Party faction leader Noboru Takeshita became the target of a protest campaign by a right-wing group called *Nippon Kōmintō* (Japan Emperor and People's Party).[4] For weeks Takeshita's neighborhood and the area around the Japanese parliament building were treated to speeches and martial music blasting from loudspeakers bolted to *Kōmintō*'s large propaganda trucks painted with slogans and flying the Japanese flag. The group's campaign tactic, known in Japanese as *homegoroshi* (killing with praise), involved praising Takeshita as Japan's top choice for the prime ministership as he was the most skilled at getting payoffs for the party. The campaign halted after Liberal Democratic Party kingmaker Shin Kanemaru intervened by requesting the assistance of *Inagawa-kai*, one of Japan's largest organized crime groups. *Inagawa-kai* interceded with another organized crime group, *Yamaguchi-gumi*, that had direct ties to *Kōmintō*.[5]

These incidents demonstrate the difficulty of determining just what the radical right is in contemporary Japan, and what it might be wrapped up in. Is the term 'radical right' merely a convenient cover for what are actually organized crime operations? Or is there a true radical right, deeply committed to the emperor and the protection of Japan's national identity in the face of foreign pressure and corrupting leftist influences? In order to sort out these questions we must look first to the roots of the modern Japanese radical right in prewar Japan, and then see how the right has responded to new constraints and opportunities in the postwar period.

Origins of the Japanese Radical Right

The core ideology of the Japanese radical right stems from the political ideas embodied in the movement to restore political authority to the hereditary emperor after many centuries of feudal military government, which culminated in the Meiji Restoration of 1868. As they developed a modern nation state modeled after Bismarck's Germany, the Meiji leaders gradually elaborated an emperor-centered nationalist ideology based on three linked ideas. First, the emperor's ancient ritual responsibilities to communicate with the gods on behalf of the people helped to transform him into a semi-sacred figure of unchallengeable authority, which in turn conferred powerful legitimacy on government actions issued in the emperor's name. Second, the concept of the emperor as the benevolent parent at the pinnacle of an all-encompassing family system symbolically united his Japanese subjects by kinship and blood, providing the foundation for relations of dominance or exclusion toward persons who were not Japanese by birth. And third, the elaboration of a state religion (state Shintō) out of ancient religious rituals associated with the emperor made the nation itself an object of worship, and elevated sacrifice for the state into a sacred duty.[6]

Through universal public primary education, universal male military conscription, and newly created public ceremonial events, these ideas were promulgated throughout the nation as state ideology. While not everyone believed the state ideology, by the early twentieth century mass media censorship and various other criminal code provisions reinforced its dominance in public discourse. The major frame breakers proposing different interpretations of events were the adherents of western universalistic political ideologies of the left (anarchism, socialism, and communism in various flavors), who became the explicit targets of these legal sanctions. At the same time, the most devoted adherents of emperor-centered nationalism developed a style of radical direct action in which individuals consummated their ideological commitment in a single dramatic gesture such as a public suicide or a suicidal military attack.

Thus while the sources and specific content of Japanese radical right ideology were clearly indigenous, they were also influenced by the ideas and institutions of western nationalism. The core ideology of the Japanese right contains ideas of racial purity and exclusive national identity that parallel those of the European radical right. It also contains similar glorification of military prowess and hostility toward the political left. As in much of Europe, from the early 1930s until 1945 these ideas were not the province of a radical fringe, but constituted the official ideology promoted by the state as its source of legitimate authority to justify a campaign of military expansion and subjugation of other peoples.[7]

Postwar Settlements and the Radical Right

Although the emperor-centered state ideology was officially discredited in the immediate postwar era and its institutional supports were largely dismantled by the reforms of the Allied occupation, a constellation of circumstances has preserved their salience for the past 50 years. The primary factor underlying the postwar status of radical right ideology was the decision of the Allied powers to permit Japan to retain the emperor after the surrender, in the belief that it would prevent social disorder and facilitate the post-surrender demilitarization and reform process.[8]

The Allied occupation under US direction worked through the existing Japanese governmental structure, bureaucracy, and political leadership to demilitarize the country and reform its political and social institutions. The occupation conducted war crimes trials in Tokyo and purged military and civilian officials who had been directly responsible for certain policies, but this process stopped well short of the emperor. A new constitution written under close occupation supervision shifted the source of political authority from the emperor to the Diet (national assembly) and the people, but retained the emperor as symbol of the nation.

The constitution also strongly protected the free expression of political ideas in speech and in print. Constitutional protection of public gatherings, political organizations, and labor unions facilitated the development of an organized left in Japan, but the same legal protection also promoted the re-emergence of the right, which identified its mission as protecting emperor-centered nationalism against perceived threats from the left.

The consequence of these new arrangements was that although the criminal laws that had provided special protection to the emperor were struck down and the pre-1945 ideological content was purged from educational materials, informal and unofficial taboos remained to preserve the symbolic ghosts of the past. While the expression of critical political ideas in speech or in print was constitutionally protected, the major mass media organizations cooperatively agreed on certain standards for public references to the emperor that later came to inhibit full discussion of any issue associated with the monarch, including the war that had been fought in his name. This situation of a seemingly wide open arena for the constitutionally protected discussion and promotion of ideas across the full political spectrum, but with a soft spot for matters concerning the emperor, has clearly shaped the role, agenda, and tactics of the radical right.

Another factor affecting the role of the radical right in postwar Japan was the 'one-party democracy' through which Japan was governed from the mid-1950s until 1993. The postwar political system was set up as a wide-open electoral arena designed to encourage minority representation, and the radical right lost no time in establishing a new political base. In the first general election following the war, in April 1946, more than 400 political parties vied for seats. In addition to the main parties, right-wing groups were in particular evidence. Some of the groups were clearly continuations of prewar right-wing organizations. New parties were also formed within veterans' groups and from the ranks of Japanese who returned to Japan from settlements in the colonies.[9]

None of these extreme right parties was successful in displacing the mainstream parties. Instead a subsurface alliance developed between the radical right and the center-right coalition in power, which later coalesced into the Liberal Democratic Party (LDP).[10] In the early years this alliance was based on a deep-seated fear of the newly resurgent communist and socialist parties and their major power base, the labor union movement, which both the mainstream and right-wing parties viewed as challenges to the development and maintenance of conservative power.

A key factor complicating the postwar political situation was a series of occupation policies designed to demilitarize Japan, which included both the dissolution of Japanese military forces and the decentralization, depoliticization, and disarming of the civilian police. These reforms left postwar Japan initially with no means of controlling domestic disturbances in the new, open climate of political organization and protest. Individuals and corporations also continued the traditional practice of using private resources such as organized crime groups and various sorts of marginal fixers for debt collection and the enforcement of other moral and legal obligations, areas where the police and the courts were either not available or deemed inappropriate.

As the Cold War developed and US policies implemented in the occupation changed, Japan did build up a military self-defense force with strong American encouragement, but did not permit it to intervene in domestic political disturbances. The civilian police did not develop trained riot-police units until considerably later. In the interim, the government found itself forced to rely on private groups to maintain order on various occasions. From very early on this institutional weakness of the state legitimized the formation of private armies under the banner of right-wing causes and reinforced the ideological element of militarism in the postwar radical right, despite the dominance of themes of peace and demilitarization in the general public discourse of postwar Japan.

The politics of the postwar era and the development of the contemporary radical right have been played out within these structural constraints. We contend that these circumstances have facilitated the development or re-emergence of (1) complex links and overlapping memberships between right-wing political groups, organized crime groups (*yakuza*), and professional corporate extortionists (*sōkaiya*); (2) considerable tolerance or even encouragement by state authorities of the use of violence and intimidation by all of these groups as forms of private policing; and, especially since the late 1970s; (3) the formation of bogus right-wing organizations to facilitate extortion, intimidation, and political corruption under cover of the legal protections afforded to political organizations.

The Radical Right, the Political Elite, and the Underside of Japan

Japanese scholars and commentators generally divide the postwar history of the right into three or four main stages of development. The first stage was in the early 1950s when nationalists, purged by the Allied occupation, were rehabilitated and re-entered top government positions. They immediately began a campaign against left-wing groups, which had gained strength under occupation reforms. The second stage began with the blatant use of right-wing and gangster organizations in the suppression of the left during the 1960 Japan-US Security Treaty crisis, and continued during the 1960s when the radical right worked closely with Liberal Democratic Party elements in anti-left activities. The third stage was a split in the right which took place in the late 1960s and widened in the 1970s as younger members grew increasingly disgusted with the behavior of older right-wing leaders and bolted, forming what today is known as the new right.[11]

As outlined above, several occupation reforms shaped the postwar political environment. However, it must not be forgotten that after the initial purge was completed and the Allies had left, those who came back into power also carried with them the prewar legacy of emperor-centered nationalism coupled with strong anti-socialist, anti-communist, and anti-union views. The constitutional guarantees installed by the occupation fostered the development of militant unions linked politically to legal socialist and communist political parties, all forms of organization that had been thoroughly suppressed prior to 1945. The radical right's strong reaction to this altered political environment laid the foundation for its close relationship with the conservative national political leadership, which remained in place for much of the first two stages of postwar right-wing development but began to crumble in the third.

An early example of the linkage between the party in power and the radical right was the 1951 attempt by Justice Minister Tokutaro Kimura to form a 200,000-man secret army composed of right-wing and gangster organizations called the *Aikoku Hankyō Battōtai* (Patriotic Drawn Sword Regiment). Kimura planned to maintain the regiment as the bulwark defense against any attempt by the communists to stage an armed revolution. A nationalist in the pre-war years who was purged from government activity in 1947 and identified as a Class D war criminal, Kimura had a fundamental fear of such a revolution, and thought that it was imminent in view of the sudden postwar strength of the Communist Party.[12] His beliefs and fears were shared by other government officials as well as those on the radical right. Although the plan was eventually terminated by Prime Minister Shigeru Yoshida, Kimura remained a trusted political official and in 1954 was named head of the Self-Defense Forces, where he continued his right-wing activities.[13]

In one sense Kimura's efforts were based on a realistic assessment of the postwar conditions created by the eradication of the Army and the dramatic weakening of police forces, combined with the new constitutional guarantees protecting the left. All of these conditions would make any real challenge to the existing government difficult to suppress or control, as major May Day clashes between left-wing demonstrators and the police in 1950 and 1952 revealed. Those clashes established the groundrule that the civilian police would not fire on unarmed demonstrators regardless of the provocation. The long and bloody conflicts between unions and companies during the 1950s further reinforced the fears of the radical right that domestic disorder could not be controlled.

The most dramatic challenge to the government's ability to maintain order came during the effort to push through a very controversial joint security treaty with the United States in 1960. The initial protests were sponsored by left-wing organizations that objected to this Cold War linkage with the United States as a violation of the Constitution's Article 9, which renounced Japan's right to war. However, the government's subsequent efforts to push the treaty through the Diet by questionable maneuvers provoked protest from a broad political spectrum of ordinary citizens, who feared that Japan's fragile postwar democratic institutions were being undermined. This conflict initiated the second stage of right-wing development, in which the radical right forged close and active ties with the Liberal Democratic Party's conservative leadership.

One man who helped set this stage was Yoshio Kodama. Kodama may be best known in the West as the 'fixer' who arranged for the sale in Japan of Lockheed Tristar jets in the 1970s by bribing politicians, the scandal which led to the disgrace of Prime Minister Kakuei Tanaka. But Kodama was also a main link between the ultra-right, the *yakuza* (organized crime) and the LDP.

Kodama was born in 1911 and joined the radical right at the age of 18 under the tutelage of two major right-wing figures, Shinkichi Uesugi and Bin Akao, the latter a perennial Diet candidate who formed the extreme right *Dai Nippon Aikokutō* (Great Japan Patriotic Party) in the postwar years. Kodama's prewar activities included sending daggers to political leaders with which they were supposed to kill themselves for disloyalty to the Emperor. During the war he served as a supply procurer for Imperial Japanese Naval Air Force headquarters, and set up his own agency in Shanghai. After the war he was tried and convicted as a Class-A war criminal and served time in Sugamo Prison until 1953.[14]

In 1959 Kodama formed the *Zen Nippon Aikokusha Dantai Kaigi,* or *Zen'ai Kaigi* (All-Japan Patriotic Organizations Conference) which included the most powerful of that era's ultra-nationalist organizations.[15] It was Kodama who promised and delivered the necessary muscle to face down any protests against the Joint US-Japan Security Treaty which might threaten the completion of the pact and President Dwight Eisenhower's imminent visit to Japan on 19 June 1960. According to one account:

> Kodama persuaded *yakuza* leaders of organized gamblers, gangsters, extortionists, street vendors and members of underground syndicates to organize as an 'effective counter-force' to ensure Eisenhower's safety.[16]

All told, Kodama promised the government 38,000 gangsters, street vendors and right-wingers for the impending event; however, at the last moment Eisenhower canceled his trip for security reasons after his advance party's car was caught in a huge anti-security treaty demonstration at the airport.

Kodama, whose organizational abilities were proven in the security treaty conflict, continued his organizing efforts to further draw the radical right and *yakuza* together. The creation of the *Tōa Dōyūkai* (East Asia Friendship Association) in 1963 was the culmination. *Tōa Dōyūkai* was meant to rationalize and strengthen the structure of organized crime groups and the ultra-nationalists by joining them into a permanent anti-communist force. In

JAPAN 273

addition, *Tōa Dōyūkai* leadership would serve as a center for negotiating peaceful settlements to any disputes which arose among member groups. Beginning in January 1963 Kodama established the organization in Tokyo and then attempted to extend it nationwide. He failed to do this, but was able to establish within the Tokyo region a potent force of 14,000 gangsters and rightists under the *Tōa Dōyūkai* umbrella.[17]

The group felt so powerful that in December 1963, it sent a letter castigating the LDP leadership for factional infighting which could only weaken political control, leaving the nation open to threats from the left. Politicians were stunned to see major crime organizations and right-wing groups directly intervening in what they considered private political affairs. Thus, in 1964, Japanese police staged the first of a series of anti-organized crime sweeps aimed at cracking the major gangs, particularly those involved in *Tōa Dōyūkai*.[18] Although the raids did not succeed in taming organized crime, relations between the LDP and the radical right-yakuza coalition would never be the same.

Nor would they have to be. Thanks to a continual build-up of riot police forces through the 1960s, the government had less and less occasion to call on private armies for security services. In response to the security treaty crisis and the continued development of an activist new-left student movement independent of the Communist Party, which again staged massive street demonstrations during the latter half of the 1960s, the government rapidly redeveloped the police resources to control domestic protest. These resources included a strong and well-equipped riot police presence in the capital, supplemented by an elite security police force designed to maintain surveillance and control of political activists, particularly those on the left.[19] By the beginning of the 1970s this aggressive policing, combined with factional divisions and a shift toward guerrilla tactics within the radical left and the resolution of the some of the left's major protest issues, had reduced the size and frequency of mass street protests.

Until that point the radical right had 'wrapped up in something long' by working in close concert with the conservative LDP political leadership. The LDP had legitimized the radical right even as it coopted its issues, but by the late 1960s the government had less need of the private protective services of radical right groups. Moreover, the close alliance between the radical right and *yakuza* organizations was beginning to have unsavory implications for Japanese politics. Yet even though the government no longer needed them, the governing party could not so easily disentangle itself from the right-wing and gangster organizations wrapped in its coat-tails.

The situation was complicated further by the involvement of a new element, Japan's resurgent large corporations, and the private security they hired for various purposes. Formal private security services were first established in Japan in 1962 to bolster security services traditionally handled in-house by corporations. The field expanded rapidly with the 1964 Olympics in Tokyo. Prior to the enactment of a law regulating security businesses in 1972 the industry was plagued by scandals.

> Of the 321 companies that existed in March 1971, 20 presidents were convicted criminals, including two members of organized crime. While private guards assisted police in 72 cases in 1970, they also committed 95 Criminal Code offenses (comparable to felonies in the United States) .... They were employed to physically suppress farmers and radical students opposing the construction of the Narita Airport [outside Tokyo], minority shareholders at shareholder meetings, or union members during strikes. In short, membership and activities of this industry indicated elements of organized crime.[20]

By the end of the 1960s, anti-war and anti-pollution protests began to target the corporations that were perpetrating what the protesters labeled as socially irresponsible behavior. In particular, anti-Vietnam War protests staged by *Beheiren* (*Betonamu ni Heiwa o Rengo*, or Alliance for Peace in Vietnam) and anti-pollution demonstrations with the victims of Minamata disease at the fore challenged corporations through the use of the one-share stockholder movement tactic.[21] This tactic involved buying single shares of stock and using shareholder rights as guaranteed under the Commercial Code to attend shareholder meetings and directly protest corporate war profiteering and pollution.

Corporations could not easily get the police to move against these groups, who were acting under the umbrella of law. Under conditions similar to those the government itself had faced in the 1950s and early 1960s, the corporations chose the same solution: they sought protection from right-wing groups to supplement private security guards and their own employees. Acting in concert with the right were *sōkaiya*, or 'stockholder's meeting men'. Put simply, *sōkaiya* are racketeers who prey on corporations but work both sides of the street. They either shake down corporations for payments not to disrupt stockholders meetings themselves, or sell their protection services to the company. For a fee, they will shout down or physically suppress any other shareholder who attempts to disrupt the meeting with questions about corporate policy or the actions of corporate officers and directors. Street fighting and assaults inside and outside shareholder meetings became commonplace. The police could not prevent the shareholders from exercising their shareholder rights but they could refuse to intervene in a 'private matter' if corporations hired their own security force, particularly if that force consisted at least partly of right-wing groups that were also exercising their own constitutional rights.[22]

As changes in tactics and philosophy were taking place on the left, the same was happening on the right, with the slow but growing split among right-wing groups giving birth to a phenomenon called the new right. Perhaps the signal event of this developing split was the 1970 ritual suicide of novelist Yukio Mishima. The suicide followed a haranguing speech to the Self-Defense Forces calling for a return to traditional and pure Japanese values.

> In his last appeal, standing on a balcony, he emphasized that all chances for passing a constitutional amendment had been lost on 21 October 1969. On that day the largest [left-wing] mass demonstration of the late 1960s did not lead, as Mishima had hoped, to a mobilization of the Self Defense Forces and a *coup d'état*. Instead the demonstration was contained successfully by the police.[23]

Mishima's dissatisfaction with the political system, his disappointment with the response of the Self-Defense Forces and his suicide seemed to hark back nostalgically to prewar right-wing actions which valued deeds over words. But the events of that day had a stunning impact on younger members of the right who began to question their own motives, tactics and goals. Mishima's suicide inspired them to a stronger sense of commitment to purity of ideas and actions.

Further adding to the split was the implication of Yoshio Kodama as a main fixer involved in the sale of American passenger jets to Japan in the mid-1970s. Those who were already chastened by Mishima's acts and those of other young leaders of the growing new right, could now clearly see that the old right had sold itself out to the LDP. Worse yet, old right leaders with the stature of Kodama were acting not in the interests of Japan but in their own economic interests. Since that time, identification as a member of the new right has constituted a badge of honor, carrying obligations of action and thought that are decidedly non-economic in nature.

However, the widening split with the new right was not the only effect of the public revelations of the involvement of prominent right-wing figures in their own economic aggrandizement. It also gave permission for others to assume the right-wing mantle and use it for their own ends. By the late 1970s an increasing number of *yakuza* and *sokaiya* racketeers were taking on right-wing identities to perpetrate their racketeering enterprises.[24] *Sōkaiya* in particular could extort money from corporations using issues espoused by the ideological right. Already committed to the principle of peace at any price, Japanese companies would pay these annoying right-wing groups to leave them alone. Standard *sōkaiya* extortion activities such as selling advertising space in *sōkaiya* newspapers and magazines or selling tickets to golf competitions and seminars were further refined by these pseudo right-wing organizations. A refusal to make a political donation or pay for advertising or subscriptions could be tagged as unpatriotic and lead to further harrassment by the pseudo-right wing *sōkaiya*.[25] The tactic spread further as an increasing number of *yakuza* organizations created their own pseudo-right wing groups to carry out the same kinds of activities.

Thus, by the late 1970s there was a confusing mixture of groups operating under the right-wing banner. They could be true right-wing groups with historical ties to gangsters stretching to the prewar or early postwar years, or *sōkaiya* racketeers or *yakuza* who were rightists in name only. Whereas earlier the radical right had 'wrapped up in something long' by attaching itself to powerful political figures in order to re-establish the legitimacy of its causes, now gangsters and racketeers were 'wrapping up in something long' by using the legitimacy of the radical right as a cover for their own economic purposes. They could get away with these tactics not only because of the constitutional protections afforded to political organizations, but also because of the longstanding Japanese practice of using marginal fixers and various forms of private policing to manage private disputes.[26]

Trying to sort out the legitimacy of right-wing groups was extremely difficult, though efforts were made. In 1978 *Shūkan Daiyamondo*, a weekly business-oriented magazine, attempted to map out the ties between *sōkaiya*, *yakuza* and pseudo-right wing groups. [27] The reportage revealed a network of connections between major groups and individuals, tracing them back to the early 1970s. That same year a listing by an academic organization dedicated to the study of public security issues revealed the ties of well-known right-wing groups to *yakuza* and *sōkaiya* organizations. They were able to identify the *yakuza* connections of 14 rightist groups with a combined membership of 939 persons.[28]

A Conceptual Map of the Contemporary Radical Right

We have attempted to illustrate this confusing situation in Figure 1, which shows two continua along which the groups and activities of the contemporary radical right can be located. The horizontal line represents the spectrum of possible participants in the radical right, ranging from purely gangster organizations on the left of the spectrum to purely political organizations on the right. The vertical line represents the spectrum of action these groups might take, ranging from purely political acts at the top of the spectrum to those acts done solely for economic gain at the bottom.

Theoretically, we would expect the politically-motivated activities of right-wing organizations to fall into the upper right quadrant of the diagram and economic extortion by racketeers and organized crime groups to fall into the lower left quadrant, with no overlap between them. In Japan, however, activities associated with the radical right can be located all over the diagram. We can now attempt to place on the diagram some of the acts described earlier in this article, but even this cannot be done with certainty. The suicides of Nomura and Mishima probably belong in the upper right quadrant, as acts which were purely political and without economic motivation. Acts committed by gangster groups such as *sōkaiya* or *yakuza* under the guise of political action probably fall into the lower left quadrant.

FIGURE 1
CONCEPTUAL DIAGRAM OF CONTEMPORARY JAPANESE RADICAL RIGHT
GROUPS AND ACTS

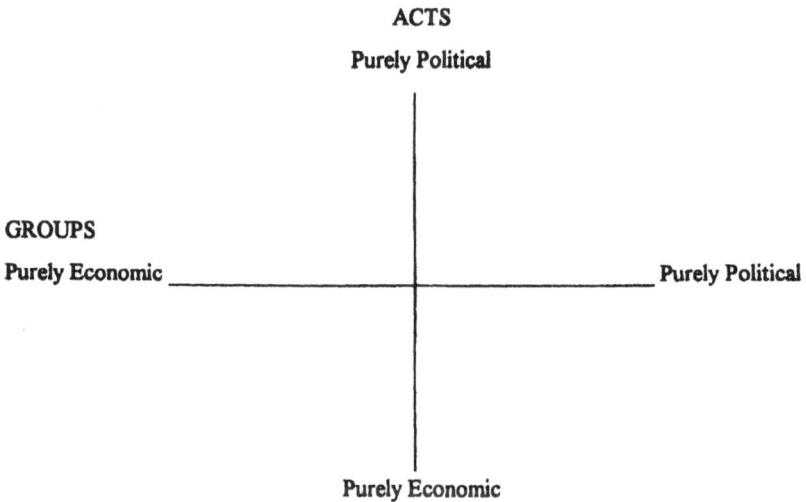

ACTS
Purely Political

GROUPS
Purely Economic _____|_____ **Purely Political**

Purely Economic

When gangster organizations provided a counter-force for the 1960 anti-security treaty demonstrations or actively participated in Kodama's anti-communist *Tōa Dōyūkai*, they were most likely placing themselves in the upper left quadrant, as economic organizations enlisted into a genuinely political cause. On the other hand, in 1989 the radical right group *Seiki Juku* was involved in clearly extortionate acts against corporations using political issues as an excuse, thus locating it in the bottom half of the diagram, but its placement into the lower left or lower right quadrant depends on how genuine one considers the group's right-wing credentials to be. The shooting of the mayor of Nagasaki by a member of this group would suggest a legitimate right-wing commitment, since the act was clearly political in nature and did not produce any economic gain for its perpetrator. Yet one could just as easily argue that the shooting was powerful advertising for any extortionate demands the group may make in the future.[29]

If a third dimension of time were added to the diagram, it would be possible to map a much larger number of right-wing activities and examine shifts in their distribution over the past 50 years, but such an enterprise is beyond our present scope. Even this simplified conceptualization, however, demonstrates the enormous difficulty of distinguishing clearly the motivations of a particular group, let alone any specific action of a group. With this major caveat, it is now possible to draw some general outline of radical right groups and their activities in contemporary Japan in the usual sociological terms of population, issues, and tactics.

Population, Issues, and Tactics

One of the basic problems in examining the Japanese radical right is that no one seems quite sure how large a movement it really is. For example, Table 1 represents official National Police Agency (NPA) population and group estimates of the radical right between the years of 1972 and 1980. While the estimated number of organizations varied considerably, the police estimate of 120,000 persons involved in the radical right never changed.

TABLE 1
JAPANESE RADICAL RIGHT GROUP AND POPULATION ESTIMATES, 1972–1980

Year	Groups	Population
1972	500	120,000
1973	550	120,000
1974	500	120,000
1975	550	120,000
1976	550	120,000
1977	600	120,000
1978	600	120,000
1979	650	120,000
1980	700	120,000

Source: National Police Agency 1973–1981

Whether it was out of embarassment or the recognition that no more precise estimate could be made, the police stopped reporting population estimates after 1980. Police white papers usually report that increases in the number of groups represent splits within existing groups or groups which formed but are not active, thus representing no change in the total population.[30] Although population estimates were no longer provided in the white papers, police still continued to report group numbers at major protests. And in interviews with police officials, the official count is still approximately 120,000 members.[31]

Private estimates of the size of the radical right are more wide-ranging. Takagi reports the radical right population as ranging from 120,000 to 125,000 but estimates group numbers at approximately 1,700 groups. This is based on his own investigation and the list includes the names of leaders, the addresses of the groups' headquarters and even phone numbers.[32]

A well-known voice within the right-wing community, Kunio Suzuki (a journalist and now leader of the new right group *Issui-kai*) notes the propensity for the police to report 120,000 members while group totals change. He concedes that the changing group numbers may indicate splits within the existing groups, adding that the term 'group' may be misleading in that many 'groups' are a single person. But he argues that the entire radical right population is probably no more than 12,000 individuals. These are persons who, if asked, would readily identify themselves as active members of the right-wing, and who regularly participate in radical-right demonstrations and other activities.[33] He further contends that police estimates, while outrageously high in terms of active members, ignore many persons who sympathize with the right-wing agenda. He cites the case of the late Bin Akao, a well-known leader of *Dai Nippon Aikokutō* (Great Japan Patriotic Party) who had been active in the radical right since before World War II. Akao generally earned 120,000 votes when he ran for a seat in the Diet. Similarly, when *Kaze no Kai*, another right-wing party, fielded candidates in the 1980s it drew approximately 220,000 votes. Moreover, police estimates do not include patriotic religious and educational groups (such as *Seichō no Ie*) which actively support right-wing causes.[34]

This difficulty in estimating the size of the radical right is a common phenomenon in the study of social movements, only complicated in the case of Japan by the problem of distinguishing 'true' and 'false' right-wing groups. The issues of the Japanese radical right are much easier to set forth. Although various sources might define the issues in slightly different terms and offer slightly shorter or longer lists, there is very broad consensus that the basic issues pressed by the postwar Japanese right include the following.

1. Protection of the emperor and restoration of his pre-1945 status. The radical right argues that with the elimination of the various legal sanctions that protected the emperor from slander, disrespect, and physical harm, it is the duty of right-wing organizations to provide that protection. The right generally does not concern itself with what private individuals think and say about the emperor, but it responds vigorously to the publication or even attempted publication of anything disrespectful to the emperor in the mainstream mass media.[35]

II. The Yalta-Potsdam System. Particularly espoused by the new right which developed in the late 1960s and 1970s, this is a codeword for all of the conditions imposed upon Japan through its defeat in World War II, and implies a desire to restore Japan to its prewar emperor-centered nationalist order. The new right argues that the world political order established by the Yalta Agreement of February 1945 and the Potsdam Declaration of July 1945 relegates Japan to second or even third-class world citizenship. The Potsdam Declaration is seen as an anti-emperor, anti-nationalist set of political notions forced on the Japanese by the Western powers.

This is a rather convenient all-encompassing platform for many right-wing groups in that anyone who seeks to support the political and economic order initially enforced by the Allied Occupation forces can become a target. Thus, the old rightists, Liberal Democratic Party politicians, major corporations and business organizations have all at one time or another been subject to attacks by right-wing groups based on anti-Yalta-Potsdam System ideology.

III. Communism, socialism and unionism. With the Japan Communist Party heading their lists, right-wing groups stage ongoing protests against left-wing political and labor organizations. They claim such unions as *Sōhyō* (the General Council of Trade Unions of Japan) and *Nikkyōsō* (the Japan Teachers' Union) are organizations working for the corruption and overthrow of Japanese society. In particular, police note the annual gathering of several thousand rightists protesting at *Nikkyōsō* rallies and study groups each year. Since the 1970s these protests have become more and more ritualized, and do not appear to have much potential for escalation into violence.

IV. The Soviet Union. Until its downfall, the Soviet Union was a major target for the Right. On 9 August of each year, right-wing groups would gather to commemorate the Soviet abrogation of its neutrality treaty with Japan on 9 August 1945 and its occupation of what have become known as the Northern Territories (the Kurile island chain just off the coast of Hokkaido, Japan's northernmost island). The right, along with more mainstream parties such as the LDP, continue to demand the return of these islands from the present Russian government. The December 1979 invasion of Afghanistan, the shooting down of the Korean Air Lines jet in September 1983, the sale of high-technology products and information by Japanese companies to the Soviet Union and Soviet-bloc countries (the sale of submarine propeller milling equipment by Toshiba Corporation in the early 1980s, for example) all added fuel to the anti-Soviet and now anti-Russian protests. The Northern Territories issue remains a prominent feature of rightist ideology.

V. The Yasukuni Shrine. The right has long held that the government should support the Yasukuni Shrine where, in a state-sponsored elaboration of ancient *Shintō* religious ideas, the spirits of Japan's war dead are gathered and enshrined. Japan's postwar constitution stipulates separation of church and state, and the shrine itself was privatized with the dismantling of state *Shinto* in 1945. Conservative politicians have been pressured by the right to make symbolic visits to the shrine and thereby honor the memory of the war dead, but whenever they do so the left protests loudly that they are violating the constitution. Thus even though the visits are staged as mass media events, politicians are generally careful to emphasize that they are visiting the shrine as private citizens. Still, the implications are not lost on neighboring Asian nations. China has been particularly sensitive to the visits to the shrine, denouncing them as evidence of rising Japanese militarism. The right argues that, in addition to demonstrating one of many flaws with the postwar Yalta-Potsdam system and the Allied-influenced constitution, criticisms by other nations are an unwarranted interference in Japanese affairs, and the fact that politicians pander to the criticism reveals their true colors.

VI. War responsibilities. The denial of wartime victims' claims, and resistance to demands for apologies and reparations, have become a more explosive public issue since the emperor taboo weakened in the late 1980s in anticipation of the death of Emperor Hirohito. In the immediate postwar period Japan was forced to make certain reparations to Asian countries it had invaded. However, the reparations were undertaken in the political environment of the Cold War, and therefore systematically excluded certain potential claimants such as North Korea. In addition, some issues such as the Nanking Massacre (1937), biological experimentation by the Japanese military (1932–45), and the claims of Asian women who were conscripted into providing organized sexual services for the Japanese military were not aired fully at that time, and they subsequently receded behind the mist of respect for the emperor. While other Asian nations have called repeatedly upon Japan as a nation and the emperor in particular to make formal apologies for this wartime conduct, the right has vehemently opposed such apologies and even denied that the events in question happened. Only since the death of the Shōwa emperor (Hirohito) in 1989 have the government and the new emperor (Akihito) begun to make such formal apologies. While this issue on the surface concerns specific wartime acts, the underlying ideological element is the blood ideology that views the Japanese as both racially and culturally unique and by extension, entitled to a position of dominance over other peoples.

All of these issues are legitimate political concerns of the ideological right in postwar Japan. The difficulty is that the same issues can provide a safe haven for groups and individuals whose purpose is not political but economic extortion, when they are coupled with the tactics commonly used by Japan's radical right. These tactics range from the purely symbolic gesture to direct physical attacks, but themes of physical intimidation and violence permeate the entire array.

Perhaps the most common tactic associated with the contemporary radical right in Japan is the use of decorated sound trucks. Radical right organizations can freely organize, publish, run candidates for election, and conduct various sorts of public meetings and demonstrations. There is no limit on such activities, although police maintain surveillance of certain groups and individuals on both the left and the right. Because political parties are prohibited by law from making direct contact with voters during election campaigns, they frequently use cars or trucks with sound equipment to carry their message to the public. During the 1980s the radical right developed this tactic into a high art, using large trucks painted and decorated like military vehicles and equipped with powerful sound equipment.

Massed sound trucks are used at the right-wing's own political rallies, and for counter-protests at large rallies of Japan-Communist Party-affiliated groups and unions, as shown in Table 2. With a ratio of only three or four participants per vehicle, the use of massed sound trucks permits a relatively few individuals representing many separate small radical right organizations to generate an impressive effect. The fact that so many small groups can use this capital-intensive tactic also attests to the affluence of both the radical right and the high-technology society of which it is a part.

The trucks are also used individually on a regular basis for the campaigns of individual right-wing organizations. In addition to cruising the streets of major cities blasting out old military music at a high decibel level, the trucks can be parked in front of a building to harangue the occupants and disturb the neighborhood. Since this calls embarrassing attention to the misdeeds of the target of the attack and simultaneously makes the victim complicit in the disruption of neighborhood calm, the victim is often willing to submit to the attacking group's demands in order to stop the harrassment. The demand may be political, but often the trucks can be silenced with an appropriate monetary donation.

By 1990 harrassment by right-wing sound trucks had become such a public nuisance that the police initiated measures to limit their decibel level. Zones were established around the parliament building and 36 other locations (primarily foreign embassies and consulates) within which the use of high decibel sound trucks is prohibited. These regulations have presumably been effective in reducing attacks against these symbolic political targets, since the police report only one or two violations per year. However, the regulations do not control the use of sound trucks to harrass a corporation or individual.[36]

TABLE 2
APPEARANCES OF RIGHT-WING GROUPS, INDIVIDUALS, AND SOUND TRUCKS, 1987

Event	Location	Groups	Persons	Trucks
Protests at Japan Communist Party Events				
August Party Conference	Yamanashi pref.	39	480	120
October Red Flag Festival	Tokyo	66	680	170
November Party Congress	Shizuoka pref.	40	250	70
Protests at JCP Teachers Union Events				
March Union Congress	Hyogo pref.	140	950	250
May National Education Mass Meeting	Tokyo	203	1,670	400
Anti-Soviet Protest Rallies by the Right				
August Anti-Soviet Day Rallies	34 prefectures	396	3,370	820
Protest of Soviet Fishing Vessel Port Calls	(total for year)	432	2,450	700

Source: NPA, Keisatsu Hakusho, 1988, p.279.

Sound trucks decorated as military vehicles invoke the military imagery of Japan's pre-1945 military prowess, but they also relate to another tactic, the radical right's penchant for organizing private armies to defend the emperor or the state against a perceived threat. While a big sound truck with one or two people in it can be used to suggest an army, various groups actually have raised private armies to support right-wing goals in postwar Japan. The most famous case internationally was the writer Yukio Mishima's private army *Tate no Kai*, a band of eager young people whom he outfitted with fancy military uniforms and treated to regular philosophical discussion sessions at his home. Mishima also arranged for his army to receive special training from the Japanese Self-Defense Forces, but it never conducted any particular military actions. Instead, the uniformed *Tate no Kai* became part of the stage-set before which Mishima dramatically committed suicide in 1970, after which it simply disbanded.[37]

Postwar Japan is a nation of readers and writers, and virtually every political organization publishes its own newspaper or magazine. While the basic purpose of these organs is to communicate the organization's ideas, since the 1970s they have become useful devices for intimidation and extortion by right-wing organizations. At its mildest, buying either copies of the publication or advertising space in it is a way of making donations to the organization. After the reform of the commercial code in 1982 prohibited payments by corporations to *sōkaiya*, this became a convenient way to make extortion payments, since political organizations are constitutionally protected. In more severe cases of intimidation, politicians or corporations often buy up whole issues of a publication to prevent the public disclosure of information that an organization threatens to reveal. Hence an organization needs only to maintain a publication and to collect embarrassing information in order to be in business, and setting up shop in the name of a right-wing political ideology provides constitutional protection for the whole operation.

At the most extreme ends of the tactical range are dramatic public suicides for political expression, on the one hand, and assassination attempts on the other. Both of these tactics have a long, romantic history in the prewar Japanese right. They also can be combined in a group suicidal attack for political purposes, such as the *coup d'état* attempts that marked the 1930s and that Mishima hoped to revive. While there has been no evidence of serious right-wing *coup d'état* attempts in postwar Japan, there have been several isolated assassination attempts aimed at politicians who said or symbolized things that are anathema to the radical right. Unlike the 'deranged lone political assassin' of American politics, these attacks generally involve an individual with strong affiliations in the radical right, acting in explicit retaliation for something the victim has recently said or done. When the target of such an attack is not a politician but a corporation the circumstances become murkier and the possibility of economic motives increases, even when the attack is committed overtly in the name of radical right ideology.

Dramatic ritual suicide is a traditional Japanese form of protest glorified in the romantic literature of the right. Suicide in this case does not mean the instrumental use of someone's body to transport and aim a weapon of destruction, as found in the *kamikaze* pilot or the suicide bomber. Rather, it is the act of committing suicide formally, in a staged public confrontation with one's enemy. Within Japanese culture such a suicide symbolizes the ultimate personal commitment to a goal that cannot be achieved, and thus serves both to lay responsibility for the failure at someone else's doorstep, and to rally future supporters through one's martyrdom. Although some radical left activists have committed suicide while in police custody for various reasons, ritual suicide as a dramatic gesture of political protest is a distinctively right-wing tactic. It refers directly to the values of personal loyalty, purity of motive, and noble self-sacrifice that were glorified in the imperial period to which the radical right would like Japan to return. And although the violence in this case is self-inflicted, it can have a powerful public impact.

Theoretically, the issues upon which the postwar radical right stakes its claim could be pursued by many different kinds of tactics, so the tactics that do appear most frequently represent a deliberate selection from a very wide array of available means. Most of the tactics currently used by the right fall into the general category of vehicles for harrassment and intimidation which sometimes lend themselves to mass protest, but which can readily be used by relatively few individuals to make a focused attack or a symbolic point. In this respect the right is quite different from the postwar Japanese left, which has an entirely different repertoire of protest tactics oriented largely around mass protest demonstrations. Even the underground guerrilla tactics of the left differ from those of the right, with the left favoring homemade grenades, bombs, and rockets rather than assassination attempts using swords, knives, or guns.[38] These differences relate to fundamental ideological orientations toward political organization in the left and the right, but they also reflect the extent to which the ideology and tactics of the radical right have been appropriated by individuals and small groups with non-political motives.

Overall, this picture of the population, issues, and tactics of the contemporary Japanese radical right reinforces the argument that there is a relatively stable but unknown number of individuals in Japan who are committed to the ideology and activities of the radical right, and an equally uncertain but not necessarily stable number of individuals who capitalize on the availability of the ideology and tactics of the right for private economic purposes. This raises the question of how the state controls these activities.

Domestic Security and the Radical Right

Police report a substantial number of arrests for right-wing protest activities each year, most of which are for minor misdemeanors. The overall number of incidents leading to arrests peaked at 690 arrests for 475 incidents in 1982 and then decreased to a low of 352 arrests for 249 incidents in 1988, the last year for which overall arrest figures have been reported. Since the death of the Shōwa emperor in early 1989 the number of guerrilla incidents attributed to radical right-wing organizations has increased, and recent police white papers have reported only these more serious incidents. There have been a reported 111 guerrilla or terrorist incidents attributed to the radical right from 1984 to 1994, 28 of them involving guns. Twenty-two of the gunfire incidents have occurred since 1989. The most recent was a gunshot fired toward ex-Prime Minister Motohiro Hosokawa on 31 May 1994, to protest the apologies he had made to foreign countries for Japan's wartime behavior. While these figures are probably lower than the number of gunshot incidents per night in major American cities, it must be remembered that guns are extremely scarce in Japan, and handguns are owned mostly by the police and *yakuza*.

It must also be emphasized that most radical right activities did not produce arrests. They were either not illegal or, in the case of successful intimidation or extortion, not reported. In terms of police reaction to the radical right, the problematic nature of distinguishing what is a purely political act from a criminal act perpetrated for economic gain is overshadowed by constitutional issues as well as police responsibility. While the police publicly recognize the right of free speech, thought, association and assembly as guaranteed under the constitution, they are also mandated by article two of the police law to preserve the public peace. Thus they acknowledge the difficulty of taking action against a particular group while stopping short of violating that group's constitutional rights. The chronic inability of police to control such activities undertaken in the name of right-wing political organizations is one of the themes underlying two important recent developments in Japanese law enforcement. These are the passage of a new law aimed at countering criminal groups and the advancement of a new crime classification that better focuses police and lawyers' resources.

The *Bōryokudan Taisakuhō* (Violent Group Countermeasures Law) took effect on 1 March 1992 and is designed to control the increasingly strident activities of organized crime groups. The law provides a mechanism for designating an organization as a violent group on the basis of the criminal records of its membership, after which a variety of sanctions can be invoked against the organization as a whole. Among the provisions is the opportunity for local citizens to bring a complaint against designated violent criminal organizations and their affiliates and have local government respond. To the extent that right-wing political organizations operate as organized crime affiliates, they may also fall within the purview of this law.

The new crime classification is known as *Minji Kainyū Bōryoku*, hereafter *Minbō* (Violent Intervention in Civil Affairs). *Minbō* is not, in itself, a crime. It is a description of a range of crimes committed by a person or a group intervening in civil affairs by violence or the threat of violence. The National Police Agency established the Violent Intervention in Civil Affairs Countermeasures Center in December 1979. It operates within the Criminal Investigation Bureau's Number Two Section, the section charged with investigating and controlling organized crime activities. The Japan Federation of Bar Associations established its own Violent Intervention in Civil Affairs Countermeasures Committee in March 1980. Centers run by both groups are now established nationwide, offering consultation services to citizens who believe they are victims of *minbō* activities. Although the two *minbō* centers would appear to be doing the same work, this is not the case due to differing definitions. The police define *minbō* as the use of violence or threats of violence by *bōryokudan* (literally 'violent groups'), a term usually, but not entirely, limited to organized crime or *yakuza*. The interventions usually involve a member of a violent group portraying himself as having been harmed in some way by the actions of the target individual or corporation and demanding monetary compensation by threatening violence. At times, the violent group may present itself as an interested third party that is attempting to settle the alleged grievance for another person, who may or may not exist.[39] The lawyers' association has a similar definition but does not limit the perpetrators to violent groups. Its definition includes acts by anyone with the intention of blocking the exercise of legally mandated rights to dispute settlements. Both the police and the lawyers' association recognize a variety of activities as *minbō* interventions. Classified by descriptions of the actors and their actions, the interventions include real estate scams, attempts to settle traffic accident claims, and other disputes which would normally be settled in a court of law or through mediation. Also included in the category are extortionate acts by gangster organizations which assume the guise of right-wing or civil rights groups.

The *minbō* classification is thus a recognition by the police of the excesses inherent in existing informal methods of private dispute settlement, and an attempt by police and lawyers to bring such practices under better control. While *minbō* as a named phenomenon encompasses a far more pervasive problem of intimidation and extortion in contemporary Japanese society, both police and the lawyers association explicitly recognize the use of false right-wing organizations in order to accomplish these goals as a subcategory of *minbō*. What is not yet clear is how the constitutional aspects of the application of *minbō*, or of the Violent Group Countermeasures Law, to ostensibly right-wing political organizations will be decided.[40] It is also not yet clear that either of these developments will have much impact on a problem that has been out of control for a very long time.

Ironically, the establishment of the *minbō* category may serve only to obfuscate further the distinction between 'real' and 'false' right-wing organizations. Genuine, ideologically-motivated radical right organizations, particularly those in the new right, explicitly dissociate themselves from the corrupt economic motives of other groups waving the right-wing banner. Yet in order to continue 'wrapping up in something long' so they can intimidate and extort funds in the name of a constitutionally protected right-wing ideology, 'false' right-wing groups must also demonstrate their legitimacy, which may lead them to engage more visibly in dramatic political acts without direct economic return. This impulse may lie behind the recent increase in right-wing incidents involving guns, which would be most readily available to individuals and groups associated with the *yakuza*.

Current Structural Changes and Predictions for the Future

This analysis has focused heavily on the largely unintended consequences of postwar structural changes for the development of relationships between the radical right and other groups in contemporary Japan. There are some indications that these structures and their consequences have now run their course, and that new patterns are beginning to emerge in the 1990s.

The death of the Shōwa emperor has clearly removed a powerful symbol from the radical right. While the new emperor still has the same legal status as his father had under the postwar constitution, he himself is very much a postwar man who has moved quickly to defuse the potentially inflammatory symbols and bring some long-overdue closure to the unfinished business of World War II. He has deliberately reduced the status gap between the imperial family and the rest of Japan both linguistically, by using normal polite Japanese in public instead of the stilted special language of the imperial household, and by blood, following up on his own marriage to a commoner in the 1950s with the much publicized recent marriages of his two sons, also to commoners. He has both approved and participated personally in the political initiative of offering official apologies for Japan's conduct during the war. All of these actions undercut the *raison d'être* of the radical right and gently delegitimize some of its central ideas, while leaving little room for the right to protest. In the 1930s it was possible for a radical right group to think about getting rid of Emperor Hirohito in favor of his more sympathetic brother, but such an idea seems entirely remote today.

In 1993 the weight of corruption finally broke apart the Liberal Democratic Party and toppled it from power after nearly 40 years, ushering in a coalition government composed of some fragments of the old LDP plus most of the longstanding minority parties except for the Japan Communist Party. This coalition managed to pass a basic change in the electoral system to a combination of single member districts and proportional representation seats before its popular leader, Morihiro Hosokawa, resigned when vestiges of the old LDP corruption reached him as well. After a wobbly attempt to continue under Noboru Hata as Prime Minister, the opposition coalition was succeeded by a bizarre coalition between the remainder of the LDP and its erstwhile enemy the Socialist Party, which has disillusioned ideological loyalists on both the left and the right. The prognosis is for a period of relatively unstable coalition governments for the next several years until new political alignments coalesce into parties under the changed political conditions. While the search for coalition partners can produce some strange bedfellows, it seems likely that overall this process will also tend in the long run to reduce the political influence of the radical right.

One early indication of this was the swift sacking in May 1994 by Noboru

Hata's minority coalition government of a justice minister who said in public that the Nanking Massacre never occurred, and that Japan had no war responsibility toward other Asian countries because it had fought the war to liberate them from Western colonialism. While there is a grain of truth to the latter notion at least as domestic rhetoric, what is most important is that until recently, such radical right ideas were sufficiently legitimate in LDP circles that their public utterance would not have been considered a political liability despite the diplomatic implications. LDP ministers have had a long history of uttering diplomatic embarrassments, in part because the party's hold on power was so firm that politicians were completely insulated from the pressures of public opinion. The justice minister's firing may have been essential to appease China, but it also sent a very clear message to the radical right that such views are no longer politically palatable.

The combination of the diminished symbolic value of the emperor, the delegitimization of important radical right issues, and the debased coinage of personal links to the LDP all serve to isolate the radical right. The standard prediction would be that such isolation would provoke the radical right into more extreme behavior in an attempt to regain its influence, but in the Japanese case such a prediction must be tempered by considering how difficult it is to assess how large a real radical right there is that might be deeply affected by these changes. To the extent that the active radical right is populated by economic opportunists, one would expect them simply to move on to some more effective gimmick if radical right ideology loses its effectiveness.

A further new factor is the influx of foreign workers from Asia and the Middle East that has brought highly visible social problems to Japan. In a country of 125 million people whose largest visible minority until recently was 650,000 long-term Korean residents, the relatively sudden influx of an estimated two million foreign workers, most of them illegal, has had a significant impact. The general potential for racism inherent in this situation could feed on radical right ideology and lead to the sort of violence associated with radical right skinhead movements in the west. Moreover, to the extent that the police and government have employed various sanctions to control foreign workers, most of whom are illegal immigrants, the situation becomes still more ominous. One might argue that state efforts to control foreign workers forcibly legitimize anti-foreign sentiment, and raise the possibility of a new basis for alliance between government and the private security forces of the right.

What may militate against that, ironically, are the longstanding links between the radical right and *yakuza* groups, and the direct investment of organized crime in these foreign minorities. There is an unusual multi-ethnic quality to Japan's organized crime groups, some of which contain high proportions of Burakumin (a native Japanese minority group) and Koreans. In recent years the *yakuza* have also developed international ties in Taiwan and Southeast Asia in connection with the drug trade. The *yakuza* are heavily involved in the recruitment of foreign labor, especially women for work in the sex industry, and *yakuza* also traditionally control the day laborer markets where much male foreign labor is now dispatched to jobs. It seems likely, therefore, that the ties between *yakuza* and the radical right would tend to limit overt anti-foreign violence, even as those same links might encourage exploitation and rationalize relations of dominance over non-native labor.

Equally important, Japan has a chronic labor shortage, particularly at the unskilled level and for dirty jobs. Despite record levels of unemployment in the current recession, the long-term capacity of the Japanese economy to attract and absorb foreign labor remains high. In fact, if it does not do so, the Japanese economy will be unable to grow over the next two or three decades. Many smaller businesses in Japan already need foreign labor in order to survive. Most significantly, there is no large segment of the Japanese labor force being displaced by foreign labor, and thus no pool of the disadvantaged and disgruntled who would be particularly susceptible to an ideological movement directed against foreigners. So while there is certainly a latent possibility of anti-foreign sentiment becoming a new issue for the radical right, it is not at all clear that things will move in that direction.

Some observers also see signs of movement in exactly the opposite direction, toward an ideological *rapprochement* between the new left and the new right centering on the concept of Asianism. There have been discussions on this subject between representative thinkers in the two camps for the past year or two, and both sides sense that the new younger generation of potential activists finds this arena attractive.[41] Both the left and the right have been down this road before, however, and it is not clear yet how a new Japanese ideology of Asianism for the twenty-first century could steer clear of the rocks that grounded it half a century ago. There is a substantial danger that it could not, and instead would re-legitimize Japanese nationalism and imperialist ambitions for a new generation. Even more problematic is the impact of a Japanese-inspired notion of Asianism on the rest of Asia, which is now in a very different state but still smarting from the events of 50 years ago. Still, it is precisely the issues related to Asia and to the emperor that in the past have divided the Japanese radical right and radical left most sharply, so any movement that proposes to bring them together is worthy of close observation.

At this juncture, the future of the Japanese radical right remains quite uncertain. While the right may no longer have anything long to wrap up in, some of the core ideas of Japanese radical-right ideology may be transformed into a new radical movement for the coming century. If such a movement arises out of the common interests of the new left and new right it will be free of the entanglements with organized crime that have plagued its predecessors, and it could have surprising moral force among young people in the next century.

Theoretical Implications

In this account of Japan's radical right we have subscribed implicitly to a political process model of social movements, linking the behavior of the radical right to broader historical and structural changes in Japanese society, and particularly to changes in political opportunities. We share with Sprinzak and the other authors in this volume a desire to place the most extreme acts of the radical right into context as part of a broader continuum of activity by organizations and individuals, and to search for common patterns and processes across different national cases that may help to explain rather than simply describe the phenomenon.

As we have shown, there is activity in contemporary Japan that the police classify as radical right-wing terrorism, and which occurs in a broader context of harrassment and intimidation by right-wing groups. There are ideological elements in Japan's radical right that parallel the themes of racial purity, militaristic nationalism, and glorification of violence found in European radical right movements; and the postwar situation of Japan's radical right resembles that of the German Nazis and Italian Fascists in some respects. Moreover, since the 1980s an unprecedented influx of illegal immigrant labor from Asia and the Middle East has become a visible foreign element in the otherwise quite ethnically homogenous environment of urban Japan.

Yet our analysis suggests that these factors do not add up to the same radical right equation that is found in Europe and the United States, and that Sprinzak's theory of split delegitimization does not provide a very robust explanation of the Japanese case. The goal of Sprinzak's theory is to explain the process by which ordinary people in certain ideological organizations come to be able to carry out brutal acts of terror by 'delegitimizing' their opponents. For particularistic groups such as those found on the radical right, he proposes a theory of split delegitimization to account for the fact that the main target of such groups is not generally the state itself, as it is for universalistic radical left groups. Instead, the targets are either enemies on the political left, other ethnic and religious groups, or elements in the government that are judged to be derelict in performing their duties.

Our analysis of the Japanese case indicates that ethnic and religious minorities are not the primary target of radical right attacks, although there is both historical precedent and contemporary opportunity for such behavior. And while the left has been a continuous object of symbolic protest for the radical right in Japan, it too has not been the major target of radical right violence and intimidation for at least the past decade. Instead, the major targets of right-wing violence in contemporary Japan have been mainstream political figures and economic institutions. Moreover, we do not find strong evidence that the Japanese radical right has in fact delegitimized and demonized the targets of its violent attacks. On the contrary, the targets remain highly personalized, and violence is simply a calculated escalation of intimidation tactics. We submit that the missing factor in the Japanese equation is economic motives, which have become so hopelessly entangled with ideological and political motives in the Japanese radical right that neither the police nor the movement's participants, let alone academic researchers, can distinguish them completely.

On the basis of this one mismatch of theory and observation we do not wish either to reject the potential utility of Sprinzak's theory for other situations, or to accept the conclusion that the Japanese case is not amenable to general theoretical explanation. Although it is not possible to do so systematically here, we believe that a careful analysis of the specifics of the Japanese situation for each of the five types of particularistic terror Sprinzak proposes, including the economic factors we have outlined, might explain why the patterns he describes have not come about in the same way in Japan. More generally, we suggest that the similarity of elements present in at least the Japanese, Italian, and German cases (taking into account both postwar German states) warrants a closer look to see if there are economic motives and underworld entanglements in these cases that have heretofore been overlooked. In short, we suggest that the Japanese case should not be dismissed as unique or inexplicable, but instead should serve as a critical test of the robustness of theory, and should contribute to further theoretical development.

Postscript

As this work was going to press, details were still unfolding about a group that may be responsible for a 20 March 1995 coordinated nerve gas attack in the Tokyo subway system that killed 12 persons and sickened more than 5,000. This was an unprecedented use of chemical weapons by terrorists against the commuters of a modern capital city. Almost immediately after the attack, search warrants were produced and several thousand security police wearing chemical protective gear and gas masks and carrying canaries launched a massive search of the business and residential properties of a religious cult called Aum Shinri Kyō. These searches turned up enormous stocks of chemicals and chemical production facilities, large quantities of cash, gold, and guns, and about 50 cult members in poor physical condition, some of whom were unconscious.[42]

The messianic Buddhist-inspired cult, which had attracted about 10,000 followers in Japan and an equal number in Russia in recent years, had apparently been under police surveillance for some time, and was implicated in two earlier, small-scale releases of the same nerve gas, sarin. The writings of the cult's leader, Shoko Asahara, contain references to Hitler's writings and a fascination with poison gas.[43]

Since the attack on the subway system cult members have been arrested in connection with earlier reported kidnappings of cult members and associates, but no one has as yet been arrested for the nerve gas incident. The cult has denied responsibility for the subway attack, claiming not only that the police were trying to harrass and frame them, but that they themselves were the victims of poison gas attacks.[44]

Three weeks after the sarin attack in the Tokyo subway system, 20,000 police were mobilized in an intense security watch over the city of Tokyo, because the cult leader's writings had predicted a doomsday cataclysm in Tokyo on 15 April. At one point it was estimated the nationwide mobilization of police involved about a third of the total police forces in Japan, even greater than the numbers mobilized for the emperor's coronation ceremonies in 1990. Nothing untoward happened on 15 April 1995, but a week later a smaller release of chemicals at three sites in the Yokohama subway station injured over 500 people. Neither the chemical agent nor the perpetrators have yet been definitely identified as of this writing.[45]

While we have not yet had an opportunity to study the ideas and activities of Aum Shinri Kyo ourselves, the news reports suggest several points of connection to the argument of this essay.

First, this is the first instance we have found in Japan in which terrorist acts have been linked to the writings of Adolf Hitler, but the link does not follow the pattern one might predict from the cases in other countries. As yet, there is no indication that Aum Shinri Kyo members identify themselves as neo-Nazis or adopt skinhead dress and behavior; instead they are described as chanting unintelligible syllables for hours in front of train stations. Even within the Japanese context, the group is identified as a religious cult whose beliefs derive from Buddhism rather than Shinto, and they do not seem to be associated with the standard themes of Japanese right-wing discourse. Further confounding matters, one of the sect's top officials was subsequently stabbed by a known rightist. Nevertheless, the reported prominence of references to Hitler's ideas in the cult leader's writings suggests that those ideas are reaching a receptive audience in contemporary Japan, a phenomenon that warrants further investigation.

Second, the group's possession of a sizable cache of guns, gun parts, and machinery for making bullets has been publicly attributed to the presence of its high-ranked 'Minister of Security', a convert from the *yakuza* organization Yamaguchi-gumi. This underscores once again the pervasive role of organized crime in the provision of private security in Japan, but we do not know if the cult has any links to right-wing organizations through this channel.[46]

Third, the rapid and extensive mobilization of security police in this case parallels the scale and style of response Japan has developed in the past three decades to deal with threats to public security from the political left. This is the first time in postwar Japan that such an intensive security police mobilization has been directed against a religious organization. It is clear that the religious cult was the object of considerable surveillance prior to the nerve gas attack on the Tokyo subway system.

To our knowledge, there has never been a similar surveillance and mobilization against any right-wing political organization in Japan. This raises the important question of why the police have not conducted such operations against right-wing organizations or their criminal affiliates, since they have the organizational capacity to do so. As we have argued, these groups have committed numerous terrorist acts and have engaged in pervasive intimidation tactics. They are at least as visible and accessible to law enforcement agencies as are religious cults and the radical left. Based on our discussion, we suggest that the police have not acted because these groups continue to enjoy both political and corporate protection. That is, they remain 'wrapped up in something long'.

NOTES

1. A group by the same name advocating the restoration of imperial rule existed just prior to the Meiji Restoration of 1868. Police investigating the *Asahi* attacks discovered that they followed the same geographic route as the earlier namesake group's attacks. Masaru Fujimoto, 'Attack Still Haunts Asahi Newsroom One Year After', *Japan Times*, 3 May 1988, p.4.
2. Kasane Kiriyama, *'Paruchizan Densetsu' Jiken* [The 'Partisan Legend' Incident] (Tokyo: Sakuhinsha, 1987), Chs. 1–2, pp.8–13.
3. Steven R. Weisman, 'Japanese Gunman Tied to Crime Ring', *New York Times*, 20 Jan. 1990, p.3.
4. Use of the pre-1945 pronunciation of the name of the country as 'Nippon' rather than the softer postwar 'Nihon' conveys a decidedly right-wing, restorationist flavor to the organization's name.
5. It is not clear who hired *Kominto* to conduct its campaign. Some contend it was a reprisal from organized crime for Takeshita's role in a bank scandal, but suspicion also falls on members of the LDP political faction once led by former prime minister Kakuei Tanaka. Takeshita had quit the faction and this insult to Tanaka as well as the weakening of the

faction's numerical strength were not forgiven. See Atsushi Mizoguchi, *Gendai Yakuza no Ura Chishiki* [Behind-the-scenes Knowledge of Today's Yakuza] (Tokyo: Nihon Purintekusu, 1993), pp.116–25.

6. See Carol Gluck, *Japan's Modern Myth* (NY: Columbia UP, 1985) and Helen Hardacre, *Shinto and the State, 1868-1988* (Princeton, NJ: Princeton UP, 1989). It must be pointed out that these beliefs and practices functioned as a state or civil religion, and did not constitute an exclusive, oppositional religious commitment until the late 1930s and early 1940s, when the state began to prosecute some small religious groups whose beliefs were thought to undercut primary loyalty to the emperor. In general, religious belief in modern Japan tends to be non-exclusive and therefore an unlikely basis for political conflict.

7. See Gregory Kasza, 'Fascism from Below? A Comparative Perspective on the Japanese Right, 1931–36', *Journal of Contemporary History* 19/4 (1984).

8. The initial terms of surrender established by the Allies at Yalta and formalized in the Potsdam Agreement of July 1945 called for unconditional surrender, but the Japanese government negotiated successfully to preserve the position of the emperor. Declassified wartime records indicate that the American Office of Strategic Services recommended preservation of the emperor as early as 1944 for essentially the same reasons.

9. Kenji Ino, *Uyoku* [the Right-Wing] (Tokyo: Gendai Shokan, 1988), p.145. The political parties with prewar predecessors included *Zenkoku Rodosha Domei* (prewar: *Kokusui Taishuto*), *Nippon Kokuminto* (prewar: *Kyoa Seinen Undo Honbu*) and *Shin Nipponto* (prewar: *Aikokusha*).

10. The Liberal Democratic Party, which remained internally a collection of distinct political factions, nonetheless managed to win election after election and retain continuous control of Japanese politics from the early 1950s until 1993. The LDP maintained control by effective use of Japan's multi-member, single-vote election district system, an occupation innovation intended to preserve a minority voice in Japanese politics by facilitating the ability of smaller parties to win the third or fourth seat even though they could never hope to win the highest number of votes in the district. The electoral system made it possible for small parties of the left and right to maintain a tiny foothold in Japanese electoral politics. However, the LDP was able to turn this structural opportunity to its own benefit by running multiple candidates from various factions in the same district. In rural areas dominated by longstanding political figures (many with an established prewar base), it was sometimes possible for the LDP to split its vote fairly precisely between two candidates and not 'waste' any unnecessary votes on the front-runner. Despite the urbanization of Japan over the ensuing decades, the LDP resisted redistricting which would undercut its rural power base. Along with other factors related to power and policy influence in the Diet and bureaucracy, the phenomenon of several LDP candidates with indistinguishable political platforms chasing a shrinking number of rural votes helped to produce the money politics that eventually brought down the LDP and led to the 1993 change to smaller single-member districts.

11. See Koji Nakamura, 'The Samurai Spirit', *Far Eastern Economic Review* 74/42 (1971), pp.22–4: and Masayuki Takagi, *Uyoku: Katsudō to Dantai* [The Right-wing: Activities and Groups] (Tokyo: Bijitsusha, 1989), pp.48–59 for brief analyses of postwar developments.

12. The Japan Communist Party enjoyed unusual political legitimacy in the immediate postwar period because it was the last political voice to have steadfastly opposed Japan's military expansion, and its leaders had remained in prison or in exile throughout the war because of their beliefs. The JCP, along with the less organized anarchists, were also the only groups that had openly opposed the emperor system before the war, which made the communist postwar resurgence appear particularly threatening to the radical right.

13. Ino (note 9), p.149.

14. Numerous recountings of Kodama's life exist. See his autobiography, published in English as Yoshio Kodama (Robert Booth and Taro Fukuda, trans.), *I Was Defeated* (Tokyo: Mainichi Shinbun Shakai-bu, 1951); John Carroll, 'The Enigma of Yoshio Kodama', *Tokyo Journal* (July 1988), pp.90–6; Nakamura (note 11); and Takagi (note 11), among others.

15. Carroll (note 14), p.95.

16. Nakamura (note 11), p.24.

17. Ino (note 9), pp.155–6.
18. Mainichi Shimbun Shakai-bu, *Soshiki Bōryoku o Ou* [On the Trail of Organized Violence] (Tokyo: Mainichi Shinbunsha, 1992), pp.223–31.
19. Peter J. Katzenstein and Yutaka Tsujinaka, *Defending the Japanese State: Structure, Norms and Political Responses to Terrorism and Violent Social Protest in the 1970s and 1980s.* Cornell East Asian Series (Ithaca, NY: East Asia Program. Cornell University, 1991), pp.62–8.
20. Setsuo Miyazawa, 'The Private Sector and Law Enforcement in Japan', in William T. Gormley, Jr. (ed.), *Privatization and Its Alternatives* (Madison, WI: Univ. of Wisconsin Press, 1991), p.249.
21. See Thomas R. Havens, *Fire Across the Sea: The Vietnam War and Japan, 1965–1975* (Princeton, NJ: Princeton UP, 1987) for further detail on *Beheiren,* and Frank K. Upham, *Law and Social Change in Postwar Japan* (Cambridge, MA: Harvard UP, 1987) for background on the Minamata disease protests.
22. See Frank Baldwin, 'The Idioms of Contemporary Japan VII: Sokaiya', *The Japan Interpreter* 8/4 (1974), pp.502–9; and Kenneth Szymkowiak, 'Sokaiya Criminal Groups and the Conflict for Corporate Power in Postwar Japan', *Asian Profile* 20/4 (1992) for details of the *Beheiren* and Minamata incidents.
23. Katzenstein and Tsujinaka (note 19), p.32. The event that so disappointed Mishima was a massive, violent anti-war demonstration staged by an array of radical left groups on International Anti-War Day, an occasion commemorating opposition to the 1966 bombing of North Vietnam and subsequent US expansion of the Vietnam War. The 1968 International Anti-War Day protests involved 288,000 demonstrators from unions, the Communist and Socialist parties, and the student movement at locations all over Japan. The student demonstrations in Tokyo were the most violent, and at their peak over 2,000 students rampaged through Shinjuku station, Tokyo's largest commuter rail station. In response the police invoked the anti-riot law against student demonstrators for the first time. A year later the police were braced for even more violent conflict in the streets. Student radicals from the newly-formed Red Army Faction introduced pipe bombs and 'Peace can bombs' into demonstrations for the first time, but the police managed to contain the disorders with mass arrests. In retrospect, Mishima's hope that this event would lead to calling out the Self-Defense Forces and a right-wing *coup d'état* was on the same level of fantasy as the radical left student demonstrators' hopes that the mass protests would lead to revolution.
24. Still other groups disguise themselves as representing the Burakumin minority and use accusations of discrimination to extort payoffs or other economic concessions from corporations. See Nihon Bengoshi Rengōkai, *Minji Kainyū Bōryoku* [Violent Intervention in Civil Affairs] (Tokyo: Shōji Hōmu Kenkyūkai, 1986), p.15.
25. Following the 1982 reform of Japan's commercial code, an increasing number of *sōkaiya* turned to right-wing disguises to hide their operations. The reform made it illegal to use corporate funds to purchase the use or control of shareholder rights – what, in effect, *sōkaiya* sell. Thus, it was illegal for corporations to provide economic benefits to *sōkaiya* in exchange for their not exercising their right to speak at meetings. The *sōkaiya* population as tracked by the police plummeted after code reform, largely reflecting the shift from their direct operations into right-wing activities. Takagi notes the heavy dependence of the radical right on corporate funding. In 1982 an investigation of income and expenditure reports required by the Political Funding Control Law (*Seiji Shikin Kisei Hō*) found that 34 to 43 per cent of right-wing group income came from corporate political donations. By contrast, about 25 per cent of left-wing group income was derived from donations but fully 40 per cent of the funds were private donations from individuals. In addition to direct donations from corporations, the radical right depends upon additional sources of income from subscriptions and advertising purchases for the group's newspaper or magazine. See Takagi (note 11), pp.68–9.
26. Such practices are not unique to Japan. See Anton Blok, 'The Peasant and the Brigand: Social Banditry Reconsidered', *Comparative Studies in Society and History* 14/4 (1972), pp. 494–503; Anton Blok, *The Mafia of a Sicilian Village, 1860–1960* (NY: Harper & Row, 1974); Eric Hobsbawm, *Bandits* (NY: Pantheon Books, 1981); Paul Rock, 'Law and Order

and Power in Late Seventeenth and Early Nineteenth-Century England', in Stanley Cohen and Andrew Scull (eds.), *Social Control and the State* (NY: St. Martin's Press, 1983), pp.191–221; Steven Spitzer, 'The Political Economy of Policing', in David Greenberg (ed.), *Crime and Capitalism* (Palo Alto, CA: Mayfield, 1981), pp.314–40; and Dwight C. Smith, Jr., 'Paragons, Pariahs, and Pirates: A Spectrum-based Theory of Enterprise', *Crime and Delinquency* (July 1980), pp.358–86.

27. 'Zōka suru "bōryoku sōkaiya" no gokuhi risuto hatsukokai' [The First Secret List of the Increasing 'Violent Sōkaiya' Made Public], *Shūkan Daiyamondo* 27 May 1978, pp.82–5 and 'Yamaguchi-gumi, Matsuba-kai no "Kigyō Kyōkatsu" no Teguchi' [The Mōdus Operandi of Yamaguchi-gumi and Matsuba-kai's 'Company Extortion'], *Shūkan Daiyamondo*, 3 June 1978, pp.94–7.

28. Goro Fujita, *Kōan Hyakunen Shi* [A Hundred-Year History of Public Security] (Tokyo: Koan Mondai Kenkyū Kyōkai, 1978), pp.687–91, 709–10.

29. Recent interviews suggest that the Japanese police regard any highly visible right-wing organization using sound trucks and direct approaches to corporations to be an economically-motivated group masquerading as a false right-wing organization, on the theory that 'true' right-wing patriots eschew such tactics, but this criterion also may be problematic. Interviews by Kenneth Szymkowiak in Kobe, Osaka and Tokyo, 1993–94.

30. See National Police Agency, *Keisatsu Hakusho* [Police White Paper] (Tokyo: Ōkurasho Insatsukyoku, 1975), p.373 for an example.

31. Kenneth Szymkowiak interviews with police officials in Kobe, Osaka and Tokyo, 1993–94.

32. Masayuki Takagi, 'The Japanese Right Wing', *Japan Quarterly* (July–Sept. 1989), pp.301, 174–273.

33. Kunio Suzuki, *Kore ga Atarashii Nihon no Uyoku Da* [This Is the New Japanese Right-wing] (Tokyo: Nisshin Hōdō, 1993), p.51.

34. Ibid., p.50.

35 Kunio Suzuki, *Datsu Uyoku Sengen* [Escape the Right Manifesto] (Tokyo: IPC Inter Press Corporation, 1993), pp.32–5.

36. When the Tokyo Metropolitan Police proposed in 1992 to limit sound vehicles to a maximum of 50 decibels at 10 meters distance, the radical Right found an unlikely ally in the Left, which argued that this was an inappropriate restriction on free political speech, since the tactic is also used by labor unions to remonstrate with recalcitrant companies, and the ban could easily be extended to the small battery-operated megaphones used universally in protest demonstrations and rallies. See 'Tōkyō-tō Kakuseiki Kisei Jōrei: Genron Chin'atsu Rippō o Yurusanai!' [The Tokyo Municipal Loudspeaker Regulation Ordinance: Do Not Permit Legislation Suppressing Speech!], (Tokyo: Kakuseiki Kisei Jōrei Seidō Seitei Sōshi Tokyo Renraku Kaigi, 10 Sept. 1992), pamphlet.

37. Patricia G. Steinhoff interview with Manabu Shinohara, a former member of *Tate no Kai*, Sept. 1990.

38. One could argue for a certain amount of overlap in guerrilla tactics, but the differences far outweigh the similarities. See Patricia G. Steinhoff, 'Protest and Democracy' in T. Ishida and Ellis Krauss (eds.), *Democracy in Japan* (Pittsburgh, PA: Univ. of Pittsburgh Press, 1987) and Patricia G. Steinhoff, 'Hijackers, Bombers and Bank Robbers: Managerial Style in the Japanese Red Army', *Journal of Asian Studies* 48/4 (Nov. 1989).

39. Nihon Bengoshi Rengōkai, *Minji Kainyū Bōryoku* (1986), pp.3–4.

40. A similar law that was designed to control radical left groups, the Anti-Subversive Activities Law (*Hakai Katsudō Hōshi Hō*), has been applied only a few times since it was passed in the early 1950s. Some of those cases are still in the courts, but the current Japanese judiciary is unlikely to declare the law unconstitutional.

41. Patricia G. Steinhoff interview with Kōji Takazawa, May 1994.

42. 'Japan police raid cult', *Honolulu Advertiser*, 22 March 1995, pp.1–2; Nicholas D. Kristof, 'Police Find More Chemicals Tied to Sect', *New York Times*, 25 Mrach 1995, p.5; 'Sarin genzairyo "Oumu" chotatsu ruto kaimei' [sarin ingredients: 'Aum' supply route revealed], *Yomiuri Shsinbun* satellite ed., 25 March 1995, p.1; 'Oumu kyo ajitto sosaku' [Aum sect hideout searched], *Asahi Shinbun*, 10 April 1995, p.19. We caution that this discussion is

based entirely on newspaper articles, which in turn are based largely on information released by the Japanese police with limited independent confirmation.

43. 'Japan police raid cult' (note 42), p.2.
44. 'Asahara denies sarin production', *Yomiuri Shimbun,* 25 March 1995, p.27 (English page of Japanese satellite ed.); David Thurber, 'Shrine reveals secret chemical lab, storage', *Detroit Free Press,* 28 March 1995, p.5A..
45. Kenzo Moriguchi, 'Police Stretching Powers to Pin Down Aum', *Japan Times,* 15 April, 1995, p.3.
46. 'Moto kumiin no Oumu kanbu taihō' [Aum official, a former gangster, is arrested], *Asahi Shinbun,* 14 April 1995, p.1.

Notes on Contributors

Tore Bjørgo is a Research Fellow at the Norwegian Institute of International Afairs. A social anthropologist by training, he is conducting research projects on right-wing violence and terrorism in Scandinavia, and on responses to racist violence. His main works in English include *Conspiracy Rhetoric in Arab Politics* (1987), *Maritime Terrorism* (1991), and several articles on racist violence and neo-Nazism. He has co-edited *Racist Violence in Europe* (1993), and co-authored (in Norwegian) books on terrorism, and political communication.
E-mail: tore.bjorgo@nupi.no

Jeffrey Kaplan is currently an assistant professor of History at the Arctic Sivunmun Ilisagvik College in Barrow, Alaska. His recent articles include: 'The Context of American Millenarian Revolutionary Theology: The Case of the "Identity Christian" Church of Israel' (1993); 'America's Last Prophetic Witness: The Literature of the Rescue Movement' (1993) [both in *Terrorism and Political Violence*, Vol.5]; and 'The Anti-Cult Movement in America: An History of Culture Perspective' (1993).
E-mail: RFJJK@aurora.alaska.edu

Heléne Lööw is a historian and Research Fellow at the Centre for Research in International Migration and Ethnic Relations (CEIFO), Stockholm University. Her present fields of study are national socialism, racism, state response, racist violence and national socialist women. She is the author of 'Hakkorset och Wasakšrven; En studie av nationalsocialismen i Sverige 1924–50' (doctoral dissertation, Gothenburg, Sweden) and many articles in books and journals.
E-mail: helene.loow@ceifo.su.se

Peter H. Merkl is Professor Emeritus of Political Science at the University of California, Santa Barbara. He is a co-editor (with L. Weinberg) of *Encounters with the Contemporary Radical Right* and an author and editor of books on German politics and political parties.
E-mail: merkl@alishaw.ucsb.edu

Ehud Sprinzak is Professor of Political Science at the Hebrew University of Jerusalem. He is the author of *The Ascendance of Israel's Radical Right* (1991) and numerous essays on religious violence and the evolutionary dynamics of insurgent terrorism.
E-mail: mssprin@pluto.mscc.huji.ac.il

Patricia G. Steinhoff is Professor of Sociology at the University of Hawaii. Her research focuses primarily on conflict between Japanese radical groups and the state. Some recent titles include 'Hijackers, Bombers and Bank Robbers: Managerial Style in the Japanese Red Army', 'Death by Defeatism and Other Fables: The Social Dynamics of the Rengo Sekigun Purge', and 'Radical Outcasts and Three Kinds of Police: Japanese Anti-Emperor Protest in the 1990s'.
E-mail: steinhof@uhunix.uhcc.hawaii.edu

Kenneth Szymkowiak is a former journalist in the United States and Japan who is currently a doctoral candidate in sociology at the University of Hawaii. He has just completed 15 months of field research in Japan under a Fulbright Doctoral Dissertation Fellowship, and is writing a dissertation on *sokaiya*. His recent publications include 'Sokaiya Criminal Groups and the Conflict over Corporate Power in Postwar Japan'.
E-mail: kens@uhunix.uhcc.hawaii.edu

Leonard Weinberg is a Professor of Political Science at the University of Nevada, Reno. He has been a Fulbright senior research fellow in Italy as well as a visiting professor at the University of Florence. His books include *After Mussolini: Italian Neo-Fascism and the Nature of Fascism*, *The Rise and Fall of Italian Terrorism* (with William Eubank) and *The Transformation of Italian Communism*.
E-mail: weinbrl@scs.unr.edu

David Welsh is a Professor in the Department of Political Studies at the University of Cape Town. His principal scholarly interest is South African politics. He is the author of *The Roots of Segregation* (1971) and *South Africa's Options* (with F. van Zyl Slabbert, 1979).
Fax: +27-21-650-3726.

Helmut Willems, Dr, is Sociologist at the University of Trier, his special interests are in Youth Sociology, Political Sociology, Social Movements, Violence and Conflict Resolution. He was J. F. Kennedy Memorial Fellow at the CES, Harvard University, Cambridge, 1991. He has published the books *Demonstranten und Polizisten* (1988); *Soziale Unruhen und Politikberatung* (1992); *Konfliktintervention* (1992); and *Fremdenfeindliche Gewalt* (1993).
E-mail: willemsh@pcmail.uni-trier.de

Select Bibliography

Abeldas, Michael and Alan Fischer (eds.), *A Question of Survival – Conversations with key South Africans* (Johannesburg: Jonathan Ball Publishers, 1987).

Adam, Heribert and Kogila Moodley, *Negotiated Revolution – Society and Politics in Post-Apartheid South Africa* (Johannesburg: Jonathan Ball, 1993).

Aho, James, *The Politics of Righteousness: Idaho Christian Patriotism* (Seattle, WA: University of Washington Press, 1990).

Almirante, Giorgio and F. Palamenghi-Crispi, *Il movimento sociale italiano* (Milan: Nuova Accademia,1958).

Almirante, Giorgio, *Autobiografia di un 'fucilatore'* (Milan: Edizioni del Borghese, 1974).

Anselmi, Tina, 'Il complotto di Licio Gelli: relazioni di Tina Anselmi, residente dellacommissione parlamentare sulla P2', Special Supplement, *L'Espresso* (20 May 1984).

Anti–Defamation League, *The Committee of the States*, ADL Special Report (October 1987).

—— *The Hate Movement Today: A Chronicle of Violence and Disarray*, ADL Special Report (1987).

—— *Extremism on the Right: A Handbook* (New York: ADL, 1988).

—— *Hate Groups in America: A Record of Bigotry and Violence* (New York: ADL, 1988).

—— *Holocaust 'Revisionism': Reinventing the Big Lie*, ADL Research Report (Summer 1989).

—— *The KKK Today: A 1991 Status Report*, ADL Special Report (New York: ADL, 1991).

—— *Sounds of Hate, Neo-Nazi Rock Music from Germany; An ADL Special Report* (New York: 1992).

—— *The German Neo-Nazis: An ADL Investigative Report* (New York, 1993).

—— *Young Nazi Killers, The Rising Skinhead Danger: An ADL Special Report* (New York: 1993).

Atkinson, Graeme, 'Germany: Nationalism, Nazism and Violence', in Tore Bjørgo and Rob Witte (1993).

Baldwin, Frank, 'The Idioms of Contemporary Japan VII: Sokaiya', *The Japan Interpreter* 8/4 (1974).

Bandura, Albert, 'Mechanisms of Moral Disengagement', in Walter Reich (ed.), *Origins of Terrorism* (New York: Cambridge University Press, 1990).

Barbieri, Daniele, *Agenda Nera* (Rome: Coines edizioni, 1976).

Barker, M., *The New Racism* (London: Junction Books, 1981).

Barkun, Michael, 'Millenarian Aspects of "White Supremacist" Movements', *Terrorism and Political Violence*, 1/4 (Oct.198), pp.409–34.

—— 'Review of J. Aho: The Politics of Righteousness: Idaho Christian Patriotism', *Terrorism and Political Violence* 3/3 (Autumn 1991), pp.149–57.

—— 'Reflections After Waco: Millennialists and the State', in James R. Lewis (ed.), From the Ashes: Making Sense of Waco (Lanham, MD: Rowman & Littlefield, 1994).

—— *Religion and the Racist Right: The Origins of the Christian Identity Movement* (Chapel Hill, NC: University of North Carolina, 1994).

Barrett, Stanley R., Is God A Racist?: The Right Wing in Canada (Toronto: University of Toronto Press, 1987).

Beam, Louis, *Leaderless Resistance* (pamphlet).

—— 'On Revolutionary Majorities', *Inter-Klan Newsletter and Survival Alert*, No.4 (19840.

—— 'We Are At War', *The Seditionist*, No.10 (Summer 1991).

Beck, U., *Risikogesellschaft. Auf dem Weg in eine andere Moderne* (Frankfurt: Suhrkamp, 1986).

Bennett, David H., *Demagogues in the Depression* (New Brunswick, NJ: Rutgers University Press, 1969).

Berger, P.L., B. Berger and H. Kellner, *Das Unbehagen in der Modernität* (Frankfurt: Suhrkamp, 1973)

Billig, Michael, 'The Extreme Right: Continuities in Anti-Semitic Conspiracy Theory in Post-War Europe', in Eatwell and O'Sullivan (1989).

Bjørgo, Tore, *Conspiracy Rhetoric in Arab Politics: The Palestinian Case* (NUPI Report No.111, Oslo: October 1987).

—— 'Militant neo-Nazism in Sweden', *Terrorism and Political Violence* 5/3 (Autumn 1993), pp.28–57.

—— 'Role of the Media in Racist Violence', in Bjørgo and Witte (1993).

—— 'Terrorist Violence against Immigrants and Refugees in Scandinavia: Patterns and Motives', in Bjørgo and Witte (1993).

—— and Daniel Heradstveit, *Politisk terrorisme* (Oslo: TANO, 1993).

—— and Rob Witte (eds.), *Racist Violence in Europe* (Basingstoke/New York: Macmillan/St. Andrew Press, 1993).

Blok, Anton, 'The Peasant and the Brigand: Social Banditry Reconsidered', *Comparative Studies in Society and History* 14/4 (1972).

—— *The Mafia of a Sicilian Village, 1860–1960* (New York: Harper & Row, 1974).

Bowling, Ben, 'Racial Harassment and the Process of Victimisation: Conceptual and methodological implications for the local crime survey', *British Journal of Criminology* 33/2 (Spring 1993).

Brown, Richard Maxwell, 'The American Vigilante Tradition', in Hugh Graham and Ted Robert Gurr, *Violence in America* (New York: Signet Books, 1969).

Buijs, Frank J. and Jaap van Donselaar, *Extreem-rechts* (Leiden: LISWO, 1994).

Bundesministerium des Innern, *Verfassungsschutzbericht 1991* (Bonn: Bundesministerium des Innern, 1992).

—— *Verfassungsschutzbericht 1993* (Bonn: Bundesministerium des Innern, August 1993).

Calhoun John C. and Louis R. Beam, 'The Perfected Order of the Klan', *Inter-Klan Newsletter and Survival Alert*, No.5 (1984)

Campbell, Colin, 'The Cult, the Cultic Milieu and Secularization', in *A Sociological Yearbook of Religion in Britain*, No.5 (1972), pp. 119–36.

Capaldo, Giancarlo *et al.*, 'L'Eversione Di Destra a Roma Dal '77 Ad Oggi', *Questione Giustizia* 2/4 (1983), pp.935–79.

Carrol, John, 'The Enigma of Yoshio Kodama', *Tokyo Journal* (July 1988).

Chalmers, David M., *Hooded Americanism* (Chicago, IL: Quadrangle Paperbacks, 1968).

Cheles, Luciano, Ronnie Ferguson and Michalina Vaughan (eds.), *Neo-Fascism in Europe* (London and New York: Longman, 1991).

Coates, James, *Armed and Dangerous: The Rise of the Survivalist Right* (New York: Hill and Wang, 1987).

Cohen, Naomi W., *Not Free to Desist* (Philadelphia, PA: Jewish Publication Society of America, 1972).

Coombe, Deneys, 'The Trust Feed killings', in Anthony Minnaar, Ian Liebenberg and Charl Schutte (eds.), *The Hidden Hand – Covert Operations in South Africa* (Pretoria: Human Sciences Research Council, 1994).

Council of Europe, *Report on Racial Violence and Harassment in Europe*, prepared by Mr Robin Oakley (Strasbourg, 1992).

D'Agostini, Fabrizio, *Reggio Calabria* (Milan: Feltrinelli, 1972).

D'Oliveira, John, *Vorster – The Man* (Johannesburg: Ernest Stanton, 1977).

Dahl, Hans Fredrik, Bernt Hagtvet and Guri Hjeltnes, *Den norske nasjonalsosialismen* (Oslo: Pax, 1990).

Dahl, Hans Fredrik, *Vidkun Quisling, I-II* (Oslo: Aschehoug, 1991/1992).

Demker, Marie, 'Stäng gränserna!?'; Svenskarnas Åsikter om flyktingmottagning', in Sören Holmberg and Lennart Weibull (eds.), *Perspektiv på krisen* (SOM No.9, 1992).

Dennis, Lawrence and Maximillian St. George, *A Trial on Trial: The Great Sedition Trial of 1944* (Torrance, CA: Institute for Historical Review, 1945, 1984).

Donselaar, Jaap van, 'The Extreme Right and Racist Violence in the Netherlands', in Bjørgo and Witte (1993).

Drake, Richard, *The Revolutionary Mystique and Terrorism in Contemporary Italy* (Bloomington: Indiana University Press, 1989).

Eatwell, Roger and N. O'Sullivan (eds.), *The Nature of the Right: American and European Politics and Political Thought Since 1789* (London: Pinter Publishers, 1989).

Farin, Klaus and E. Seidel-Pielen, *Krieg in den Städten* (Berlin: Rotbuchverlag, 1991).

—— *Skinheads* (Munich: Beck, 1993).

Ferracuti, F. and F. Bruno: 'Psychiatric Aspects of Terrorism in Italy', in I.L. Barac-Glantz and C.R. Glantz (eds.), *The Mad, the Bad and the Different* (Lexington, 1981).

Ferraresi, Franco, 'I riferimenti teeorico-dottrinali della destra radicale', *Questione Giustizia* 2/4 (1983), pp. 881–92.

—— 'La destra eversiva', in idem (ed.), *La destra radicale* (Milan: Feltrinelli, 1984).

—— *Fascismo Di Ritorno* (Rome: Edizioni della Lega per le autonomie, 1973).

Flowers, Stephen E., 'Revival of Germanic Religion in Contemporary Anglo-American Culture', *Mankind Quarterly* 21/3 (Spring 1981).

Flynn, Kevin and Gary Gerhardt, *The Silent Brotherhood: Inside America's Racist Underground* (New York: The Free Press, 1989).

Forster, Arnold and Benjamin R. Epstein, *The New Anti-Semitism* (New York: McGraw-Hill, 1974).

Frankel, Philip H., *Pretoria's Pretorians – Civil-Military Relations in South Africa* (Cambridge: Cambridge University Press, 1984).

Freda, Giorgio, *La disintegrazione del sistema* (Padova: Edizioni AR,1969).

Friedman, Robert I., *The False Prophet: Rabbi Meir Kahane – From FBI Informant to Knesset Member* (New York: Lawrence Hill Books, 1990).

Frigaard, Iver, 'Terrorism in Nordic Perspective', in E. Ellingsen (ed.), *International Terrorism as a Political Weapon* (Oslo: The Norwegian Atlantic Committee, 1988).

Furlong, Paul, 'Political Terrorism in Italy: Responses, Reactions and Immobilism', in Juliet Lodge (ed.), *Terrorism: A Challenge to the State* (Oxford: Martin Robertson, 1981).

Galleni, Mauro (ed.), *Rapporto sul Terrorismo* (Milan: Rizzoli, 1981).

Gamson, William, *The Strategy of Social Protest* (Homewood, IL: Doresy Press, 1975).

Gluck, Carol, *Japan's Modern Myth* (New York: Columbia University Press, 1985).

Gordon, Paul, 'The Police and Racist Violence in Britain', in Bjørgo and Witte (1993).

—— Racial Violence and Harassment (London: Runnymede Trust, 1990).

Graumann, C.F. and S. Moscovici (eds.), Changing Conceptions of Conspiracy (New York: Springer Verlag, 1987).

Gregor, James A., 'Fascism: Philosophy of Violence and the Concept of Terror', in David C. Rapoport and Yona Alexander (eds.), The Morality of Terrorism (New York: Pergamon Press, 1982).

Grundy, Kenneth W., The Militarization of South African Politics (Bloomington, IN: Indiana University Press, 1986).

Guzzanti, Paolo, Il neofascismo e le sue organizzazioni paramilitari (Rome: PSI,1973).

Hainsworth, Paul (ed.), The Extreme Right in Europe and the USA (London: Pinter Publishers, 1992).

Hamm, Mark, American Skinheads: The Criminology and Control of Hate Crime (Westport, CT: Praeger, 1993).

—— (ed.), Hate Crime: International Perspectives on Causes and Control (Cincinnati, OH: Anderson Publishing/Academy of Criminal Justice Sciences, 1994).

Harber, Anton and Barbara Ludman (eds.), Weekly Mail and Guardian A-Z of South African Politics (London: Penguin Books, 1994).

Hardacre, Helen, Shinto and the State, 1868–1988 (Princeton, NJ.: Princeton University Press, 1989).

Hasselbalch, Ole, Viljen til modstand ('The Determination to Resist') (Tidehvervs forlag, 1990).

Heitmeyer, Wilhelm, Rechtextremistische Orientierungen bei Jugendlichen, 4th edition (Weinheim/München: Juventa Verlag, 1992).

—— Die Bielefelder Rechtsextremismus-Studie (Weinheim, München: Juventa-Verlag, 1992).

—— 'Hostility and Violence towards Foreigners in Germany', in Bjørgo and Witte (1993).

Hobsbawm, Eric, Bandits (New York: Pantheon Books, 1981).

Hoffman, Bruce, 'Right-Wing Terrorism in Europe', Conflict 5/3 (1984).

Horne, Alistaire, A Savage War for Peace: Algeria 1954–1962 (London: Macmillan, 1977).

Huggins, Martha K., 'Introduction: Vigilantism and the State – A Look at South and North', in M. K. Huggins (ed.), Vigilantism and the State in Modern Latin America: Essays on Extralegal Violence (New York: Praeger, 1991)

Husbands, Christopher T., 'Militant Neo-nazism in the Federal Republic of Germany in the 1980s', in Luciano Cheles et al., (1991).

—— 'Racism and Racist Violence: Some Theories and Political Perspectives', in Bjørgo and Witte (1993).

Ibara, Carlos F., 'Guatemala: The Recourse of Fear', in Huggins (1991).

Ignazi, Piero, *Il Polo Escluso* (Bologna: Il Mulino, 1989).

—— 'The Changing Profile of the Italian Social Movement', in Merkl and Weinberg (1993).

Ino, Kenji, *Uyoku* [the Right-Wing] (Tokyo: Gendai Shokan, 1988).

Irish, Jenny and Howard Varney, 'The KwaZulu Police: Obstacle to Peace?' in Minnaar (1993).

Jackson, Kenneth T., *The Ku Klux Klan in the City, 1915–1930* (Chicago, IL: Ivan R. Dee Publisher, 1967, 1992).

Jeansonne, Glen, 'Combating Anti-Semitism: The Case of Gerald L. K. Smith', in David A Gerber (ed.), *Anti-Semitism in American History* (Urbana, IL: University of Illinois Press, 1986).

Jeansonne, Glen, *Gerald L. K. Smith: Minister of Hate* (New Haven, CT: Yale University Press, 1988).

Jellamo, Anna, 'J. Evola, il pensatore della tradizione', in Ferraresi (1984), pp.215–52.

Jensen, Erik, 'International Nazi Cooperation: A Terrorist Oriented Network', in Bjørgo and Witte (1993).

Jha, Prem Shankar, 'The Fascist Impulse in Developing Countries: Two Case Studies', *Studies in Conflict and Terrorism* 17/3 (July–Sept. 1994).

John D. Klier, 'The Pogrom Tradition in Eastern Europe', in Bjørgo and Witte (1993).

Kahane, Meir, *40 years* (Miami Beach: Institute of the Jewish Idea, 1983).

Kane-Berman, John, *Political Violence in South Africa* (Johannesburg: SA Institute of Race Relations, 1993).

Kaplan, Jeffrey, 'The Anti-Cult Movement in America: An History of Culture Perspective', *SYZYGY* 2/3–4 (Summer/Fall 1993).

—— 'The Context of American Millenarian Revolutionary Theology: The Case of the "Identity Christian" Church of Israel', *Terrorism and Political Violence* 5/1 (Spring 1993), pp.30–82.

—— 'The Millennial Dream', both in James R. Lewis (ed.), *From the Ashes: Making Sense of Waco* (Lanham, MD: Rowman & Littlefield, 1994).

—— 'The Reconstruction of the Ásatrú and Odinist Traditions', in James Lewis (ed.), *Magical Religions and Modern Witchcraft* (Albany, NY: SUNY, forthcoming).

Kasza, Gregory, 'Fascism from Below? A Comparative Perspective on the Japanese Right, 1931–36', *Journal of Contemporary History* 19/4 (1984).

Katrin Reemtsma, *Roma in Rumänien. Menschenrechtsreport der Gesellschaft für bedrohte Völker* (Göttingen, 1992).

—— 'Between Freedom and Persecution: Roma in Romania', in Bjørgo and Witte (1993).

Katzenstein, Peter J. and Yutaka Tsujinaka, *Defending the Japanese State: Structure, Norms and Political Responses to Terrorism and Violent Social Protest in the 1970s and 1980s.* Cornell East Asian Series (Ithaca: East Asia Program, Cornell University, 1991).

Kemp, Arthur, *Victory or Violence – The Story of the AWB* (Pretoria: Forma Publishers, 1990).

Kenneth Johansson, *Political violence in Sweden; A study of three cases of systematic use of political violence by Swedish organizatons and the international influences on their use of violence* (Statsvetenskapliga institutionen, Lunds Universitet, mastersutbildning, VT 1993).

Klanwatch, 'The Ku Klux Klan: A History of Racism and Violence', *Klanwatch Special Report*, 4th edition (1991).

Klassen, Ben, *Nature's Eternal Religion* (Otto, NC: Church of the Creator, 1973).

—— *Rahowa! The Planet is Ours* (Otto, NC: Church of the Creator, 1989).

—— *The Klassen Letters , Vol. 1–2* (Otto, NC: Church of the Creator, 1988).

—— *The White Man's Bible* (Otto, NC: Church of the Creator, 1981).

Knutson, Jeanne N., 'Social and Psychodynamic Pressures Towards a Negative Identity: The Case of an American Revolutionary Terrorist', in Yona Alexander and John M. Glison (eds.), *Behavioral and Quantitative Perspectives on Terrorism* (New York: Pergamon Press, 1981).

Lane, David, '88 Precepts', *WAR* 1/1 (n.d.).

—— 'Divided Loyalties', *NSV Report* 8/3 (July–Sept. 1990).

Lange, Anders; and Charles Westin, *Den mångtydiga toleransen; Färhållningssätt till invandring och invandrare 1993*, preliminary version (CEIFO, Stockholms universitet, November 1993).

Lange, Anders; and Charles Westin, *Ungdom om invandringen II: Färhållningsätt till invandring och invandrare 1993*, preliminary version (CEIFO, Stockholms universitet, Nov. 1993).

Laqueur, Walter, *The Age of Terrorism* (London: Weidenfeld, 1987).

Larsen, Stein Ugelvik et al., *Who were the Fascists?* (Oslo: Universitetsforlaget, 1980).

Laurence, Patrick, *Death Squads – Apartheid's Secret Weapon* (London: Penguin Books, 1990).

Levine, M., *Les Ratonnades d'Octobre, un mentre collectif à Paris en 1961* (Paris: Ramsay, 1985).

Lindquist, Hans, *Fascism idag; Färtrupper eller eftersläntare?* (Stockholm: Federativ, 1979).

Lipset, Seymor Martin and Earl Raab, *The Politics of Unreason: Right-Wing Extremism in America 1790-1970* (New York: Harper & Row, 1970).

Lodenius, Anna-Lena and Stieg Larsson, *Extremhögern* (Stockholm: Tiden, 1991).

Lööw, Heléne, *Hakkorset og Wasakärven: En studie av nationalsocialismen i Sverige 1924-1950* (Ph.D. dissertation from Historiska Institutionen, Göteborg, 1990).

—— 'Återkommande mänster', *Invandrare & Minoriteter*, Nos.5–6 (1990).

—— 'Från 'nassar' til 'seriösa samlare av uniformer", *Tvärsnit* (No.3, Oct. 1991).

—— 'Dom har ockuperat mitt land', *Anno* 1992.

—— 'Tant Brun: Män och kvinnor i vit makt värden och i de nationella leden', *Historiskt tidsskrift*, No. 4 (1992).

—— 'The Cult of Violence: The Swedish Racist Counterculture', in Bjørgo and Witte (1993).

—— 'Vit makt – en mörk historia', in *Uppväxtvillkor* nr. 3 (1993).

Lunde, Henrik, *Aller ytterst: De rasistiske grupperinger i dagens Norge* (Oslo: Antirasistisk Senter, 1993).

Lyttelton, Adrian, 'Fascism and Violence in Post-War Italy: Political Strategy and Social Conflict', in Mommsen and Hirshfeld (1982).

—— 'Italy: The Triumph of TV', *New York Review of Books*, 11 August 1994.

Macdonald, Andrew (pseudonym for William L. Pierce), *The Turner Diaries* (Hillsboro: National Vanguard Books, 1980).

—— *Hunter* (Hillsboro, NC: National Vanguard Books, 1989).

Majocchi, Luigi (ed.), *Rapporto sulla Violenza Fascista in Lombardia* (Rome: Cooperativa Scrittori, 1975).

Mario, Giovana, *Le nuove camicie nere* (Turin: Edizioni Dell'Albero, 1966).

Martinez, Thomas; with John Gunther, *Brotherhood of Murder* (New York: Pocket Books, 1990).

Marty, Martin E. , *A Nation Of Behavers* (Chicago, IL: University of Chicago Press, 1976).

Marty, Martin E., *Modern American Religion Volume 2: The Noise and the Conflict 1919–1941* (Chicago, IL: University of Chicago Press, 1991).

Mason, James, *Siege* (Denver, CO: Storm Books, 1992).

Merkl, Peter H., *Political Violence Under the Swastika: 581 Early Nazis* (Princeton, NJ: Princeton University Press, 1975).

—— 'Rollerball or neo-Nazi Violence', in Peter H. Merkl (ed.), *Political Violence and Terror: Motifs and Motivations* (Los Angeles, CA: University of California Press, 1986).

—— *The Making of a Stormtrooper* (Boulder, CO: Westview Press, 1987).

—— 'Conclusion: A New Lease on Life for the Radical Right?' in Merkl and Weinberg (1993).

—— 'Are the Old Nazis Coming Back?' in Merkl (ed.), *The Federal Republic at Forty-five* (London: Macmillan, 1994).

—— and Leonard Weinberg (eds.), *Encounters With the Contemporary Radical Right* (Boulder, CO: Westview Press, 1993).

Merton, Robert K., 'Sozialstruktur und Anomie', in F. Sack und R. König, *Kriminalsoziologie* (Frankfurt: Suhrkamp, 1979).

Miles, R., *Racism* (London: Routhledge, 1989).

Mills, A. Rud, *The Odinist Religion: Overcoming Jewish Christianity* (Melbourne, Australia: self-published, c.1930).

Minnaar, Anthony (ed.), *Patterns of Violence – Case Studies of Conflict in Natal* (Pretoria: Human Sciences Research Council, 1993).

Miyazawa, Setsuo, 'The Private Sector and Law Enforcement in Japan' in William T. Gormley, Jr., (ed.), *Privatization and Its Alternatives* (Madison, WI: University of Wisconsin Press, 1991).

Mizoguchi, Atsushi, *Gendai Yakuza no Ura Chishiki* [Behind-the-scenes Knowledge of Today's Yakuza] (Tokyo: Nihon Purintekusu, 1993).

Mommsen, W.J., and Gerhard Hirshfeld (eds.), *Social Protest, Violence, and Terror in Nineteenth and Twentieth-Century Europe* (New York: St Martin's Press, 1982).

Mullins, Eustace, *The Curse of Canaan: A Demonology of History* (Staunton, VA: Revelation Books, 1987).

Myrdal, Arne, *Sannheten skal fram* [The Truth Must be Told], (Oslo: Lunderød Forlag, 1990).

Nagyn, Géza, 'Främlingsrädsla och invandrarfientliga opinionsyttringar i Sverige: Från anonyma brev till organiserad rasism', in *Kulturmöte konflikt eller samarbete, Papers in Anthropological linguistics II* (Göteborg, 1982).

Nakamura, Koji, 'The Samurai Spirit', *Far Eastern Economic Review*, 74/42 (1971).

Noakes, Jeremy, 'The Origins, Structure and Functions of Nazi Terror', in Noel O'Sullivan (ed.), *Terrorism, Ideology and Revolution* (Boulder, CO: Westview, 1986).

Nola, Alfonso Di, *Antisemitismo in Italia 1962/1972* (Florence: Vallecchi editore, 1973).

Nolte, Ernst, *Three Faces of Fascism* (New York: Mentor Books, 1965).

Otto, Hans-Uwe and Roland Merten (eds.), *Rechtsradikale Gewalt im vereinigten Deutschland: Jugend im gesellschaftlichen Umbruch* (Opladen: Leske + Budrich, 1993).

Pansa, Giampaolo, *Borghese mi ha detto* (Milan: Palazzi,1971).

Parry, Albert, *Terrorism: From Robespierre to Arafat* (New York: The Vanguard Press, 1976).

Pauw, Jacques, *In the Heart of the Whore – The Story of Apartheid's Death Squads* (Johannesburg: Southern Book Publishers, 1991).

Petersen, Jens, 'Violence in Italian Fascism', in Mommsen and Hirshfeld (1982).

Peterson, Thomas; Mikael Stigendal, Björn Fryklund, *Skånepartiet; Om folkligt missnöje i Malmö*, (Lund, 1988).

Porta, Donatella della and Maurizio Rossi, *Cifre crudelli: bilancio del terrorismi italiani* (Bologna: Istituto Cattaneo, 1983).

Post, Jerold M., 'Notes on a Psychodynamic Theory of Terrorist Behavior', *Terrorism: An International Journal* 7/3 (1984).

Rhodes, James M., *The Hitler Movement: A Modern Millenarian Revolution* (Stanford, CA.: Hoover Institution Press, 1980).

Roberts, Archibald, *Emerging Struggle for State Sovereignty* (Ft Collins, CO: Betsy Ross, 1979).

Rock, Paul, 'Law and Order and Power in Late Seventeenth and Early Nineteenth-century England', in Stanley Cohen and Andrew Scull (eds.), *Social Control and the State* (New York: St Martin's Press, 1983).

Rockwell, George Lincoln, *This Time the World* (Arlington, VA: Parliament House, 1963).

Ronchey, Alberto, *Accadde in Italia 1968–1977* (Milan: Garzanti, 1977).

Rooyen, Johann van, *Hard Right – The New White Power in South Africa* (London: I.B. Tauris, 1994).

Rosenbaum, Jon H. and Peter C. Sederberg, 'Vigilantism: Analysis of Establishment Violence', *Com*

Rosenbaum, Petra, *Il nuovo fascismo* (Milan: Feltrinelli,1975).

Rosenthall, A. M. and Arthur Gelb, *One More Victim: The Life and Death of a Jewish American Nazi* (New York: Signet Books, 1967).

Salierno, Giulio, *Autobiografia di un picchiatore fascista* (Turin: Einaudi, 1976).

Sampson, Steven, '"The Threat to Danishness": Danish Culture as seen by Den Danske Forening', in Jan Hjarnø (ed.), *Proceedings of the 9th Nordic Seminar on Migration Research* (København: Nordisk Ministerråd, forthcoming).

Santarelli, Enzo, *Fascismo E Neofascismo* (Rome: Riuniti, 1974).

Sassano, Marco, *La Politica della Strage* (Padova: Marsilio, 1972).

Scobie, William, 'Gladio: The War That Never Was', *World Press Review* 38/2 (1991).

Secchia, Pietro, *Lotta AntiFascista e giovani generazioni* (Milan: La Pietra, 1973).

Seymour, Cheri, *Committee of the States: Inside the Radical Right* (Mariposa, CA: Camden Place Communications, 1991).

Simone, Cesare De, *La Pista Nera* (Rome: Editori Riuniti, 1972).

Skolnick, Jerome H., *The Politics of Protest* (New York: Ballantine Books, 1969).

Sloan, John, 'Terrorism in Latin America', in Michael Stohl (ed.), *The Politics of Terrorism* (New York: Marcel Dekker, 1979).

Smith, Dwight C. Jr., 'Paragons, Pariahs, and Pirates: A Spectrum-based Theory of Enterprise', *Crime and Delinquency* (July 1980).

Smith, Tim, 'The Warlord and the Police', in Minnaar (1993).

Sørensen, Øystein, *Hitler eller Quisling?* (Oslo: Cappelen, 1989).

Spitzer, Steven, 'The Political Economy of Policing', in David Greenberg (ed.), *Crime and Capitalism* (Palo Alto, CA: Mayfield, 1981).

Sprinzak, Ehud, 'From Messianic Pioneering to Vigilante Terrorism: The Case of Gush Emunim Underground', in David C. Rapoport (ed.), *Inside Terrorist Organizations* (London: Frank Cass, 1987).

—— 'The Psycho-political Formation of Extreme Left Terrorism in a Democracy: The Case of the Weathermen', in Walter Reich (ed.), *Origins of Terrorism* (New York: Cambridge University Press, 1990).

—— 'The Process of Delegitimation: Towards a Linkage Theory of Political Terrorism', *Terrorism and Political Violence* 3/1 (Spring 1991), pp.50–68.

—— 'Violence and Catastrophe in the Theology of Rabbi Meir Kahane; The Ideologization of the Mimetic Desire', *Terrorism and Political Violence* 3/3 (Autumn 1991), pp.48–70.

—— *The Ascendance of Israel's Radical Right* (Oxford University Press, 1991).

Stanton, Bill [Klanwatch] *Bringing the Ku Klux Klan to Justice* (New York: Grove Weidenfeld, 1991).

Steinhoff, Patricia G., 'Protest and Democracy' in T. Ishida and Ellis Krauss, *Democracy in Japan* (Pittsburgh, PA: University of Pittsburgh Press, 1987).

—— 'Hijackers, Bombers and Bank Robbers: Managerial Style in the Japanese Red Army', *Journal of Asian Studies* 48/4 (Nov. 1989).

Stenberg, Leif, 'När Kimstad blev riksbekant', *Pockettidningen R*, Nos. 2–3 (1991).

Sternhell, Zeev, 'Fascist Ideology', in Walter Laqueur (ed.), *Fascism: A Reader's Guide* (Berkeley, CA: University of California Press, 1976), pp.320–37.

Suzuki, Kunio, *Datsu Uyoku Sengen* [Escape the Right Manifesto] (Tokyo: IPC Inter Press Corporation, 1993).

—— *Kore ga Atarashii Nihon no Uyoku Da* [This Is the New Japanese Right-wing] (Tokyo: Nisshin Hodo, 1993).

Szayna, Thomas, 'Ultranationalism in Central Europe', *Orbis* 37/4 (Fall 1993).

Szymkowiak, Kenneth, 'Sokaiya Criminal Groups and the Conflict for Corporate Power in Postwar Japan', *Asian Profile* 20/4 (1992).

Takagi, Masayuki, 'The Japanese Right Wing', *Japan Quarterly* (July–Sept. 1989).

Takagi, Masayuki, Uyoku: *Katsudo to Dantai* [The Right-wing: Activities and Groups] (Tokyo: Bijitsusha, 1989).

Tamm, Ditlev, *Retsopgøret efter besettelsen* (Copenhagen: Jurist- og økonomforbundets forlag, 1984).

Trelease, A.W., *White Terror: The Ku Klux Klan Conspiracy and the Southern Reconstruction* (New York: Harper Torchbooks, 1971).

Tydén, Mattias, *Svensk antisemitism 1880–1930*, uppsala Multiethnic Papers 8 (Uppsala :Centre for Multiethnic Research, 1986).

Weinberg, Leonard, 'The American Radical Right: Exit, Voice and Violence', in Merkl and Weinberg (1993).

—— 'The American Radical Right in Contemporary Perspective', paper presented at IPSA Panel RC 6.2, 'The Revival of Right-Wing Extremism', IPSA World Congress, Berlin, August 1994.

Wilcox, Laird; and John George, *Nazis, Communists, Klansmen and Others on the Fringe* (Buffalo, NY: Prometheus, 1992).

Wilkinson, Paul, *The New Fascists* (London: Grant McIntyre, 1981).

Willan, Philip, *Puppetmasters* (London: Constable, 1992).

Willems, Helmut, 'Gewalt und Fremdenfeindlichkeit: Anmerkungen zum gegenwärtigen Gewaltdiskurs', in Hans-Uwe Otto und Roland Merten, *Rechtsradikale Gewalt im vereinigten Deutschland* (Bonn: Leske + Budrich, 1993).

—— 'Kollektive Gewalt gegen Fremde: Historische Episode oder Genese einer sozialen Bewegung von Rechts?', in Rainer Erb und Werner Bergmann (eds.), *Neonazismus und rechte Subkultur* (Berlin: Metropol Verlag, 1994).

—— R. Eckert, S. Würtz, L. Steinmetz, *Fremdenfeindliche Gewalt: Einstellungen, Täter, Konflikteskalation* (Opladen: Leske + Budrich, 1993).

—— S. Würtz and R. Eckert, *Analyse fremdenfeindlicher Straftäter* (Bonn: Texte zur Inneren Sicherheit, Bundesministerium des Innern, Dec. 1994).

Zeskind, Leonard, *The 'Christian Identity' Movement: Analyzing Its Theological Rationalization for Racist and Anti-Semitic Violence* (Atlanta, GA: Center for Democratic Renewal, 1986).

Index

Note: Figures in **bold** type indicate a figure or table on the page.

INDEX

INDEX

INDEX 321

Bureau of Immigration (SIV) 131, 139;
support for *prisoners of war or politics*
128; 'White Power activists' 125, 141;
World War II and 182
Swedish anti-immigration groups, *Bevara
Sverige Svenski* (Keep Sweden Swedish)
121, 141, 143, 148; *Framstegpartiet* (The
Progressive Party) 121, 138; *Ny
Demokrati* (New Democracy) 121, 131;
Sjobopartiet (The Sjöbo Party) 121;
Skanepartiet 149; *Svenska Folkets Väl*
(The Swedish League) 148;
Sverigedomokraterna (SD Swedish
Democratic Party) 121, 138–9, 143,
147, 149, 187
Swedish anti-racist groups, *Ariska
Frihetsfonden* (Aryan Liberation
Foundation) 128; *Ben Klassen Academy*
123; *Den Reorganiserade Kreativistens
Kyrka* (The Reoganised COTC) 123;
DeVries Instituet 123; *Föreningen
Sveriges Framtid/Riksfronten*
(Association for Sweden's Future/Nation
Front) 198; *Hisingens kommunalförening*
143 *Kreativistens Kyrka* (COTC Church
of the Creator) 123, 126, 144, 198;
Nyhedniska Fascistpartiet (The National
Neo–Pagan Fascist Party) 146–7;
Nordiska Rikspartiet (NRP The Nordic
National [Reich] Party) 24, 120, 122,
129, 139, 143–5, 146–8, 201–3;
Nysvenska Rörelsen (NRS the New
Swedish Movement) 142, 145–6, 148;
Riksaktionsgruppen (RAG National
Action Group) 120; *Riksfronten* (National
[Reich] Front) 24, 124, 133; *Svensk
Socialistisk Samling* (Sweden National
Socialist Party) 120; *Unga
Nationalsocialister i Sverige* (Young
national Socialists in Sweden) 143; *Vitt
Ariskt Motstand* (VAM White Aryan
Resistance) 24–6, 38, 109, 137, 148,
182–3, 187, 197–9, 202, 206, 222
Swedish anti–Semitic groups, *Frisprakig
Nationell Förening* (The Outspoken
National Association) 141;
NS–Information (National Swedish
Information) 142; *Organisation Svenske*
(The Swede organisation) 148; *Svenska
Antisemitiska Föreningen* (Sweden's
Anti–Semitic Organisation) 142
Swedish racial violence, age at time crime
committed (1990–93) **132**; age
distribution among convicted activists
151; comparison of number of

racist/xenophobic crimes (1993) **136**;
distribution of different categories of
perpetrators **152**; numbers of refugees,
relatives and other migrants (1987–93)
130; serious attacks against asylum
seekers (1990–92) **134**
Swedish refugee policy 130 –1
Swedish right–wing extremist groups,
Demokratisk Allains (Democratic
Alliance) 120; *Sveriges Nationella
Förbund* (SNF Swedish National
Association) 120–1
Swift, Wesley 51, 53
Symbionese Liberation Army 82
Szymkowiak, Kenneth 6, 9–10, 13,
265–98

Takagi, Masayuki 279
Takeshita, Noboru 266
Tate no Kai 283
tax protest movements 67–8, 98
Terrorism and Political Violence (journal)
6, 45, 72, 77
Thatcher, Margaret 111
'theft of culture' 46, 80
'The International Jew' (1920 series of
articles) 51
The Odinist (1971) 60–2
The Order 1, 38, 57–8, 74, 98, 123, 129,
222; Aryan Nations and 53; assassination
of Alan Berg 77; tax protest movement
67–8
The Turner Diaries (novel) 1, 57–8, 82–4,
85, 196, 207
Thuleringen (The ring of Thule) 124
Tito 27
Tōā Dōyukai (East Asia Friendship
Association 1963) 272–3, 277
Togliatti, Palmiro 227
Tokyo subway nerve gas attack (20 March
1995) 292
Tolkien, J.R.R. 234
Toshiba Corporation 280
traitors, identification 192–3, 204;
'resistance' against 188–96; treatment
191, 206
transformational delegitimization 20
Treurnicht, Dr A.P. 241, 260
Tribulation, preparation for 86
Trochman, Randy (MOM) 83
Truth Commission (South Africa) 247
Turks in Germany 1, 99, 166
typology of right–wing terrorism 22–3;
millenarian 22, 33–5; racist 22, 31–3;
reactive 22, 26–9; revolutionary 22, 23–6;

For Product Safety Concerns and Information please contact our EU
representative GPSR@taylorandfrancis.com
Taylor & Francis Verlag GmbH, Kaufingerstraße 24, 80331 München, Germany